International
Relations Theory
and South Asia

International
Relations   Theory
South   Asia
Identities
Images   s
Security
Political   Economy
DomesticPolitics
Identities
Images   s
International
Relations   Theory
South   Asia
Identities
Images   s
Security

International Relations Theory and South Asia

edited by

E. SRIDHARAN

VOLUME I

Security,
Political Economy,
Domestic Politics,
Identities, and Images

OXFORD
UNIVERSITY PRESS

OXFORD
UNIVERSITY PRESS

Oxford University Press is a department of the University of Oxford.
It furthers the University's objective of excellence in research, scholarship,
and education by publishing worldwide. Oxford is a registered trademark of
Oxford University Press in the UK and in certain other countries

Published in India by
Oxford University Press
YMCA Library Building, 1 Jai Singh Road, New Delhi 110 001, India

First Edition published in 2011
Oxford India Paperbacks 2014

ISBN-13: 978-0-19-945341-2
ISBN-10: 0-19-945341-1

Typeset in Adobe Garamond 10.5/12.6
by Le Studio Graphique, Gurgaon 122 001
Printed in India by Replika Press Pvt. Ltd., Haryana 131 028

In memory of S.K. Singh

Contents

Part I

REGIONAL COOPERATION MODELS, PROCESSES, AND OBSTACLES

Part II

DOMESTIC POLITICS AND ITS FOREIGN POLICY IMPLICATIONS

Part III

POLITICAL ECONOMY AND REGIONAL COOPERATION

Tables and Figures

Preface

This volume is the first of a two-volume set which is part of a project entitled 'International Relations Theory and South Asia'. The first output of this project was a single volume published in 2007.* The project was initiated and carried out under my guidance by the University of Pennsylvania Institute for the Advanced Study of India (UPIASI) in New Delhi. It was a multi-year project, generously supported by the Ford Foundation. It attempted to engage scholars from the South Asian region working in the discipline of international relations with each other, drawing upon their varied perspectives to question their own understanding of conflict and cooperation in the region in various issue areas and their relationship to international relations theory and wider social science theorizing. However, while it invited scholars to write on the problems of conflict and cooperation in the region seen in the light of international relations theory as well as, importantly, other related social science theorizing, most of the writing was also based on cross-border fieldwork in countries other than the scholar's own. The project was thus both consciously theoretical and also broke new ground in empirical work. As a by-product, it created a pool and network of scholars who had engaged in fieldwork in countries of the region other than their own. An initial conference was held in July 2002, followed by four others in August 2003, July 2004, March 2005, and March 2006. This volume contains a selection of the research so conducted, duly updated, and revised several times after the referees' comments.

I would like to thank the Ford Foundation, particularly the then representative in New Delhi, Gowher Rizvi, and later the Program

* E. Sridharan (ed.), *The India–Pakistan Nuclear Relationship: Theories of Deterrence and International Relations* (Delhi and Abingdon, UK: Routledge, 2007).

Officer for Local and Global Governance, Bishnu Mohapatra, for financial support. I would also like to thank the late S.K. Singh, former governor of Rajasthan and Arunachal Pradesh, former foreign secretary of India, and founding secretary-general and governing council member of UPIASI, for helping facilitate the project in innumerable ways. Francine Frankel, director of the Center for the Advanced Study of India (CASI), University of Pennsylvania, hosted me at CASI during periods coinciding with the project, as did her successor Devesh Kapur in summer 2009, enabling me to accomplish invaluable work. On behalf of all the contributors, I would like to thank the three anonymous referees of Oxford University Press for their comments which greatly helped in improving the original drafts. I would like to thank Adil Tyabji for copyediting the manuscript. Last but not least, I would like to thank Adnan Farooqui for research and editorial assistance in earlier years, and Sucharita Sengupta in later years, as well as the staff of UPIASI—S.D. Gosain, Ruchika Ahuja, and Desh Raj—for their hard work on the project.

Abbreviations

AL	Awami League
ASEAN	Association of Southeast Asian Nations
BNP	Bangladesh National Party
CHT	Chittagong Hill Tracts
DoD	Department of Defence
ECSC	European Coal and Steel Community
EEC	European Economic Community
EU	European Union
FDI	foreign direct investment
FTAA	Free Trade Agreement of the Americas
GDP	gross domestic product
IMF	International Monetary Fund
IPKF	Indian Peace-Keeping Force
IR	international relations
ISAF	International Security Assistance Force
ISLFTA	Indo-Sri Lanka Free Trade Agreement
JVP	Janatha Vimukthi Peramuna
LDC	least developed country
LeT	Lashkar-e-Taiba
LTTE	Liberation Tigers of Tamil Eelam
MBT	main battle tank
MFN	most favoured nation
MNNA	major non-NATO ally
MoD	Ministry of Defence
MoU	memorandum of understanding
NAFTA	North American Free Trade Agreement
NATO	North Atlantic Treaty Organization
NGO	non-governmental organization
NSC	National Security Council
NTB	non-tariff barrier

OAS   Organization of American States
PPP   Pakistan Peoples Party
RSC   regional security complex
SAARC   South Asian Association for Regional Cooperation
SAFTA   South Asian Free Trade Area
SAPTA   South Asian Preferential Trade Area
SLFP   Sri Lanka Freedom Party
UN   United Nations
UNDP   United Nations Development Program
UNF   United National Front
UNP   United National Party
UPIASI   University of Pennsylvania Institute for the Advanced
                Study of India
WTO   World Trade Organization

International Relations Theory and South Asia

Security, Political Economy, Domestic Politics, Identities, and Images

E. Sridharan

This book is part of a two-volume set, which follows another volume published in 2007.[1] It sets out the research that emerged from a project entitled 'International Relations Theory and South Asia'. In this project, a diverse group of scholars from the region go beyond conflict management to begin thinking through the longer-term difficulties of gradually resolving conflict and building a larger South Asian regional entity in a world of growing regional integration. It attempts to draw upon the insights of international relations (IR) theory, and more broadly upon social science theorizing, and relate them to South Asian conflicts—the major bilateral conflict between India and Pakistan and the other bilateral and multilateral problems of regional cooperation-building—incorporating extra-regional factors and the superpower/ global regime. The aim is to undertake theoretically grounded research that is at the same time empirical and based on comprehensive fieldwork to conceptualize possible solutions to South Asian conflicts and encourage cooperation over the long run. Most chapters in both volumes are based on fieldwork in a South Asian country other than the author's own. While scholars contributing to the project were encouraged to think theoretically on the broad theme of conflict and cooperation, selecting issues that interested them, no single central approach or template was imposed on them. This was because the nature of the conflicts in the region—between India and its various neighbours—being more bilateral than regional and centred on diverse issues covering not only security but also political economy, precluded a centralizing approach to the project and volume. This might have been feasible had the scope of the project been limited to, say, India–Pakistan relations and security issues.

This project has thus brought together not only a loose community of scholars employing IR theory and broader social science theorizing to come to grips with South Asian conflict resolution and cooperation-building, but also a pool of scholars who have engaged in fieldwork in another South Asian country in the 2000s, including interviews with political functionaries and policymakers. The aim of the project was also to focus, in as theoretically informed a way as possible, on issues that are usually neglected and on which there is very little literature, particularly the interrelationship between distinct issue areas, in contrast, for example, to those on which there is already a large body of literature, such as Kashmir, nuclear stability, or regional economic cooperation taken as stand-alone issues. It addresses a wide range of issues in the two volumes: for example, questions such as integrating nuclear deterrence issues with the possibilities for economic cooperation (E. Sridharan); foreign policy shifts and domestic politics (Mohammed Ayoob, Rajesh M. Basrur, Nalini Kant Jha); such shifts and the domestic political economy (Rahul Mukherji, Asad Sayeed); domestic politics of minorities and foreign policy (Mohammad Waseem); education and the creation of images (Akbar Zaidi); the question of whether economic cooperation can lead to peace-building or whether political and security preconditions are necessary for such cooperation (Akbar Zaidi, E. Sridharan, Humayun Kabir); India's possible regional leadership role in comparative perspective (Varun Sahni); the determinants of post-Cold War US policy in the region (K.P. Vijayalakshmi); the role of identities, ideas, interests, and fears in regional integration (Pratap Bhanu Mehta); diasporas and conflict in the region (Sanjay Chaturvedi); minority rights and state restructuring (Jayadeva Uyangoda); the possibility of a regional normative regime for human rights (Siddharth Mallavarapu); and the Hindutva world-view and inter-state relations in the region (Sanjay Chaturvedi).

In South Asia, regional conflict resolution and cooperation-building face several intertwined obstacles, covering the issue areas of security, political economy, and regional architecture, and operating at the levels of both foreign policy and domestic politics, with the politics of identities, images, and norms spanning all issues and levels. The India–Pakistan conflict has acted as a barrier to any form of regional security treaty or institution and, therefore, to the South Asian Association for Regional

Cooperation (SAARC) becoming an effective regional organization. The problem, first and centrally, is how this barrier can be overcome, that is, how India–Pakistan nuclear deterrence can be stabilized as a first step, and then how the conflict over Kashmir (which is an amalgam of territory, borders, and national identity) can be resolved, ameliorated, or sidestepped.[2] Second, and almost equally important, are the usual regional cooperation barriers in terms of sharing the costs and benefits of economic cooperation, which is inevitably linked to domestic politics that is in turn concerned with perceived intentions, national identities, images of various 'others', and political norms. For South Asian security cooperation, all the aforementioned barriers need to be overcome, and all this achieved in the unique context of one country, India, being both geographically central (no other country in the region shares a common border) and overwhelmingly dominant in area, population, and economy. However, the reality is that the region is not unipolar but effectively, if lopsidedly, bipolar, given Pakistan's nuclear capability. Any study of South Asian cooperation has to also factor in US and Chinese policies in the region. There is thus a need to think through, in an integrated way, the problem of stability of nuclear deterrence between neighbouring states with disputed territory/borders along with the problems of building regional security, economic and other cooperation.

The collection of essays in these two volumes analyse South Asian conflict and cooperation in the post-Cold War and post-1998—the nuclear-tests period—in the light of diverse strands of IR and other relevant social science theories. These diverse strands link three issue areas—security, political economy, and possible regional cooperation architectures—at two levels of analysis: foreign relations and domestic politics, with both levels including the construction of images, identities, and norms. The latter can be treated both as a level of analysis, if applied to leaders/policymakers, or as a distinct constructivist theoretical approach that treats structure and actor in international relations differently from neo-realist and neoliberal institutional theorizing.[3] This collection encompasses the interaction of these issue areas, levels of analysis, and theoretical approaches.

SOUTH ASIAN CONFLICT RESOLUTION AND COOPERATION ACTIVITY

There has been a proliferation of non-official dialogues, academic research, and allied activities on South Asian conflict resolution and regional cooperation since 1991, primarily focused on the Indo-Pakistan conflict, largely triggered off by the near-war crisis of May 1990.[4] The principal activities have been of the following seven kinds.

First, there have been Track Two dialogues, more or less explicitly aimed at influencing foreign policies in the short run; for example, most prominently, the Neemrana and Indo-Bangladesh dialogues. The participants have largely comprised former senior policymakers from the diplomatic, military, and civil services; the media; and academia.

Second, there have been 'Track Three' or grass roots or people-to-people dialogues, seeking to build links across borders between diverse groups from all walks of life. A leading example is the India–Pakistan People's Association for Friendship and Cooperation.

Third, there have been multilateral dialogues, usually pan-South Asian, which are again primarily policy-oriented, issue-specific, and aimed at suggesting policy frameworks for regional institutions. The participants are either non-governmental organizations (NGOs), such as the South Asian Forum for Human Rights (SAFHR) and the South Asian Free Media Association (SAFMA), professional groups such as lawyers, media persons, and environmentalists, or former policymakers as in Track Two dialogues.

Fourth, there have been initiatives that seek to strengthen business links at both bilateral and multilateral levels, the participants being principally business associations such as the SAARC Chamber of Commerce or the India–Pakistan Chamber of Commerce and Industry.

Fifth, there are regular exchanges and dialogues between research institutes and think tanks in the region, including, prominently but not exhaustively, the Centre for Policy Research, Institute for Defence Studies and Analyses, Institute of Peace and Conflict Studies, Delhi Policy Group, Observer Research Foundation (all at Delhi); International Centre for Ethnic Studies (Colombo and Kandy), Regional Centre for Strategic Studies (Colombo); Bangladesh Institute for International and Strategic Studies, Centre for Policy Dialogue (both at Dhaka); Islamabad Policy Research Institute, Institute for Regional Studies, Institute for Strategic Studies, and Sustainable Development Policy Institute (all at Islamabad). The idea of a South Asian University has been agreed to and is in the start-up stage as of 2010, but regular inter-university academic exchanges are still virtually non-existent.

Sixth, there are also dialogue initiatives outside South Asia aimed at bringing South Asians together, such as those organized by the US Institute of Peace, Stimson Center, Program in Arms Control,

Disarmament, and International Security (ACDIS) at the University of Illinois at Urbana-Champaign, Wilton Park Conferences, Chatham House, Queen Elizabeth House at Oxford University, and Japan–South Asia Forum. Some of these have the character of academic research while others are essentially dialogue fora. More of the participants have an academic background than is usually the case in the other categories mentioned earlier.

Seventh is interaction among South Asian nationals at international fora even when the central agenda is not South Asia focused; for example, Parliamentarians for Global Action, the Asia Society's annual Asia Pacific Roundtables and Williamsburg meetings, and the annual conferences of the United Nations Regional Centre for Peace and Disarmament in Asia and the Pacific.

Most of these efforts have a short-term focus and are policy-oriented without being conceptual and theoretical, that is, not drawing upon or situated in IR or other social science theorizing. It is my surmise that the failure, by and large, to stabilize and institutionalize South Asian security, conflict resolution, and regional cooperation is substantially because of the failure to ground policy in a deeper theoretical understanding. The essays in these volumes are a first attempt towards doing this by addressing issues in the three interrelated areas of security, political economy, and possible regional architectures at the levels of both foreign policy and domestic politics, and incorporating the construction of images, identities, and norms. The interrelationship exists because regional architectures depend upon consensus, which in turn depends upon the domestic politics of security concerns and political economy of each of the countries of the region, and also their perceptions of the intentions of other countries. These perceptions are again strongly influenced by the politics of identity, construction of images, and the norms institutionalized in the domestic and international politics of each country. Equally, bilateral and regional conflict resolution and cooperation, whether on economic or security issues, can feed back positively (or negatively, in the case of discord) on the domestic politics of each country.

INTERNATIONAL RELATIONS THEORY AND SOUTH ASIA

The starting point for assessing the usefulness of IR theory for analysing conflict between states in South Asia is the neo-realist–neoliberal debate and its recent evolution which seeks to transcend the terms of both sides of the debate.[5] The extended debate between neo-realism and neoliberal institutionalism saw considerable criticism of neo-realism.[6] The following issues are important in theorizing about South Asia. First, unlike neo-realism's assumption that preferences are exogenous, it has been widely argued that it is necessary to explain the origins of states' preferences. Most fundamentally, anarchy does not necessarily imply neo-realist assumptions or conclusions and their implications for state behaviour. Robert Keohane showed that a repeated prisoner's dilemma game could lead to cooperation under anarchy through a learning process in which, as Robert Axelrod demonstrated, actors operating under uncertainty about other actors' intentions can develop cooperation through a naturally evolving tit-for-tat strategy that rewards cooperative responses and penalizes non-cooperation.[7] Joseph Grieco responded that Keohane assumed that absolute gains drive behaviour; what are relevant are relative gains.[8] To elaborate (as this point is very important for South Asia), neo-realists like Grieco hold that states are more sensitive to relative gains than to absolute gains in cooperation. In neo-realist theory, states in an anarchic world system seek power and the balance of power to safeguard their security, and as power is relative, they are sensitive to relative, not absolute, gains. Hence, cooperation can be successful only if it does not upset the relative gains balance, no matter what absolute gains one can point to as the fruits of cooperation.[9] That is, even if a cooperative deal yielded absolute gain to a state, it would still be willing to forgo the resulting gain if it believed that other states would gain relatively more. The basic drift of this line of criticism is that it is necessary to define anarchy and its consequent behaviour pattern by reference not only to the lack of a common government but also to the means available to states, that is, force, and within that category, nuclear or conventional weapons. Where nuclear weapons exist, balancing may not occur even under anarchy; rather, there may be cooperation to prevent war. This is because nuclear weapons can lead not only to deterrence—that is, balancing—but also to minimal deterrence if the latter is seen as adequate, and hence to confidence-building measures and arms control to prevent an unacceptably devastating war.

Robert Powell makes the case that neo-realists have mistaken effects for causes, arguing that concern for relative gains is primarily an effect and not a cause.[10] While neo-realists assume that states under anarchy are preoccupied with relative gains in transactions with other states, neoliberals argue that the degree of a state's concern for relative gains is conditional and depends upon the intensity of the security dilemma it faces. A predominant concern with relative gains is an effect of the state's perceived strategic situation. Citing Grieco, Powell argues that a state's sensitivity to relative gains depends upon six factors, two of which are the fungibility of power across issues, and whether relative gains or losses occur over the military or the economic sphere, with the relative gains sensitivity being greater in the former sphere but also existing in the latter. Thus, Powell argues that the degree of sensitivity to relative gains is part of the outcome or effect of the perceived strategic setting (the latter situation being a *perception*, not a given fact), influenced by several factors—an effect but not a cause or an explanation of the presence or absence of international cooperation. Thus, it is not just structure but *perceptions*, and what goes into their shaping that are critical to policy and hence to outcomes.

Stephen Walt brings in perceptions more explicitly, arguing that whether states balance or bandwagon depends, inter alia, on the *perceived* intentions of the adversary, which brings us to the importance of images.[11] Perceptions of threat and intentions, and hence the construction of images and calculations of interest, thus connect structure to foreign policy. However, images are formed through repeated interaction. Therefore, images, and hence perceived intentions, are crucially linked to the history of the interaction of states-in-the-making and nations-in-the-making, and whether the process has been antagonistic or peaceful.

Neo-realism's focus on structure and outcomes, and its indeterminacy as regards policy, makes it unsuitable for foreign policy analysis, conflict resolution, and cooperation-building. Neo-realism is a theory of outcomes or, if one follows Powell, a theory of preference over actions, not over outcomes: the pursuit of power as a means to whatever end is assumed to be the operational motive. Neo-realists like Stephen Krasner argue that in the long run rational power calculations will prevail, whatever ideas and internal processes determine short-term foreign policy.[12] Power alone does not, however, explain action as traditional realism acknowledges. Power and situation set limits on options but almost never reduce the number of options to one. In this context, Robert Keohane and Judith Goldstein argue that ideas and internal processes have independent causal significance.[13]

The neo-realist–neoliberal debate has thrown into relief the *effects of anarchy* and the *degree of concern about relative gains*, both sides in the debate accepting that balancing behaviour and a heightened concern for relative gains are conditional upon the strategic setting. Grieco makes a useful beginning by specifying six factors influencing concern for relative gains. The challenge is to specify more closely, in regional and issue regimes, the conditions which lead to such behaviour and the institutions which can lead to the realization of cooperation and joint gains.

BANDWAGONING VERSUS BALANCING: LARGE AND SMALL STATES, AND REGIONAL COOPERATION IN POST-COLD WAR SOUTH ASIA

Specifically, what do larger/dominant countries in alliances or regional security pacts need to do to obtain the voluntary cooperation of smaller partners, and what do smaller countries in such situations fear and what do they require from larger countries in order to bandwagon rather than balance? There is an extended debate on balancing versus bandwagoning when new poles of power emerge, which basically concludes that weaker states' decisions to balance or bandwagon depends upon the threat perception from the emerging pole, and whether there are shared *interests* or not, and by implication, the kind of deal—implicit or explicit—or accommodation or side payments offered as inducements by the emerging pole to potential allies.[14] In the case of USA, the leader of the most successful alliance in the twentieth century, it is clearly understood, both within USA and by its allies, that a key factor in the stability of the alliance has been the biggest partner's willingness and ability to shoulder a disproportionate share of the costs of alliance, including post-war aid to ravaged allies, the bulk of the defence burden, and relatively greater economic openness to movements of goods, capital, and people than its allies, enabling them, crucially, to catch up on the basis of such openness.[15]

What are the incentives for small and large states to ally, in general, and in a regional security alliance? Hans Morgenthau argued that alliances are formed to maintain the balance of power in an uncertain world, while Stephen Walt modified his argument to maintain that states balance not against power per se but against threat, and maintain the balance of threat, thus bringing in the perceptual factor of what constitutes an actual or potential threat.[16] The North Atlantic Treaty Organization (NATO) after the Cold War is an apparent exception, in that while there is no longer any Soviet threat, it still persists and expands its membership and area of operation. As regards small states, the overall benefits-versus-costs calculus is crucial. Does the increased security that an alliance with a larger power brings outweigh the loss of autonomy or other options? Does the risk of such 'entrapment' outweigh the risk of abandonment in a crisis? Is neutrality or 'hiding', as against bandwagoning or balancing, an option? Small states may opt to join an alliance for economic benefits and support for their regimes rather than purely security benefits: for example, post-Cold War Central and Eastern Europe joining NATO despite the retreat of Russia. In some alliances, as in the Conference on Security and Cooperation in Europe or in NATO, small states were able to acquire influence through institutionalized norms of equality and negotiation over confrontation.

The alliance literature is not always clear about what an alliance is. Broadly speaking, one can distinguish between three types of alliances.[17] The first is a defence pact in which countries mutually or multilaterally commit to come to each other's defence in the event of a security threat. This can be an asymmetrical pact, as for example, between USA and Japan or South Korea. The second is a non-aggression or neutrality pact in which countries commit not to attack or threaten each other. The third is an entente, which commits them merely to consultation (for example, the Indo-Soviet Treaty of 1971). The second and third types of alliances tend to be weak owing to lack of military commitments, particularly lack of military bases on each other's soil, which become hostages in war and hence tripwires that trigger commitment, and the existence of an exit option because of a lack of concrete commitment. Olson and Zeckhauser argue that major powers contribute disproportionately to alliances while minor powers free-ride.[18] There are two assumptions here: (i) alliance-based security is a public good which cannot be withheld from any one ally in an alliance; (ii) more powerful states are more influential. Joanne Gowa and Edward Mansfield argue that an important benefit of alliances is increased trade with allies.[19] This could be the motivation for post-Cold War Central and Eastern European countries to join NATO and the European Union (EU). Douglas Gibler argues that territorial settlement treaties are more likely than all other alliances to end the incidence of war.[20] This would make such treaties vitally important for relationships between countries and within regimes where there are territorial disputes and which have had a history of partitions on religious and ethnic lines and wars over territory and borders.

Alliance theory does not seem to fit the behaviour of weaker powers. It has been found by many scholars (Acharya 1998; Holsti 1998) to be useless for developing countries as there have been virtually no stable alliances between weak states, and whatever alliances there have been have often had a major power behind what appears to be an alliance between weaker states (Handel 1981).[21] During the Cold War, most Third World states were either non-aligned or allied to one of the superpowers, not to each other. Even Cold War-inspired regional alliances of weaker states such as the Southeast Asia Treaty Organization (SEATO) and Central Treaty Organization (CENTO) were notably unsuccessful. South–South coalitions for joint defence of their interests even in the economic sphere vis-à-vis the developed countries have been notably weak. Alliance theory is wanting because its motives for alliances, namely, to bolster security against external threats, ignore the very significant motive in developing states-in-the-making of security against internal threats, usually ethnic or ideological in nature, or more fully, internal threats allied to external actors.[22]

Why do India's smaller neighbours, in particular Pakistan, and to a lesser degree, Bangladesh, Sri Lanka, and Nepal, not bandwagon with India in the post-Cold War, post-liberalization period? Why has their behaviour pattern been one of trying to balance India? Classical realist and neo-realist theorizing on state behaviour, particularly Great Power behaviour, in a fundamentally anarchic world has maintained that states seek survival and act to maintain the balance of power towards that end. That is, when any state becomes too powerful, other states seek to balance it by forming countervailing alliances (apart from self-help, that is, arming themselves). The alternative view is that states could seek security by bandwagoning with the most powerful or threatening state. Recent literature on alliances in history has shown that bandwagoning has been much more common than was known.[23] States also have third options such as 'hiding', buck-passing, or transcending conflicts.[24] While Walt (1987) modifies balance of power theory by arguing that states balance against threat, not power itself, he considers bandwagoning a form of capitulation with a threatening power. Schweller distinguishes between security-driven and non-security-driven bandwagoning.[25] He cites cases of 'piling on' or bandwagoning with the victors at the end of wars. Schweller (1998), Fritz and Sweeney (2004), and Sweeney and Fritz (2004) argue that what determines bandwagoning or balancing is *interest*, not power; the latter authors explicitly bring in bandwagoning for profit.[26] This applies particularly to weak powers as does bandwagoning behaviour in general. The literature on bandwagoning emphasizes that alliances have often been for profit alone, not against a common enemy.[27]

Stephen Walt and Michael Sheehan argue that the perception of threat is necessary and can arise from one or more of any of the following: geographical proximity, territorial disputes, ideological hostility, and perceived aggressive intentions.[28] Michael Barnett points to the importance of non-material, ideational factors in defining threat perceptions.[29] Conversely, bandwagoning can result from perceived common interests and identities including, as the literature on democratic peace suggests, similar political regimes and values.[30] However, 'regime similarity need not necessarily mean interest similarity; the latter can exist without the former and vice versa'.[31] That is, a similarity of regime is neither necessary nor sufficient for common interest and does not have a strong effect on the probability of bandwagoning. More recently, the democratic peace theory has itself been questioned, with Gibler advancing the argument that democracy and peace are symptoms not causes of the eradication of territorial issues between neighbours.[32] To this we can add that perhaps a democracy which inherits territorial and ideological conflicts as initial conditions, as in South Asia after independence and partition in 1947, may not be conducive to the compromises necessary for peace-building as it gives free play to competitive patriotism and hard-line parties. The general finding is that threat is the key to balancing alliances while *interests* exclusively drive bandwagoning, and that weak states, not sufficiently investigated in the literature, might bandwagon out of fear or for profit.[33]

Barry Buzan points to a possibly fruitful way forward in emphasizing that in focusing on the state and internal conflict, critics of neo-realism as applied to the Third World should not ignore system-level theory for unit-level analysis but complement the former by focusing on the hitherto neglected structural differentiation of the units.[34] That is, they should focus on how the unit states are organized and constructed, and by extension, how they are articulated within the regional and world system. However, before discussing that, let us briefly review the limited literature on IR theory's application to South Asia.

The vast literature on the international relations of South Asia is largely diplomatic–historical and, more broadly, contemporary–historical or descriptive. Very little can be said to fall within the rubric of contemporary IR theorizing.[35] Perhaps the earliest and most comprehensive IR-theoretic account of South Asia's international relations is that by Buzan, elaborated for the post-Cold War period by Buzan and Waever.[36] Buzan argues for the conceptual recognition of a regional security complex (RSC) as an intermediate level between global dynamics and internal dynamics, consisting of the level of the dynamic of security relations between local sub-systemic states. The rationale for choosing the region as a distinct level, in contrast to structural realism's world-as-a-single-system think-ing, is that military threats travel more effectively to adjacent countries. This was an attempt to deal with the problem of the seamless web in security studies, security being relational. However, there is no widely accepted definition of region. In order to form an RSC, a region does not have to be economically or politically integrated because an RSC is not an alliance, merely a geographically adjacent set of states that affect each other's security even if antagonistically. However, IR theorizing, both traditional realist and neo-realist, tends to be global-systemic and does not recognize sub-systemic levels as distinct levels of analysis apart from the very traditional notion of local or regional balances of power. However, Buzan argues that power and balance of power are inadequate concepts to define regional security subsystems. A useful regional sub-system concept can be based on security itself.

For a useful definition of security for the purpose of identifying a regional security subsystem or complex, we need to consider power in combination with the historical dynamic of amity and enmity, which is only partly related to balances of power. This historical dynamic is much more rigid than the more fluid balance of power, even where it is related. Thus, an RSC is a regionally bounded historical pattern of amity and enmity as well as distribution of power. Cultural and racial ties too are important in constituting RSCs insofar as they focus states' attention on each other. An important point is that external actors have a much lower impact on the historical patterns of amity and enmity than they do on the distribution of power. Indeed, they tend to acquiesce in local patterns of amity and enmity.

An RSC may or may not have an insulator state at the edge or a buffer state in the middle (for example, neutral Switzerland and Austria during the Cold War). A standard RSC can be either unipolar or multipolar (including bipolar, as in South Asia) and does not have a great power (system-level power). RSCs can undergo either internal or external transformation.

There can be a hierarchy of higher- and lower-level security complexes. In the Cold War era there could be four levels: domestic, regional, super-regional, and global. For example, for India, the four levels can be India, South Asia, South Asia plus China, and the global level. Alternatively, to conceive of India's situation in another way, the South Asian RSC can be said to be surrounded by three other RSCs or super-complexes: the Southeast Asian complex to the East, the Sino-Russian-Central Asian super-complex to the north, and the Middle East and Gulf super-complex to the West, with Afghanistan and Myanmar occupying ambiguous or multiple positions.

Barry Buzan and Ole Waever argue in RSC theory that after the Cold War, the structure of the international system is characterized by one superpower, four great powers, and several regions.[37] Buzan and Waever see two possible paths for the South Asian RSC: either internal transformation into Indo-centric unipolarity caused by the decline of Pakistan's relative power, or external transformation due to intensified Sino-Indian rivalry and the emergence of India as a third Asian great power, the latter being unlikely. The possibility and objective of the Gujral Doctrine, according to them, was the transcending of South Asia by India by 'pacify[ing] its smaller neighbours, make[ing] accommodative agreements with them and increase[ing] intra-regional trade. This policy was based on the understanding that India had no hope of being taken seriously outside the region until it could stabilize its own local environment.'[38] They conclude that South Asia is still very far from a Deutschian definition of a 'security community' in which the actors cannot imagine a war.[39] In South Asia, regional security cooperation is intimately linked to national identity and nation-building processes. For smaller states in South Asia, territorial disputes are linked to identity, rivers, and the like, as well as to the fear of loss of autonomy combined with a lack of economic incentives.

Although the aforementioned literature, except for Buzan and Waever, is principally about the great powers, not middle powers like India or weak states, and largely world-systemic not regional, it can profitably be applied to South Asia. What insights do these findings provide us in relation to South Asia? In South Asia, Pakistan has a major territorial and border dispute with India, a history of wars, an ideological hostility intertwined with its identity and nation-building process, and has systematically balanced India both by military, including nuclear self-help, and alliances. However, even in case of the other states, apart from Bhutan and Maldives, which are micro-states with few options, we do not see bandwagoning behaviour towards India (and even Bhutan renegotiated in early 2008 its special relationship with India whereby it would no longer consult the latter on foreign relations). For the other three smaller states—Nepal, Sri Lanka, and Bangladesh—the situation is ambiguous, in that relations with India have not been hostile, with no history of wars and serious territorial/border disputes, barring the Indian intervention in Sri Lanka in 1987–90 (Maldives in 1988 was at the request of and in support of the regime). Bandwagoning behaviour would then heavily depend on shared interests. What could these shared interests be? Gains from trade and economic cooperation could play a major role in inducing bandwagoning. However, pre-1991, India was essentially a closed, intensively import-substituting economy and, therefore, there was no incentive for its smaller neighbours to integrate with it. Have things changed since then? Can India's increasing economic openness and rapid growth create incentives for economic and political integration with it, either bilaterally or through the SAARC process? Alternatively, are there countervailing threat perceptions based on India's domestic developments (for example, the rise of Hindu majoritarianism) and the image of India as somehow being a threat to national identity.

In this context, what does a preponderant state such as India need to do to induce bandwagoning towards itself and therefore create over time a regional community that *voluntarily and on the basis of interest* accepts its leadership. The incentives for India to create such a community are clear even if it means short-term sacrifices of self-interest for long-term political and economic gains. If India can create a vibrant regional economic community around itself, then the gains are not only or even mainly economic but also geopolitical in both the Asian and world contexts, and India will be the major consumer of those long-term benefits. The first thing that India needs to diligently pursue is to settle outstanding border, including maritime border, issues with its smaller neighbours, particularly Bangladesh and Sri Lanka. As Gibler (2007) shows, territorial settlement treaties are more likely than anything else to end the incidence of war. The next most important thing is to promote economic cooperation in a way that creates incentives without the fear of being dominated or losing one's autonomy for the smaller states.

The literature indicates that typically the largest state has to be prepared to bear a disproportionately large share of the costs of regional cooperation-building and maintenance, and obtain only a disproportionately small share of the benefits, at least in the short run, for example, by non-reciprocal economic openness, in order to be able to make the usually necessary side payments to smaller partner countries. In other words, act like a benevolent hegemon. This insight is derived from coalition theory as applied to states in an anarchic world system, which shows that it is in the interest of smaller partners to coalesce with a larger partner both in a legislative setting and in international politics, particularly when the larger partner is willing and able to make side payments that make sharing of the payoff disproportionate. As Bruce Bueno de Mesquita puts it:

If the benefits derived from a winning coalition are distributed so as to preserve the initial relative distribution of resources among the winners, then the largest member of the coalition must get the largest share of the benefits. Of course, the ratio of this actor's size to that of each of its partners remains constant... but its absolute size moves closer to the system's definition of the size required to win.[40]

The argument is essentially that the largest partner, even when bearing and taking only a proportionate share of the costs and benefits respectively, is making a disproportionate quantum gain by being enabled to cross an international size/power/status threshold that makes it a qualitatively more important international player. That is, an effective South Asian regional organization led by India can disproportionately boost India's position in the global hierarchy of powers without correspondingly lifting any of its regional supporters. Therefore, they would need to be compensated more than proportionately in cost- and benefit-sharing for it to be in their interest to be in such a regional coalition, and for the same reason, it would be in the interest of the big country in such a coalition to so compensate them. What needs to be analysed are the kinds of cross-issue linkages and tradeoffs, such as between economic and security issues, and foreign and domestic policy changes affecting international relations, that are involved in the role played by the largest state and the transactions between it and the smaller ones.

IMAGES, IDENTITIES, NORMS, AND PERCEIVED INTENTIONS

In South Asia, the domestic politics affecting the prospects for regional conflict resolution and cooperation-building is less about political economy, given the current low level of economic integration, but principally about the perceived intentions of neighbours. It is important, as mentioned earlier, to understand how this is linked to images, identities, and domestic political norms. A further offshoot of the neo-realist versus neoliberal debate, also as a reaction to and in dissatisfaction with both schools, is constructivism.[41] Constructivism stands halfway between neo-realist and neoliberal theories, both rational choice approaches, and postmodernism. The neo-realist–neoliberal debate, sketched earlier, has several gaps that can be filled by constructivist perspectives in explanatorily useful ways. For example, the neoliberal criticism that the *origins* of states' preferences need to be explained gets scholars into the territory of ideologies, beliefs, experiences, and knowledge, all hitherto neglected by neoliberal as well as neo-realist theories. The criticism of neo-realism on the need to consider agents and structure as mutually constitutive is taken a step further by constructivism. Constructivist approaches stress the mutual constitution of agents and structure across levels of analysis. They stress the role of agency as against the inexorable structural determinist bias of neo-realism, and reach back to the English international history school to stress the role of agent identity and interest, and hence connect with decision-making approaches to foreign policy analysis.

Most importantly, constructivism stresses the *force of norms* upon agents and hence, interactively, on international relations. Norms are collective understandings important for behaviour. They constitute actor identities and interests, and do not just regulate or constrain behaviour, and do not merely constitute a superstructure. Domestic political and regime norms have deeper cognitive effects. Thomas Risse-Kappen, for example, argues that in NATO, the member states have functioned in a relatively more democratic and consensual manner than could be expected from the distribution of capabilities alone, because 'democracies externalize their internal norms when cooperating with one another. Power asymmetries will be mediated by norms of democratic decision-making'.[42] Thus, norms constitute identities and interests, in the process screening out 'illegitimate' identities and interests, for example, the norms embodied in the European Union (EU) as they have developed over decades of integration screen out certain threatening kinds of nationalism of an earlier era. Audie Klotz's work on South Africa, where the force of public opinion, ultimately norms, compelled Western governments with major economic and strategic interests in South Africa to impose sanctions against the apartheid regime, is a crucial case study that supports the constructivist approach and negates the neo-realist approach.[43]

The constructivist approach and its social construction of 'legitimate' and 'illegitimate' norms, following from this, would appear to be particularly relevant to the study of the construction of national identities and national interests.[44] Sagarika Dutt, citing Lapid and Kratochwil, argues that as homogeneous nation-states are a dwindling minority, national identity based on territory and that based on 'ethnicity'/culture have become contradictory.[45] In theory, however, there can be a civic liberal nationalism that does not place great importance on ethnicity or culture, for example, USA. This is extremely important in the South Asian context of the legacy of religio-ethnic partitions and wars, disputed territory and borders, majoritarian states, minority disaffection, separatist movements, terrorism, and perceived threats from neighbouring states.

Some scholars have attempted to give the constructivist approach micro-foundations in cognitive psychology, borrowing from the learning argument, social psychology, and the symbolic interactionist theory in sociology, since identities and interests are forged in social learning. Applied concretely as cognitive-strategic research to foreign policy analysis, Richard Hermann and Michael Fischerkeller argue that *strategic images*, defined as a subject's cognitive construction or mental representation of another actor in the political world, are vital in explaining actions not outcomes.[46] Confronting the cognitive revolution's implications in IR is essential. For South Asia, what needs to be explored is how images of various other countries are created by examining how that country is taught, researched, and written about; its media coverage, particularly how history and contemporary politics and portrayed; and especially the treatment of minorities and minority-dominated regions.

Constructivism also enables the development of approaches to understanding identity conflict that have the potential to transcend and resolve such conflicts. Jonathan Mercer argues that identities being malleable, such conflicts can be overcome by transcending given to larger identities, for example, national to pan-European identity in the case of European integration.[47] A vital part of creating this pan-European identity, I would argue, is that apart from economic integration, there is the creation of a common *normative* framework within which the rights of all minorities in member-states are assured, thus eradicating suspicions and hostility on the grounds of maltreatment of linguistic, religious, and ethnic minorities in some states which might be the majority group in another state, besides also assuring the rights of immigrants from poorer states. The much broader Council of Europe, whose membership has expanded in the post-Cold War period, has had a European Convention for the Protection of Human Rights and Fundamental Freedoms, and associated institutions of a European Commission of Human Rights and European Court of Human Rights, now merged into a single European Court of Human Rights. The important point here is that member countries agree to be judged by this court—which can be moved by individuals, groups, or states—on their adherence to the convention. In 1998, a Framework Convention for the Protection of National Minorities came into effect as a derivative of the former agreements and institutions, and was the first-ever legally binding instrument devoted to the general protection of national minorities. These are the kinds of agreements that generate confidence in the goodwill of partner states towards each other's peoples, and hence positively affect the *perception of intentions*, and therefore need to be studied for their lessons for South Asia. The members of the Association of Southeast Asian Nations (ASEAN) also, in practice, eschew majority chauvinism, and have power-sharing arrangements and prominent representation of minorities in national political and economic life. In contrast, SAARC, as a regional organization, not only has no common normative framework—even on minorities or minority-dominated regions despite its history of wars, partitions, and separatist movements—but also bars discussion of domestic and bilateral issues. Reinforcing this negatively is the fact that seven of the eight states are formally religio-majoritarian, privileging Islam, Buddhism, or (in Nepal till 2008) Hinduism, and India too—despite democracy, federalism, and secularism—has its share of unaddressed injustices to minorities as well as separatist movements, all of which play a role in forming its image and its perception as a potential or actual threat by its neighbours. Thus, majoritarian political norms, as well as the politics of minorities and minority regions, lead to the construction of negative images and antagonistic national/ethnic/religious identities, feed threat perceptions, and play a vital role in impeding regional conflict resolution and cooperation-building. Hence, any theorizing or policy for regional conflict resolution and cooperation needs to understand how images are generated, how they affect the self-images as well as perceptions of others (including perceptions of intentions), and, for South Asia, how the treatment of minorities in the domestic politics of the countries of the region is absolutely crucial in shaping images and identities.

POLITICAL ECONOMY OF TRADE AND ECONOMIC REGIONALISM

How do political economy and domestic politics affect the relations between states in the region and conduce to conflict resolution and cooperation-building, or otherwise. First, the level of economic integration in South Asia is very low, partly because a group of low-income, labour-intensive economies are largely competitive rather than complementary (although the recent literature on product differentiation and intra-industry trade would indicate that this is not a barrier to trade and investment integration), but primarily because the Indian economy was relatively slow to open up.[48] It is also because India's smaller neighbours have had reservations about integration with India not only due to the usual economic interest group rationale of fearing Indian takeover of their markets and nascent industries, but also due to political reasons that are linked to national, religious, and ethnic identities and images of India as somehow threatening. In case of the smaller South Asian countries, economic integration with India and increased access to, but also dependence upon, the Indian market, while bringing economic benefits, could also make them vulnerable to changes in Indian policies. That is, they would not only become more sensitive to Indian market fluctuations, but also more vulnerable to Indian trade policy shifts and hence political pressures.[49] Despite the gradual growth of preferential trade since the 1990s among the countries of South Asia under the auspices of SAARC, the South Asian Preferential Trade Area (SAPTA), initiated in 1995, went through four rounds of negotiations towards intra-regional trade liberalization based on a commodity approach. The SAARC summit of January 2004 led to a Framework Agreement to achieve a South Asian Free Trade Area (SAFTA), which formally came into existence from January 2006.[50] However, despite the rapid growth of trade since 2003 with Pakistan and Sri Lanka, the share of trade with its neighbours in India's (non-petroleum) total trade remains a mere 2.74 per cent. If one takes exports alone, it still remains only 5.75 per cent.[51] Thus, the SAFTA area will probably be marginal in terms of India's trade growth even as an export market.

India–Pakistan bilateral trade has remained at a very low level. Following the thaw after the successful SAARC summit of January 2004 at which the Indian and Pakistani heads of government met and agreed to promote economic cooperation along with a schedule of talks on all issues, the past six years have seen a dramatic quadrupling of trade, albeit from a very low base, though direct investment and joint ventures are non-existent.

SAFTA came into existence in January 2006 and is expected to roll out to full free trade by 2016.[52] There is also the India–Sri Lanka Free Trade Agreement of 1998, effective 2000, which has now reached the stage of zero-duty imports subject to rules of origin of 35 per cent value-added or 25 per cent value-added if there is 10 per cent Indian content, barring a rather large negative list of items on both sides (429 for India, 1,180 for Sri Lanka), but which can be imported at SAFTA rates. As of March 2008, India has unilaterally reduced duties to zero for imports from the four Least Developed Countries (LDCs) in South Asia—Bhutan, Maldives, Nepal, and Bangladesh—subject to a negative list of items which can be imported at SAFTA rates. However, among the items for which India allows duty-free imports from Sri Lanka and Nepal (the only two countries with which India has bilateral trade agreements), some are subject to tariff rate quotas, that is, above a certain volume, they are not duty-free but subject to SAFTA tariffs which are somewhat and varyingly lower than regular most-favoured nation (MFN) tariffs for the rest of the world. Pakistan is the odd one out in South Asia, in that while India allows imports from that country at SAFTA rates with the same negative list as for Sri Lanka, Pakistan allows, at the latest count, only 1,075 items to be imported from India at SAFTA rates, with other items banned for import.[53] The real potential for growth in trade is in the future. This is because of the inevitable liberalization of all the economies coupled with a perhaps sustained growth rate of over 7–8 per cent in India and industrial diversification; but the real holdout on regional free trade is Pakistan, which has been unwilling to grant India MFN status (although it is only a question of time under its commitments to the World Trade Organization).

The incentives for regional economic cooperation-building for leading regional states could be analogous to that for global hegemons, from the perspective of hegemonic stability theory, for building global economic cooperation regimes, as neoliberal institutionalists Robert Keohane and Joseph Nye argue: 'Stable economic regimes require leaderships—that is, willingness to forego short-term gains in bargaining in order to preserve the regime—and that an actor is most likely to provide such leadership when it sees itself as a major consumer of the long-term benefits produced by the regime.'[54] Further, 'When the hegemonial power does not seek to conquer other states, but merely to protect its favoured position, other states may benefit as well.'[55] This argument can be modified to apply to regional economic cooperation regimes in which there is a clear regional economic power whose relative global or extra-regional status would be boosted by leading a regional group, and hence would have incentives to be 'generous' to smaller states, as has been argued by Bueno de Mesquita.[56]

However, other scholars looking at successful cases of regional economic integration would argue that there are political prerequisites for successful economic integration. The most successful case is the EU. The process of European integration began with the Schuman Plan (for the European Coal and Steel Community) presented in May 1950, the

European Coal and Steel Community Treaty in 1951, ratified to bring it into effect in 1952. Helen Milner argues that,

The Schuman Plan called for countries and their firms to relinquish control of two vital economic sectors, coal and steel, to a supranational 'High Authority' (HA). Since these sectors undergirded the rest of the economy and provided the means to make war, control over them was not just an economic issue.... Once these sectors were integrated internationally, it was felt, war between these countries would never again be possible.[57]

Thus, the treaty neutralized the Saar, Rhine, and Ruhr border areas between France and Germany, which produce coal and steel. The treaty would thus constrain Germany. Moreover, it should be noted that this treaty was preceded by the formation of NATO as a security umbrella under US leadership, the Warsaw Pact as a common threat, and the Korean War as an ongoing regional hot war in the Cold War confrontation, in addition to which there was US pressure on both France and Germany to ratify the treaty. Thus, the process of economic integration was built on political preconditions from its very inception rather than being an economic process bringing about security and political integration.

To sum up, when one theorizes political economy and domestic politics in South Asian conflict and cooperation, one is not talking principally in terms of economic interest groups as in, say, regional integration in the EU, NAFTA, ASEAN, or Mercosur, but substantially about images and identities, and relationship of both to the treatment of minorities and minority regions, the ideology of the state, and the idea of the nation in each country. This is particularly so in the case of India–Pakistan relations.

THE CHAPTERS IN THIS VOLUME

The first volume in this two-volume collection covers three broad issue areas—one, the creation of possible regional architectures; two, the political economy of trade and economic integration (at both the foreign policy and domestic political levels of analysis); three, purely domestic political issues, such as the state and minorities, which are important because they impinge on relations between states and hence on the prospects for regional integration and regional architectures. Some chapters like those by Pratap Bhanu Mehta, Jayadeva Uyangoda, and Ayesha Siddiqa are not limited to IR theory but employ broader social science theorizing, particularly political philosophy and comparative politics.

Pratap Bhanu Mehta argues that interests and ideas alone do not propel regional integration. So long as states depend on the fear of an 'other' as a basis for their identity and internal unity, regional integration will be an uphill task. It will depend crucially upon the states in the region reaching a stage of maturity where they do not need the fear of an 'other' to secure their sense of self and identity. Regional integration requires sovereignty tradeoffs, in that it requires the creation of supranational, trans-border institutions and rules that require the surrender of at least some components of sovereignty in some spheres to such supranational authorities. Because sovereignty is closely tied to identity, that is, a sense of distinctness and particularity, such sovereignty tradeoffs are politically difficult in a way that goes beyond arguments about material interests or convergence of ideas or ideology between states.

Mehta's chapter reviews the literature on the conditions for regional integration, taking into account sub-regional conflict, ideas, interests, and identities, and analyses South Asia in the context of these.

Varun Sahni, taking a Buzanian RSC perspective, explores the concepts of 'regional power' and 'regional security', and links them to the under-theorized concept of 'regional leadership' through a comparative analysis of the regional power and leadership profiles of three emerging powers, all 'middle powers' which lack system-shaping capabilities but which cannot be ignored by the great powers in their respective regions: India, Brazil, and South Africa. The underlying argument is that 'while the exercise of regional power is essentially a control operation, the establishment of regional leadership requires the generation of consent'. India is thus a regional power but not a regional leader, whose status as such is contested not only by Pakistan but also by several of its smaller neighbours. However, he hints at the scope for policy initiatives by India to break the regional deadlock.

Aparajita Biswas critiques the neo-realist approach and argues that a variant of neoliberal institutionalism at the regional level, namely, the cobweb or 'bottom-up' Nordic model of cooperation is the only feasible model for SAARC as a regional cooperation institution at the present juncture. Regional cooperation should begin with the 'low politics' issues of economic and infrastructural cooperation and with non-traditional security issues such as economic and human security, and build upwards gradually to the 'high politics' of traditional security. Such an approach, resembling also the ASEAN model, is more effective and much needed to build trust between the countries of the region. It is better than trying to construct a premature and, hence, inevitably weak and unstable regional security cooperation architecture.

Turning to domestic politics and its implications for relations between states, Ayesha Siddiqa analyses civil–military relations in four South Asian countries—India, Pakistan, Bangladesh, and Sri Lanka—going beyond the narrow focus of most scholars on civilian command and control of the armed forces. Borrowing from Charles Tilly and Fredric Lane, she situates the narrower issue of command and control within the larger framework of state–society relations in post-colonial societies and focuses on authoritarianism and the role of force in the larger political culture and how it shapes civil–military relations. Pakistan and India are the polar cases in South Asia. The key factors increasing the military's political role and power include the perceived primacy of military security in the leadership's political objectives. Internal conflict is also a key factor, and following from this, the political leadership's propensity to use the armed forces for political purposes. Granting the military such a role in domestic politics is bound to increase its overall power and importance over time.

Jayadeva Uyangoda's chapter explores the 'conceptual possibilities for reworking the Sri Lankan state in conjunction with a negotiated political settlement to the ethnic conflict that addresses ethnic minority grievances'. Its detailed analysis of various possibilities, while entirely focused on Sri Lanka, is hugely important for the possibility of a common normative framework for the treatment of minorities, from both the rights and power-sharing perspectives, and hence for the possibility of a regional cooperation and integration framework based on such a common normative framework, the latter being virtually necessary in the context of South Asia for the creation of perceptions of benign intentions towards the peoples of other states. The chapter is, therefore, extremely important for thinking through the domestic political basis of stable and sustainable regional integration in South Asia and neatly complements the other chapters of the volume.

Rajesh M. Basrur analyses the policy reversal of Sri Lanka towards India from the 1990s, from distancing and attempted balancing to bandwagoning, at all three levels—structure, domestic politics, and leadership initiatives. He argues that structure, or distribution of power, remained the same and supports the arguments of neoclassical realists and liberals that structure does not necessarily determine foreign policy and can be transcended in certain contexts. The decision to bandwagon was a conscious leadership choice in Sri Lanka based on revised perceptions and preferences, and this was not due to a crisis but was evolutionary, and was not based on business or bureaucratic interest groups (these being very weak). What was crucial for the policy reversal were the opportunities offered by the liberalization of the Indian economy as well as by a more cooperative Indian attitude to Sri Lanka's domestic ethnic conflict, and hence the emergence of a common security interest in a negotiated political settlement of the civil war in Sri Lanka in the late 1990s and early 2000s.

Nalini Kant Jha, in his study of the domestic politics of Bangladesh's policy towards India, argues that domestic factors, such as Dhaka's sense of insecurity arising out of its small size and 'India-locked' location, its underdevelopment and dependence on foreign aid, the dilemma of national identity, half-hearted accommodation of the religious and linguistic minorities, the political insecurity of ruling elites, and acute factionalism within the ruling establishment have interacted with each other and together shaped the country's foreign policy in general and its India policy in particular.

He finds support for his hypothesis 'that in a situation where the ruling elites' support base is narrow, they lack political legitimacy and their survival is uncertain, domestic politics is accorded greater salience in the making of foreign policy in comparison with the external environment...', and that the pursuit of 'regime interests overrides national interests'.

Rahul Mukherji examines the case of the Indo-Sri Lanka Free Trade Agreement of 1998 and its subsequent evolution to analyse the conditions under which regional trade liberalization is possible between India and its smaller neighbours. He contextualizes the Agreement against the backdrop of India's post-1991 trade liberalization and need for export markets, the opportunity costs for Sri Lanka of lacking access to the growing Indian market, the pressures on both countries from the 1997 Asian crisis, and the post-nuclear tests sanctions on India in 1998, and argues that mutual gain and a positive-sum trade relationship are necessary conditions. However, India's strategy of reciprocity-plus or asymmetrical concessions needed both an ideational change as well as an improved strategic relationship to lessen relative gains sensitivities. Both the ideational change and the improved strategic relationship followed from the Liberation of Tamil Tigers Eelam's (LTTE's) assassination of Rajiv Gandhi, combined with Sri Lanka's later move in the 1990s towards an exploration of a peace process to accommodate Tamil aspirations which India desired.

Mohammad Humayun Kabir examines, in the light of IR theory, the gamut of India–Bangladesh relations, which began on a positive note in 1971 and then progressively deteriorated. He focuses on the problem of river waters among various other issues, and draws upon the theorizing on relative gains sensitivities and on Andrew Kydd's ideas on trust and reassurance. He argues that the reasons for the failure of cooperation are Bangladesh's cumulative relative gains' fears, and fears of being locked in by India and losing an exit option in cooperation, and that these fears are in turn rooted in a lack of trust due to India's lack of reciprocity and non-reassuring postures. These have impeded cooperation between the two neighbours, particularly in the areas of transit, gas export, and water resources.

The essays in this first volume are complemented by those in the second volume of this set in which three broad issue areas—(i) security; (ii) political economy and domestic politics; and (iii) the construction of images, identities, world-views, and normative frameworks—are covered by scholars, many of whom are critical of mainstream approaches.

Notes

1. The earlier and first volume of the project was E. Sridharan (ed.), *The India–Pakistan Nuclear Relationship: Theories of Deterrence and International Relations* (New Delhi and Abingdon, UK: Routledge, 2007).

2. The issue of Kashmir is missing in this collection because the literature on it is already vast.

3. See Kenneth N. Waltz, *Man, the State and War* (New York: Columbia University Press, 1959); and Arnold Wolfers, *Discord and Collaboration: Essays on International Politics* (Baltimore: Johns Hopkins University Press, 1962), pp. 3–24, for early but still insightful discussions of levels of analysis in international politics. For images and perceptions of decision-makers as a level of analysis, see Robert Jervis, *Perception and Misperception in International Politics* (Princeton: Princeton University Press, 1976).

4. For details of the various South Asian dialogues summarized in the rest of this section, see Navnita Chadha Behera, Paul M. Evans, and Gowher Rizvi, *Beyond Boundaries: A Report on the State of Non-Official Dialogues on Peace, Security & Cooperation in South Asia* (Toronto: University of Toronto-York University, Joint Centre for Asia Pacific Studies, 1997).

5. For the next five paragraphs I draw heavily on E. Sridharan, 'International Relations Theory and the India–Pakistan Conflict', in E. Sridharan (ed.), *The India–Pakistan Nuclear Relationship*, pp. 32–5, the first volume that came out of this project. For an excellent critical survey of the neo-realist–neo-liberal debate, see Robert Powell, 'Anarchy in International Relations Theory:

The Neorealist–Neoliberal Debate', *International Organization*, 48 (2), Spring 1994, pp. 313–44. For two book-length collections on the debate, see Robert O. Keohane (ed.), *Neorealism and Its Critics* (New York: Columbia University Press, 1986); and David A. Baldwin (ed.), *Neorealism and Neoliberalism: The Contemporary Debate* (New York: Columbia University Press, 1993). For the best statement of traditional realism, see Hans J. Morgenthau, *Politics among Nations* (New York: Alfred A. Knopf, 1948), and for the classic statement of neo-realism, see Kenneth Waltz, *Theory of International Politics* (Reading, MA: Addison Wesley, 1979). For an early and classic statement of neoliberal institutionalism, see Robert O. Keohane, *After Hegemony* (Princeton: Princeton University Press, 1984).

6. The structure of the argument and the classification of criticisms of neo-realism in the next few pages draw heavily on Powell, 'Anarchy in International Relations Theory'.

7. Keohane, *After Hegemony*.

8. Joseph Grieco, 'Anarchy and the Limits of Cooperation', in Keohane (ed.), *Neorealism and Its Critics*, pp. 116–42.

9. However, it has been shown that cooperation can also take place under conditions of sensitivity to relative gains. See Duncan Snidal, 'Relative Gains and the Pattern of International Cooperation', *American Political Science Review*, 85 (3), September 1991, pp. 701–26.

10. Powell, 'Anarchy in International Relations Theory'.

11. Stephen M. Walt, *The Origins of Alliances* (Ithaca, NY: Cornell University Press, 1987).

12. Stephen Krasner, 'Global Communication and National Power', in Baldwin (ed.), *Neorealism and Neoliberalism*, pp. 234–49.

13. Judith Goldstein and Robert O. Keohane, 'Ideas and Foreign Policy: An Analytical Framework', in Robert O. Keohane and Judith Goldstein (eds), *Ideas and Foreign Policy: Beliefs, Institutions and Political Change* (Ithaca, NY: Cornell University Press, 1993), pp. 3–30.

14. For a recent review of the bandwagoning–balancing debate and the position that bandwagoning or balancing takes place not against/with power or perceived threat but on the basis of shared interests or the lack of this, and in particular that bandwagoning is induced by shared interests and balancing takes place only in high-security situations within which weak states invariably bandwagon, see Paul Fritz and Kevin Sweeney, 'The (De)Limitations of Balance of Power Theory', *International Interactions*, 30, 2004, pp. 285–308; for the historical data revealing bandwagoning behaviour as well as excellent surveys of the bandwagoning versus balancing literature, see Kevin Sweeney and Paul Fritz, 'Jumping on the Bandwagon: An Interest-based Explanation for Great Power Alliances', *Journal of Politics*, 66 (2), May 2004, pp. 428–49.

15. This is a summary of the key features of US behaviour towards its allies in building global economic cooperation regimes in the post-Second World War period. For details, see Robert Keohane and Joseph Nye, *Power and*

Interdependence: World Politics in Transition (Boston: Little, Brown & Co., 1977); and Keohane, *After Hegemony*, which extends the neoliberal institutionalism to global institution- and regime-building in post-hegemonic distributions of power.

16. Hans J. Morgenthau, *Politics Among Nations: The Struggle for Power and Peace* [1948] (New York: Alfred A. Knopf, 1978); Stephen M. Walt, *The Origins of Alliances*.

17. For a review of the security alliance literature focusing on small states, see Volker Krause and J. David Singer, 'Minor Powers, Alliances and Armed Conflict: Some Preliminary Patterns', and Heinz Gartner, 'Small States and Alliances', both in Erich Reiter and Heinz Gartner (eds), *Small States and Alliances* (Vienna: Physica Verlag, 2001).

18. Mancur Olson and Richard Zeckhauser, 'An Economic Theory of Alliances', *Review of Economics and Statistics*, 48 (3), August 1966, pp. 266–79.

19. Joanne S. Gowa and Edward D. Mansfield, 'Power Politics and International Trade', *American Political Science Review*, 87 (2), June 1993, pp. 408–20; Joanne S. Gowa, *Allies, Adversaries and International Trade* (Princeton: Princeton University Press, 1994).

20. Douglas M. Gibler, 'Bordering on Peace: Democracy, Territorial Issues, and Conflict', *International Studies Quarterly*, 51 (3), September 2007, pp. 509–32.

21. See the chapters by Amitav Acharya and K.J. Holsti, 'Beyond Anarchy: Third World Instabilty and International Order after the Cold War', pp. 159–212, and 'International Relations Theory and Domestic War in the Third World: The Limits of Relevance', pp. 103–32, respectively, in Stephanie G. Neuman (ed.), *International Relations Theory and the Third World* (London: Macmillan, 1998); and Michael Handel, *Weak States in the International System* (London: Frank Cass, 1981).

22. Steven R. David, 'The Primacy of Internal War', in Neuman (ed.), *International Relations Theory and the Third World*, pp. 77–102.

23. See Fritz and Sweeney, 'The (De)Limitations of Balance of Power Theory'; Sweeney and Fritz, 'Jumping on the Bandwagon', for the historical data revealing bandwagoning behaviour as well as excellent surveys of the bandwagoning versus balancing literature.

24. Paul W. Schroeder, 'Historical Reality vs. Neorealist Theory', *International Security*, 19, 1994, pp. 108–48.

25. Randall L. Schweller, 'Bandwagoning for Profit: Bringing the Revisionist State Back In', *International Security*, 19, 1994, pp. 72–107, especially, p. 74.

26. Randall L. Schweller, *Deadly Imbalances: Tripolarity and Hitler's Strategy of World Conquest* (New York: Columbia University Press, 1998); Fritz and Sweeney, 'The (De)Limitations of Balance of Power Theory'; Sweeney and Fritz, 'Jumping on the Bandwagon'.

27.   Robert G. Kaufman, '"To Balance or Bandwagon?" Alignment Decisions in 1930s Europe', *Security Studies*, 1, 1992, pp. 417–47; Eric J. Labs, 'Do Weak States Bandwagon?', *Security Studies*, 1, 1992, pp. 383–416; Randall L. Schweller, 'Bandwagoning for Profit'; Randall L. Schweller, *Deadly Imbalances*; Fritz and Sweeney, 'The (De)Limitations of Balance of Power Theory'; Sweeney and Fritz, 'Jumping on the Bandwagon'.

28.   Walt, *The Origins of Alliances*; Michael Sheehan, *The Balance of Power: History and Theory* (New York: Routledge, 1996).

29.   Michael Barnett, 'Identity and Alliances in the Middle East', in Peter Katzenstein (ed.), *The Culture of National Security: Norms and Identity in World Politics* (New York: Columbia University Press, 1996), pp. 400–50.

30.   Kurt Taylor Gaubatz, 'Democratic States and Commitment in International Relations', *International Organization*, 50, Winter 1996, pp. 109–30.

31.   Sweeney and Fritz, 'Jumping on the Bandwagon', citing Henry S. Farber and Joanne Gowa, 'Common Interests or Common Polities? Reinterpreting the Democratic Peace', *Journal of Politics*, 59 (2), 1997, pp. 393–417.

32.   Gibler, 'Bordering on Peace'.

33.   Fritz and Sweeney, 'The (De)Limitations of Balance of Power Theory'; Sweeney and Fritz, 'Jumping on the Bandwagon'.

34.   Barry Buzan, 'Conclusion: System versus Units in Theorizing About the Third World', in Neuman (ed.), *International Relations Theory*, pp. 213–34.

35.   Recent exceptions focus on the limited issue of the India–Pakistan conflict for broader theorizing on war and deterrence, but not comprehensively on South Asian conflict resolution and regional cooperation, such as Devin T. Hagerty, *The Consequences of Nuclear Proliferation: Lessons from South Asia* (Cambridge, Mass.: MIT Press, 1998); Sumit Ganguly, *Conflict Unending: India–Pakistan Tensions since 1947* (New York: Columbia University Press, 2001); Sumit Ganguly and Devin T. Hagerty (eds), *Fearful Symmetry: India–Pakistan Crises in the Shadow of Nuclear Weapons* (New Delhi: Oxford University Press, 2005); T.V. Paul (ed.), *The India–Pakistan Conflict: An Enduring Rivalry* (Cambridge: Cambridge University Press, 2005); Rajesh M. Basrur, *Minimum Deterrence and India's Nuclear Security* (Stanford: Stanford University Press, 2005); S. Paul Kapur, *Dangerous Deterrent* (Stanford: Stanford University Press, 2007); Sridharan, *The India–Pakistan Nuclear Relationship*.

36.   Barry Buzan, 'A Framework for Regional Security Analysis', and Gowher Rizvi, 'Pakistan: The Domestic Determinants of Security' and 'The Rivalry Between India and Pakistan', all in Barry Buzan and Gowher Rizvi (eds), *South Asian Insecurity and the Great Powers* (London: Macmillan, 1986); Barry Buzan and Ole Waever, *Regions and Powers: The Structure of International Security* (Cambridge: Cambridge University Press, 2003).

37.   Buzan and Waever, *Regions and Powers*.

38.   Ibid., p. 120.

39. Karl W Deutsch, Sidney A. Burrell, and Robert A. Kann, *Political Community and the North Atlantic Area: International Organization in the Light of Historical Experience* (Princeton NJ: Princeton University Press, 1957), pp. 5–9.

40. Bruce Bueno de Mesquita, *Strategy, Risk and Personality in Coalition Politics: The Case of India* (Cambridge: Cambridge University Press, 1975), pp. 9–10.

41. See, for example, Alexander Wendt, 'Constructing International Politics', *International Security*, 20, Summer 1995, p. 73.

42. Thomas Risse-Kappen's chapter on NATO, in Peter Katzenstein (ed.), *The Culture of National Security: Norms and Identity in World Politics* (New York: Columbia University Press, 1996), pp. 357–99.

43. Audie Klotz, *Norms in International Relations: The Struggle Against Apartheid* (Ithaca, NY: Cornell University Press, 1995).

44. For important recent works on identity and culture in IR theory, see Rodney Bruce Hall, *National Collective Identity: Social Constructs and International Systems* (New York: Columbia University Press, 1999); Bill McSweeney, *Security, Identity and Interests: A Sociology of International Relations* (Cambridge: Cambridge University Press, 1999); Yosef Lapid and Friedrich Kratochwil (eds), *The Return of Culture and Identity in IR Theory* (London: Lynne Rienner, 1996). For foreign policy analyses that privilege identities, see David Campbell, *Writing Security: United States Foreign Policy and the Politics of Identity* (Manchester: Manchester University Press, 1992); Elizabeth Kier, 'Culture and French Military Doctrine Before World War II', in Peter Katzenstein (ed.), *The Culture of National Security* (New York: Columbia University Press, 1996), pp. 186–215; Alastair Ian Johnston, 'Cultural Realism and Strategy in Maoist China', in Katzenstein (ed.), *The Culture of National Security*, pp. 216–68.

45. Sagarika Dutt, 'Identities and the Indian State: An Overview', *Third World Quarterly*, 19 (3), 1998, pp. 411–33; Yosef Lapid and Friedrich Kratochwil, 'Revisiting the "National": Toward an Identity Agenda in Neorealism', in Lapid and Kratochwil, *The Return of Culture*, pp. 105–26.

46. Richard K. Hermann and Michael P. Fischerkeller, 'Beyond the Enemy Image and Spiral Model: Cognitive–Strategic Research after the Cold War', *International Organization*, 49 (3), Summer 1995, pp. 415–50.

47. Jonathan Mercer, 'Anarchy and Identity', *International Organization*, 49 (2), Spring 1995, pp. 229–52.

48. See the literature on product differentiation and intra-industry trade, for example, Paul R. Krugman, 'Intraindustry Specialization and the Gains from Trade', *Journal of Political Economy*, 89 (5), October 1981, pp. 959–73; Robert Balance, Helmut Forstner, and W. Sawyer, 'An Empirical Examination of the Role of Vertical Product Differentiation in North-South Trade', *Review of World Economics (Weltwirtschaftsarchiv)*, 128 (2), 1992, pp. 330–8; Paul

R. Krugman, 'Increasing Returns, Monopolistic Competition, and International Trade', *Journal of International Economics*, 9 (4), November 1979, pp. 469–79.

49. For a discussion of sensitivity interdependence and vulnerability interdependence, see Keohane and Nye, *Power and Interdependence*, pp. 11–19.

50. Government of India, *Annual Report 2004–2005* (New Delhi: Ministry of External Affairs, Government of India), pp. 129–30.

51. Government of India, Ministry of Commerce and Industry, Department of Commerce, Export–import data bank, 2007–8.

52. See www.saarc-sec.org for the activities of SAARC, including SAFTA.

53. The last count referred to was in March 2008. Informal source was ICRIER whose researchers track India–Pakistan trade including Pakistani policies.

54. Keohane and Nye, *Power and Interdependence*, p. 44. For hegemonic stability theory, see Stephen D. Krasner, 'State Power and the Structure of International Trade', *World Politics*, 28, 1976, pp. 317–47. For a critical survey of hegemonic stability theory, disaggregating its strands, see David A. Lake, 'Leadership, Hegemony and the International Economy: Naked Emperor or Tattered Monarch with Potential?', *International Studies Quarterly*, 37 (4), December 1993, pp. 459–89.

55. Ibid., pp. 44–5.

56. Bruce Bueno de Mesquita, *Strategy, Risk and Personality in Coalition Politics: The Case of India* (Cambridge: Cambridge University Press, 1975), chapter 1, for a survey of power maximization theories of coalition politics which shows that it is in the interest of smaller partners to coalesce with a larger one, in a legislative setting, particularly when the larger partner is willing and able to make side payments that make the sharing of the payoff disproportional. The argument is essentially that the largest partner is only compensating for the disproportionate quantum gain that it is enabled to make either by enabling government formation or by enabling it to cross a political threshold that makes it a qualitatively more important player in the system.

57. Helen Milner, *Interests, Institutions and Information: Domestic Politics and International Relations* (Princeton: Princeton University Press, 1997), p. 180.

Part I

REGIONAL COOPERATION MODELS, PROCESSES, AND OBSTACLES

1 Sovereignty Tradeoffs and Regional Integration

Theoretical and Comparative Reflections

Pratap Bhanu Mehta

What are the conditions under which regional integration takes place? This chapter offers some reflections on this pointedly posed question in an attempt to bring some theoretical and comparative material in dialogue with the debate over the limits and possibilities of regional integration in South Asia. The purpose is not so much to provide an exhaustive history of inter-state relations in South Asia and the recalcitrance of the states in the region to move towards greater regional integration; but only to clarify the kinds of questions we need to ask about this process in the light of comparative and theoretical considerations.

Before jumping to the central argument, I want to make a prefatory comment about international relations (IR) theory that has some bearing on the argument advanced here. It has become canonical in the literature to attribute principally two motives to the state: ideas or interests. It is assumed that for the most part, states are moved by one or the other motive or some combination of both. The language of interests does, in many instances, force an analytical clarity by insisting that an account of the kinds of gains a state is likely to achieve by a particular course of action will be crucial to explaining its behaviour. Indeed, the language of ideas does focus on the values and ideologies that might drive the state, but the language of ideas and interests greatly impoverishes our understanding of international politics (or politics in general) if viewed as exhaustive of the motives upon which state acts. For one thing, this vocabulary elides over several crucial distinctions. For instance, we can posit that states would wish to enhance their power, but it makes all the difference in the world if their acceptance of power politics is driven by *macht politik* rather than realpolitik.

More typically, states are nation-states, and as such are often driven by a sense of their own identity or a sense of honour. Their identity, and their sense of honour, is the context within which their interests are defined rather than the other way around. However, if the idea of honour cannot be subsumed under the language of interest without great contortion, it cannot be reduced to the realm of ideology either. For one thing, honour is more about moral psychology than it is about ideas or values; it enfolds within it a series of insecurities, fears, and hopes that nations have acquired through the process of their formation. Second, the objects through which these complexes express themselves need not have any determinate content; they can be differently expressed depending upon the context. In that sense their content is more elusive than that of ideas or interests. Its effect is, however, no less palpable. In some senses, IR theory needs to take on board the idea that just as in the case of an individual you lose analytical clarity by bunching all motives under the label of interest, so is the case with 'corporate' entities like nation-states. In a sense, this is a call to return to a more variegated understanding of motives that operate on the world stage; the kind of understanding embodied in Thucydides' Peloponnesian War. It is somewhat a waste of time to debate whether he was a realist or an idealist; his understanding of the motives that drive states, to aggrandizement and self-destruction alike, was far too rich to be captured by labels such as ideas or interests.

The reason for making this point as a preface to this chapter is this: As I shall argue in the following, the language of interests or ideas does not capture the forces that propel regional integration. Indeed, in the context of South Asia, there is something prior that impedes a full consideration of interest or ideas: a longing for identity. Dealing with the fragility of identity is not simply a matter of throwing more power or goods at a state; nor is it merely a matter of producing ideological convergence. It requires a complex set of historical processes that are, to some degree, still far away. Indeed, one of Thucydides's central insights was that fear of an enemy, sometimes even manufactured, was necessary to bind a state together. This was an insight that Aristotle developed strikingly and became a staple of political theory from Polybius to Machiavelli. Aristotle writes:

Constitutions are preserved, not only by keeping their destroyers at a distance, but also by sometimes keeping them near, because being afraid people will have a better grip of constitutions. Thus, those who care for the constitution should manufacture fears and bring that which is far near, so that people will guard the constitution like night watchmen without relaxing.[1]

The central question for a theory of international relations is: Under what circumstances do states need the fear of an external enemy to secure their internal identity and unity? In South Asia, to a certain extent, many of the states have relied on a fear of the other to secure their identity. The prospects of regional integration will depend not so much upon a cold calculus of material interests or an ideological convergence but crucially upon the states in the region reaching a state of maturity where they do not need the fear of an 'other' to secure their sense of self and identity. One of great lessons of the classical tradition of political thinking, from Thucydides, Sallust, and Polybius, is that this condition is rarer than one supposes. It took Europe the catastrophic experience of two world wars to recognize that fear of the other was not exactly the most constructive way of securing the identity of the state; this is a lesson South Asia is yet to learn.[2]

Part 1

Sovereignty Bargains in Comparative Perspective

The canonical model of the Westphalian state is commonly based on two components: territorial sovereignty and juridical autonomy. Political authority in this canonical view of the state is exercised over a defined geographical space. The claim to autonomy involves many things, but principally the idea that no external authority or actor enjoys authority within the borders of the state. In other words, the state is *sovereign*, in that it is not subordinate to any other institution or organization. In the classical model, sovereignty is the raison d'etre of the state. It is, in a Hobbesian sense, a resolution to the conundrum of internal authority, and a state ceases to be a state if it compromises on its sovereignty.

The Westphalian conception of sovereignty has of course been routinely compromised in the actual practice of states: through conventions, coercion, contracts, and even impositions.[3] However, increasingly, states are resorting to what might be called 'sovereignty tradeoffs'. One prominent example of such a process is the creation of regional and political unions. These unions entail sovereignty tradeoffs insofar as they often require the establishment and maintenance of structures of authority and institutions that supersede national boundaries. Such institutions often transgress autonomy and transfer control to supranational actors. The most prominent example is of course the European Union (EU), an entity that possesses the most far-reaching and wide-ranging supranational institutions of any scheme of regional integration. The EU now has powers ranging from initiating legislation to monitoring implementation, from setting policy constraints to imposing judicial sanctions.

What are the factors that justify sovereignty tradeoffs, and under what circumstances can we expect such tradeoffs to occur? The first is an explicitly normative question concerned with the desirability of such tradeoffs, the second a more empirical one and that falls squarely within the provenance of IR theory. Under what conditions can we expect such tradeoffs to take place and why would states wish to engage in sovereignty tradeoffs?

In order to get a grip on this question, it is important to make a couple of preliminary analytical distinctions. It is a truism that states will often engage in sovereignty tradeoffs because of some perceived benefits to them. It is, however, important to begin by recognizing that states would rarely wish to cede sovereignty as such; rather what they cede are particular components of sovereignty. Sovereignty is, in this view, not an all-or-nothing concept. Rather, it comprises of a cluster of elements, each of whose importance, and relationship with other elements, varies historically. Following Walter Mattli, we can identify three components of sovereignty that pull in different directions: autonomy, control, and legitimacy.[4] As he describes it, autonomy refers to independence in the formulation of policy. Control refers to the ability of states to produce the effects they desire; it refers to the actual capacities to produce outcomes. Legitimacy refers to the right of the state to formulate rules in a way that is widely accepted and recognized internally and externally. This scheme is certainly not exhaustive of the components of sovereignty. Indeed, as I argue in later sections of the chapter, sovereignty is crucially tied to identity: a sense of *distinctness and particularity* that states seek to maintain, which plays a crucial role in the behaviour of states. Indeed, the terms in which the identity of the state is defined crucially determine what its interests are. For the moment, however, it is helpful to proceed with the components of sovereignty that Mattli so well defined.

In normal international agreements, tradeoffs between these components are visible all the time. A state may be nominally autonomous, but ineffective in bringing out the results it desires. Many states confuse sovereignty with just one of its components, autonomy.

Arguably, India or Bangladesh's opposition to trade agreements was rooted in precisely such confusion. Sovereignty was collapsed into autonomy, without any regard for control or power: the ability to affect outcomes. Paradoxical as it sounds, states can sacrifice their autonomy to achieve greater power. Some international agreements also involve an autonomy–legitimacy tradeoff. Participation in international environmental regimes may, for instance, diminish both internal legitimacy and autonomy but enhance external legitimacy. The Hanseatic League had all the autonomy components of sovereignty but none of the control. The prosperity–sovereignty tradeoff often underlies the choice for regional economic unions too. Some states will sacrifice their autonomy to lock into arrangements that they think will produce prosperity. The precise tradeoffs involved in bargains over sovereignty are structured differently for different states, depending upon their particular circumstances. However, the core point is that sovereignty comprises a variety of components, and it may be the case that not all these can be secured simultaneously and that negotiations over sovereignty are not all-or-nothing affairs.

States engage in sovereignty tradeoffs through a wide variety of instruments: security pacts, trade agreements, regional unions, international treaties, and human rights conventions. The motives for engaging in such tradeoffs depend upon the particular incentive structure that states face or, more accurately, that leaders within it face.

One of the most striking features of sovereignty tradeoffs is that a large number of them are prompted by what we might call, without a pejorative connotation, neoliberal ideologies. The number of trade agreements across the world has increased strikingly, and these agreements entail serious sovereignty tradeoffs. North American Free Trade Agreement (NAFTA), for example, requires countries to accept something approaching a Washington consensus: reduce deficits, reform interest rates, realign exchange rates, liberalize foreign direct investment (FDI), protect property rights, and go in for at least some measure of deregulation and privatization. The same is true of new claimants to EU membership. Here I should clarify that neoliberal in this context means a commitment to trade and openness of economy, not necessarily a diminished role for the state or a reduction in its size. Indeed, the degree to which the openness of an economy is compatible with a welfare state or social democracy, or with regulatory intervention by the state, has proved to be a remarkably more open question than many writers have argued.

What are the conditions under which this particular set of sovereignty tradeoffs becomes attractive? While it would be difficult to argue that there is a single set of necessary and sufficient conditions, some enabling conditions can be identified. In *The Logic of Regional Integration* (1999), Walter Mattli has persuasively argued that sustained periods of economic decline make such tradeoffs more attractive.[5] For instance, 18 of the 20 applications for membership in the EU were submitted in times of economic difficulty. States did not seek integration so long as there was not a considerable performance gap between the state and the union, and only sustained performance gaps prompted a desire to seek the benefit of union. Even relatively prosperous states are more attuned towards seeking union in times of economic downturn relative to the regional performance. Second, regional integration has a self-fulfilling dynamic. It is indeed often the case that countries experience economic difficulties precisely because their neighbours are integrating into such arrangements, as was the case with Britain and the EU. Alternatively, arguably even China's entry into the World Trade Organization (WTO) is an attempt to avoid the effects of sovereignty bargains being made by other nations. Indeed, it is not entirely an accident that once a number of countries decide to engage in such bargains, others have to necessarily follow. For instance, once China entered into a free trade agreement with the Association of Southeast Asian Nations (ASEAN), it put pressure on Japan to follow; and it convinced India that it needed to enter into some kind of free trade agreement with ASEAN. The interesting question is: what is the threshold whereby the dynamics of states engaging in these tradeoffs can become self-expanding?

However, and this is the third component, regional economic unions, and free trade agreements more generally, require a commitment to something akin to a neoliberal ideology, in the sense suggested earlier. One of the more curious results of studies of European and North American economic integration is that sustained periods of economic downturn are also propitious for the rise of neoliberal ideologies. The intuitive logic behind this idea is simply that massive state expenditures and interventions are unlikely to be sustained under conditions of protracted economic slowdown. Therefore, states will begin to redefine their functions in a more 'liberal' direction and seek to break domestic logjams by seeking out international agreements and conditionalities. The striking enthusiasm for the EU from former communist states is of course a striking instance of this. In the long run, sovereignty bargains in the direction of free trade, and greater regional integration require some acceptance of neoliberal economic principles.

The most successful example of far-reaching sovereignty tradeoffs is the EU. While the conditions that brought about greater European integration are complex, and include the horrifying experience of the Second World War, greater American presence, the formation of North Atlantic Treaty Organization (NATO), and the like, the logic of integration had elements of a neoliberal model. While there are many theories of European integration, the two most powerful accounts—Andrew Moravcsik's liberal inter-governmentalism (*The Choice for Europe: Social Purpose and State Power from Messina to Maastricht*) and John Gillingham's recent history (*European Integration 1950–2003*)—point in similar directions.[6] The logic of the relationship between the EU and neoliberalism was spelt out in Hayek's classic 1939 essay, 'The Economic Conditions of Interstate Federalism'.[7] Ironically, this essay appeared in print on 1 September, the day Hitler invaded Poland, but still remains a powerful analysis.

Hayek begins the essay by arguing that open markets and gradual political interdependence go together, and the logic of his explanation bears repeating. He argues that no successful instances can be found of political federations without institutions that secure the unimpeded movement of goods, capital, and labour. The absence of trade barriers, he argues, will make it difficult for individual states to identify their interests independently of the rest of their trading partners. It will thus limit the pursuit of independent policies by member states of a federation. It will consequently be more difficult for any state to manipulate prices, set an independent monetary policy, discriminate against particular producers, levy harmful taxes, or even impose social or regional policies to any considerable degree. He argued also that the larger the size of the union, the less likely that it would be possible to undertake extensive planning at the central level. His explanation for this was based on political economy: it would be more difficult for a federation than individual states to satisfy the range of demands placed upon it, and so it would respond essentially by trying to limit itself to the proscription of anti-market policies. The weakening of federal and state power, he argued, would also mean that many of the essential tasks of the state would be conducted at regional and local levels. Competition between these constituent units would in turn provide a check on the power and growth of centralized institutions.

There is much to quibble about in the logic of this argument. While Hayek saw inter-state federalism as a bulwark against communism, the degree to which such integration is incompatible with large welfare states or interventionist states remains an open question. Moreover, Hayek underestimated the extent to which questions of regional inequality become important and certain regions need to be subsidized in federations of this kind. Indeed, one of the central lessons from the European experience is that regional integration of any kind depends in good measure upon the willingness of rich states in the region to unilaterally provide subsidies to poorer regions. It also depends in a substantial measure upon *not* dismantling such social protection and subsidies as exist; otherwise the project of integration does not receive sufficient domestic political support. However, notwithstanding serious flaws, Hayek's remains a powerfully compelling account of the logic of the EU. To put it bluntly, as many observers have argued, it is more difficult to imagine social democracy rather than some version of neoliberalism being the dominant regulatory ideology of an enlarged EU. In fact, the EU signals the demise of old style left parties. Indeed, as has been shown, even the problem of the pacification of Germany was conceived of largely in neoliberal terms. Wilhelm's Ropke's classic, *The Solution to the German Problem*, argued that:

The world calls for an application of a principle that surpasses every other in boldness and novelty. This is the principle of absolute, and even if necessary, one-sided free trade. The Allies should impose on Germany nothing more than a single measure of economic intercourse with foreign countries and bring German free trade into effect.[8]

There is substantial evidence that a neoliberal project of integration was at the heart of the origins of the EU. But more importantly for our purposes was Hayek right in making the following claims?

1. A commitment to neoliberalism, in the sense defined earlier, of some kind, facilitates or is likely to increase the probability of sovereignty bargains in the economic arena. These sovereignty bargains, in turn, sustain open economies. Whatever one may think of neoliberalism, as an economic ideology its elective affinity with sovereignty bargains is compelling. Are states, committed to free trade in the long run, more likely to see sovereignty bargains? Alternatively, to put it even more bluntly, is regional cooperation more likely or inconceivable without some deep commitment to free trade and all that it entails?[9]

2. Hayek's second claim was that once states are attuned to making sovereignty bargains in the economic arena, most of them will be functionally compelled to make more and more sovereignty bargains. Free trade is a first step towards disaggregation of sovereignty claims.

3. Greater regional integration involves a simultaneous dialectic of centralization and decentralization. On the one hand, power will devolve to supranational institutions, but it will also devolve downwards towards localities (a version of the subsidiarity principle).

4. Although Hayek did not explicitly state this, the logic of his argument suggested that regional integration can help promote the solution of sub-regional conflicts, like the Irish and the Basque problems. I want to spell out the logic for thinking this, as it is of considerable interest.

REGIONAL INTEGRATION AND SUB-REGIONAL CONFLICT

I should add a preliminary note to avoid misunderstanding. Hayek was by no means an economic determinist, as anyone familiar with his works is aware. In fact, the entire burden of his argument was that free trade is not a pre-ordained outcome, but is itself a product of *political* choice.

The mechanisms through which regional integration helps sub-regional conflict are the following. First, as states get habituated to unbundling sovereignty, they are less susceptible to seeing it as an all-or-nothing affair. Essentially, conflicts can be resolved only if the outcome is not seen as a zero-sum game. Without unbundling sovereignty into its different components, it is unlikely that any zero-sum discourse can be overcome. In particular, states used to sovereignty tradeoffs have a structure of domestic politics where such arguments as bargains are more acceptable. These are states that begin to understand that, just as in areas of trade, sovereignty tradeoffs can bring benefits and can, in principle, do so in other areas as well. Second, sub-regional devolutions undertaken in the context of wider regional settlements are easier to sell politically because they are part of a larger process of restructuring and not seen as an individual issue. Third, the parent state itself begins to redefine its core stakes in the sub-regional conflict. If its interests in trade, free movement, human rights, and rights of minorities within minorities can be secured, for instance, then it might be more willing to devolve other powers. In fact, because both the sub-regional unit and the parent state are encased in a larger supranational set of institutions, both have a credible assurance that their interests in these areas will not be unilaterally undermined. Fourth, within the logic of regional convergence, the substantive laws of all the states and the normative values they protect begin to look more and more alike. Thus, the state itself no longer remains the arena in which national differences are articulated and defended. Fifth, in cases of sub-regional issues, involving inter-state conflict, the two states in question can acquire greater experience of working together in interlocking institutions. Sixth, states are also more attuned to accepting outside mediation.

Whether or not any of the aforementioned mechanisms will lead to desired outcomes remains contingent and it would be unwise to believe in economic or political over-determination. However, if the experience of the EU is any guide, this is certainly plausible. In fact, the one case that strikingly bears out the consequences of the mechanisms discussed earlier is Britain, both in reference to Scotland and Wales, but also more importantly to Northern Ireland. It is a striking fact that devolution to Scotland and Wales was facilitated by Britain's integration into the EU. That integration provided assurances that the core British interests in these regions would not be unilaterally abridged by devolution of powers: a local assembly could not unilaterally expropriate the English or pass laws that discriminated against outsiders. One of the fears of greater devolution in places like Kashmir, and one of the arguments against it, is that it is not clear what a devolved power structure might entail by way of preserving other core values (the controversy over Kashmir's inheritance bill recently is a striking example). Devolved power within the context of supranational associations like the EU makes such fears less rational. The irony, of course, is that it is easier to devolve power when the structure of laws across the devolved units looks more similar. A greater ideological convergence makes power sharing more possible.

As has been pointed out by others, notably Sumantra Bose, the peace process in Northern Ireland was greatly facilitated by the fact that both Britain and Ireland were members of the EU, which both joined in 1972.[10] It was easier for them to engage in bilateral cooperation under an overarching regional framework of cooperation and integration. This framework, which linked the two states through supranational institutions, reduced the salience of zero-sum sovereignty discourses. It certainly involved a reorientation of Irish attitudes towards Europe, and supranational institutions involved both countries in a framework of cooperation. In a context of a *general* rethinking of devolution of powers across Europe, it was easier to relocate the Irish problem out of a particular competitive framework and place it in the context of a wider rearrangement.

Whether or not this example is applicable elsewhere is another question. It is nonetheless a dramatic illustration of sovereignty tradeoffs helping to resolve a particularly nasty conflict and a reminder that these tradeoffs were made possible because they were ensconced in a wider framework of sovereignty negotiations.

The most important thing, of course, is to recognize that sovereignty tradeoffs are possible and enduring when there is at least an implicit convergence of values. We can list the benefits from trade that resulted as a consequence of greater European integration, but in the final analysis, the project was an outcome of the catastrophic experience of the two world wars. Amongst other things, this project generated an *absolute commitment to the pacification of violence* on the European continent. Second, the project was generated by a commitment to contain Germany within the context of a larger European project; Germany in turn became an ardent enthusiast of the project because it was perhaps the only means of furthering its legitimacy in the aftermath of its horrific historical experience. Third, the project depended crucially upon all the states in the regions subscribing to democratic values of some kind. Indeed, as the EU expanded, its very presence acted as a catalyst for democracy in newly emerging states.

It is important to draw a distinction here between common values and a common culture. The European project, for the most part, was premised upon common values, not a drive to create a common culture. It is only when the question of the integration of Turkey came to the fore that the question—does Europe have a common culture grounded in Christianity—came to the forefront. If Europe shifts the discourse from common values to common culture, its potentiality for expansion and accommodating differences will be severely tested. However, perhaps most crucially it depended upon the idea that, at least within the context of Europe, a politics premised on the fear of the other had reached its logical conclusion in the two wars and that a politics premised upon securing national identities and national strength by mobilizing fear had diminishing returns. In part, what makes EU such an extraordinary political experiment is that it is premised upon nation-states, with a long history of enmity, creating structures to overcome fear.

SOVEREIGNTY TRADEOFFS AND HUMAN RIGHTS REGIMES

While much has been written on sovereignty tradeoffs in relation to trade, there is relatively little on sovereignty tradeoffs in relation to human rights instruments (the exception is Moravscik [2000][11]). Regimes, such as those established by the European Convention on the Protection of Human Rights and the Inter-American Convention on Human Rights, hold governments accountable for internal activities. Such regimes have drawn little attention, in part because most of them, like the United Nations (UN) Covenant, remain largely unenforceable. However, institutions like the European Convention for Human Rights (ECHR) empower individuals to bring suits to challenge the domestic activities of governments. They establish supranational bodies of adjudication on matters of human rights, which some might say are an ultimate sovereignty tradeoff. Whatever the details of the ECHR, the puzzle is this: why would governments favour the establishment of an independent authority, supranational in character, the sole purpose of which is to constrain its domestic sovereignty?

Moravscik has effectively rebutted the realist and idealist explanation of this phenomenon. He argues that neither coercion-based explanations nor explanations that involve simply the diffusion of ideas work in this context.[12] After all, paradoxically, just as dictatorships initially oppose such agreements, so do well-established democracies, which view them as a usurpation of sovereignty. Alternatively, in many instances, democracies see such institutions as irrelevant because they claim to have credible internal institutions to deal with such issues. Therefore, USA and the UK are notoriously more hostile to such forms of sovereignty tradeoffs. His argument is that the demand for such credible instruments comes usually not from established democracies, but from recently established and potentially unstable ones.

The logic of the argument is as follows. New and unstable democracies have leaderships that are new and precariously positioned. They are on the lookout for instruments of democratic consolidation that can lock in certain institutional commitments that are conducive to democracy. In other words, they seek insulation from the actions of future governments. Established democracies, in this view, support sovereignty tradeoffs in the sphere of human rights, largely as a response to perceived threats from others. A state may wish to 'bolster' democratic peace, buy a form of insurance policy against other states, by locking them into certain arrangements. In effect, it sees human rights instruments as a kind of long-term security bargain.

This analysis is interesting because it points to features that make for regional cooperation. The first is that states and their leaderships must experience what I call a legitimation deficit. States that are too secure in the legitimacy of their institutions are less likely to engage in sovereignty tradeoffs, as are states that simply do not care about legitimation and democratic consolidation. Some states—arguably India on occasion— can be both very secure in the confidence of their own institutions, on the one hand, and not care much about human rights violations, on the other hand. The second condition it points to is that a state might come to view enforceable human rights instruments as a guarantor of its own security: if a neighbouring state is obliged to conform to human rights and democratic norms, it might well be worth the price of trading off your own sovereignty.

The question in relation to South Asia is whether states in fact experience such a legitimation deficit. This legitimation deficit is in part a function of the ideational diffusion: do states have a political culture that takes human rights seriously? If they do not, then convergence on a regional institutional architecture is less likely. However, one of the interesting hypotheses that Moravscik's arguments generates is this: states are more likely to accede to some regional human rights commitments if they feel that doing so will enhance their legitimacy abroad and lock them into certain commitments in terms of domestic politics. As he puts it, 'Governments will sacrifice sovereignty in order to dampen domestic political uncertainty and lock in more credible policies.'[13] This is, however, a special condition that obtains only when a state does not legitimize itself through hostility to neighbours; nor is it so secure in its sense of legitimacy that it feels it irrelevant to secure external legitimacy.

The role of 'external legitimacy' is also important from another angle. In Europe's case it is sometimes easy to forget the role of a continuing American presence in the consolidation of the EU. The fact that the Cold War necessitated the consolidation of military alliances in Western Europe was a condition that facilitated unification for a number of reasons. First, it effectively brought these nations under a common security umbrella and eradicated security as a bone of contention. Second, American presence was in part instrumental in producing the convergence over values. Third, it was also a presence that, for the most part, was a source of assurance that no one major player had the ability to dominate Europe, at least in terms of military and security. In short, the role of outside powers is also important in creating the background conditions for regional integration. In South Asia this role has been considerably different.

PART 2

REGIONAL INTEGRATION IN SOUTH ASIA: THE THEORETICAL PRECONDITIONS

In examining the future prospects for regional integration in South Asia it is worth considering the conditions, referred to earlier, under which successful regional integration can occur. If regional integration has to take place, it has to dovetail hard-headed economic and political logic with a normative aspiration—not sentimentalism and rhetoric. Indeed, the burden of the previous sections was to suggest implicitly that in the case of the EU, normative commitments drove the project as much as mere material gains; indeed what material gains states choose to concentrate upon is in part a function of their values and self-identity. ASEAN, perhaps, presents an alternative model in which the convergence of values is less robust. Indeed, it prides itself on providing a mechanism enabling very diverse kinds of countries to engage in trade relations and create a modicum of constitutional culture that helps negotiate tensions without demanding the deep convergence of values that Europe requires. However, in some respects the countries of ASEAN, given their modest size and location, saw that their bargaining power with other major powers would be enhanced by some form of regional cooperation. I shall discuss later whether the ASEAN model has any implications for South Asia.

South Asia remains one of the least integrated regions in the world. According to a recent report, intra-regional trade is less than 2 per cent of Gross Domestic Product (GDP) in South Asia in comparison to over 20 per cent in East Asia; only 7 per cent of international phone calls in the region are regional as compared to over 70 per cent in East Asia; the cost of trading across borders in the region is amongst the highest in the world; and notwithstanding propitious geography, there is relatively little trading of energy.[14] These indicators, in a social and economic sense, exemplify the deep political divides in the region that make the prospects for regional integration look dim.

What are the conditions that promote regional integration? Do these conditions exist in South Asia?

We must distinguish between regional cooperation and regional integration. The former refers simply to a type of cooperation between governments. Regional integration, on the other hand, is the unleashing of a process that binds the societies and economies of neighbouring countries much more closely together. On one level, any project of greater regional integration involves what are called 'sovereignty tradeoffs'. Integration often requires the establishment and maintenance of structures of authority and institutions that surpass national boundaries. The EU is a prominent example of an entity that possesses wide-ranging, supranational prerogatives. What are the reasons justifying sovereignty tradeoffs? Under what conditions can we expect these tradeoffs to occur?

The first condition that will make South Asian integration possible is a revolution in the understanding of 'sovereignty' itself. Although nationalists wave the flag of sovereignty as if it were a mystical, indivisible whole, in truth it is no such thing. As argued earlier, sovereignty has different components that pull in different directions: autonomy, control, legitimacy, and identity. Autonomy refers to the independence a state has in making policy; control refers to the actual ability of the state to produce the outcomes it desires. Legitimacy refers to its right to make rules in ways that are widely accepted and recognized internally and externally. However, one of the things that much of the literature on regional integration ignores is identity. It is interesting that in Walter Mattli's typology of the components of sovereignty, referred to earlier, identity does not figure as one of the variables. Identity refers to the capacity of the state to endow people with an overriding sense of who they are as a collective group.

The difficulty is that these components of sovereignty do not hang together particularly well. A state may be autonomous, but may be quite ineffective in bringing about the results it desires. It might also lack control. Meanwhile, in South Asia people tend to confuse sovereignty with just one of its components: autonomy. Arguably, the post-colonial opposition to free trade that still marks most countries in the region (with the exception of Sri Lanka and now, increasingly, India) is rooted in just such a confusion. Bangladesh may nominally assert its autonomy vis-à-vis India by refusing to sell it natural gas, but by doing so it is diminishing its own power. Paradoxical as it may sound, sacrificing autonomy can sometimes enhance power. The crucial starting point for regional integration is when states begin to realize that autonomy does not necessarily create either control or power; that committing to forms of interdependence can enhance power, even though it may initially seem to diminish autonomy.

Almost all of South Asia was thus caught in a post-colonial syndrome, in which that particular, narrow understanding of sovereignty became a mark of self-respect and identity. After all, colonialism was seen to have violated just this most-cherished aspect of political identity. An obsession with sovereignty, initially the result of the colonial experience, evolved on the part of the neighbouring states into a defensive claim against possible Indian domination. India's political difficulties in the region have stemmed primarily from its relative size and power. In the interests of regional integration or the creation of free trade zones, one of two conditions must be met: either most of the countries have to be of comparable size, or the economy of a dominant country has to be so attractive that others cannot resist the allure of integration. For most of the period since independence, India's economy did not have such a status. However, with India's economy currently in the process of acquiring a new stature, this could offer a dynamic to pull the region together.

Even if New Delhi does not act threateningly, the mere possibility of its regional domination elicits a defensive response from its neighbours. Arguably, if India sins against its neighbours, it is more a sin of condescension rather than a naked desire for domination. However, for fragile states with insecure identities struggling to establish themselves, condescension might appear to be even worse than overt hostility. In consequence, India finds it very difficult to overcome the fears and anxieties of countries like Bangladesh and Nepal, which is necessary in order to stabilize relations. As a whole, the regional countries have never felt sufficiently secure as states to engage in sovereignty bargains that would be in their interest. Perhaps regional integration depends upon individual countries coming into their own as classic, full-fledged states that feel sufficiently confident to consider transcending their own limitations. However, with many not yet having achieved that status, the ruling establishments tend to become defensive at the mention of regional cooperation or integration.

The second prerequisite condition for regional integration is a commitment by the states of the region to liberal economic policies: 'liberal' in this case not in its strongly theoretical sense, but simply implying the promotion of free trade, greater mobility of citizens, and the like. Will the South Asian states recognize the benefits of an integrated common market? Certainly, all will recognize the benefits in the long run. In the short term, however, entrenched interests fear the consequences of opening up their economies; as such, they artfully disguise their immediate interests as the long-term welfare of their larger societies. The commitment to economic liberalism is arguably still very tenuous in South Asia and there is simply no example of successful regional integration amongst sovereign states that is not founded on a commitment to economic liberalism.

Here, two factors might prove to be crucial. First, India has now clearly emerged as a dynamic economy: one that has sufficient power to carry the region with it. Sri Lanka, always a pioneer in this respect, has realized that it can piggyback on India's economic success. Not only has Colombo signed a free trade agreement and relaxed its visa regime for all arrivals, it is also negotiating a comprehensive economic agreement with New Delhi. India also has a free trade agreement with Bhutan and a Trade and Transit Agreement with Nepal. However, India–Pakistan and India–Bangladesh trade relations remain deeply problematic. According to some estimates, trade between India and Pakistan has potential worth of at least 8 to 10 billion dollars, even accounting for the fact that some trade diversion may result as a consequence of a regional trade agreement.

The second factor is, in some ways, the opposite of the first. It could be argued that, precisely because India is becoming a powerful economy, its smaller neighbours will fear it even more and become more defensive. However, while this fear is often exaggerated (if the Pakistani market were to open to Bollywood, the allure of an additional 100 million consumers would transform Bollywood cinema at least as much as it would impact Pakistan), India will still need to prepare to make unilateral concessions in order to avert those fears. When it comes to economic integration with its neighbours, India must move away from a paradigm of cyclical bilateral diplomacy, where each tariff concession depends upon some reciprocal gesture from the other side. New Delhi can now easily afford to give preferential treatment to goods and services produced in the neighbourhood. This would create a long-term constituency for regional cooperation and defuse much of this fear. India has recently abandoned its insistence on reciprocity, and this will considerably improve the prospect of a more effective South Asian Free Trade Agreement (SAFTA). It has also, for the first time, recognized that it will have to take the lead in trade facilitation, by endeavouring to lower transaction costs on its borders. Regional trade had been greatly hampered by the fact that India had, for the most part, a frontier mentality towards its borders. Rather than showcasing its best infrastructure and customs facilities, it historically left the border regions underdeveloped as a kind of buffer zone. Its initiatives on trade facilitation may not resolve many of the serious obstacles in the way of trade, but they will certainly help. If the comparative reflections in Part 1 (Sovereignity Tradeoffs, Regional Integration) are any guide, all projects of regional integration depend to a certain degree upon *unilateral* concessions driving the project.

If one looks beyond strictly South Asia, regional economic integration is already on the move and the momentum is substantial. In some ways, India's strategy to look beyond the South Asian Association for Regional Cooperation (SAARC) and negotiate free trade agreements with ASEAN, Thailand, and Singapore, and possibly the Bay of Bengal Initiative for Multi Sectoral, Technical and Economic Cooperation (BIMSTEC) grouping that brings together some South and Southeast Asian states, was a clever move. As far as India is concerned, the possible free trade zone now stretches from Kabul to Manila, in which only Pakistan and Bangladesh will be excluded if they do not come on board. In the long run, they will have to join the party or pay a heavy economic price. However, politically, Dhaka and Islamabad might find it convenient to join a larger grouping than SAARC, which always carries the taint of being dominated by India. In some ways, in the rest of the world, the logic of free trade moves in concentric circles outward: a core group of territorially contiguous countries signing agreements and generating momentum for others to join in. In South Asia, this is almost reversed, with greater liberalization towards the outside world coming in as a catalyst for modest opening within the region.

Despite some modest moves towards trade integration in the region, trade is still hostage to conflict. Even the most promising trade relationship, that between India and Sri Lanka, has not had as much momentum on the improvement of their political relationship as was assumed. Indeed, the larger conclusion from the failure of trade to create a greater momentum for political relationships is that *politics is prior*. It is not a calculus of relative or absolute gains that will drive greater integration, but an overcoming of internal identity complexes that will create the space for trade.

The third condition for the emergence of greater regional integration would be the acceptance by regional states of what might be called a 'simultaneous dialectic' of greater regional integration and sub-regional power. Imagine if there were a free flow of goods and services throughout South Asia. Sri Lanka would in all likelihood develop extensive links with Tamil Nadu in India. The two Punjabs (one in India and the other in Pakistan) would share greater interdependence, as might West Bengal (in India) and Bangladesh, or parts of Rajasthan and Sindh (Pakistan). It would also mean the greater development of the border regions of current states, where growth has been deliberately slowed.

Would the region's states look upon this kind of sub-regional integration without suspicion? On the ground, regional cooperation can gather momentum only when it is based on organic links between different sub-regions of the subcontinent, not on links enforced from the centre of each country. None of these sub-regional linkages are likely to create any serious problem of secession from existing political units, though they will lead to a rediscovery of some old cultural identities. The allure of 'Punjabiyat', which has marked the recent thaw in relations between India and Pakistan, is one such instance. Regional integration will require future South Asian states to have 'strong' centres but 'weak' circumferences. The fears that regional integration would somehow swallow existing states are exaggerated; these states would emerge even more strongly, just with different definitions.

In a curious way, as has been shown by the experience of the EU, regional integration can also help to solve identity conflicts. However, if power is devolved to regions within the context of a broader regional framework, where the larger region as a whole is committed to certain, specific values, these anxieties can become less pressing. Greater regional integration in this sense has the potential of creating a new dialectic of identity in the region. However, it is precisely a concern over identity that is the most formidable obstacle to generating a political momentum over regional integration in India. In some ways, the nation-states of the Indian subcontinent were formed against the grain of natural geography and cultural links of the region. Whatever may have been the cause of the partition of the subcontinent and the subsequent violence that ensued, the fact is that the identity and raison d'etre of the nation-states in South Asia were defined in contradistinction, if not hostility, with one another. While there have been expressions of popular and political sentiment that this hostility be transcended, it is fair to say that the region is still a long way off from committing itself to the kind of absolute pacification of violence within the region that defined the EU. One way of putting aside the difference is as follows.

In Europe, for the most part, the project of regional integration took place years after the question of the core national identities of the major players had been more or less settled. The question was finding a framework for containing one another. In South Asia, the question of the identity of many of the states—Pakistan, Bangladesh, Sri Lanka, and to a certain extent, India—remains internally unsettled. It is an uncomfortable truth, but our identities impel us to invest in conflict.

That is why, in part, the debate over regional integration and identity remains a vicious circle in the region. There are those who argue that if the logic of trade, communications, and other kinds of linkages is allowed to take over, this will slowly and ineluctably lead to a diminution of the identity conflicts that beset the region. However, in a context where these identity conflicts are central to the identity of states (as say the Kashmir issue is to both Pakistan and India), yielding on issues of regional cooperation is seen not just as subject to an ordinary calculus of interests, but relevant to the fundamental identity of the state. Any concessions are seen not in the framework of bargaining, but as a fundamental act of betrayal. The core structural problem in South Asia is what might be described as the *antagonism of narratives*. For regional integration to be possible, the following will have to take in place. In the case of India and Pakistan, for example, each side will, in principle, have to answer the following question: What is it that they are willing to concede as a concession to the other side? Such a concession will have to square the following circle. It will have to be insignificant enough for the conceding party, so that it is not regarded as an act of betrayal. It will, however, have to be sufficiently significant for the other party to count it as a credible concession. This is not about the legal or moral legitimacy of claims of either party but simply stating that the way in which the countries concerned have constructed their narratives of identity make such concessions difficult.

What compounds the problem is of course the fact that this antagonism of narratives is often used by elites to shore up their own domestic power. In Pakistan, for instance, the military has used this antagonism with India to shore up its power; in a lesser vein, elites in Nepal and Bangladesh can put the fear of India to political uses. Although India has been changing, it has also been very difficult to move domestic opinion to create the condition for some concessions when targets of opportunity present themselves. In short, the dynamic of regime legitimation has often required investment in conflict rather than in its mitigation. The particular fusion of identity narratives and elite power makes it difficult for South Asian states to deal in an ordinary calculus of power. The central challenge for the region is going to be to come up with new narratives of identity that can help mitigate some of the structural contradictions of the current ones.[15]

It might also be worth thinking of the role that offshore balancing and external powers can play in producing regional convergence in South Asia. Admittedly, the historical conditions for regional integration have been difficult in the region, but it could be argued that the presence of external powers in the region has exacerbated rather than reduced the antagonisms. This is for a number of reasons. First, the presence of these powers distorted the dynamic of balancing in the region. Their economic assistance and security protections can often reduce the incentives to deal with other powers in the region. In the case of ASEAN, countries could band together to increase their bargaining power with other major powers. In South Asia, they used outside major powers to increase their bargaining power with other countries in the region. Second, the external powers themselves, in contrast to Europe, were by and large not agents of ideological convergence or convergence around values. Indeed, they were often indifferent to regime type, and often the pattern of foreign aid and assistance has shored up the power of the military in the region.

The most crucial aspect of regional integration is, however, ideological convergence across the member states. This does not mean that all politics would begin to look alike, but it would necessitate a set of commitments to which all states would abide and incorporate into their own laws. These requirements would include a commitment to basic liberal values, a respect for minority rights, a commitment to the rule of law, and the like. Unfortunately, for the moment, domestic politics throughout most of South Asia often disallows pledges on these core values. Indeed, ironically, the only ideology that calls for greater regional integration, the Bharatiya Janata Party's (BJP) dreams of an undivided India, is an obstacle for two reasons. First, its assimilationist rhetoric is threatening and itself generates conflict. It, however, also rests on a deep confusion that besets much of the discussion of regional integration in the region. The confusion is this: regional integration is not premised upon cultural commonality or a fusion of identities. It is rather premised upon a common set of *normative values*: a commitment to the pacification of violence, human rights, democracy, and trade. Democracy has emerged as a widespread aspiration in the states of South Asia. In 2009, for the first time, every single state became a democracy of some kind. There is, however, still little evidence that it is an overriding value that will trump other fears and obsessions.

On the face of it, the prospects for SAARC would appear very grim. There is no ideological convergence on the subcontinent; no deep commitment to trade as an engine of growth; and none of the states is willing to acknowledge that any solution to its problems might be found regionally, beyond its own national boundaries. On the other hand, insecurities abound in our individual states. Rather than transcending identities, the region's governments use identity politics to keep their populations hostage and to bait their neighbours. No country is sufficiently serious or willing to make a definitive break from the historical agreements and compromises that, in the final analysis, are to blame for the current impasse. Thus, we have absurd situations where SAARC countries do not collaborate on energy and hesitate to facilitate bilateral trade, even when their own populations would benefit. Meanwhile, every possible economic, geographical, or cultural link is reduced. The result is that South Asia is one of the world's most militarized areas, with states needing to protect themselves against their own region.

Notes

1. Aristotle, *Politics* (New York: Oxford University Press, 1962), 1261a, pp. 10–15.

2. See Plutarch, *Lives* XXVII. 2 (New York: Modern Library), 2001; Neal Wood, 'Sallust's Theorem: A Comment on Fear in Western Political Thought', *History of Political Thought*, 16 (2), 1995, pp. 174–89.

3. Stephen Krasner, *Sovereignty: Organized Hypocrisy* (Princeton: Princeton University Press, 1999).

4. Walter Mattli, 'Sovereignty Bargains in Regional Integration', *Review of International Studies*, 2 (2) 2000, pp. 149–80.

5. Walter Mattli, *The Logic of Regional Integration: Europe and Beyond* (Cambridge: Cambridge University Press, 1999).

6. The best books on the EU are Andrew Moravscik, *The Choice for Europe: Social Purpose and State Power from Messina to Maastricht* (Ithaca: Cornell University Press, 1998); John Gilligham, *European Integration 1950–2003: Super State or New Market Economy* (Cambridge: Cambridge University Press, 2003). For normative debates, see Glyn Morgan, *The Idea of a European Super State* (Princeton: Princeton University Press, 2005); for constitutional debates see Joseph Weiler, *The Constitution of Europe* (Cambridge: Cambridge University Press, 1999); for governance, see Fritz Scharpf, *Governing Europe* (Oxford: Oxford University Press, 1990).

7. F.A. Hayek, 'The Economic Conditions of Interstate Federalism' [1939], in F.A. Hayek, *Individualism and the Economic Order* (London: Routledge, 1948).

8. Wilhelm Ropke, *The Solution to the German Problem* (New York: Putnam and Sons, 1947), p. 16.

9. This proposition has in a different way been articulated by a modern classic: Philip Bobbit, *The Shield of Achilles: War, Peace and Course of History* (London: Penguin Books, 2002). It argues that the world is moving from an era of nation-states to an era of what he calls 'market states', where an economic logic of openness replaces traditional concerns of the state. While his account of this transition is exaggerated, the central point that market access has become a principal concern of states is very valid. This is not, however, market access gained directly by imperial domination, but by opening up trade.

10. Sumantra Bose, *Kashmir: Roots of Conflict, Paths to Peace* (Cambridge, Harvard University Press, 2004).

11. Andrew Moravscik, 'The Origins of Human Rights Regimes: Democratic Delegation in Post War Europe', *International Organization*, 54 (2), 2000, pp. 217–52.

12. Ibid.

13. Ibid., p. 249.

14. *South Asia: Growth and Regional Integration*, World Bank, 2006.

15. For this, in relation to Pakistan, see Farzana Shaikh, *Making Sense of Pakistan* (London: Hurst, 2009).

2 Regional Dynamics of Emerging Powers

Power/Control or Leadership/Consent?[1]

Varun Sahni

The primary purpose of this chapter is to examine the twin concepts of 'regional power' and 'regional security', and to link them to the relatively unexplored concept of 'regional leadership'. I approach these concepts through a comparative analysis of the regional security *problématique*s of Brazil, India, and South Africa, the three most visible 'emerging powers' in the global South. My core understanding is that regional power and regional leadership are distinct but interrelated concepts: while the exercise of regional power is in essence a control operation, the establishment of regional leadership requires the generation of consent.

However, the chapter also has a secondary objective, which is to understand the interplay between policy initiative and regional context. To what extent are the regional policies of Brazil, India, and South Africa conditioned by their respective regional contexts? While regional structures surely pose powerful constraints on the policy choices of the emerging powers, what is the role of innovative domestic and regional policy in transforming the regional context? Stated thus, it is clear that the subject matter of the chapter lies squarely within the bounds of a fundamental issue in social research, the agent–structure problem.[2]

The analysis that follows is organized in seven sections. In the first, I explain why (and how) Brazil, India, and South Africa are being compared. In the second, I identify the respective regions within which the three countries are situated. In the third section, I analyse the concepts of regional security, regional power, and regional leadership, and apply these concepts to our three cases. The fourth, fifth, and sixth sections sequentially examine the respective regional dynamics confronting Brazil,

India, and South Africa. The seventh section concludes the chapter by providing tentative answers to two important questions. First, what provides regional security to emerging powers: promoting regional peace and stability or finding the most effective route to regional dominance? Second, does the regional context determine the regional policy of each emerging power, or is the regional policy adopted by each unrelated to the constraints imposed by the regional power configuration?

THREE EMERGING POWERS

Brazil, India, and South Africa are three significant countries of the global South. It therefore makes a lot of sense to expect that they can learn a great deal from one another's experiences. Clearly, the governments of the three countries have decided that they should coordinate their respective policies and strategies, which they have done quite impressively in the context of world trade negotiations in recent years. Since 2003, the three countries have come together in the India, Brazil, and South Africa Dialogue Forum (IBSA), a new trilateral initiative. The IBSA initiative was formally inaugurated by the Brasilia Declaration of 6 June 2003.[3] Earlier that year, conversations between President Luiz Inácio Lula da Silva of Brazil, Prime Minister Atal Behari Vajpayee of India, and President Thabo Mbeki of South Africa led to the Brasilia meeting between the foreign ministers of the three countries. The explicit aim of the Brasilia meeting was to examine 'themes on the international agenda and those of mutual interest'. This implies that the three countries are similarly situated in the international system and also have similar aspirations regarding a future global role for themselves.

For all these similarities, there are significant differences between the three countries. In some obvious senses, they fit uneasily together. In terms of sheer size, for example, South Africa cannot be sensibly compared, either geographically or demographically, with Brazil or India. From the domestic political perspective, while Brazil and South Africa made their democratic transitions in the mid-1980s and mid-1990s, respectively, and are therefore recently consolidated democracies, India has been a robust, if sometimes flawed, functioning democracy since 1952. Their respective regional settings are also dissimilar: unlike Brazil and South Africa, India belongs to a fractured region. In what ways, then, does it make sense to compare the three countries?

Brazil, India, and South Africa began appearing together in lists of countries drawn up by scholars and analysts of world affairs in the late

1990s, during the first decade after the end of the Cold War. The three countries featured in Jeffrey Garten's list of the 10 large emerging markets, which were deemed important not only because they were 'the key swing factor in the future growth of world trade', but also because they were crucial to 'the avoidance of war in several critical hotspots'.[4] They also appeared on Robert Chase, Emily Hill, and Paul Kennedy's list of nine pivotal states, which were defined by their 'capacity to affect regional and international stability. A pivotal state is so important regionally that its collapse would spell transboundary mayhem: migration, communal violence, pollution, disease, and so on.'[5] Both lists, it is important to note, had a distinct regional dimension.

However, the three countries first appeared together in a list drawn up in the mid-1980s, in Carsten Holbraad's pioneering study of middle powers.[6] Like the pivotal states concept, one would intuitively expect middle powers to have a significant impact on the security of their region. However, the precise relationship between middle powers and regional security is unclear. This lack of clarity largely stems from the nebulous and protean nature of the middle power concept itself.

Middle powers could be defined on the basis of relative power, specific systemic and/or regional roles, a potential to emerge as future great powers, or just a vague sense of being 'in the middle' (geographically, economically, culturally, or diplomatically).[7] In this chapter, we define middle powers as the special category of states that lack the system-shaping capabilities of the great powers, but whose size, resources, and role, nonetheless, preclude them from being ignored by the great powers. In other words, middle powers may lack the capacity to challenge the way in which the great powers run the international system, but they are sufficiently powerful to defy any great power attempt to force them to behave in a manner against their choosing. Emerging powers, then, are a subset of middle powers: they are the middle powers on the ascendant; the states that have the capability and intention to manoeuvre their way into great power status.

It is worth emphasizing that not all middle powers are necessarily regional powers, or vice versa. As Holbraad rightly points out, 'relegating the middle powers to regional roles means excluding the possibility that such states in certain situations may play roles at other levels of international politics'.[8] Furthermore, the pre-eminent power in a region need not be a middle power. For example, in the Western hemisphere, a region comprising four middle powers (Canada, Mexico, Brazil, and Argentina), a great power (USA) is quite clearly the regional power.[9]

Again, in sub-Saharan Africa, two middle powers, Nigeria and South Africa, share influence with an extra-regional middle power, France. In the Asia-Pacific region, a host of middle powers—India, Indonesia, and Australia among them—await the coming China–US bipolarity.

As will be readily apparent from the preceding discussion, defining the respective regions of Brazil, India, and South Africa is itself a complicated issue. Nevertheless, an accurate identification of the respective 'region' to which each of the emerging powers belongs is essential. Without it, any calculus of relative power would be a meaningless and futile exercise. The next section analyses the precise regional contexts of Brazil, India, and South Africa.

THREE SOUTHERN SETTINGS

To which region does each emerging power belong? Is Brazil's region the southern cone, or South America, or Latin America, or the entire Western hemisphere? Is South Africa's region southern Africa, or sub-Saharan Africa, or the African continent, or the Indian Ocean–South Atlantic littorals? Is India's region South Asia, or some larger geographical–historical–cultural–strategic entity? Is China in India's region, or is it extra-regional? In order to answer these important questions we need conceptual clarity about what precisely a region is.

William R. Thompson, in his pioneering 1973 article on the concept of the regional subsystem, lamented the 'immaturity of the study of regional subsystems and, in causal consequence, the great lack of theory capable of explaining and relating the existing generalizations'.[10] Thompson went on to propose four 'necessary and sufficient conditions for the regional subsystem', the first of which was that the 'pattern of relations and interactions' of the regional actors 'exhibit a particular degree of regularity and intensity to the extent that a change in one point of the subsystem affects other points'. Thompson's second necessary and sufficient condition, that the actors are 'generally proximate', is one with which most analysts and observers would concur. Third, according to Thompson, it is important that 'internal and external observers and actors recognize the subsystem as a distinctive area'. The fourth condition is straightforward: that 'the subsystem logically consists of at least two and quite probably more actors'.[11]

Despite Thompson's foray into conceptual clarification three and a half decades ago, 'region' remains one of the most nebulous concepts in the study of world politics. Even though regionalism as an idea and regional integration as a process have galloped along since the mid-1970s, there are only a few satisfactory definitions of 'region' in the literature on world politics. In his effort to link regionalism with global order, Andrew Hurrell suggests that regions could be viewed either as 'containers for diversity and difference', or as 'poles or powers', or as 'levels in a system of multilevel global governance', or as 'harbingers of change in the character of international society'.[12] Another interesting characterization is by David A. Lake, who defines a regional system as a 'set of states affected by at least one transborder but local externality that emanates from a particular geographic area. If the local externality poses an actual or potential threat to the physical safety of individuals or governments in other states, it produces a regional security system or complex.'[13] However, for the purposes of this chapter, Barry Buzan's 'security complex' is the most appropriate and easily applicable conceptual tool to identify the respective regional settings of the three emerging powers.

Buzan defines the security complex as 'a set of states whose major security perceptions and concerns are so interlinked that their national security problems cannot reasonably be analysed or resolved apart from one another'.[14] The essential notion at the heart of Buzan's concept is that 'regionally based clusters' are the 'normal pattern of security interdependence in a geographically diverse, anarchic international system'.[15] The essential structure of a security complex is determined by the patterns of amity and enmity, and the distribution of capabilities among the principal states within it.[16] On the basis of this conceptual framework, we can identify the regions to which Brazil, India, and South Africa belong as, respectively, the southern cone of South America, South Asia, and southern Africa.

Besides Brazil, the security complex of the southern cone consists of Argentina, Chile, Peru, Bolivia, Paraguay, and Uruguay. The omnipresent USA is obviously a crucially important extra-regional element in the southern cone security complex. Will this security complex evolve into a security community? The nature of the integrationist project in the Americas—one hegemonic project, or several—will depend upon the answer to this question.

The South Asian security complex consists of India, Afghanistan, Pakistan, Bangladesh, Sri Lanka, Nepal, Bhutan, and the Maldives; however, India's long-standing boundary dispute with China, and Pakistan's well-established strategic relationship with China, adds an additional element to the complex. In the mid-1990s, as Burma was steadily being absorbed into the Southeast Asian security complex, Pakistan's security ties with Taliban-ruled Afghanistan made the latter a member of the South Asian security complex. Although Afghanistan's security links with Central Asia and the Middle East security complexes remain, the former is certainly a full-fledged part of South Asia, having also formally become a member of the South Asian Association for Regional Cooperation (SAARC). US military presence in the region in the context of the International Security Assistance Force (ISAF) in Afghanistan adds a formidable extra-regional power to South Asia.

The members of the security complex in southern Africa are South Africa, Namibia, Angola, Mozambique, Zambia, Zimbabwe, Malawi, Botswana, Lesotho, and Swaziland. However, the protracted conflict in the Congo could potentially merge the southern African security complex with those of central and east Africa, thereby creating an enormously complicated security system from the Cape of Good Hope to the Horn of Africa: a curious reincarnation of the 'Cape to Cairo' aspirations of South African leaders from Cecil Rhodes to P.W. Botha.

The three case studies that follow will not only analyse the relative power configurations that characterize each of these security complexes, but also justify why these security complexes are indeed the most appropriate regional settings in which to study the regional security of the three emerging powers. Before embarking on the specific cases, however, we must clarify the precise meaning of the concept of regional security, and its various empirical implications. In the following section I will elucidate the concepts of regional security, regional power, and regional leadership through an examination of the regional settings of Brazil, India, and South Africa.

REGIONAL SECURITY, POWER, AND LEADERSHIP

Regional security involves more than merely situating national security within the regional context, that is, relating the regional configuration of power to the national security problématiques of the states that constitute it. Rather, the location of security at the regional level does more than just create an intermediate level between international security and national security simply because 'security' has very distinct *meanings* at the three levels. By international security we conventionally mean the *prevention of war*, particularly systemic war, in the international system. National security, on the other hand, usually alludes to *protection from existential threats*, actual or potential. Regional security, it would appear, is a hybrid concept encapsulating *both* connotations of security.

In other words, regional security simultaneously implies the absence of war within the region *and* the protection of the region from extra-regional threats. In that sense, the formation of a cohesive region requires not only the resolution of internal conflicts but also the binding influence of a common external threat. For example, the European Union (EU), product of Franco–German amity and the Soviet menace, and Association of Southeast Asian Nations (ASEAN), resulting from the end of the Indonesia–Malaysia *konfrontasi* and the shared Chinese threat, are powerful empirical evidence in favour of this conceptual understanding of regional security. It follows, therefore, that regional security has both an internal and an external dimension. Therefore, when studying a region, the following questions need to be asked: What is the geostrategic configuration of each region? What is the distribution of power resources in each region? What are the historic patterns of amity and enmity (alliance structure) in each region? What is the history of extra-regional intervention in each region? In what ways has the regional configuration of power evolved? What is the respective level of regional cohesion? Does each region have an ongoing process of regional cooperation and integration, and how successful is this process? These regional characteristics are closely related to the attributes of power of each emerging power, as well as its policy perspective vis-à-vis its neighbours.

Depending upon the distribution of capabilities among the regional states, a regional power could be expected to enjoy a position of primacy, dominance, or supremacy within its region. Primacy suggests a situation of primus inter pares; dominance suggests the lack of a convincing regional rival; and supremacy suggests the untrammelled ability to set the regional agenda. However, a calculus of relative power in a region must take into account both the military capability and socio-economic levels for the following reason. Military capability is zero-sum or negative-sum in nature, and therefore tends to be divisive at the regional level. Faced with the concentration of military power in a region, the weaker states seek to balance their powerful neighbour. Thus, analysing the regional distribution of capabilities solely on the basis of military prowess creates a distorted picture of regional rupture. A high socio-economic level, on the other hand, is attractive. Regional states tend to build links with a wealthy neighbour, which increases regional cohesion. While regional power, based on the distribution of military capabilities, is inherently divisive, regional leadership depends upon attracting the neighbours towards a cohesive regional project.

In conceptual terms, it is important to differentiate regional power from regional leadership: while the former is necessarily a control operation, the latter presupposes the generation of consent.[17] It is quite remarkable how often the most powerful state in a region is not the *leading* state in the sense of providing leadership; indeed, it would appear that the type of regional superiority—primacy, dominance, or supremacy—enjoyed by the regional power is only one half of the regional equation.[18] In order to get the complete picture of regional dynamics, we must take into account the attitude of neighbouring states. Three possibilities exist: a regional power's primacy/dominance/supremacy could either be acknowledged by the neighbouring states, or contested by them, or else be an extraneous or irrelevant factor in regional dynamics.[19] The other important point about the reactions of the respective neighbouring states is their context-specificity. Friendships can get converted into rivalries, and vice versa. For example, the 'German Problem' was the core of the European regional security problématique not so long ago, and until the mid-1990s the 'Front-line States' were loathe to recognize South African regional supremacy.

In the three sections that follow, Brazil, India, and South Africa are studied in their respective regional settings. The geographical boundaries, historical evolution, cultural characteristics, and power dynamics of each region are analysed. In the concluding section, the various threads that make up this study are drawn together in a comparative assessment of the regional security policies of the three emerging powers.

BRAZIL IN THE SOUTHERN CONE: EXTRANEOUS PRIMACY

Brazil's security complex has a long geopolitical history and is now evolving in interesting directions. The following five interlocking components can be discerned: (i) Brazil, by far the largest country in its continent, has historically not dominated its regional space given its relatively low socio-economic levels, its inability to integrate and leverage its continental dimensions, and its cultural distinctiveness as the only Portuguese-speaking country in a Spanish-speaking region; (ii) since the 1960s, Brazil has advanced technologically and economically while its traditional regional rival, Argentina, has not only stagnated but declined; (iii) Brazil has been largely successful in integrating its regional space into a zone of peace, with multiple projects for regional cooperation, including important bilateral projects; (iv) the Brazilian Amazon, long a formidable barrier between Brazil and its Pacific and Caribbean neighbours (Peru, Ecuador, Colombia, Venezuela, Guyana, Suriname, and French Guiana), is rapidly being occupied and integrated into its national territory; and (v) Brazil is now engaged in a high stakes game of challenging US hemispheric hegemony by ensuring that there are two integrationist projects in the Western hemisphere rather than a single one. In this section we will examine each of these strands in some detail.

As Table 2.1 indicates, Brazil's total population is much larger than that of Argentina, Bolivia, Chile, Paraguay, Peru, and Uruguay

TABLE 2.1   Military Capability in the Southern Cone: Brazil and Its Neighbours

	Brazil	Its Neighbours*
Total population	191,908,598	114,839,290
Total armed forces (active)	326,435	332,692
Total paramilitary forces	395,000	202,560
GDP in 2008 (US$ billion)	1,330	640.1
Military budget in 2008 (US$ billion)	20.15	6.3[a]
Main battle tanks	224	878
Light tanks	130	351
Armoured reconnaissance vehicles	422	445
Armoured infantry fighting vehicles	0	420
Armoured personnel carriers	842	1,494
Artillery (towed & self-propelled)	1,862	4,083
Air defence guns	72	722
Surface-to-air missiles	39	434
Principal surface combatants (warships)	16	34
Patrol & coastal combatants	33	254
Submarines	5	13
Combat aircraft	333	364
Armed helicopters	57	37

Source: The International Institute for Strategic Studies, 'Caribbean and Latin America', *The Military Balance 2009* (London: Routledge, 2009), pp. 61–96.

Notes: * Argentina, Bolivia, Chile, Paraguay, Peru, and Uruguay.
[a] Military budget figure for Uruguay is for 2007.

taken together. Brazil's military and paramilitary forces, taken together, are larger than the combined forces of all its neighbours. Brazil's gross domestic product (GDP) is significantly larger than the combined GDP of its southern cone neighbours, as is its military expenditure. However, in terms of crucial weapon platforms, such as main battle tanks (MBT), submarines, and combat aircraft, the other southern cone countries distinctly outnumber Brazil.

Table 2.2 gives us a picture of the relative socio-economic levels in the region. Although Brazil is by far the largest country in the region in terms of land area and population, comparisons of other socio-economic indicators are not in its favour. Argentina, Uruguay, and Chile enjoy much higher GDP per capita and much better infant mortality and female adult illiteracy rates. In the entire region, only Bolivian women have a shorter life expectancy than their Brazilian counterparts. Thus, in terms of socio-economic levels, Brazil does have several regional rivals with which it has yet to catch up. Therefore, while Brazil's sheer size—in terms of geography, demography, and economics—ensures its primacy in the region, it cannot in any significant sense be said to dominate the southern cone.

Geographically, Brazil dominates the South American landmass and shares land borders with every South American country, barring Ecuador and Chile. While Brazil does not itself have a Caribbean or Pacific coast, several of its neighbours do. We therefore need to explicitly justify our analytical confinement of Brazil's regional security problématique to the southern cone. Why do I consider Chile, which does *not* border Brazil, as a part of Brazil's security region, but exclude Colombia, which *does* share a land border with Brazil, from this analysis of Brazil's regional complex?

My conception of Brazil's security region as the southern cone also runs counter to declared Brazilian policy. The National Defence Policy, enunciated in November 1996, declared that Brazil is 'a country of different regions and a diversified profile—belonging simultaneously to the Amazon, Atlantic, Southern Cone, and River Plate basin'.[20] In line with this understanding, the *National Strategy of Defense*, issued by President Luiz Inácio Lula da Silva on 18 December 2008, is explicit about the need to redeploy Brazil's military forces:

The main Army units are deployed in Southeast and South Brazil. The Navy fleet concentrates in the Rio de Janeiro city. Almost all of the Air Force technological premises are located in São José dos Campos, São Paulo. The most critical defense concerns are, however, in the North, West and in the South Atlantic regions.

TABLE 2.2 Geographic, Demographic, and Socio-economic Indicators: Countries of the Southern Cone

Country	Human development index/rank (2006)	Area (km²)	Total population (thousands, 2006, est.)	GDP per capita (US$, 2008)	GDP per capita PPP (int'l $, 2006)	Female life expectancy at birth (years, 2006)	Infant mortality rate (per 1,000 births, 2000–5)	Adult literacy rate (per cent, 2000–7)	Ratio of adult literacy rate of females to males (per cent, 2000–7)	Sustainable access to improved drinking water sources (per cent, 2006)	Sustainable access to improved sanitation facilities (per cent, 2006)
Argentina	0.860/46	2,780,400	39,134	8,358	15,795	78	15	98	100	96	91
Bolivia	0.723/111	1,098,581	9,354	1,723	2,984	67	48	90	90	86	43
Brazil	0.807/70	8,511,965	189,323	8,311	9,054	75	20	91	101	91	77
Chile	0.874/40	756,626	16,465	10,091	12,655	81	8	97	100	95	94
Paraguay	0.752/98	406,752	6,016	2,581	5,054	78	24	94	99	77	70
Peru	0.788/79	1,285,216	27,589	4,471	6,624	75	17	91	90	84	72
Uruguay	0.859/47	177,414	3,331	9,610	11,451	79	12	98	101	100	100
Southern Cone	–	15,016,594	291,212	–	–	–	–	–	–	–	–

Source: Statistics and indicators are provided by the UN Statistics Division from http://data.un.org, accessed on 24 January 2010. Dashes indicate 'data unavailable/unreported'.

Without ignoring the need to defend the largest demographical concentrations and the largest industrial centers of the country, the Navy shall be more intensely present in the region of the Amazon river mouth, and in the large Amazon and Paraguai–Paraná river basins. The Army shall deploy its strategic reserves at the central region of the country, from where troops can be moved towards any direction.[21]

The Amazonian region remains a perennial source of concern for Brazilian defence planners. The National Defence Policy of 1996 had (i) referred to 'the actions of armed groups that are active in neighbouring countries, on the edge of the Brazilian Amazon',[22] (ii) underlined the importance of 'borders and boundaries that are precisely defined and internationally recognized',[23] and (iii) given 'priority to the development and reinvigoration of the strip of land along Brazil's borders, especially in the northern and central western regions'.[24] The last point refers to the Brazilian army's Projecto Calha Norte (Northern Ditch Project), aimed at demarcating, controlling, and protecting Brazil's Amazonian territories.[25] The *National Strategy of Defense* document of 2008 also makes a pointed reference to 'strengthening the Programa Calha Norte defense approach'.[26] In concrete terms, this implies an 'increase in the participation of military and civilian government organizations in the plan to vivify and to develop the strip of the Amazon region border, *employing the strategy of presence*'.[27] The 2008 document also states that the Brazilian navy 'will start studies and will get ready to establish, at the relevant venue, as near as possible to the mouth of the Amazon river, a multiple-use naval base that is comparable, in terms of scope and density of its means, to the Naval Base of Rio de Janeiro'.[28]

Jack Child underlines the deep-seated belief among Brazilian geopolitical and security analysts that their country must ensure that it 'fully and effectively occupies all its territory and that it is the dominant power in the vast empty spaces of the South American heartland'.[29] According to the 2008 document, 'The sustainable development of the Amazon region will, from now on, be also seen as an instrument of national defense: it is the only thing that may consolidate the conditions to ensure national sovereignty in that area.'[30] This finds emotional expression in the slogan '*A Amazônia é nossa*' ('*Amazônia* is ours') and is an essential element in the 'seemingly inevitable Brazilian path to *grandeza*, the code word for the moment when (and never *if*) Brazil will become the first superpower to emerge from the Southern Hemisphere'.[31] As the *National Strategy of Defense* (2008) states:

Brazil will be watchful to the unconditional reaffirmation of its sovereignty upon the Brazilian Amazon region. It will repudiate, by means of actions of development and defense, any attempt of external imposition on its decisions regarding the preservation, development and defense of the Amazon region. It will not allow organizations or individuals to serve as instruments for alien interests—political or economic—willing to weaken the Brazilian sovereignty. It is Brazil that takes care of the Brazilian Amazon region, at the service of mankind and at its own service.[32]

If the Amazonian region is so central to Brazilian security thinking, how can I exclude it from our analysis of Brazil's military security? My reasoning is simple: despite its rhetorical and programmatic emphasis on the Amazonian region, Brazil does *not* yet face any significant security threats from the north. As Child convincingly argues, 'The vast interior areas of the Orinoco and Amazon Basins serve as a buffer between the Caribbean Basin and the Southern Cone.'[33] Colombia, Venezuela, Guyana, Suriname, and French Guiana, 'more Caribbean than South American',[34] comprise a distinct security complex in which Brazil does not feature. While initiatives like the Calha Norte Project will *eventually* make Brazil a player in the Caribbean basin security complex, for the next decade or two Brazil's regional security concerns will remain embedded in the security complex of the southern cone.

The southern cone can be defined as the system of power politics involving major actors such as Brazil, Argentina, Chile, and Peru, and smaller buffer states such as Uruguay, Bolivia, and Paraguay, with the remaining South American states somewhat on the periphery of this power relationship.[35] The security complex of the southern cone has evolved from two nineteenth-century balance of power systems in South America: the Pacific System involving Chile, Peru, and Bolivia; and the River Plate/Atlantic System comprising Argentina, Brazil, Uruguay, and Paraguay. The southern cone region is dominated by Argentina, Brazil, Chile, and Peru, and is organized around two 'diagonal alliances' between Brazil–Chile and Argentina–Peru.[36] The central political relationship in this geopolitical space has traditionally been the rivalry between Argentina and Brazil to influence the southern cone.

From a historical perspective, the Argentina–Brazil rivalry has a heritage that goes back nearly five centuries to the arrival of the Iberian powers in South America. The present borders of Brazil are a consequence of adventurous exploration and settlement by Portuguese and later Brazilian *bandeirantes* (flag-bearers or pioneers), backed by the dexterous diplomacy of the Portuguese and Brazilian states, all at the cost of Spain's imperial possessions and, later, Spain's several successor states. Brazil's history of territorial conquest through stealth and diplomacy, exemplified by its constant move westwards towards the Pacific, aroused the fear and suspicion of its neighbours, which were more than matched by Brazilian fear of 'encirclement' by its Hispanophone neighbours. Towards the south, Brazil's expansion was met by Argentina. Rivalry between the two took the form of acquisition of influence in the buffer states of Bolivia, Uruguay, and Paraguay whenever the opportunity arose. Through much of the nineteenth and early twentieth centuries, Brazil and Argentina were combatants, either against each other or on the same side, in a series of wars: the Cisplatine war between Argentina, Uruguay, and Brazil over the Banda Oriental (1825–8); Brazilian intervention in 1852 in the Argentine civil war (between Buenos Aires and the provinces); the war of the Triple Alliance of Argentina, Brazil, and Uruguay against Paraguay (1865–70); and the Chaco war between Bolivia and Paraguay (1932–5).[37] Thus, Argentine–Brazilian rivalry has historically been a feature of international relations in South America. However, there are two aspects of this rivalry that must be underlined. First, Argentine–Brazilian rivalry was never based on a territorial dispute or an identity conflict, but essentially a competition about influence in the region. Second, it has been a long time since the two countries faced each other in battle: they fought a war in 1828 and Brazil intervened in an Argentine civil war in 1852.

An underlying theme of the Argentine–Brazilian rivalry was the suspicion of the Hispanophone states that Lusophone Brazil was merely acting as surrogate for the Anglophone hegemonic powers, Great Britain and USA. This of course added an important extra-regional dimension to the southern cone rivalry, Portugal having been the longest-standing British ally in the European continent. Brazil, for its part, assiduously sought, for 30 years following the Second World War, to cement its wartime alliance with USA, during which an entire Brazilian division had fought against the Axis powers in Italy. Driven partly by its fears of encirclement and partly by its dreams of *grandeza* (grandeur), Brazil in effect offered a *barganha leal* (loyalty bargain) to USA: Brazil would remain loyal to the regional hegemony of USA and would in return be accorded the status of junior partner or sub-hegemon. During these decades, Argentina was scathingly critical of this arrangement, which it viewed as the principal impediment to the creation of an anti-US Latin American identity under its own leadership. USA, it must be added, never fully accepted the deal offered by the Brazilians. As Philip Kelly notes, 'The Argentine–Brazilian contention preserved the buffer states' autonomy, restricted regional economic integration, allowed the United States' "divide-and-conquer" diplomacy toward South America, and checkmated both Brazil's and Argentina's global participation.'[38]

If the effects of the Argentine–Brazilian rivalry were so apparently negative, why did both countries persist with this negative-sum relationship for so long? Here, it is important to recognize that the behaviour of the two South American states had an economic basis. Unlike the Brazilian and US economies, which are complementary in nature, Argentina's agricultural exports of beef and wheat were directly competitive with US production. Thus, Argentina's historic anti-US orientation is based on its need to build a durable relationship with the European continent, especially—the Falklands/Malvinas dispute notwithstanding—with Great Britain. Argentina's traditional affinity to Europe can also be explained by the predominantly European composition of its population. Thus, the Argentine–Brazilian rivalry was based on much more than mere policy preferences.

By the 1970s, a nuclear dimension had entered the Argentine–Brazilian rivalry. Nevertheless, the nuclear rivalry between Buenos Aires and Brasilia was never more than a subset of their larger competition for regional influence. Thus, the rivalry did not generate into open conflict. Indeed, Child characterizes this competitive relationship as 'low-key and even cordial, but...nevertheless a present and constant factor'.[39]

In the mid-1970s, Brazil broke away from its subservient relationship with USA. The critical event that forced Brazil to revaluate its relationship with USA was the latter's opposition to the Brazilian–West German nuclear agreement of 1975. During the Carter administration, US bilateral relations with both Argentina and Brazil reached their nadir, largely as a result of Carter's human rights policy. The two South American countries were therefore able to overcome their traditional hostility when they discovered a community of interests that outweighed their antagonism. Faced with shared pressure from USA, the generals on both sides broke the ice and initiated a new era of understanding. In 1980 the military governments of generals (and presidents) Jorge Videla of Argentina and João Figueiredo of Brazil signed an agreement on the peaceful uses of nuclear energy, which marks the beginning of the Argentine–Brazilian entente. Nuclear rapprochement was greatly strengthened by Brazil's support for Argentina during the Falklands/Malvinas war against the UK in 1982. For the Argentine generals, this conclusively demonstrated that Brazil, unlike Chile, which actively helped British forces during the war, was not Argentina's enemy. After the war, the Brazilian Embassy in London handled Argentine interests in the UK until the UK and Argentina reestablished diplomatic relations.

Thus, when the democratic transition took place in Argentina and Brazil, in 1983 and 1985 respectively, the new civilian presidents found that their generals had already opened up the path to bilateral nuclear cooperation. One of the first acts of the two civilian governments was the Iguassu Falls declaration on the peaceful purposes of the Argentine and Brazilian nuclear programmes in 1985. In 1987, a Brazilian delegation visited the Pilcaniyeu gas diffusion enrichment plant in Argentina, which was followed a year later by an Argentine visit to Brazil's Aramar ultra-centrifuge enrichment plant. By 1991, nuclear cooperation between the two countries was in full swing, culminating in the setting up of the Brazilian–Argentine Agency for Accounting and Control of Nuclear Materials (ABACC).[40]

The 'nuclear understanding' between the two South American giants was the essential first step that initiated a new process of regional cooperation and integration. Mercosur or Mercosul (Spanish: Mercado Común del Sur; Portuguese: Mercado Comum do Sul; English: Common Market of the South) is self-evidently based on the new strategic relationship between Argentina and Brazil. In that limited but crucial sense, Mercosur is no different from the EU or ASEAN: regional integration necessarily required the transformation of the cardinal bilateral relationship from enmity to friendship. The entire southern cone region has benefited from the new cooperative dynamic between Argentina and Brazil. Mercosur was constituted by Argentina, Brazil, Paraguay, and Uruguay on 26 March 1991 by the Treaty of Asunción, later amended and updated on 16 December 1994 by the Protocol of Ouro Preto; Venezuela signed a membership agreement on 17 June 2006, but its entry into Mercosur still awaits ratification by the Brazilian and Paraguayan parliaments. Bolivia, Chile, Peru, and Ecuador have signed Agreements of Economic Complementation (Acuerdos de Complementación Económico) with Mercosur, thereby becoming associate members of the regional organization. Going beyond the economic domain, Mercosur/l with its associate members Bolivia and Chile signed the Protocol of Ushuaia on Democratic Commitment in July 1998; on that occasion the members and associate members also signed a political declaration that designated the territories of Mercosur, Bolivia, and Chile as a zone of peace. On 18 February

2002, the members of MERCOSUR signed the Protocol of Olivos for the Resolution of Controversies between the States Parties, thereby establishing a dispute settlement mechanism within the organization.[41]

MERCOSUR still accounts for only a small share of Brazil's foreign trade: in 2008, trade with its MERCOSUR partners constituted 10.3 per cent of Brazil's exports and imports. While MERCOSUR may not be that important to Brazil in commercial terms, the reverse is not true, as Brazil drives intra-MERCOSUR trade: in 2008, Brazil accounted for 52.3 per cent of intra-MERCOSUR exports and 34.9 per cent of intra-MERCOSUR imports.[42] Due to the international financial crisis, 'world trade collapsed in 2009 and intra-MERCOSUR trade was no exception'.[43] Nevertheless, for Brazil's partners, MERCOSUR trade with Brazil during the crisis was 'a moderating factor in the compression of trade they had been suffering'.[44] Finally, 'prospects for 2010 are encouraging': in January 2010, intra-MERCOSUR trade was 54 per cent higher than in January 2009.[45] Thus, both the political and economic outlooks for the regional integration processes in the southern cone remain positive.

The impact of Mercosur has been entirely positive and beneficial for Argentina and Brazil. In Philip Kelly's words, 'rapprochement between the two states...has relaxed tensions in the area, increased regional integration and development, kept U.S. influence at bay, and heightened international status for both Brazil and Argentina'.[46] The integrationist project in the southern cone is a 'cooperative Argentine–Brazilian condominium'[47] that aims at breaking the geographical isolation of the region by making it a force in the world economy. According to Kelly, Brazil's foreign policy has traditionally fluctuated along a spectrum, ranging from imperialist to balance-of-power participant, to US surrogate, to great power aspirant, to regional hegemon, to regional integrationist. In Kelly's view, Brazil's foreign policy today is 70 per cent integrationist, but it still retains a residual 30 per cent element of regional hegemony.[48] Brazil's National Defence Policy statement of 1996 lauds the formation, through 'positive and concrete diplomatic action', of 'a veritable ring of peace' around Brazil, based on Mercosur, the Amazon Cooperation Treaty, the Community of Portuguese-speaking Countries, and the South Atlantic Zone of Peace and Cooperation.[49] The *National Strategy of Defense* (2008) states that the integration of South America 'not only will contribute to the defense of Brazil, but it will also allow the country to promote regional military cooperation and the integration of the defense industrial bases'.[50]

MERCOSUR is only the latest, albeit most impressive, example in a long history of Brazilian initiative to shape Brazil's regional neighbourhood through cooperative initiatives, especially those involving disputes with regional neighbours. There is perhaps no better example of this predisposition than the construction of the Itaipu Binacional hydroelectric project over the Paraná river, which forms a border that has been disputed by Brazil and Paraguay since the mid-eighteenth century. In 1750, Spain and Portugal had signed the Exchange Treaty, but the treaty text itself was vague about the boundaries between the areas on the right bank of the Paraná river, especially in the Seven Falls area. The dispute, later inherited by Paraguay and Brazil as the respective successor states, remained unsettled despite several diplomatic attempts. The War of the Triple Alliance (1865–70), involving Brazil, Argentina, and Uruguay against Paraguay, once again kindled the Brazil–Paraguay dispute about the borders in the Seven Falls area. According to the Peace Treaty of 1872, the disputed territories were to be divided by the Paraná river up to the Seven Falls; however, due to topological complications and disagreement between the parties, demarcation of the disputed area petered out 20 km short of the Seven Falls area.

However, in the early 1960s, after the full hydroelectric potential of the Paraná river was recognized, the idea of the two countries coming together to generate electricity was considered for the first time. To bolster Paraguay's confidence in this massive collaborative venture, Brazil constructed in 1965 the Friendship Bridge, connecting its own town of Foz do Iguaçu with the Paraguayan town of Ciudad del Este, thereby enabling the export of Paraguayan products through Brazilian ports. On 22 June 1966, after intense negotiations, the two foreign ministers signed the Iguazu Minutes, a study of the water resources jointly held by the two countries along the Paraná river. The Itaipu project involved the inundation of a large part of the area in dispute, thereby ending forever the Brazil–Paraguay dispute over the Seven Falls. A small portion of the area in dispute that escaped inundation was converted into a binational ecological reserve. In 1967, a Mixed Committee was created to implement the Iguazu Minutes, and on 26 April 1973 Brazil and Paraguay signed the Itaipu Treaty, the legal instrument that authorizes both countries to use the Paraná river for hydroelectric purposes. Soon after, in May 1974, the Itaipu bi-national company was created to manage the power plant's construction.

It is noteworthy that the Brazilian government was solely responsible for procuring resources for the project, while the benefits of the project went to both countries. Itaipu was financed by short-term credits from private financial institutions and public foreign banks; the debt will be fully repaid in 2023. Built between 1975 and 1991, the Itaipu power plant is currently the largest hydroelectric power plant in the world as regards the generation of energy, with 20 generator units and 14,000 MW of installed power. In 2009, the plant generated 91,651,808 megawatts-hour (MWh) of electricity. It now provides 20 per cent of Brazil's and a massive 94 per cent of Paraguay's energy supplies. Thus, a long-running boundary dispute has been transformed, largely due to Brazilian vision and effort, into a shining example of bilateral cooperation in infrastructure development.[51]

As far as external influences in the region are concerned, USA remains the dominant extra-regional actor in the southern cone. Brazil's attempts to distance itself from USA, a foreign policy trend that began in the mid-1970s, have been pursued forcefully since 1995 by the administrations of Fernando Henrique Cardoso and Luiz Inácio Lula da Silva. However, just as Brazil moved away from its hitherto close relationship with USA, the traditionally anti-US Argentina began moving ever closer to the hemispheric hegemon. In the decade 1989–99, Argentine diplomacy even evolved a new doctrine of *realismo periférico* (peripheral realism) which explicitly recognized US leadership in the Western hemisphere.[52] During these years, Argentina had one of the most pro-US foreign policy policies in the Americas, culminating in its designation by USA as a major non-NATO (North Atlantic Treaty Organization) ally (MNNA). However, after its disastrous economic crisis of 2001, which Argentina's public opinion blamed squarely on the country's close adherence to the neoliberal Washington Consensus, Argentina's foreign policy has veered away from quasi-alliance with USA and is now focused on strengthening MERCOSUR and the strategic partnership with Brazil. This new Argentina–Brazil coordination found concrete expression during the Fourth Summit of the Americas, held on 4–5 November 2005 at Mar del Plata, Argentina, during which the leaders of MERCOSUR countries openly disagreed with USA and 29 other members of the Organization of American States (OAS) over the proposed Free Trade Agreement of the Americas (FTAA). This latest change in Argentina's policy is entirely in Brazil's interest because it ensures that a single integrative project, led by USA, will not take root in the Western hemisphere.

US hemispheric policies notwithstanding, Brazil's regional policy will be most impacted by decisions taken by three South American countries in the coming years: Chile, Venezuela, and Argentina. Chilean choices, especially following the signing of the US–Chile Free Trade Agreement in 2004, are significant because they could lead to a breaking of ranks in the southern cone; integrating South America will be extremely difficult if the most dynamic economy in the region, and the *southernmost* country in the world, decides to integrate with North America instead. The trajectory of the Venezuela-led ALBA (Spanish: Alianza Bolivariana para los Pueblos de Nuestra América; English: Bolivarian Alliance for the Peoples of Our America) is a second challenge for Brazilian policy, because ALBA represents an alternate, fiercely anti-US model for integrating South America. Argentina's future policy is a concern for Brazil because Argentina has erratically oscillated from one policy extreme to another for the past seven decades, making it a rather unreliable partner. Thus, despite Brazil's diplomatic dexterity in generating consent among its neighbours, several factors in its region will continue to remain beyond its control.

INDIA IN SOUTH ASIA: CONTESTED DOMINANCE

India's regional security problématique is made up of three interlocking components: (i) while India dominates its region, its dominance is severely contested, particularly by Pakistan; (ii) as a consequence, India's region is neither internally peaceful nor externally cohesive; and (iii) China, although an extra-regional player, now rivals India for influence in India's neighbourhood and may well end up exercising significant regional leadership in South Asia. An additional, and complicating, component is the presence of US forces in Afghanistan as the bulk of the ISAF (International Security Assistance Force): US interests in the Af-Pak region, and its need for Pakistan's cooperation in combating terrorism in the area, exert some additional pressures upon Indian foreign policy. In this section I will explicate each of these components.

In military terms, India clearly dominates its region. As Table 2.3 reveals, while India's population is 2.8 times larger than of the countries neighbouring it, its GDP and military expenditure are four times as large as those of its regional neighbours. India's military and paramilitary forces vastly outnumber (1.6 times) those of its neighbours, as do the weapon systems and platforms in its arsenal. The only categories of weapons in which India is outgunned are armoured personnel carriers and patrol and coastal vessels, a lack of numbers that is more than compensated

TABLE 2.3 Conventional Military Capability in South Asia: India and Its Neighbours

	India	Its Neighbours*
Total population	1,147,995,898	404,695,204
Total armed forces (active)	1,281,200	1,047,353
Total paramilitary forces	1,300,586	492,100
GDP in 2008 (US$ billion)	1,078	264.8[a]
Military budget in 2008 (US$ billion)	25.3	6.3[b]
Main battle tanks	4,065	2,755
Light tanks	0	8
Armoured reconnaissance vehicles	110	58
Armoured infantry fighting vehicles	1,700	62
Armoured personnel carriers	817	1,777
Artillery (towed & self-propelled)	12,412	5,625
Air defence guns	2,395	2,273
Surface-to-air missiles	3,500	3,160
Principal surface combatants (warships)	47	12
Patrol and coastal combatants	92	225
Submarines	16	8
Combat aircraft	632	496
Armed helicopters	32	49
Strategic airlift aircraft	24	0

Source: The International Institute for Strategic Studies, 'Central and South Asia', pp. 342–59.

Notes: * Afghanistan, Bangladesh, Nepal, Pakistan, and Sri Lanka (Bhutan and Maldives not included).
[a] GDP data for Afghanistan and Nepal are for 2007
[b] Military expenditure data for Afghanistan is for 2007.

by India's crushing superiority in armoured infantry fighting vehicles, capital ships, and submarines.

However, Table 2.4 convincingly demonstrates that India's depressingly low socio-economic level remains its enduring weakness. Notwithstanding its enormously larger land area, population, and GDP, India's infant mortality rate, female life expectancy figures, and adult illiteracy rate are similar to those of Bangladesh, Pakistan, and Nepal, and significantly worse than those of Sri Lanka and the Maldives. India's

TABLE 2.4 Geographic, Demographic, and Socio-economic Indicators: Countries of South Asia

Country	Human development index/rank (2006)	Area (km²)	Total population (thousands, 2006, est.)	GDP per capita (US$, 2008)	GDP per capita PPP (int'l $, 2006)	Female life expectancy at birth (years, 2006)	Infant mortality rate (per 1,000 live births, 2007)	Adult literacy rate (per cent, 2000–7)	Ratio of adult literacy rate of females to males (per cent, 2000–7)	Sustainable access to improved drinking water sources (per cent, 2006)	Sustainable access to improved sanitation facilities (per cent, 2006)
Afghanistan	Unranked	652,090	26,088	466	–	43	165	28	29	22	30
Bangladesh	0.524/147	143,998	155,991	494	2,217	63	47	54	82	80	36
Bhutan	0.613/131	47,000	649	1,933	5,703	67	56	56	63	81	52
India	0.609/132	3,287,590	1,151,751	1,061	3,827	64	54	66	71	89	28
Maldives	0.749/99	298	300	4,131	–	73	26	97	100	83	59
Nepal	0.530/145	147,181	27,641	465	1,596	63	43	57	62	89	27
Pakistan	0.562/139	796,095	160,943	1,010	2,553	63	73	55	59	90	58
Sri Lanka	0.742/104	65,610	19,207	2,030	5,081	76	17	92	96	82	86
South Asia	–	5,139,862	1,542,570	1,155	–	–	59	63	71	–	–

Source: Statistics and indicators are provided by the UN Statistics Division from http://data.un.org (accessed on 24 January 2010). Dashes indicate 'data unavailable/unreported'.

consistent socio-economic underperformance, both in absolute and relative terms, explains why it does *not* enjoy regional supremacy: while none of its neighbours, not even Pakistan, can convincingly challenge its domination of South Asia, they are nevertheless unwilling to concede regional leadership to India. This is true not only of elite opinion in the neighbouring countries but also in their respective public opinions: apart from democracy, there is no other attribute of India that its neighbours seem to wish to emulate. Thus, as the Indian economy grows and becomes a dynamic part of the global economy, close engagement with India could well become a more attractive policy option for its regional neighbours.

Since the India–Pakistan war of 1971, which led to the creation of Bangladesh, South Asia as a region has remained prey to structural insecurity. The Indo-centric nature of South Asia is a fact of history and geography, a structural element that India cannot avoid and its neighbours cannot afford to ignore. Geographically, India forms the core of South Asia, and its neighbours, the periphery. The formal entry of Afghanistan into SAARC in April 2007 is significant, among other reasons, because it brings into the region a country that does *not* share a border with India. Earlier, while India had shared borders with each of the other countries in the region, none of its neighbours had shared a land border with any South Asian country other than India.

As we have seen in Table 2.3, Indian military power in conventional terms far outweighs the collective power of *all* its regional neighbours. Thus, the only way the other countries of South Asia could contend with Indian power was by resorting to external balancing, that is, seeking extra-regional intervention, which India has always resolutely opposed. Until Pakistan's nuclear tests in May 1998, there seemed to be no way out of this security dilemma. However, by gaining strategic parity with India, Pakistan has shattered the structural insecurity that has plagued South Asia and opened the possibility of durable peace in the region.

India–Pakistan antagonism, it must be emphasized, is distinct from the structural insecurity problem outlined earlier. India's conflict with Pakistan has its roots in ideology and identity rather than in an asymmetry of power. Indeed, among important sections of the Pakistani policy elite, the obsession of parity with India, a country seven times larger than their own, has a certain hallucinatory quality. For most Indians, it is clear that a central problem for India–Pakistan relations remains the 'original sin' of the 'two nation theory', a divisive ideology that conferred distinct national identities on Hindus and Muslims of the Indian subcontinent, thereby leading to the partition of India and the founding of Pakistan in 1947. For most Pakistanis, on the other hand, 1947 is a year to be celebrated. The year of shame for Pakistan is 1971, when its eastern wing seceded under the pressure of Indian military action and became the new nation-state of Bangladesh.

While nuclearization gives Pakistan strategic parity with India and thereby security in perpetuity from India, it does not diminish the power asymmetry that exists between the two countries. What strategic parity does is give Pakistan a relatively free hand in waging asymmetrical war on India.[53] Although the two countries are officially at peace, India has accused Pakistan, not without proof, of openly pursuing a low-cost and moderately effective strategy of supporting insurgent and terrorist groups against it.[54] The two countries almost went to war during the military mobilization crisis of 2001–2, after a terrorist attack on the Indian Parliament, which New Delhi attributed to Pakistan.

Since 2001–2, India's attitude towards Pakistan has fluctuated between frigidity and fury. From 2004 to 2008, the two countries were involved in a Composite Dialogue that had its roots in the Pakistani leadership's commitment to its Indian counterpart on 6 January 2004 that Pakistan would no longer permit any territory under its control to be used to support terrorism against India. Consequently, according to the official report of the Indian foreign ministry in 2005, India pursued 'a proactive policy of constructive engagement to establish peaceful, friendly, and cooperative relations with Pakistan with the larger objective of cementing a viable structure of peace and stability in South Asia'.[55] Nevertheless, progress in the dialogue remained slow, as the Indian foreign ministry noted in its official report of 2007: 'India–Pakistan relations remained well short of their potential and are yet to be fully normalized.'[56] For India, the sticking point remained its position on terrorism in Kashmir and other parts of India being allegedly supported by Pakistan.[57]

Even during the years of Composite Dialogue, the Indian military establishment remained extremely cautious about security threats emanating from Pakistan, as clearly affirmed in successive official reports of the Indian defence ministry from 2005 to 2008. In 2005, the defence ministry stated that there was 'no evidence of any significant Pakistani effort to dismantle the infrastructure of terrorism, such as communications, launching pads, and training camps on its eastern borders with India comparable to Pakistan's operations in the war against terrorism on its western borders with Afghanistan'.[58] According to the defence ministry's official report in 2006, 'Attempts at infiltration [of terrorists into India] continue and the infrastructure [of terrorism] in Pakistan has not been dismantled.'[59] (Infiltration is the term used by the Indian government to denote the entry of terrorists from Pakistan-controlled territory to India and the hard indicator employed by the Indian government to assess Pakistan's willingness to abet and sponsor terrorism in India.) In 2007, the defence ministry reported that, 'Terrorist groups continue to operate freely in Pakistan. They also find shelter, support and training for operations across the border...from elements in Pakistan.'[60] The defence ministry report of 2007 further asserted that the Composite Dialogue with Pakistan

hinges on building an atmosphere of trust and confidence, free from violence and terror. Infiltration has to stop and Pakistan needs to take decisive action on dismantling the infrastructures of terrorism. For an effective end to terrorism, the training camps, launching pads and communication networks of terrorist organizations must be eliminated.[61]

The terrorist attack on Mumbai in November 2008 by the Lashkar-e-Tayyiba (LeT), a group that is based in, and India insists is supported by, Pakistan, has sent bilateral relations back into deep freeze. In 2009, the Indian foreign ministry asserted that 'terrorism and non-implementation of the 6 January 2004 commitments by Pakistan has eroded the fundamental premise of the Dialogue process'.[62] The official report notes that 'subsequent actions by Pakistan were dilatory and obfuscatory, and are yet to bring the perpetrators to justice or to dismantle the infrastructure in Pakistan for terrorism against India'.[63] There has therefore once again been 'a sharp deterioration in bilateral relations'.[64] The Indian defence ministry noted in 2009 that, 'The unimpeded growth of extremist and terrorist organizations in Pakistan was marked by an increase in ceasefire violations, continued infiltrations across the LoC, as also major terrorist attacks.' It alludes to 'clear evidence' that the terrorist attack on Mumbai in November 2008 'was planned and launched by Pakistan'.[65] The hard line taken by the Indian defence establishment can be gauged from the following sentences:

The expanding footprint of extremist and terrorist organisations in Pakistan and the fact that many of them have a known record of terrorist attacks against India amounts to a security challenge with serious implications for us. The continuing links of these organisations with organs of the Pakistan State adds greater complexities and dangers to the evolving situation confronting us... Pakistan's history of military and quasi-military adventurism underscores the seriousness of the threat we face.[66]

The Indian foreign ministry's official report in 2010 clearly states that 'there can be a meaningful dialogue with Pakistan only if it fulfils its commitment, in letter and spirit, not to allow its territory to be used in any manner for terrorist activities against India'.[67] Ashley Tellis appositely describes Pakistan's asymmetric war strategy against India as 'bleeding India through a thousand cuts, but not wounding it to a point that automatically embarrasses Pakistan or precipitates a major subcontinental war'.[68]

Apart from terrorism, the other fundamental security problem for India is the construction of a relationship of nuclear deterrence with Pakistan.[69] Having only very recently acquired an overt nuclear weapons capability, both countries are still learning the basics of nuclear deterrence, as the military mobilization crisis of 2001–2 clearly demonstrated. Nuclear risk-reduction measures and direct communications between the two national command authorities are urgently needed. Unfortunately, Pakistan has tended to drag its feet on this issue, as a larger nuclear 'comfort zone' for India is understandably not in Pakistan's interest.

It is undoubtedly true that Pakistani insecurity vis-à-vis India lies at the heart of the regional security problématique in South Asia. However, a securer Pakistan is a necessary (but not a sufficient) prerequisite for durable peace in South Asia. There are a number of other factors standing in the way of regional peace. Throughout South Asia there are clear signs that radical ideas are permeating religious groups, often on the lines of inter-generational cleavages. While most pronounced in Islamic communities, this phenomenon exists in all religions. The 'Talibanization' of Bangladesh, however exaggerated, has become a pressing concern for India.[70]

Most of the countries of South Asia also face centrifugal and fissiparous tendencies, often as a result of years of misgovernance and maladministration. Usually, neighbouring countries have played a role in establishing and supporting these movements. A prime example is the Tamil Tigers (LTTE) group in Sri Lanka, now comprehensively defeated by the Sri Lankan military forces, which was first supported and later combated by India.[71] Finally, although some variant of democracy is now seen as the best form of government across most of the globe, many South Asian countries, perhaps because they have lacked democracy for many years, still suffer from the violence of groups wishing to overthrow the state for ideological reasons. The Maoist movement in Nepal is an excellent example. Again, the linkages between Nepal's Maoists and

India's many Naxalite (Maoist) groups are self-evident and have major security implications for India.[72]

What seems notable regarding the aforementioned factors is the extent to which these security concerns, although supposedly *internal*, have pronounced cross-border linkages; they invariably involve neighbouring countries. While India has a multitude of internal security concerns of its own, its central location in the region ensures that it cannot isolate itself from the spillover effects and explicit linkages that arise from the internal security challenges of its neighbours. Finally, it is also worth noting that there is little or no security cooperation between the countries of South Asia to deal with these security threats, challenges, and concerns.

As we have seen, South Asia is hopelessly divided internally. Furthermore, it does not cohere externally: the countries in the region do not have either a shared sense of vulnerability or a coalesced sense of regional identity. The partition of India introduced a zero-sum political logic in the way India and Pakistan, the two successor states to British India, viewed the external world. Indeed, no external presence in the region was *ever* perceived by either state in similar terms. Immediately after the victory of the Chinese revolution, India tried to build strong ties with the Chinese Communist leadership while Pakistan was drawn into the US alliance structure to contain the Soviet Union and 'Red China'. India viewed the US alliance structure as a threat to the region, a perspective that Pakistan, as a US ally, obviously did not share. Later, as India's relations with China deteriorated, leading to the border war of 1962 between the two Asian giants, Pakistan's relations with China improved dramatically, culminating in the 'all-weather friendship' between Beijing and Islamabad. Pakistan was one of the few countries with which China maintained close diplomatic and political relations even during the Cultural Revolution.

After the Sino-Soviet rift, India moved to cement its relations with Moscow, over time becoming a close friend of the Soviet Union. After the signing of the Indo-Soviet Treaty of Peace, Friendship, and Cooperation in 1971, the two countries became virtual allies. Although the Indian leadership was greatly perturbed by the Soviet invasion of Afghanistan in 1979, India did *not* publicly oppose the invasion. Pakistan, meanwhile, became the frontline state through which USA and other Western powers funnelled billions of dollars to the anti-Soviet mujahideen. After the 9/11 attacks upon USA, Pakistan hesitated only very briefly before choosing once again to become a frontline state and partner of USA, this time against the Taliban regime and Al-Qaeda in Afghanistan. Ostensibly, both India and Pakistan have been on the same side of the 'Global War on Terror' since 2001. In reality, they are deeply suspicious of each other. Hence, a cohesive South Asian view has once again not evolved.

Thus, it should be clear that the countries of South Asia have never shared a common perspective on outside powers. This is principally because the cardinal relationship in the region (India–Pakistan) is still driven by a zero-sum perception. However, another factor of importance is that it is not always easy to identify an 'external presence'. In particular, is China extra-regional in the South Asian context or not? Even the two principal agencies of the Indian government responsible for foreign and security policy have not always agreed on the composition of India's strategic neighbourhood. For instance, the official report of India's defence ministry in 1999 linked India's security 'directly with its extended neighbourhood', a term that 'particularly includes India's neighbouring countries and the regions of Central Asia, Southeast Asia, the Gulf and the Indian Ocean'.[73] In this definition, pride of place is given to China, 'India's largest neighbour'.[74] The report went on to assert that 'India has a direct stake in the security of this entire region but is not hemmed in by it'.[75] In the same year, the official report of India's foreign office had a rather different understanding of which countries constituted India's neighbours: (i) the western neighbours (Afghanistan, Iran, and Pakistan), (ii) eastern and southern neighbours (Bangladesh, Myanmar, Maldives, and Sri Lanka), and (iii) the northern neighbours (Bhutan and Nepal).[76] The most notable difference between the two reports is that India's largest neighbour, with whom India contests the largest disputed land border in the world, is not listed as a northern neighbour by the Ministry of External Affairs (MEA) but is tucked away in East Asia, together with Japan and the two Koreas.[77] Clearly, this curious classification of China has less to do with geostrategic realities than with MEA's internal bureaucratic organization.[78]

Clearly, China is *not* a part of South Asia; the Himalayas have for five millennia defined the northern limits of the region. Nevertheless, China is a critical element in South Asian regional security. China is at the very heart of Asia: it is the only Asian country that skirts every sub-region of Asia, whether it is Northeast Asia, Southeast Asia, Central Asia, Inner Asia, or South Asia; there can thus be no Asia without China. Any geostrategic (as opposed to merely geographic) definition of South Asia must necessarily include China. Viewed from New Delhi in particular, this is a totally defensible proposition. China is a country against which India has fought and lost a war in 1962. Nearly half a million Indian soldiers are deployed on India's disputed northern border with China. Furthermore, as the Indian defence ministry reported in 2006, 'Close defence exchanges and nuclear and missile cooperation between China and Pakistan continue to elicit concern.'[79]

Till recently, most analysts tended to ignore the China factor in India's security planning, drawing instead a spurious equation between India and Pakistan. India, with a population of 1.1 billion, is nearly 85 per cent of China's size (population of 1.3 billion) and eight times larger than Pakistan (population of 147 million). Nevertheless, India's attempt to contend with China has been seen as hopelessly over-ambitious, while Pakistan's determination to match India step-for-step has been viewed as being perfectly natural. With the rise of China and the emergence of India, the flawed perception of an India–Pakistan equation is at last being laid to rest.

On China, India's foreign office and defence establishment do not in recent years appear to be speaking with one voice. In 2005, while the Indian foreign ministry was of the view that 'Cooperation between India and China is not only conducive to their socio-economic development and prosperity, but also to strengthening multi-polarity in the world and enhancing the positive factors of globalization',[80] the Indian defence ministry felt that 'the nascent challenge posed by a rapidly-growing and modernizing China was too strong to be ignored'.[81] In 2007, the Indian foreign ministry was almost celebratory:

India–China relations continued to develop steadily. The year 2006 was celebrated as the India–China Friendship Year with a number of commemorative activities. The process of high-level interactions, which has contributed to mutual understanding and cooperation, was sustained. The visit of President Hu Jintao of China to India was a milestone in bilateral relations and resulted in a number of significant understandings, which have further substantiated the strategic and cooperative partnership between the two countries.[82]

The Indian defence ministry, while agreeing that 'India–China relations are progressing',[83] nevertheless focused on the security implications of China's rise in its 2007 report:

China's military modernization, with sustained double-digit growth in its defence budget for over a decade and continued upgrading its nuclear and missile assets, development of infrastructure in the India–China border areas and its growing defence links with some of India's neighbours continue to be monitored closely. The Chinese assistance to Pakistan's nuclear and missile programme has been a matter of concern as it has adversely impacted on India's national security environment.[84]

India's foreign ministry remained positive about India–China relations in 2009:

Bilateral relations with China were further consolidated during 2008.... The situation along the India–China border remained peaceful while the boundary question continued to be addressed by the Special Representatives. The Expert Level Mechanism on trans-boundary rivers continued to expand its work. Defence cooperation between the two countries has contributed to enhancement of mutual trust.[85]

The report of the foreign ministry in 2009 also notes the 'firm commitment' of both countries 'to resolving all outstanding differences through peaceful negotiations, while ensuring that such differences are not allowed to affect the positive development of bilateral relations'.[86]

Referring to India's 'strategic and cooperative partnership' with China, the official report of India's defence ministry in 2009 suggests that the two countries are 'seeking to build a relationship of friendship and trust, based on equality, in which each is sensitive to the concerns and aspirations of the other'. Joint military exercises, a regular defence dialogue since 2007, and exchanges of military delegations are also 'building greater understanding'. Furthermore, India and China 'have agreed to maintain peace and tranquillity in the border areas through the implementation of mutually agreed confidence building measures, pending the final settlement of the boundary issue'.[87] However, after these initial pleasantries, the defence ministry's report turns the heat on India's largest neighbour:

India has taken note of China's statement ... that it will never seek hegemony or engage in military expansion now or in the future, no matter how developed it becomes. India has also taken note of the double digit growth in Chinese defence expenditures over the previous 20 years, which has led to significant modernization of its defence forces, both in terms of quality and quantity. China's stated objectives...of developing strategic missile and space-based assets and of rapidly enhancing its blue-water navy to conduct operations in distant waters, as well as the systematic upgrading of infrastructure, reconnaissance and surveillance, quick response and operational capabilities in the border areas, will have an effect on the overall military environment in the neighbourhood of India. Consequently, China's defence modernization needs to be monitored carefully in the foreseeable future for the implications that it can have on the security and defence of India.[88]

The report further states that China's 'military assistance and coopera-tion with Pakistan and other countries in our neighbourhood ... [has] direct military implications for India'. Thus, 'India will engage China to seek greater transparency and openness in its defence policy and posture, while taking all necessary measures to protect the national security, territorial integrity and sovereignty of India'.[89]

However, the biggest challenge that China poses to India has nothing to do with the border dispute, its military modernization, or even its military assistance to India's neighbours. Over the past three decades, China has built strong political and economic links with nearly all of India's neighbours in South Asia. While India has failed to present a feasible regional vision and invest heavily in it, China has worked systematically, step by step, to create an alternate incentive structure for the countries neighbouring India. The net result, by Chinese design and Indian default, has been to tie India within a regional framework that is inimical to India's interests and ambitions.

It is only over the past few years, specifically from around 2005, that the Indian policy elite has begun to focus on the importance of taking the lead in establishing regional infrastructure projects. Unsurprisingly, this change has coincided with India's emergence as a major player in international politics and the world economy. Perhaps the best expression of this new neighbourhood vision is the establishment of a largely Indian-funded yet genuinely regional South Asian University in New Delhi.[90] The seed of this exciting project was sown in a comment made by Indian Prime Minister, Manmohan Singh, during the 13th SAARC Summit, held in Bangladesh in November 2005:

The people of our subcontinent are at the cutting edge of scientific and technological research and in the front ranks of the knowledge society across the world. Wherever an enabling environment and world class facilities are made available to our talented people, they excel. My suggestion to you is, why cannot we ... pool our resources to create a centre of excellence, in the form of a South Asian University, which can provide world class facilities and professional faculty to students and researchers from every country of our region?[91]

A superb project in terms of both its vision and its connection with the real needs of the region, the South Asian University may yet signal a reversal in the hitherto negative and sterile trajectory of India's regional policy. However, it could also, tragically for India and its region, be a case of too little, too late.

To summarize this section, South Asia is neither peaceful internally nor cohesive externally. Pakistan internally and China externally have ensured that India, although the regional power in South Asia, is able neither to pacify its region nor make it cohere. India's region is not a launching pad but a drag anchor. This perhaps explains why India has increasingly turned its back on its region and instead looks outwards.[92]

SOUTH AFRICA IN SOUTHERN AFRICA: ACKNOWLEDGED SUPREMACY

South Africa's security complex is configured around several contradictory elements: (i) although by far the most powerful country in southern Africa, South Africa was defied by its much weaker neighbours until it transformed itself, internally and externally; (ii) having transformed itself internally, South Africa was able to embark on its mission to transform its region and its continent; (iii) once the most destructive power in the region, South Africa is now playing the part of peacemaker on the African continent; (iv) by not seeking regional or continental hegemony, South Africa has followed a policy of political self-abnegation, but its technologically superior corporations have nevertheless penetrated and dominated markets across Africa; and (v) South Africa has sought, in partnership with Nigeria, to change the way politics is conducted across Africa, but it has been unable to transform politics in its 'near abroad', specifically the regime of Robert Mugabe in Zimbabwe. This section will analyse each of these strands.

To fully understand the link between superior socio-economic levels and regional supremacy, no better example exists than South Africa. Table 2.5 sheds light on the peculiar nature of South Africa's regional superiority. Although South Africa is outnumbered by its regional neighbours in terms of population and military–paramilitary personnel, it could potentially spend much more than they can on military capability for the simple reason that its GDP is 2.5 times as large as that of its neighbours combined. In fact, South Africa spends less on its military capability in comparison to its neighbours. The military balance in southern Africa reflects these military budgets: South Africa is outgunned, at least nominally, in several crucial categories, including MBT, artillery, and combat aircraft. While this is partly attributable to large quantities of unusable Soviet-made materiel in Angola, it is also the result of deliberate South African policy.

TABLE 2.5   Military Capability in Southern Africa: South Africa and Its Neighbours

	South Africa	Its Neighbours*
Total population	43,786,115	77,859,515
Total armed forces (active)	62,082	187,800
Total paramilitary forces	0	42,200
GDP in 2008 (US$ billion)	264[a]	106.6[b]
Military budget in 2008 (US$ billion)	2.8	3.4[c]
Main battle tanks	167	430
Light tanks	0	85
Armoured reconnaissance vehicles	176	883
Armoured infantry fighting vehicles	1,200	290
Armoured personnel carriers	810	744
Artillery (towed & self-propelled)	1,467	2,090
Air defence guns	76	1,266
Surface-to-air missiles	0	1,031
Principal surface combatants (warships)	4	0
Patrol and coastal combatants	26	35
Submarines	3	0
Combat aircraft	12	191
Armed helicopters	11	26

Source: The International Institute for Strategic Studies, 'Sub-Saharan Africa', *The Military Balance 2009* (London: Routledge, 2009), pp. 288–327.

Notes: * Angola, Botswana, Lesotho, Malawi, Mozambique, Namibia, Zambia, and Zimbabwe (Swaziland not included).
[a] GDP figure for South Africa is for 2007.
[b] GDP data for Lesotho and Zimbabwe are for 2007.
[c] Military budget data for Botswana, Lesotho, Malawi, Mozambique, and Zambia are for 2007 (data for Zimbabwe not available).

As Table 2.6 indicates, although marginally smaller than Angola in land area, South Africa has the largest population, the largest GDP per capita, and lowest infant mortality rate (after Botswana), the lowest adult illiteracy rate, and longest female life expectancy figures (after Namibia) in southern Africa. As South African policymakers realize, the last thing that the neighbouring countries need or want is a situation of conflict with the leading state in the region. Thus, South Africa's supremacy in

TABLE 2.6 Geographic, Demographic, and Socio-economic Indicators: Countries of Southern Africa

Country	Human development index/rank (2006)	Area (km²)	Total population (thousands, 2006, est.)	GDP per capita (US$, 2008)	GDP per capita (PPP) (int'l $, 2006)	Female life expectancy at birth (years, 2006)	Infant mortality rate (per 1,000 births, 2000–5)	Adult literacy rate (per cent, 2000–7)	Ratio of adult literacy rate of females to males (per cent, 2000–7)	Sustainable access to improved drinking water sources (per cent, 2006)	Sustainable access to improved sanitation facilities (per cent, 2006)
Angola	0.484/157	1,246,700	16,557	1,942	2,678	43	116	67	65	51	50
Botswana	0.664/126	569,582	1,858	6,108	13,089	52	33	83	100	86	47
Lesotho	0.496/155	30,350	1,995	788	3,592	44	68	82	123	78	36
Malawi	0.457/162	118,480	13,571	278	731	51	71	72	82	76	60
Mozambique	0.366/175	801,590	20,971	440	1,345	51	115	44	58	42	31
Namibia	0.634/129	824,292	2,047	4,143	8,142	63	47	88	99	93	35
South Africa	0.670/125	1,221,037	48,282	5,566	11,960	53	46	88	98	93	59
Swaziland	0.542/141	17,364	1,134	2,369	5,137	43	66	80	97	60	50
Zambia	0.453/163	752,618	11,696	1,144	1,098	43	103	68	78	58	52
Zimbabwe	Unranked	390,757	13,228	314	2,011	43	59	91	94	81	46
Southern Africa	–	5,972,770	131,339	5,293	–	–	–	–	–	–	–

Source: Statistics and indicators are provided by the United Nations Statistics Division from http://data.un.org, accessed on 24 January 2010. Dashes indicate 'data unavailable/unreported'.

southern Africa has a socio-economic rather than a military basis: its overwhelming socio-economic superiority in the region virtually makes its military capability redundant.

In terms of relative capabilities, South Africa's predominant position in southern Africa is self-evident. Even during the apartheid years, South Africa was 'the "mover-and-shaker" in southern African affairs: the state with by far the greatest capability to affect and influence the course of regional events'.[93] However, South Africa's peculiar domestic arrangements under apartheid stood in the way of regional leadership. As Robert Jaster expressed it in 1986, 'The paradox of regional politics is the fact that South Africa has been unable as yet to translate this overwhelming military and economic power into anything like a comparative degree of political influence in the region.'[94] On the contrary, for all its military and economic power, South Africa's sense of isolation within its region only increased during the last decade of the apartheid system. A contemporary observer had then noted that 'regional policy is today very much a matter of military survival'.[95] It was this notion of regional security, of being under siege, which underlay the 'destabilization policy' of the P.W. Botha government (1978–89). The officially declared objective of destabilization was 'to cripple SWAPO and the ANC militarily'[96] and 'to create such military and economic pressure on the sanctuary states...that they would be forced to deny the guerrillas sanctuary'.[97] However, as Jaster points out, 'The destabilisation policy had a third and overriding objective: to bring about a regional detente on terms imposed by South Africa and formalized in a series of bilateral accords; in short, nothing less than a *Pax Pretoria*.'[98]

The new policy of 'clubbing [its] neighbours into submission'[99] was legalized through the amendment of the Defence Act in 1977. The amended legislation allowed the South African Defence Force (SADF) to operate not only 'in any part of the Republic of South Africa' but also, for the first time, in 'neighbouring states'.[100] By 1984, two of South Africa's neighbours buckled under its military and economic might and sued for peace. At the negotiating table, South Africa successfully hammered out the Luanda Accord establishing a ceasefire with Angola, and the Nkomati Accord of mutual non-aggression with Mozambique. In Jaster's opinion, 'There is no doubt that it was the destabilization policy and the punishing blows it dealt to Angola and Mozambique which led those two states to agree to sign such politically distasteful and costly pacts with the apartheid regime.'[101] Thus, from a strictly security perspective, there can be no doubt of South Africa's ability to have its way in southern Africa.

However, even the purposeful exercise of South African power by the Botha administration was unable to win regional leadership for the apartheid regime. In 1979, South Africa proposed the creation of a 'constellation' of 10 regional states under its leadership for regional cooperation and detente, but the idea quickly fizzled out.[102] In a rapid counter move, Botswana, Angola, Zambia, Mozambique, and Tanzania set up the Southern African Development Coordination Conference (SADCC), with the explicit aim of 'reducing the region's economic dependence on South Africa'.[103] The regional states in SADCC included Botswana, Lesotho, and Swaziland (the so-called BLS states), all of which had 'close economic links with South Africa through the Southern African Customs Union'.[104] South Africa was the source of 90 per cent of the imports of the BLS states, while the Customs Union provided two-thirds of the total budget revenues of Lesotho and Swaziland.[105] Other front-line states were also heavily dependent on South Africa's economy and infrastructure.

In a show of its economic muscle in the region, South Africa withdrew 25 locomotives on loan to Zimbabwe in 1981, strategically timed to disrupt a bumper grain harvest, and relented only under strong US pressure.[106] Nevertheless, its economic and military muscle notwithstanding, during the apartheid years South Africa did not 'gain political influence in the region commensurate with its military and economic clout...[and] thus failed to meet the criteria of a true regional power'.[107] In other words, while South Africa could bring overwhelming power to bear on its neighbours, it was not able to force them to acknowledge its supremacy in southern Africa.

The establishment of multiracial democracy after the elections of April 1994 and the ending of apartheid both had 'profound political and strategic consequences'.[108] As the White Paper published by South Africa's Department of Defence (DoD) in 1996 put it, 'The government is no longer unrepresentative and at war with its own people and neighbouring states in Southern Africa.'[109] The White Paper also points out that '[after] two and a half decades of isolation...[the] country's foreign relations have been transformed from an adversarial mode to bilateral and multi-lateral co-operation'.[110]

The impact of South Africa's domestic changes on the regional security context has been huge. The DoD's *Defence Review 1998* notes, in its chapter on regional security, that the most significant strategic development 'is South Africa's new status in Southern Africa, previously an arena of intense conflict'.[111] South Africa's relations with neighbouring states 'have shifted from animosity to friendship and co-operation'.[112] This change is fully reflected in South Africa's assessment of its national security, and provides a marked change from the feeling of being isolated and besieged, which dominated the final years of white minority rule.

The White Paper also states that South Africa 'is not confronted by an immediate conventional military threat, and does not anticipate external military aggression in the short- to medium-term'.[113] This has important implications for force design: 'the size and capability of the SANDF...should not be seen as threatening by the other states of Southern Africa'.[114] The White Paper suggests that 'reductions in South Africa's force levels and weapons holdings might stimulate a broader process of disarmament in Southern Africa'.[115] It, however, adds the important proviso that 'force reductions should be kept within reasonable proportions if South Africa is to play an active supportive role in the region'.[116] The bottom line, in both the White Paper and the *Defence Review*, is that 'South Africa has a common destiny with Southern Africa.'[117] Nelson Mandela expressed this sentiment succinctly in 1993, several months before his inauguration as state president: 'South Africa will resist any pressure or temptation to pursue its own interests at the expense of Southern Africa.'[118]

In its official documents during the democratic transition, the South African government has repeatedly reiterated its interest in instituting confidence- and security-building measures (CSBMs) in the region. Some of the CSBMs emphasized include: annual consultation and exchange of information; the establishment of a regional arms register; notification, on-site inspection, and verification of military exercises; and a communications network and crisis hotline.[119] Apart from CSBMs, 'defence co-operation with other Southern African states is a priority'[120] for South African defence planners. As the *Defence Review* points out, 'South Africa now engages in defence co-operation with a number of countries and participates in regional security arrangements under the auspices of the Southern African Development Community (SADC).'[121] To this end, South Africa is seeking to 'strengthen the security and defence forums of SADC'[122] and 'encourage the development of a multi-lateral, "common security" approach in Southern Africa'.[123] However, the one area of security cooperation that the Mandela government particularly focused on was multilateral peace support operations, both in the region and on the continent.

The White Paper points to the 'expectations that South Africa will become involved in multi-national peace support operations on the continent'.[124] As a precondition to participate in such operations, South Africa insists that operations 'in Southern Africa should be sanctioned by SADC and undertaken with other SADC states. Similarly, operations in Africa should be sanctioned by the OAU [Organization of African Unity]'.[125] Furthermore, peace 'enforcement operations which take place under the auspices of the OAU or SADC require prior endorsement by the UN Security Council'.[126] While noting that 'a standing peacekeeping force in the region is not required or feasible',[127] the *Defence Review* asserts that 'the SADC states are committed to regional co-operation in preparing for peace support operations'.[128] In order to achieve this, '[c]ombined training should be undertaken with the forces of countries with which South Africa is likely to be involved in peace support operations'.[129]

A decade plus after the White Paper (1996) and the *Defence Review* (1998), how much importance should we accord to these fundamental documents of the post-apartheid transition period? Len Le Roux has pointed out that the SANDF today 'acts as a force for crisis prevention and intervention rather than preparing to defend South Africa against a conventional onslaught'.[130] The 'steady and pragmatic shift away from the written policy'[131] has occurred because 'some of the assumptions underlying South Africa's defence policy have not been fully realised'.[132] Le Roux points to the

de facto move away from the policy of a small regular force backed by a significantly large part-time force towards a larger, full-time force with out-of-area support requirements. Similarly, a force design predicated on short logistic lines for highly mechanised mobile forces prepared to fight in defence of the territorial integrity of South Africa has given way to preparations for out of area force projection and support requirements in distant places including Burundi and the Democratic Republic of Congo.[133]

During the initial years of the democratic transition, with Nelson Mandela as its iconic president, South Africa was confident that the 'miracle' of its transition held lessons for all of Africa: 'For the first time in the continent's history, a country marked its own path to peace, uniting all factions to a prolonged conflict through democratic change. Africans demonstrated that they could find their own solutions—and that these were more durable than anything imposed externally.'[134] Glowing in the righteousness of its own internal transformation, South Africa 'has been a constant architect of Africa's new peace and security architecture, an advocate of new diplomatic norms, and a tireless contrarian voice in the international community on behalf of the world's least developed regions'.[135]

However, the new South Africa soon learnt that it continued to be viewed with suspicion in many parts of Africa, including in its own region of southern Africa. When the military regime in Nigeria, led by General Sani Abacha, carried out its death sentence of Ogoniland activist (and novelist) Ken Saro-Wiwa in November 1995, a disgusted Mandela, then participating in the Commonwealth summit in Auckland, called for oil sanctions against Nigeria and its expulsion from the Commonwealth. However, South Africa on that occasion failed to carry its southern African neighbours along with itself, and Mandela found his decision being criticized across much of Africa. Worse still, South Africa was 'accused by many African leaders of becoming a western Trojan horse sowing seeds of division in Africa and undermining African solidarity'.[136] The Nigeria episode has proved to be a salutary lesson in foreign policy for the leaders of democratic South Africa. Nevertheless, the moral dimension remained an important strand in South Africa's regional and continental policy during the Mandela years. Thus, as Sisa Ngombane argues, 'South Africa's increasing involvement in the Great Lakes crises under Mandela was both a trial of fire for South Africa and a moral repudiation of the international community's indifference.'[137]

South Africa's involvement in the Congo crisis is a good example of its diplomatic approach to regional conflicts, as also of the limits of South African regional policy. Ngombane suggests that

whilst involvement was incremental it was understood that in order to succeed it had to be continuous and multifaceted. Thus peace-brokering led to constitution making, followed by transitional rule, preparation and holding of elections and development cooperation with technical assistance on the security sector (army and police), public sector reform and home affairs, during the pre- and post-election period.[138]

However, the South African initiative in the Democratic Republic of the Congo (DRC) was 'openly defied by Zimbabwe, Namibia, and Angola which sent troops to the DRC in 1998',[139] during the last year of the Mandela presidency. The situation in DRC thus became the first diplomatic challenge faced by Thabo Mbeki after taking over the South African presidency in June 1999. In April 1999, Zimbabwe crafted a military assistance pact with Namibia, Angola, and the DRC, principally to prop up militarily regimes in the latter two countries, both of which are facing serious insurgencies.[140] The Congo conflict transcended the southern African region because Rwanda and Uganda actively supported the Congolese rebels. Zimbabwe's initiative, by de facto splitting SADC, put it on a collision course with South Africa, which had been attempting to reach a negotiated settlement to the Congo conflict.

With Robert Mugabe, Zimbabwe's long-ruling president, in a militant mood both domestically and externally, South Africa under Thabo Mbeki found that the regional agenda was spinning out of its control. Not willing to repeat the experience of Mandela in 1995, Mbeki decided that he needed to build an understanding with Nigeria's democratically elected president, General Olusegun Obasanjo, relating to South Africa's regional and continental initiatives. Adebajo remarks that 'Pretoria's alliance with Abuja [was] therefore a marriage of necessity for Mbeki.... South Africa has reached out to Nigeria, Africa's most populous state, and coordinated efforts in diplomatic fora.'[141]

Zimbabwe has presented the most difficult regional challenge to South African policy since the democratic transition. Despite repeated pressure from the Western powers for a more proactive policy, Thabo Mbeki stuck to his 'softly-softly' approach towards Zimbabwe and Mugabe during his presidency (1999–2008). Thus, the lessons from Mandela, Nigeria, and 1995 were well learnt. How Jacob Zuma, South Africa's president from May 2009, will approach the issue of Zimbabwe still remains to be seen. Chris Landsberg has made the interesting suggestion that 'South Africa and Zimbabwe represent the Germany and France of southern Africa. Just like the latter are indispensable for European stability and integration, so the former two are pivotal in the southern African context.'[142] One thing is clear: the disintegration of Zimbabwe after almost three decades of one-party and one-person rule, and especially the destruction of Zimbabwe's economic base, holds up a mirror to South Africa itself and reminds many South Africans that the consolidation of their multiracial democracy is essential.

After over 15 years of South African conflict-mediation in its region and continent, it is possible to assess the success of South Africa's regional policy. Several criticisms have been levelled against its approach to conflict mediation in Africa. For instance, Kurt Shillinger has argued that 'South Africa has seemed almost blinded by enthusiasm for its own model', although many of the conflicts that South Africa has sought to mediate have 'lacked one or more factors critical to the success of its model—the most important being the mutual recognition of all parties that continued conflict is no longer a viable alternative to resolution.'[143]

Daniela Kroslak points to the discrepancy 'between its rhetoric and practice, between its policy and strategy in peace processes, between highly qualified and renowned negotiators and facilitators and the lack of capacity at the middle level of implementation' as undermining 'South Africa's role and credibility as a peacemaker'.[144] Kwesi Aning remarks that there is 'mounting concern that South Africa's approach to mediation is statist. Put differently, that South Africa will usually support a state party in a conflict with combatants.'[145] Nevertheless, Aning admits that 'While there are cases of irritation about South Africa's power, there is also general acceptance—from both rebels and state parties—of the role Pretoria can play.'[146]

How then should we evaluate South Africa's policy in its regional neighbourhood and on its continent? Landsberg has argued quite forcefully that the new South Africa 'behaves like a revisionist power when it makes the promotion of democracy in Africa a central plank of its foreign policy, but it remains essentially a status-quo power when it pursues unfriendly policies toward its smaller neighbours'.[147] Adebajo, on the other hand, suggests that post-apartheid South Africa is 'neither a messiah nor a mercantilist power. It is simply an aspiring middle power seeking to punch above its weight in global politics'.[148] Adebajo further argues that while South Africa 'simply lacks the economic and military muscle and political legitimacy' that it would need to become Africa's messiah, it is not a mercantilist power either because it 'is gradually loosening its protectionist policies in southern Africa, it has restructured SACU [Southern African Customs Union] and SADC [Southern African Development Community] to render greater benefits to its other members, and is at last conscious of the need to promote investment and industrialisation policies that benefit its neighbours'.[149]

It is clear that 'Africa has embarked on a grand project of self-correction', and that South Africa 'will continue to play a primary role in this metamorphosis'.[150] In its *Strategic Plan 2010–2013*, South Africa's Department of International Relations and Cooperation lists 'Continued Prioritisation of the African Continent' and 'Improving Political and Economic Integration of the SADC' as the first and second priorities of South African foreign policy.[151] Adebajo is essentially correct in asserting that

South Africa is becoming an African power, and can aspire to global middle-power status through its current policy of working through key African allies, as well as Brazil and India, in international fora in which South Africa's voice is widely respected. But Pretoria's future lies in Africa and its global status can only be achieved by being accepted as a leader on its own continent.[152]

On the face of it, South Africa's neighbours have recognized, and to a certain extent even welcomed, its supremacy in the region. This, however, could be a transitory phase based on the extended honeymoon that South Africa enjoyed thanks to the moral stature of Nelson Mandela and its remarkable exit from apartheid to multiracial democracy. We should also bear in mind the relative economic decline of South Africa vis-à-vis its neighbours and the social costs of the AIDS (acquired immune deficiency syndrome) pandemic, both of which have also contributed to South Africa's regional supremacy looking increasingly tattered. Referring to the two middle powers in sub-Saharan Africa, Adebajo and Landsberg remark that

it would be naive of South Africa and Nigeria to expect that other regional states will stand idly by while they form an alliance to lead Africa to the promised land. Unless the two 'giants' take the interests of such states into account, and constantly find ways of reassuring them of their desire for mutual benefits from regional cooperation, they should not be surprised if counter-hegemonic alliances are formed to balance their own power.[153]

STRUCTURAL CONSTRAINTS, POLICY INNOVATION

A comparative analysis of the regional security problématiques of Brazil, India, and South Africa must attempt to provide at least tentative answers to a number of important questions. What can we say about the pathways adopted by the three countries in the context of their regional security? Does the comparative analysis suggest that one pathway is 'better'? What do we understand by a 'better' pathway to regional security: promoting regional peace and stability or finding the most effective route to regional dominance? How important is the regional context? Does the regional context in effect determine the pathway taken by each emerging power? Or is the policy adopted by each emerging power in some ways unrelated to the constraints imposed by the regional power configuration?

My study suggests that the role of a regional power depends upon at least three factors. The first two, military capacity and socio-economic levels, determine the relative capability of the emerging power within its own region. However, the patterns of regional enmity and amity, a product of past history and current policy, are also a critical factor in the reaction of the neighbouring states to the regional role of the emerging power.

South Africa was able to gain undisputed leadership in its region once it abandoned the divisive domestic policy of apartheid. The Brazil–Argentine entente, on the other hand, was based much more on a change in perception than policy. In South Asia, the India–Pakistan relationship remains a hostage to history. In the latter region, perceptions about the past continue to place a limit on the possibilities for the future. Viewed in this light, it makes little sense to talk about a 'better' route to regional security, as policy breakthroughs are only one element in a complex web of factors, regional and extra-regional, that define the security problématique of a region.

However, to state the aforementioned is not to suggest that policy choices do not matter. The constraints imposed by structural factors such as the regional power configuration, the role of extra-regional powers, and the perceptions of neighbouring states may seem overwhelming but are not insuperable. Perceptions may constrain policy, but policy can alter perceptions. The clearest example of the significance of policy choices is South Africa, an emerging power which has taken on a new and constructive role in its region as a direct result of a single (and singular) policy change: the decision to abandon apartheid. If South Africa's supremacy in southern Africa is widely acknowledged, and in many cases even welcomed, by its neighbours today, a change in policy lies at the base of this startling change. The contrast between the new policy of multilateral peace support operations and the regional destabilizing policy of the apartheid state could not be any sharper.

The case of Brazil is also extremely interesting in terms of the links between the policy choices of the emerging powers and regional security. At first glance, rapprochement between Argentina and Brazil is a fairly recent phenomenon, initiated by the military dictatorships in the context of nuclear rivalry, but later broadened and deepened by the newly installed civilian regimes in both countries. However, as an explanation of the irrelevance of Brazilian primacy in the southern cone, the Argentina–Brazil entente is not, by itself, sufficient. Why do Brazil's neighbours not fear this huge continental state much more than they actually do? To understand 'why' requires an explanation that takes note of persistent Brazilian policy to establish regional stability, which goes back over 150 years. This policy has several strands: an active policy of frontier management from the days of the Baron of Rio Branco, the legendary foreign minister (1902–12) who settled all of Brazil's border disputes peacefully; establishment of a strong diplomatic presence in its neighbours' countries to diffuse tension; and the creation of a regional infrastructural network, such as the Itaipu project, to bind the neighbouring states together and to itself.

In sharp contrast to Brazil and South Africa, India appears to be a prisoner of its regional context. The India–Pakistan relationship remains one of enduring rivalry, enemy imaging, and zero-sum calculations. Notwithstanding socio-cultural kinship and economic complementarities, these two neighbouring countries have, given a divergent ideology, both a disputed geography and a divided history. This situation is unlikely to change any time in the near future. However, even in this extreme case of regional constraints, it would appear that policy has a positive role to play. Indeed, over the years India has resorted to a variety of strategies to enhance its regional security, fluctuating from bullying tactics (a blockade of Nepal in the late 1980s), on the one hand, to offering unilateral concessions (resolving a river waters dispute with Bangladesh on extremely generous terms), on the other. The so-called 'Indira Doctrine', enunciated during the later years of the Indira Gandhi period, virtually declared South Asia to be an Indian sphere of influence into which external powers were not welcome. The Gujral Doctrine of the late 1990s, in sharp contrast, was a strategy aimed at giving unilateral concessions to regional neighbours without insisting on reciprocity, all with the aim of reducing regional tensions and promoting regional cooperation. Vis-à-vis Pakistan, India's policy has fluctuated between extreme belligerence (the nuclear tests of May 1998) and a genuine desire to bury the hatchet (then prime minister Vajpayee's bus journey to Pakistan in February 1999). Thus, even in the constrained context of South Asia, there is a role for policy initiatives aimed at breaking the regional deadlock.

In conclusion, I will advance two interrelated yet superficially contradictory propositions about the three emerging powers and their respective regional contexts. The first is that emerging powers are *not* merely regional powers; indeed, they are characterized as 'emerging' precisely because they appear to be transcending their own region and acquiring a systemic (trans-regional) presence and impact. The second is that an emerging power will not in fact emerge as a systemic player without first consolidating and pacifying its region through a process of positive transformation into a zone of growth and peace. It is noteworthy that Brazil, India, and South Africa all find themselves in regions that are outside the zones of economic dynamism in the contemporary international system. The regional security context, that is, whether their respective regions will serve as launching pads or as drag-anchors, is thus a critical factor for the emerging powers in their quest to transcend regional bounds and achieve a global impact. What this chapter suggests is that regional leadership, by building consent, is a surer way to achieve this objective than a futile exercise of regional power.

Notes

1. This comparative chapter on Brazil, India, and South Africa, begun over a decade ago, has had an uncomfortably long gestation which I am relieved is finally over. In its initial version, the research on which the chapter is based was published as a working paper in Mexico: Varun Sahni, 'Brazil, India and South Africa: Three Pathways to Regional (In)security', *Documento de Trabajo EI-46, División de Estudios Internacionales* (Centro de Investigación y Docencia Económicas [CIDE]: Mexico City, 1999). Later, an abridged and updated version was published in Pakistan as a chapter in a book: Varun Sahni, 'Primacy, Dominance and Supremacy: A Comparison of the Regional Security Contexts of Brazil, India and South Africa', in Jamshed Ayaz Khan (ed.), *Prospects of Peace, Stability and Prosperity in South Asia* (Islamabad: Institute of Regional Studies, 2005), pp. 274–90. Yet another version, translated into Spanish, was later published in Argentina as a chapter in a book: Varun Sahni, 'Ancla flotante o plataforma de lanzamiento? Dinámica regional de los poderes emergentes', in Juan Tokatlian (ed.), *India, Brasil y Sudáfrica: El impacto de las nuevas potencias regionales* (Buenos Aires: Libros del Zorzal, 2007), pp. 97–125. In a related study, the following chapter, comparing military industry, nuclear policy, and HIV/AIDS strategy in the three countries, was published in Brazil: Varun Sahni, 'Tangential yet Tangible: IBSA in the Context of India's Security Concerns', in Alcides Costa Vaz (ed.), *Intermediate States, Regional Leadership and Security: India, Brazil and South Africa* (Brasilia: Editora Universidade de Brasília [University of Brasilia Press], 2006), pp. 87–113. Finally, parts of the analysis in this chapter appeared in a chapter in a book published in Germany: Varun Sahni, 'India in Asia: An Emerging Power in a Proto-Region', in Hans J. Giessmann (ed.), *Security Handbook 2008: Emerging Powers in East Asia: China, Russia and India: Local Conflicts and Regional Security Building in Asia's Northeast* (Baden-Baden: Nomos Verlagsgesellschaft, 2008), pp. 138–56.

2. As Dessler neatly points out, the agent–structure problem 'emerges from two uncontentious truths about social life: first, that human agency is the only moving force behind the actions, events, and outcomes of the social world; and second, that human agency can be realized only in concrete historical circumstances that condition the possibilities for action and influence its course.' (David Dessler, 'What's at Stake in the Agent–Structure Debate?', *International Organization*, 43 (3), 1989, p. 443). This in turn suggests, in the words of Wendt, 'that human agents and social structures are, in one way or another, theoretically interdependent and mutually implicating entities. Thus, the analysis of action invokes an at least implicit understanding of particular

social relationships (or "rules of the game") in which the action is set—just as the analysis of social structures invokes some understanding of the actors whose relationships make up the structural context.' (Alexander E. Wendt, 'The Agent–Structure Problem in International Relations Theory', *International Organization*, 41 (3), 1987, p. 338).

3. The text of the Brasilia Declaration (2003) can be downloaded from http://meaindia.nic.in/jshome.htm, accessed on 30 October 2005.

4. Jeffrey E. Garten, *The Big Ten: The Big Emerging Markets and How They Will Change Our Lives* (New York: Basic Books, 1997), p. 3.

5. Robert S. Chase, Emily B. Hill, and Paul Kennedy, 'Pivotal States and U.S. Strategy', *Foreign Affairs*, 75 (1), 1996, p. 37. For a fuller treatment, see Robert Chase, Emily Hill, and Paul Kennedy (eds), *The Pivotal States: A New Framework for U.S. Policy in the Developing World* (New York: W.W. Norton, 1998).

6. Carsten Holbraad, *Middle Powers in International Politics* (London: Macmillan, 1984).

7. For a thorough discussion on the characterization of middle powers, see Holbraad, *Middle Powers*, pp. 67–75.

8. Holbraad, *Middle Powers*, pp. 74–5.

9. This was one of the conclusions reached at an international workshop on '*Las relaciones de seguridad en el Hemisferio Occidental: Cuatro Potencias Medias y los Estados Unidos*' ('Security Relations in the Western Hemisphere: Four Middle Powers and the US'), held at the Centro de Investigación y Docencia Económicas, Mexico City, on 11–12 November 1999.

10. William R. Thompson, 'The Regional Subsystem: A Conceptual Explication and a Propositional Inventory', *International Studies Quarterly*, 17 (1), 1973, p. 115.

11. Thompson, 'The Regional Subsystem', p. 101.

12. Andrew Hurrell, *On Global Order: Power, Values, and the Constitution of International Society* (Oxford: Oxford University Press, 2007), p. 247.

13. David A. Lake, 'Regional Security Complexes: A Systems Approach', in David A. Lake and Patrick M. Morgan (eds), *Regional Orders: Building Security in a New World* (University Park: The Pennsylvania State University Press, 1997), pp. 48–9.

14. Barry Buzan, Ole Wæver, and Jaap de Wilde, *Security: A New Framework for Analysis* (Boulder: Lynne Rienner, 1998), p. 12. This is Buzan's latest definition of a concept he first proposed in 1983.

15. Buzan *et al.*, *Security*, p. 11.

16. Barry Buzan, *People, States and Fear*, 2nd Edn (Boulder: Lynne Rienner, 1991), p. 211.

17. Andrew Hurrell suggests that a regional power arises because it is 'so overwhelmingly dominant within a region that it is the "natural hegemon" and can enforce its will, or because it succeeds in creating consensual hegemony within a region (maybe by providing economic benefits or underpinning regional security, or by claiming to embody a particular view of the world or a

set of values)'. See Hurrell, *On Global Order*, p. 251. Clearly, enforcing one's will and creating consensus represent two very different processes.

18. As Hurrell trenchantly remarks, 'Regional leaders need regional followers ... the other states in the region can be very resistant to being led by what outsiders may consider to be the "natural" leader of the region...'. See Hurrell, *On Global Order*, p. 251.

19. This aspect relates closely to regional patterns of amity and enmity in Buzan's formulation.

20. República Federativa do Brasil, Presidencia da República, *Política de Defensa Nacional* (Brasília: Imprensa Nacional, 1996), pt. 2.7, hereafter referred to as *PDN Brasil*. Official English translation downloaded from http://www. brasil.emb.nw.dc.us./fpst10de.htm, accessed on 3 June 1998.

21. Brazilian Government, Ministry of Defence, *National Strategy of Defense*, 14, accessed from https://www.defesa.gov.br/eventos_temporarios/2009/ estrategia/arquivos/estrategia_defesa_nacional_ingles.pdf, on 13 March 2010. Hereafter referred to as *Brazilian National Strategy of Defense*.

22. *PDN Brasil*, pt 2.12.

23. Ibid., pt 4.2.

24. Ibid., pt 5.1l.

25. An excellent, if somewhat controversial, academic account of the Brazilian military institutional interest in the Amazonian region can be found in Daniel Zirker and Marvin Henberg, 'Amazônia: Democracy, Ecology and Brazilian Military Prerogatives in the 1990s', *Armed Forces & Society*, 20 (2), 1994, pp. 259–81.

26. *Brazilian National Strategy of Defense*, p. 45.

27. Ibid., p. 49 (my emphasis).

28. Ibid., p. 22.

29. Jack Child, *Geopolitics and Conflict in South America: Quarrels among Neighbors* (New York: Praeger Publishers, 1985), p. 36.

30. *Brazilian National Strategy of Defense*, p. 26.

31. Child, *Quarrels among Neighbors*, p. 34.

32. *Brazilian National Strategy of Defense*, p. 14.

33. Child, *Quarrels among Neighbors*, p. 7.

34. Ibid., p. 7.

35. Ibid., p. 7.

36. Ibid., p. 100.

37. The Chaco War activated economic competition between Argentina and Brazil over petroleum resources in the disputed Gran Chaco region. It also resulted in a diplomatic tussle between Argentina and Brazil to mediate between the opposing sides, a competition won eventually by Argentina, whose foreign minister, Carlos Saavedra Lamas, was awarded the Nobel Peace Prize in 1936.

38. Philip Kelly, *Checkerboards and Shatterbelts: The Geopolitics of South America* (Austin: University of Texas Press, 1997), pp. 52–3.

39. Child, *Quarrels among Neighbors*, p. 99.

40. See http://www.abacc.org, accessed on 14 April 2004.

41. For the milestone treaties, protocols, and declarations in the short history of MERCOSUR, see http://www.mercosur.com/in/info/tratados_acuerdos.jsp, accessed on 17 April 2004.

42. 'Intra-MERCOSUR Trade in a Crisis Year: A View through Brazilian Figures', *INTAL Monthly Newsletter* 162, January–February 2010, p. 1, accessed from http://www.iadb.org/intal/aplicaciones/uploads/publicaciones/i_INTAL_ICM_162_MERCOSUR1_2010.pdf, on 27 March 2010.

43. 'Intra-MERCOSUR Trade in a Crisis Year', p. 2.

44. Ibid., p. 3.

45. Ibid., pp. 3–4.

46. Kelly, *Checkerboards and Shatterbelts*, p. 53.

47. Child, *Quarrels among Neighbors*, p. 99.

48. Kelly, *Checkerboards and Shatterbelts*, pp. 176–80.

49. *PDN Brasil*, pt 2.10.

50. *Brazilian National Strategy of Defense*, p. 17.

51. See http://www.itaipu.gov.br, accessed on 15 March 2010, for more information on the Itaipu Binacional hydroelectric project.

52. On the Argentine doctrine of 'peripheral realism', see Carlos Escudé, *Foreign Policy Theory in Menem's Argentina* (Gainesville: University Press of Florida, 1997).

53. On this important point, see Varun Sahni, 'The Stability–Instability Paradox: A Less Than Perfect Explanation', in E. Sridharan (ed.), *The India–Pakistan Nuclear Relationship: Theories of Deterrence and International Relations* (London: Routledge, 2007), pp. 185–207.

54. As Ashley Tellis has recently noted,

Jihad undertaken by sub-national groups with state support [became] the instrument that allowed Pakistan to punch above its geopolitical weight...when it became clear that the strategy of sustaining domestic insurgencies against India was simply not paying off in the manner expected—a sorry record that goes back to Pakistan's earliest experiments in 1947 in Kashmir—Islamabad responded with a new strategy of fomenting terrorism instead.

Ashley J. Tellis, 'Bad Company: Lashkar e-Tayyiba and the Growing Ambition of Islamist Militancy in Pakistan', Congressional Testimony, United States House of Representatives, Committee on Foreign Affairs, Subcommittee on the Middle East and South Asia, 11 March 2010, 2–3, accessed from http://www.carnegieendowment.org/publications/index.cfm?fa=view&id=40330, on 12 March 2010.

55. Government of India, Ministry of External Affairs, *Annual Report 2004–2005* (New Delhi: Ministry of External Affairs, 2005), p. 6. Hereafter *MEA Annual Report*.

56. *MEA Annual Report 2006–2007*, p. iv.

57. *MEA Annual Report 2005–2006* (2006), p. 14.

58. Government of India, Ministry of Defence, *Annual Report 2004–2005* (New Delhi: Ministry of Defence, 2005), 10. Hereafter *MoD Annual Report*.

59. *MoD Annual Report 2005–2006*, p. 7.

60. *MoD Annual Report 2006–2007*, p. 4.

61. Ibid., p. 5.

62. *MEA Annual Report 2008–2009*.

63. Ibid., p. ii.

64. Ibid., p. v.

65. *MoD Annual Report 2008–2009*, p. 5 (pt 1.12).

66. Ibid., p. 5 (pt 1.13).

67. *MEA Annual Report 2009–2010*, p. 16.

68. Tellis, 'Bad Company', p. 5.

69. Sahni, 'The Stability–Instability Paradox'.

70. See Hiranmay Karlekar, *Bangladesh: The Next Afghanistan?* (New Delhi: Sage Publications, 2005).

71. V.K. Shashikumar, 'Recruited by RAW, Trained by Army: LTTE', *CNN-IBN*, 2 July 2006, accessed from http://ibnlive.in.com/news/recruited-by-raw-trained-by-army-ltte/14462-3-1.html, on 7 September 2010.

72. See S.D. Muni, *Maoist Insurgency in Nepal: The Challenge and the Response* (New Delhi: Rupa and Observer Research Foundation, 2003).

73. *MoD Annual Report 1998–1999*, p. 2 (pt 1.2).

74. Ibid., p. 2 (pt 1.4).

75. Ibid., p. 2 (pt 1.2).

76. *MEA Annual Report 1998–1999*, pp. 1–10.

77. Ibid., pp. 31–3.

78. A quick glance through the *Annual Reports* of the Indian Ministry of External Affairs makes it clear that the non-categorization of China as India's neighbour in *MEA Annual Report 1998–1999* was not an aberration. See, for instance, *MEA Annual Report 2000–2001*, pp. 1–13, 27–29.

79. *MoD Annual Report 2005–2006*, pp. 9–10.

80. *MEA Annual Report 2004–2005*, p. 4.

81. *MoD Annual Report 2004–2005*, p. 8.

82. *MEA Annual Report 2006–2007*, p. iii.

83. *MoD Annual Report 2006–2007*, pp. 5–6.

84. Ibid., p. 6.

85. *MEA Annual Report 2008–2009*, p. i.

86. Ibid., p. iv.

87. *MoD Annual Report 2008–2009*, p. 5 (pt 1.14).

88. Ibid., pp. 5–6 (pt 1.15).

89. Ibid., p. 6 (pt 1.15).

90. For more information, see http://www.southasianuniversity.org, accessed on 7 September 2010.

91. Statement by Prime Minister Dr Manmohan Singh at the 13th SAARC Summit, Dhaka, 12 November 2005, accessed from http://www.saarc-sec.org/main.php?id=164&t=7.1, on 26 March 2010.

92. While this aspect cannot be further explored in this chapter, it has been examined in Varun Sahni, 'Change and Stasis in India's Regional Policy: Bypassing and Surpassing South Asia', in N. Jayaram and R.S. Deshpande (eds), *Footprints of Development and Change: Essays in Memory of Professor V.K.R.V. Rao Commemorating His Birth Centenary* (New Delhi: Academic Foundation, 2008), pp. 225–55.

93. Robert S. Jaster, *South Africa and Its Neighbours: The Dynamics of Regional Conflict, Adelphi Paper 209* (International Institute for Strategic Studies, London, Summer 1986), p. 6.

94. Jaster, *South Africa and Its Neighbours*, p. 6.

95. Philip H. Frankel, *Pretoria's Pretorians: Civil–Military Relations in South Africa* (Cambridge: Cambridge University Press, 1984), p. 104.

96. The South West African People's Organisation (SWAPO) and the African National Congress (ANC).

97. Jaster, *South Africa and Its Neighbours*, p. 14.

98. Ibid., p. 16.

99. Ibid., p. 17.

100. Republic of South Africa, *White Paper on Defence, 1977* (Pretoria: DoD, WPF-1977), 9, cited in Frankel, *Pretoria's Pretorians*, p. 58.

101. Jaster, *South Africa and Its Neighbours*, p. 21.

102. Ibid., p. 45.

103. Ibid., p. 46.

104. Ibid.

105. Ibid., p. 67.

106. Ibid., p. 12.

107. Ibid., p. 65.

108. Republic of South Africa, DoD, *Defence in a Democracy: White Paper on National Defence for the Republic of South Africa* (May 1996, ch. 1, pt 1), hereafter *DoD White Paper 1996*.

109. Ibid., ch. 1, pt 5.

110. Ibid., ch. 1, pt 4.

111. Republic of South Africa, DoD, *South African Defence Review 1998* (ch. 4, pt 3), hereafter *SADR 1998*.

112. Ibid., ch. 1, pt 41.

113. *DoD White Paper 1996*, ch. 4, pt 3.

114. *SADR 1998*, ch. 2, pt 20.1. The South African National Defence Force (SANDF) was established in 1994 through the integration of former statutory and non-statutory forces. The former category includes the South African Defence Force (SADF) and the forces of the four 'homelands' (Transkei, Ciskei, Venda, and Bophutatswana); the latter, guerrilla forces such as the ANC's Umkhonto we Sizwe (Spear of the Nation).

115. *DoD White Paper 1996*, ch. 4, pt 28.

116. Ibid., ch. 4, pt 28.

117. Ibid., ch. 4, pt 29; *SADR 1998*, ch. 4, pt 15.
118. Nelson Mandela, 'South Africa's Future Foreign Policy', *Foreign Affairs*, 72 (5) 1993, p. 91.
119. *SADR 1998*, ch. 4, pt 11.3.
120. *DoD White Paper 1996*, ch. 4, pt 6.4.
121. *SADR 1998*, ch. 1, pt 4.
122. *DoD White Paper 1996*, ch. 4, pt. 6.4. The structures of SADC include the Summit, the Organ on Politics, Defence, and Security, and the Inter-State Defence and Security Committee.
123. *DoD White Paper 1996*, ch. 4, pt 12.
124. Ibid., ch. 4, pt 2.
125. *SADR 1998*, ch. 5, pt 5.3.
126. Ibid., ch. 5, pt 15.
127. Ibid., ch. 4, pt 13.
128. Ibid., ch. 4, pt 14.
129. Ibid., ch. 5, pt 33.
130. Len Le Roux, 'Revisiting the South African Defence Review', *African Security Review*, 13 (1), 2004, p. 107.
131. Ibid., p. 106.
132. Ibid., p. 105.
133. Ibid., p. 106.
134. Sisa Ngombane, 'Mediating Conflict in Africa: Challenges, Priorities, Lessons', in Kurt Shillinger (ed.), *Africa's Peacemaker? Lessons from South Africa's Conflict Mediation* (Auckland Park: SAIIA/Fanele, 2009), p. 6.
135. Kurt Shillinger, 'Learning from South African Engagement in African Crises', in Kurt Shillinger (ed.), *Africa's Peacemaker? Lessons from South Africa's Conflict Mediation* (Auckland Park: SAIIA/Fanele, 2009), p. 17.
136. Adekeye Adebajo, 'The Pied Piper of Pretoria', *Global Dialogue*, 10 (1), February 2005, p. 2, accessed from http://www.ccr.org.za/images/pdfs/piedpiper_adebajo_2005.pdf, on 28 March 2010.
137. Ngombane, 'Mediating Conflict in Africa', p. 9.
138. Ibid., p. 12.
139. Adebajo, 'The Pied Piper of Pretoria', p. 3.
140. Iden Wetherell, 'Mugabe Forms New Defence Pact', *The Mail & Guardian*, Johannesburg, 16 April 1999, accessed from http://www.africanews.org, 28 March 2010.
141. Adebajo, 'The Pied Piper of Pretoria', p. 3.
142. Chris Landsberg, 'New Powers for Global Change? South Africa's Global Strategy and Status', *FES Briefing Paper* 16 (Johannesburg: Friedrich Ebert Stiftung, November 2006), p. 6, accessed from http://library.fes.de/pdf-files/iez/global/04135.pdf, on 20 March 2010.
143. Shillenger, 'Learning from South African Engagement in African Crises', p. 20.

144. Daniela Kroslak, 'South Africa's Implementation of Its Own Peacemaking Model in Africa: A Reality Check', in Kurt Shillinger (ed.), *Africa's Peacemaker? Lessons from South Africa's Conflict Mediation*, (Auckland Park: SAIIA/Fanele, 2009), p. 41.

145. Kwesi Aning, 'Healer or Hegemon? Assessing Perceptions of South Africa's Role and Motivation in African Mediation', in Kurt Shillinger (ed.), *Africa's Peacemaker? Lessons from South Africa's Conflict Mediation*, (Auckland Park: SAIIA/Fanele, 2009), p. 55.

146. Aning, 'Healer or Hegemon?', pp. 55–6.

147. Chris Landsberg, 'Promoting Democracy: The Mandela–Mbeki Doctrine', *Journal of Democracy*, 11 (3), 2000, p. 115.

148. Adebajo, 'The Pied Piper of Pretoria', p. 4.

149. Ibid.

150. Shillenger, 'Learning from South African Engagement in African Crises', p. 23.

151. Republic of South Africa, Department of International Relations and Cooperation, *Strategic Plan 2010–2013*, accessed from http://www.dfa.gov.za/department/strategic%20plan%202010-2013/strategic%20plan%202010-2013.pdf, on 28 March 2010.

152. Adebajo, 'The Pied Piper of Pretoria', p. 3.

153. Adekeye Adebajo and Christopher Landsberg, 'South Africa and Nigeria as Regional Hegemons', in Mwesiga Laurent Baregu and Christopher Landsberg (eds), *From Cape to Congo: Southern Africa's Evolving Security Challenges* (Boulder: Lynne Rienner, 2003), p. 197.

3 SAARC

The Search for a Regional Security Model

Aparajita Biswas

The late twentieth century was marked by profound changes in international politics and the concept of security. This period witnessed the end of the Cold War and of other major conflicts in several regions. It also encompassed the transition from the Cold War security order to the beginning of a post–Cold War regional security dynamic. Paradoxically, although there has been greater strategic uncertainty during the period, the pursuit of new concepts and approaches towards security has raised hopes for the achievement of peace and stability. In the conceptual space that has replaced Cold War imperatives, new security ideas and institutions have begun to emerge. Modifiers such as 'comprehensive', 'common', and 'cooperative' have been added to the trope of 'security' and have entered the parlance of regional security planners.

This chapter explores the ideas that fall under the expanding rubric of 'South Asian regional security' in the light of contemporary developments in social and international relations theory, primarily neoliberalism. It questions the validity of the claims of neo-realists and argues that the international and regional institutions created by the major powers to bolster international stability can alleviate the problem of anarchy at the regional level. According to Robert Keohane, one of the founders of neoliberal institutionalist theory, conflict is inherent in the international system. Institutions are the key to mitigating the anarchical character of international relations and minimizing the incidence of violent conflict and enhancing welfare.[1] The chapter argues that the Nordic 'cobweb' model of low-political cooperation is what the South Asian Association for Regional

Cooperation (SAARC) has been about, and that this path can build the trust necessary for security cooperation, unlike neo-functionalist and Deutschian 'security community' concepts for supranational or regional integration.

Robert Keohane in his study *After Hegemony* (1984) advanced a theory of why and how international cooperation and governance flourish in the absence of a hegemonic power imposing order on the system.[2] The central line of reasoning of liberal institutionalists is that international cooperation is neither a product of hegemony nor an altruistic response on the part of states; rather, it is a rational response to conflict between states among whom there is considerable interdependence. Liberal institutionalists emphasize that cooperation helps in strengthening the flow of information between actors. It enhances political transparency, builds trust, and increases the predictability of state behaviour. By creating norms and rules designed to guide state action, cooperation has a legitimizing effect on international relations. Keohane believes that international institutions, whether formal organizations such as the World Trade Organization (WTO) or informal agreements dealing with issues such as counter-terrorism or proliferation of missiles, 'empower governments rather than shackle them'. As he puts it, 'Institutionalists do not elevate international regimes to mythical positions of authority over states; on the contrary, such regimes are established by states to achieve their purposes. Facing dilemmas with regard to coordination and collaboration under conditions of interdependence, governments demand international institutions to enable them to achieve their interests through limited collective action.'[3] It follows then that institution-building is an important prerequisite for peaceful settlement of disputes.[4]

Keohane and Nye, in their seminal study *Power and Interdependence* (1977), which challenged realism's state-centrism, characterized the international system as one of 'complex interdependence' in which there are innumerable interactions at inter-governmental, inter-state, and transnational levels.[5] They asked why and under what circumstances do states engage in international cooperation and institution-building. According to them, globalization is a process that strengthens various aspects of internationalization, leading to even greater complex interdependence. Consequently, in the later version of their masterpiece, they argue that globalization is a step forward in globalism. This globalism can be construed as interdependence among nations spread far and wide across the globe.[6] It implies that in the globalized era, the world market is so powerful that it penetrates and dictates to national economies, which are increasingly compelled to lose some of their 'nationness'. For neoliberals, globalism represents the logic of a post-Westphalian world in which the traditional boundaries of nation-states are becoming less important.

Neoliberals stress the importance of 'good governance'. The extensive implications of globalization and the restructuring of the nation-state make it imperative to go beyond state-centrism in the global system and, instead, think in terms of a more complex, multi-level political structure in which the state is reorganized and performs different functions.[7] If globalization is defined in terms of a technological revolution, increasingly mobile foreign investment, and a loosening of governmental control over its firms or markets, then it follows that states will seek mutual survival strategies. In addition, this need for survival is accentuated by new hazards associated with globalization and contemporary security issues that are environmental, demographic, ethnic, and cultural in nature.

Regional organizations today tend to be regarded as a natural outgrowth of international cooperation. Barry Buzan has noted that the removal of the earlier configuration of superimposed great power influence has encouraged multi-polarity and contributed towards an international system in which 'regional arrangements can be expected to assume greater importance'.[8] Further, regionalism has been encouraged by democratization and new attitudes towards international cooperation in which absolute rather than relative gains have begun to dominate.[9]

A coherent theory for the new emerging regions can be found in the studies of Bjorn Hettne. The vigorous movement towards multi-polarity, the creation of new political structures both above and below the nation-state, and the avoidance of clearly directed and thematically focused forms of cooperation, leading instead to a multifaceted agenda, form the core of Hettne's definition of new regionalism. Above all, a defining characteristic is that it occurs in a multi-polar global context (contrasted to the bipolarity of the Cold War world), making it extroverted and open, which is one way of coping with the global economy.[10]

The establishment of the North American Free Trade Area (NAFTA), the deepening integration in the European Union (EU), and the growing economic interdependence in East Asia are a few examples of emergent regional organizations.[11] An important characteristic of the new regionalism is the wide variation in the levels of institutionalization, with many regional groupings lacking the institutional and bureaucratic structures of the regionalist model represented by the EU.[12]

This explains the emerging framework of cooperation between the states of South Asia in the post–Cold War period, notwithstanding different types of regimes and various unresolved issues in the region. A key objective of this chapter is to focus on the fundamental restructuring of the patterns of interaction between the countries of the South Asian region against the backdrop of an increasingly complex interplay between geo-economics and geopolitics. It will also focus on the potential of common projects that recognize the reality of profound interdependence among the South Asian nations, both in the economic and security spheres, while taking into consideration the fact that the states concerned would act in accordance with their self-interest.

In the late twentieth century South Asia was characterized by an incongruous blend of increasing political instability, on the one hand, and a cautious yet resolute fostering of regional consciousness on the other hand. For example, the testing of nuclear weapons by India and Pakistan in 1998, the return of military rule in Pakistan in 1999, limited war between India and Pakistan in 1999, the rise of Hindu nationalism in India, civil war in Sri Lanka, and political chaos in Nepal appeared to have stifled any future progress towards internal or inter-state security in the subcontinent. Coupled with this, the events following the 11 September 2001 terrorist attacks in USA led to the rise of political extremism and religious fundamentalism in the domestic politics of Pakistan and Bangladesh. This resulted in a spectacular deterioration of relations between the countries of the region. Even so, these negative developments carried within them the seeds of a radical transformation in the South Asian region. Regional initiatives by nations to familiarize themselves with other nations and pull together received a strong impetus, both due to developments within and outside the region.

From a neoliberal perspective, this chapter analyses the policies of South Asian states towards regional security institutions and cooperation. What drives the South Asian states' behaviour towards regional cooperation on security in the post–Cold War situation? Will relations be guided by the decades-old perceptions formed on mutual distrust and hostility, or will economic interests push South Asian countries towards greater cooperation?

The Emergence of SAARC and the Security Scenario in South Asia

Since the 1960s, the study of regionalism has occupied an important space in the discipline of international relations. The 1960s were a period that witnessed unprecedented European cooperation in the midst of intense Cold War tensions. In fact, going back a little further in time, the concept of regional integration had attracted the attention of scholars like Karl Deutsch, Ernst Haas, and Leon Lindberg at a time when the European unity movement flourished in the 1950s: first as the European Coal and Steel Community (ECSC) and thereafter as the European Economic Community (EEC) or the Common Market. The progress towards European unity could not be explained simply as a new form of alliance that reflects the traditional notion of balance of power. This unity among European nations was an attempt to take advantage of opportunities for mutual growth as much as creating a front against perceived threats.[13]

Scholars drew inspiration from regional integration analysis, especially the work of David Mitrany in which he challenged the power-centric realist approach and emphasized the separability of the developmental and welfare-oriented dimensions of integration from its power–political dimensions.[14] Consequently, Karl Deutsch and Ernst Haas did pioneering work on integration theory to understand the politics of western European economic integration in the 1950s.

Let us explore the concepts of neo-functionalism and 'security community', initiated by Haas and Deutsch.[15] During the Cold War, when international relations theory was almost totally dominated by the realist paradigm, Deutsch defined integration in terms of turning 'previously separate units into components of a coherent system'.[16] He emphasized the setting up of a 'security community'.[17] His concept of and framework for a security community were based on three pillars: integration, sense of community, and peaceful change. Haas highlighted the interests of different groups consisting of elites, bureaucratic officials, and political leaders, and the extent to which they altered their behaviour through learning.[18] Deutsch and his co-workers, in *Political Community and the North Atlantic Area* (1957), on the other hand, questioned the circumstances under which the security community came into being. Both Haas and Deutsch downplayed the nation-state as the basic unit of analysis and did not rely on the traditional concept of national interest.

Neo-Functionalism

Neo-functionalism has played a critical role in the development of theories of European integration. In *The Uniting of Europe* (1958), Haas explained the strategy of political leaders in the European integration movement, linked it with the interests of parties and groups, and put it in a theoretical perspective that strongly influenced scholars of international relations to pursue further studies of regional integration. He applied the concept of 'spillover' to the ECSC which, by creating a common market in the coal and steel production sectors, necessitated the integration of the energy resources of the Community, such as nuclear energy, covered by the Euratom Treaty in 1957, and oil and gas covered by the EEC Treaty. This eventually led to the establishment of a common market for all goods and services.

Set between the rationalist and revolutionist traditions of international relations, neo-functionalism—also known as 'federal functionalism'—mingles some elements from both functionalist and federal theories. Integration is considered a process for the creation of a 'political community' which resembles the 'supranational state' proposed by federalists.[19] However, neo-functionalism differs from federalism in its method of reaching the ultimate goal. The method of integration pursued by neo-functionalism is taken from functionalism. Contrary to federalism and similar to functionalism, neo-functionalism proposes a step-by-step method, beginning with economic sectors and spreading through the political sphere for the creation of a supranational political community.

However, 'the study of regional integration is concerned with explaining how and why states cease to be wholly sovereign, how and why they voluntarily mingle, merge, and mix with their neighbours so as to lose the factual attributes of sovereignty while acquiring new techniques for resolving conflict between themselves'.[20] The suggestion here is that states balance the partial loss of sovereignty following rationalization with some advantage derived from collective action. In relation to the latter, Haas argues that the augmentation of regional integration depends on when these collective actions are 'made incrementally, based often on consequences not initially intended by the actors (governments and important interest groups)'.[21] According to neo-functionalists, leaders of political groups support policies enhancing integration not on the basis of general principles or ideologies, but advantages perceived in specific situations. The leaders of a particular region would tend to opt for integration when there is a perception of the benefits of enhanced regional cooperation being equitable.

Exponents of the neo-functionalist school, led by Ernst Haas, Joseph Nye, and others, emphasized that integration was a process leading to the formation of a new political unit, superseding the nation-states participating in it. Neo-functionalism explained the process of integration as a set of functional (that is, economic) spillovers, leading to economic and political integration, with actors transferring their expectations and loyalties to a supranational central authority. In essence, neo-functionalism is an integration theory proposing a model to achieve the establishment of a political community at the end of the integration process. As the process advances, the nation-state is no longer the basic unit of analysis, and transnational interaction beyond the management and control of national governments becomes increasingly frequent.[22]

In this model, neo-functionalism postulates a linkage between economic and political integration. It claims that after the realization of economic integration within the framework of a supranational organization, political integration will follow almost automatically. Unlike functionalism's universalist tenets, neo-functionalism placed immense stress on the establishment of regional integration.[23] However, both theories have highlighted the concept of spillover, described by Leon Lindberg as 'a situation in which a given action, related to a specific goal, creates a situation in which the original goal can be assured only by taking further actions, which in turn creates a further condition and a need for more action, and so forth'.[24]

Again, in the process of integration, neo-functionalists accept the dichotomy between 'high' and 'low' politics. Haas sees the political sphere divided into two distinct levels, those of high and low politics. He was sharply cognizant of the difficulty of achieving regional integration in the sphere of high politics, which includes diplomacy, strategy, defence, and national ideologies. In the neo-functionalist conceptualization, nation-states are reluctant to lose their sovereign authority in the sphere of high politics. Therefore, Haas proposed that the integration process begin from the low politics of the economic and technical spheres.[25] Integration in the sphere of high politics would be a natural consequence of the spread of the integration process. During the functional spillover process, the supranational organization created on the principle of the delegation of sovereign authority gains new areas for exercising its supranational control. In fact, supranational institutions were seen as the most effective means of resolving common problems, 'beginning with technical and non-controversial issues but "spilling over" into the realm of high politics and leading to a redefinition of group identity around the regional unit'.[26]

Another major concern of neo-functionalists revolved around the process of socialization which results from 'the combined effects of the organizational context of decision-making, the pressures of the crisis situation, the force of habits and procedure, interaction with other political actors, the awareness of a commitment or need to agree, and similar features of the political setting, to force actors to a redefinition of their situation, interests and methods'.[27] As Lindberg elucidated, members who actively participate in the central institutions may develop various viewpoints, some form of personal bonding, and 'camaraderie of expertise, all of which may reflect back upon the national governments and affect future national policy-making'.[28] Interestingly, neo-functionalism recognizes the same conditions of complex interdependence described by neoliberalism, but attributes inter-state cooperation to political rather than economic reasons. Second, neo-functionalism argues that inter-state cooperation assumes a self-perpetuating character as the issue areas in which states cooperate begin to 'spill over' to other issue areas. Basically, neo-functionalism revolves around the idea of 'spillover' whereby issue-based regional cooperation in areas of 'lesser salience' could eventually push national actors towards a path of cooperation in areas of 'higher salience', including political and security cooperation. Accordingly, if functional regional groups could successfully foster economic integration, the need for regional security would ensure that the actors would learn over time to resolve conflicts peacefully and cooperate on common security issues.[29] The essence of neo-functionalism, therefore, is a step-by-step process of economic decisions, a process which is more effective than big decisions at the level of high politics.

SECURITY COMMUNITY

Two classics on the study of security communities are the works of Deutsch (1957) and Adler and Barnett (1998). Deutsch's work set the tone for the study of security communities, while Adler and Barnett contributed by refreshing the framework, about 40 years after the original, having conducted extensive research within the framework of the former.[30] In the 1950s, Deutsch and his colleagues conducted an extensive enquiry into the means by which war had been eliminated in certain geographic areas and historical periods through the formation of security communities. 'A security community is a group of people which has become "integrated", where integration reflects the "attainment within a territory of a sense of community", by turning previously separate units into components of a coherent system and by fostering transactions between societies and changes in public attitudes within societies.'[31] The security community paradigm is viewed as a socially based phenomenon premised on the notion that 'common social problems must and can be resolved by peaceful change'.[32] Here, 'peaceful change' means the resolution of social problems through institutions, without resorting to use of large-scale physical force. Barry Buzan introduced the concept of 'regional security complex' to study regional security or what he calls 'regional pattern of amity and enmity'.[33] A regional security complex is 'a group of states whose primary security concerns link together sufficiently closely so that their national securities cannot be considered apart from one another'.[34] This is the kind of 'we-feeling' identified by Deutsch as a key feature of management of regional conflict.[35] Thus, peaceful change is the most significant aspect of this concept. For instance, Richard Merritt and Bruce Russett equate expectations of peaceful change to security communities.[36] Thus, peaceful change is conditional, not merely acquiescent, and there has to be a spirit of accommodation of other people's requirements, not just the continuation of the past. The extent to which the regional institutions and sub-regions have continued to adjust and adapt to changes in their environment is a crucial factor.

At its most basic, a security community has been defined as a group of states that have renounced the use of force as a means of resolving intra-regional conflict. Ben Resmond defines security community as 'a group of states amongst whom the prospects of war is eradicated, a situation achieved via processes described as transnational'.[37] However, much is dependent on the ability of the group to manage conflicts peacefully rather than the absence of conflict per se. This distinguishes a security community from other types of security relationships. Conflicts are often prevented through regional integration processes which thus serve as the foundation of a security community.

For Deutsch, the principal goal of integration is not only the preservation of peace but also the achievement of some specific task or the acquisition of some common identity. With regard to the inter-state security system, Deutsch emphasizes two different kinds of communities: the amalgamated political community, where supranational institutions play a major role; and a pluralistic community, where a common centre for decision-making does not exist. He believes that integration can be both something static and a process. In a pluralistic community, the members would remain formally independent. According to Ronald Yalem, 'security communities are characterized by mutual interdependence of diverse political units; mutual responsiveness of political units; and simply pacification or the abandonment of the use of force among political units'.[38] For example, the Nordic system is primarily based on a sense of solidarity and not on a common political and economic goal.

Deutsch foresaw that the objective of integration could only be realized when a high volume of international communication and transactions characterizes the 'political community consisting of an international system of developed nation-states. Closer diplomatic and commercial contacts foster "a sense of shared community and trust" which makes war between members inconceivable'.[39] 'Thus, the concept of security community, as defined by Deutsch and later by Adler and Barnett, arises when different states, which are structurally independent, do not target each other militarily'.[40] According to Nye, states are regarded as stable units and are also expected to have compatible values and predictable interests, with elites holding similar policy aims. The democratic institutional framework is also an essential factor in a regional security structure.[41]

Similar views have been voiced by Asberg and Wallesteen. They characterize the security community as an agreement by states to share some values, for example, democracy. Asberg and Wallesteen believes that mutual responsiveness refers to 'an ability to predict the behaviour of other states and requires extensive contacts and communications as well as psychological and political adjustment'.[42] Survival of the state and sovereignty form the core values of the security community as the state is the ultimate provider of security. Baylis and Renggers have listed the key characteristics of security community as follows: mutual compatibility of values; multifaceted social, political, and cultural transactions; a growing number of institutionalized relationships; mutual responsiveness; and mutual predictability of behaviour.[43] One can argue on the basis of the aforementioned hypothesis that where there is a security community, there is integration. Haas concluded that the communication theory encompasses the following hypothesis: 'if élite responsiveness increases, then a security community will arise.'[44] This definition is similar to Andren's cobweb integration which occurs 'when the mutual dependence of its components is increased. Interdependence is a function of élite responsiveness, which in turn produces a security community'.[45]

Thus, a security community at the conceptual level poses a serious challenge to the core assumptions of realist theory. Realism holds that there is always a fear of military confrontations in the anarchic structure of the international system, resulting in security competition among the states. Although states do not engage in war all the time, they must not exclude the possibility that they might be attacked, and they must at all times be prepared for war. Contrary to these views, states that embrace a security community regard the use of force against each other as unthinkable and abstain from fighting one another. As Deutsch put it, 'There is a real assurance that the members of that community will not fight each other physically, but will settle their dispute in some other way.'[46] It is this belief of peaceful change, Keohane indicates, that clearly distinguishes Deutsch and his colleagues from the realist tradition of international relations.[47]

However, despite its political and theoretical importance, Deutsch's theory of communication was neglected during the Cold War period. It came into prominence only in the 1990s, when the world was metamorphosing from Cold War rhetoric to post–Cold War uncertainties. It was during this period that the liberal tradition of international relations regained its dynamism. Not only the realists but even the liberals were surprised by this unexpected change. Adler and Barnett claimed that in the post–Cold War paradigm, there was a need to rethink the role of the state because, although states pretend that their 'actions are performed in the interest of the wider community, their actions derive from much more selfish concerns'.[48] Moreover, they construct an analytical framework in which mutual trust and collective identity within a group of states are the necessary conditions for a dependable expectation of peaceful change, the benchmark of a security community. They identify the 'existence of common values as the wellspring for close security cooperation' and believe that this deepens shared values and transnational linkages. It is these transnational linkages—which Adler and Barnett identify as trade, migration, tourism, cultural and educational exchanges, and physical communication flows within and between states—which are in fact accurate indicators of the growth of human communities. They regard communication as the 'cement of social groups in general and political communities in particular, which consequently enables a group to think together and to act together'. These features follow the hypothesis of Deutsch's communicative approach to integration, in which the building of a political unit largely depends upon the flow of communication within the unit as well as between the unit and the outside world.[49]

Yet another dimension of the security community paradigm is the expectation of the state that the community would protect its natural security and hence make it possible for it to undertake developmental activities. In this way, the security community paradigm advocates the expansion of security from its military dimensions to other areas, including economic, environmental, and social welfare concerns. It is in this context that an elaboration of the regional organization of the Nordic countries is relevant, avoiding as it does the sphere of high politics and concentrating on regional cooperation in non-controversial areas.

THE NORDIC MODEL OF INTEGRATION OR COBWEB INTEGRATION

The Nordic effort to promote regional integration without formal institutions dates back to the mid-nineteenth century. The Nordic system involves close cooperation between the Scandinavian states, particularly since the Second World War. The unique characteristics of the Nordic system are manifested in the model of the Nordic welfare state, in its anti-militarism, and in a largely shared rational, enlightened way of thinking. The distinction between high politics and incremental economic goals is particularly significant. It must be noted that at the time of establishment of the Nordic Council in 1952, it was decided that all matters relating to the defence and foreign policies of the participating countries would be excluded from the Nordic Council's agendas and proceedings. It was by the exclusion of these vital matters from the discussions that the members of the Council obtained an inbuilt assurance that the Council would not be able to interfere in the sphere of the high politics of the member states.

Nils Andren has developed the dominant arguments in theoretical discussions of the Nordic pattern of economic cooperation and integration, which is very different from the integration model of the EU. Andren emphasizes that Nordic economic cooperation and integration developed from a combination of ideological Nordism and pragmatism. An ideological core in the member states working for Nordic economic cooperation and integration, supported by the Nordic Council, pushed Nordic economic integration forward. Thus, when the interacting countries develop needs that can be met on a mutual basis, they will move to a point where either their immediate goals are fulfilled or obstacles thwart further progress. This process is repeated as they progress in cooperation in other areas involving other institutions.[50]

Andren labelled this pattern as 'cobweb' integration. It 'projects the visual pattern of a web, with a thread linking the Nordic countries together in a variety of directions and forms. Furthermore, all these happen in a pre-planned pattern. However, over a long period of time, the cobweb will present a network of ties, commitments and channels that always grows thicker and always invites further cooperation'. Thus, 'integration is a process which transforms a system in such a manner that the mutual interdependence of its components is increased'.[51]

Another important characteristic that distinguishes Nordic cooperation from the European integration model is its opposition to strong integration, and a critical stance towards any form of supranationality. Unlike the European experiment, the Nordic model did not have larger political ambitions that could continually push economic integration forward. It sought to establish economic cooperation through informal meetings and consultations among the member states. Therefore, intergovernmental cooperation and non-governmental organizations (NGOs) have been the essence of the Nordic cooperation network.

In the course of studying South Asian regional integration, it appears that SAARC has adopted the Nordic model of regional cooperation, that is, an avoidance of the 'constitutional' approach, understanding that the national political system would remain unaltered as the political basis of cooperation, which would be directed towards the areas of relatively 'low' political content, and the exclusion of areas of 'high' political content, such as national security, from regional cooperation. The rule of unanimity has been accepted by the member countries at all levels of decision-making, and domestic, bilateral, and contentious issues have been excluded from the deliberations of SAARC. The policy of incrementalism on the lines of the Nordic model was necessary given the predominance of political determinants of inter-state relations in South Asia. The countries in this region were required to take a political decision to establish a dialogue before initiating any discussion on technical, social, cultural, or other matters. The predominance of the political in inter-state matters permitted only a slow start to cooperation.[52]

ANALYSING SOUTH ASIAN REGIONAL COOPERATION

This section analyses the origins, dynamics, and consequences of regional security cooperation in South Asia from a multi-level perspective. In doing so, it draws on the neo-functionalist approach, which has proved to be a useful, albeit open-ended, analytical tool for understanding the dynamics of linkages between regional economic integration and peace and security in the South Asian region. It revolves around the liberal view that there should be greater cooperation and integration at the regional level in South Asia in order to avoid or end bilateral, regional, and even domestic conflicts.

Earlier, South Asia was referred to as a region without any semblance of regionalism, but aware of the increasing trend towards regional association. In fact, the area has been categorized by Bjorn Hettne as one with a very low level of 'regionness'[53] because of the antagonism between the two major powers, India and Pakistan. India, Pakistan, and Bangladesh were once part of a single political entity—British India. The disruption of the economic and political unity of India in 1947, followed by India–Pakistan hostility over Kashmir and other issues, forced the two major powers in the region to build divergent economic links with each other. The severance of political links between India and Pakistan in the late 1940s and early 1950s was the consequence of decisions based on political and security calculations and not economic considerations. Therefore, intra-regional trade collapsed. In 1948–9, the first full year after Partition, 32 per cent of Pakistani imports came from India while India bought 56 per cent of Pakistan's exports. Fifty-five years later, the situation was dramatically different.[54] In 2004–5, India imported only 0.42 per cent of Pakistan's exports and provided only 0.13 per cent of the latter's imports.[55]

Likewise, Bangladesh, except in the years immediately following its liberation, was not interested in enhancing economic cooperation with India. Even railway and road networks that once united British India were subject to severe economic and political barriers after Partition. The North Western Railway that linked Karachi with Delhi and the fabled Grand Trunk Road that connected Peshawar with Calcutta (now Kolkata) through Delhi were disconnected. Natural ports were cut off from their hinterlands such as Chittagong from India's north-east and Kolkata from the western part of East Pakistan (now Bangladesh). Twin commercial cities like Mumbai and Karachi have become distant neighbours. Indeed, border trade has never been encouraged by the

South Asian states after Partition. The primacy of the political factor thus demonstrated in the early years of independence has continued to hamper all succeeding endeavours aimed at promoting economic cooperation within South Asia.[56]

Moreover, since 1947 there was continuing tension and conflict between the two largest countries in the region, which led to three major wars, two of which were centred on Kashmir in 1947–8 and 1965, and one around the issue of Bangladesh's independence in 1971. There were also near-war situations in 1984, 1987, and 1990, reflected in numerous clashes between India and Pakistan. Additionally, in the summer of 1999, India and Pakistan fought a 73-day military conflict in the upper reaches of Kashmir at Kargil, located 120 miles from Srinagar (the capital city of Jammu and Kashmir). The conflict was a clear manifestation of a 50-year-old subcontinental rivalry that contains risks of a nuclear conflagration affecting global peace and security. Against this background of minimal regional cooperation, in 1985, the then Bangladesh President Ziaur Rahman mooted the idea of setting up an ASEAN-like (Association of Southeast Asian Nations) organization in South Asia. This initiative was seen as a landmark effort in moving the South Asian countries towards a more cooperative relationship and in giving the South Asian region a more visible and influential presence in world affairs. The birth of SAARC in 1985 marked a new beginning for the seven South Asian countries—India, Pakistan, Sri Lanka, Bangladesh, Nepal, Bhutan, and Maldives. For the first time, these countries made an institutional effort to forge cooperation between themselves. A careful study of its objectives and principles reveals that the South Asian regional organization, SAARC, was envisaged as being complementary to and not a substitute for bilateral and multilateral cooperation. The basis of this cooperation was to be guided by accepted international principles of inter-state relations, namely, sovereign equality, territorial integrity, political independence, non-interference in the internal affairs of the other states, and mutual benefit. The primary emphasis was on the welfare of the people of the region: to improve their quality of life through the acceleration of economic growth, social progress, and cultural development; providing all individuals the opportunity to live in dignity; and promoting collective self-reliance among the countries of South Asia. The objectives were also defined to go beyond the sphere of socio-economic development and encompass spheres of mutual trust, understanding of each other's problems, and cooperation in international forums on matters of common interest.[57]

Yet if one assesses the role of SAARC in the last 25 years, its success has been quite limited when compared to ASEAN, primarily because bilateral conflicts between individual South Asian states (mostly between one of the smaller countries and India) prevented either the initiation or the implementation of multilateral arrangements which could benefit all members. SAARC evolved at a time when relations between India and most of the other member countries had been characterized by mistrust and suspicion. The single-most important issue for all of India's neighbours was how to relate to India, the focal point of their threat perceptions. These perceptions dominated inter-state relations in the region, especially India's apprehension about the intentions of other nations in the region towards it, and the other nations' fear of India's hegemony. Further, it was a fear of the Indian state that compelled the other nations in South Asia to search for their own separate identities, and in the process, ignoring affinities that existed with India.

Again, the India–Pakistan political and military conflicts are the most important matters in this context, with Pakistan being reluctant to deal with India on the economic matters to which SAARC has so far confined itself.[58] Moreover, the sheer territorial size and the centrality of location of India in South Asia have given the region a certain distinctiveness of character, and have mostly determined inter-state affairs in the region. India's size, population, resources, and power potential make for its implicit predominance in the prevailing asymmetric power structure in South Asia. The Indo-centric nature of the region has been a major source of dissonance.[59] That most of the less powerful South Asian countries are geographically in close proximity to India but not to each other means that they are more likely to have disputes with India than with one another. For example, Bangladesh does not have cooperative ties with India; and India's relationship with Nepal, which shares a porous land border of over 1,800 km together with some of the religious and cultural values based on Hinduism, remains trouble-prone. Sri Lanka has its own bag of problems, including the Tamil separatist issue, keeping it suspicious of India's motives. Bhutan's worries are several, but a 1949 friendship pact prevents it from publicly airing its grievances against New Delhi. The Maldives' position is not strikingly different from Bhutan's, apart from the fact that Bhutan is a landlocked country and the other is an island nation.

Also, over the years, tension has been mounting between India and Bangladesh over the sharing of waters of their 54 common rivers. India, lying upstream, controls the main waters flowing into Bangladesh and Pakistan. Any withdrawal of water (for irrigation and, in the case of the Hooghly River, for shipping) affects Bangladesh's agriculture, fisheries, shipping, and ecology. Again, for a country like Pakistan, which relies heavily on irrigation and has built the largest irrigation system in the world, water surely could become a casus belli. However, as a rare example of political farsightedness, India and Pakistan signed the Indus Waters Treaty in 1960, providing for the allocation of the waters of the three western rivers (Indus, Jhelum, Chenab) to Pakistan, and those of the three eastern rivers (Ravi, Sutlej, Beas) to India.[60]

India's latest initiative to interlink some of the major river systems running through its territory has set off a regional controversy, raising the level of concerns in both Nepal and Bangladesh. Once implemented, this mega-project could deprive both its neighbours of a crucial natural resource: water. Nepal would be prevented from making consumptive use of river water as it would affect the flow downstream into India, and Bangladesh would find itself dry if India goes ahead with its plan to dig deep canals on the upper reaches to divert the rivers that have traditionally been the principal source of water for Bangladesh.

Nepal too is completely dependent on India for its economic development, covering foreign assistance and crucial imports, including oil, petroleum, cement, and coal. Over 700,000 Nepalese are employed in India in addition to some 20,000 Gurkha personnel in the Indian army. In 1989, when India cancelled the supply of essential commodities to Nepal as a consequence of serious disagreement between the two countries over trade and transit issues, the limited nature of Nepal's economic autonomy was exposed.[61]

The dismemberment of Pakistan in 1971 and India's role in it, India's nuclear test in 1974, its annexation of Sikkim in 1975, and its intervention in Sri Lanka in 1987–90 and in Maldives in 1988, have only added to the insecurity and fear of Indian hegemony among its neighbours. It was because of perceptions of India as a threat and causes of conflicts such as demarcation of borders and sharing of water flows from international rivers that differences arose in the foreign policy orientations of the countries of the region. Their foreign policies accorded greater importance to extra-regional linkages, which were responsible for introducing superpower rivalry in South Asia during the Cold War, thereby contributing to intra-regional hostilities.[62]

A study of the trends in regional cooperation in SAARC points towards two contradictory phases in its evolution. The first is the formative phase from its inception in 1985 until the end of 1990s when one notices initial uncertainties and scepticism among the countries about arriving at some form of regional cooperation agreement. It also coincided with serious internal conflicts in the region, such as the LTTE problem in Sri Lanka and the Sikh separatist movement in India. This was also a phase in which an effort was made to formulate the basic framework of regional cooperation and the first tentative efforts were made to widen the scope of cooperation.

The initial euphoria about formulating a framework of cooperation appears to have lasted through the first two or three summits. For example, at the Dhaka Summit of 1985, a three-year agreement on sharing the Ganges waters was reached between the then prime minister of India, Rajiv Gandhi, and the then president of Bangladesh, General H.M. Ershad. At the Bangalore Summit of 1986, the prime ministers of India and Pakistan met to discuss and clarify some misconceptions surrounding nuclear issues and border tensions. The growth of confidence was visible during the Kathmandu Summit of 1987, at which the delicate issue of the Siachen Glacier in Kashmir and the crucial issue of cross-border drug-trafficking and terrorism were taken up by the prime ministers of India and Pakistan.

However, in 1989, at the time of the proposed Colombo Summit, trouble began to brew when Sri Lanka stated that it was not in a position to hold the Summit until the withdrawal of the Indian Peace Keeping Force (IPKF) from the island. The differences of opinion between India and Sri Lanka over the presence of IPKF resulted in the postponement of the summit. India's relations with all its neighbours had reached a dead end during this period. India's tough stance of imposing a trade embargo against Nepal and its intervention in Sri Lanka had an adverse impact in the region. Coupled with this, increasing Chinese influence over the subcontinent in the past two decades—in the form of deepening strategic relations with Pakistan, and expanding links with Nepal, Bangladesh, and Sri Lanka—happened at a time of increasing complexity of India's own relations with its immediate neighbours.

The second phase of the evolution of SAARC began with the end of the Cold War and resultant changes in the global order. This phase witnessed an attempt by the SAARC member states to redefine its role. The post–Cold War economic imperatives provided the momentum for regional cooperation in South Asia. Pressure from the International

Monetary Fund (IMF) as well as the dynamics of General Agreement on Tariffs and Trade (GATT) and WTO demanded that the region adopt policies aimed at export promotion, remove barriers to imports, and integrate with the global economy. On the one hand, as a part of the trend towards globalization, regionalization has become a very influential phenomenon of integration among countries of specific regions. The policies of economic liberalization and the unleashing of the private sector are nudging the South Asian states to integrate their markets. It has also made it imperative that greater and more sustained efforts be made to promote better bilateral relations among neighbouring countries which could help develop a congenial atmosphere for economic development, including joint ventures, expansion of trade, transfer of technology, and the like, at the regional level. On the other hand, there are internal pressures from the region, forcing the states to act more purposefully.[63]

After a series of low-intensity crises and actual wars, India and Pakistan have finally acknowledged the significance of upholding bilateral agreements that entail both bilateral cooperation and conflict resolution. Moreover, the South Asian countries have finally accepted the fact that the civil wars or low-intensity conflicts in the region need to be approached diplomatically and politically rather than through hostile means.

Through the 1990s, relations between India and its smaller neighbours improved dramatically. This period posed new challenges for India's foreign policy. There was a pressing need to recast India's approach towards its neighbours. Moreover, some important political developments in the neighbourhood induced India to reshape and realign its regional foreign policy. The return of democratic governments in Bangladesh and Nepal by 1991 and the return to power of the Chandrika Kumaratunga-led People's Alliance in Sri Lanka in 1994, the installation of the United Front government in India in 1996, all combined to push the concerned parties on to a more pragmatic path.

In 1996, treaties on river waters were signed between India and Nepal and India and Bangladesh. The government of India had also permitted the transit of Nepalese cargo to Bangladesh by road via the Kakarbitta–Phulbari–Banglabund route in September 1997. India's quest for a new approach towards its neighbours remained central to the foreign policy debate throughout the 1990s, and was more explicitly articulated in the famous Gujral Doctrine. This essentially promoted the accommodation of the interests of the neighbouring states, without expectation of reciprocity.[64]

The change of attitude was reflected at the Sixth SAARC Summit held in Colombo in 1991. A decision was made to establish a multilateral trade arrangement known as the South Asian Preferential Trading Arrangement (SAPTA). SAPTA began as 'a contractual agreement' providing only a set of rules and 'modalities' for gradual trade liberalization among the SAARC members, but the intention was to remove tariffs and other trade barriers in a 'negotiated step-by-step' manner. The idea was to expand trade within South Asia and eventually transform it into South Asian Free Trade Area (SAFTA). Subsequently, the SAPTA agreement was signed during the Seventh SAARC Summit held in Dhaka in April 1993. The signing of this agreement established an umbrella framework of rules providing for step-by-step liberalization of intra-regional trade in such a way that countries in the region would equitably share the benefits of trade expansion. In the agreement, provisions for safeguard action and balance of payments measures were also incorporated to protect the interests of member states during critical economic circumstances. The agreement provides scope for trade liberalization with a combination of four approaches and procedures. These are the product-by-product approach, across-the-board tariff reductions, a sectoral approach, and direct trade measures.[65]

In SAPTA I, which came into force in 1995, after being ratified by all the SAARC member states, trade concessions were offered on 226 commodities by all the member states. Subsequently, in 1997, SAPTA II offered trade concessions to 1,871 products, along with the removal of various non-tariff barriers (NTBs) for the least developed countries (LDCs), that is, Bangladesh, Nepal, Bhutan, and the Maldives. For example, India offered tariff concessions on 500 consumer goods from the LDCs. Consequently, Bangladesh was able to sell goods such as textile and leather items with a decreased duty of almost 50 per cent. The agreement also envisaged the establishment of a free trade area SAFTA by 2001. In SAPTA III, trade concessions were offered not only on commodities but also on several sectors at the two-digit level. By the end of the third round, over 4,600 tariff lines out of a total 6,000 were covered by preferential access. India offered the largest number of concessions, followed by Bangladesh, Pakistan, and Nepal. The LDC member states within SAARC have also been offered a large share of such concessions vis-à-vis the non-LDC members. Although the total concessions offered to all member states remain limited, it has been a beginning, even if a modest one.[66]

At the bilateral level, in 1998, India and Sri Lanka signed a Free Trade Agreement in the process of pursuing a Comprehensive Economic Partnership Agreement, to integrate their economies as closely as possible. This was a landmark treaty aimed at removing customs tariffs on all but few items traded between the two countries. The treaty, which came into effect from 1 March 2000, is expected to facilitate a massive increase in trading links between India and Sri Lanka. It has been observed that with this treaty, there is a considerable increase in Sri Lankan exports to the Indian market. Consequently, Sri Lanka has emerged as the fifth largest supplier of imports to India. However, it is also true that a large proportion of the Sri Lankan preferential exports consists of intermediate products required for the Indian industry, rather than final products for direct consumption.[67]

There was a spillover effect of these developments on the political front. India and Bangladesh signed a historic 30-year treaty on sharing of the Ganga waters in December 1996. The resolution of the Ganga water dispute opened up fresh opportunities for the management of water and environment-related issues. In 1997, the Chakma leaders and the Bangladesh government concluded an agreement for the repatriation of an estimated 50,000 refugees from India belonging to the Chittagong hill tracts in Bangladesh. This influx from Bangladesh to the north-eastern states of India had caused serious ethnic problems. Earlier, in 1996, India had achieved an important breakthrough on the issue of sharing river water resources by signing the Mahakali River Treaty with Nepal.

The river-water sharing projects and development of barrages between India and its neighbours were aimed at linking the states in a network of interdependence to enhance agrarian production. Apart from linkages through water sharing, India supported an initiative to establish a road link between Nepal and Bangladesh. This enabled Nepal to trade through the Chittagong port in Bangladesh. Similarly, India has also been looking for a route via Bangladesh to its north-eastern states. There were, however, a few unresolved issues that existed between Bhutan and Nepal, on the one hand, and Bangladesh, on the other, but these never became major irritants in the region.[68]

A scrutiny of the intra-regional trade data in the SAARC region reveals that, contrary to expectations, there has hardly been any improvement in the share of such trade. In 1995, when SAPTA was being implemented, only 3 per cent of all South Asian trade was conducted within the region.[69] So far, the improvements in regional trade have been marginal. The success of SAPTA, and later SAFTA, in creating a free trade area in South Asia was hampered by several economic and political factors.

On the economic front, the unequal size of markets has obstructed the expansion of trade. Even the share of intra-regional trade is not substantial because, given that India's economy is roughly three times as large as that of the other six taken together, the volume of intra-regional trade is restricted by the much smaller production and absorption capacities of India's regional trading partners. Moreover, the lack of complementarities in South Asia poses other obstacles. The South Asian economies are basically competitive rather than complementary in nature. Most of the export products of the SAARC countries seem to be fairly similar primary and consumer goods.[70]

Another major stumbling block in the progress of SAARC and SAPTA has been the nuclear tests conducted by India and Pakistan in 1998, followed by events in Kargil and the creation of a new war-like situation in mid-1999. *The Kargil Review Committee Report* states that

instead of seeking a stable relationship on the basis of nuclear options capabilities, Pakistan used nuclear deterrence to support aggression. Kargil indicated that armed with nuclear weapons, Pakistan had increased confidence that it could raise the conflict thresholds with India. It demonstrated a willingness to take greater risks in conflict escalation. Instead of seeking nuclear stability, Pakistan demonstrated greater propensity to sustain instability, by seeking military conflict.[71]

It is here that SAARC could have played a role, providing a forum for continuing dialogue between India and Pakistan on various levels: from heads of state down to the technical committees. Moreover, as SAARC provides a multilateral forum, it allows for a continuing dialogue even when bilateral talks break down. So long as the dialogue continues, there is hope that a major war can be avoided. There were other issues that intensified the already tense relations in the region and contributed to blocking the 'political side of SAARC' from functioning. These included the return of military rule in Pakistan in late 1999 and India's aversion to it, the hijacking of an Indian Airlines flight from Kathmandu and the alleged involvement of Pakistan's intelligence agency in it in December 1999. These factors resulted in the deterioration of the security environment, which eventually led to the indefinite postponement of the Eleventh SAARC Summit scheduled to be held in 1999. Subsequently, the return to power of Khaleda Zia in the Bangladesh elections of 2001, in alliance with fundamentalist Islamic groups, and the mayhem in Nepal after the assassination of the royal family in the region in June

2001, further complicated relations between the states. It was only in January 2004 that the Twelfth SAARC Summit was held, this time in Islamabad.

The WTO imperative of trade liberalization compelled the member states to set aside political vendettas and move towards an economic agenda. The member states signed the South Asian Free Trade Agreement in 2004, which was designed to help bring down customs duties, promote cross-border investment, and, more crucially, formalize the trade conducted through third countries and surreptitious channels. The aim was to achieve removal of all trade barriers among SAARC member states by 2016. At the 14th SAARC Summit in 2007 India also submitted a proposal to create a South Asian Economic Union with a common currency on the lines of the EU. However, for Pakistan, Kashmir and terrorism remain complicated and unresolved issues. Pakistan has refused to grant Indian goods the Most Favoured Nation (MFN) status, mandatory under WTO norms, unless India makes concessions on Kashmir. Nonetheless, the signing of the South Asian Free Trade Agreement by the SAARC member states and its commitment to a free trade area, juxtaposed with the developments under WTO, will have significant consequences for intra-regional trade in the coming years, with spillover effects in the political and security spheres.

Finally, 'conflict resolution through the pursuit of common programmes for the future without referring to the quarrels of the past', proposed by Mircea Malitza,[72] is a useful reference point in the case of economic cooperation among the SAARC member states. 'In practical terms,' as E. Sridharan argues, 'the approach means finding a common project that can produce common interests, overlap diverging interests, and have minimal culture, value of belief consideration.'[73] In South Asia, the energy sector is one possible area for economic cooperation. For example, a gas pipeline and export of electricity could enliven economic cooperation and act as a catalyst in the formation of an energy cooperation regime in the region.

With the economic agenda of SAARC countries gaining importance, there is a plan to build an energy grid in the region to ensure a two-way flow of power, natural gas, and oil. The strategy is to offer economic benefits and open a gateway for trade with ASEAN countries and also create a more congenial environment for regime formation in the energy sectors. To facilitate the plan for an energy grid, SAARC set up its first-ever senior and technical energy committees in late 2003. The seven heads of states signed off on an energy ring and harmonized energy efficiency standards for the region at the Islamabad Summit in January 2004.

In 2005, there was a noticeable improvement in India–Pakistan relations, with confidence-building measures from both sides. One of the major breakthroughs that might be witnessed between the two estranged neighbours is the laying of a 2,600-km gas pipeline originating in southern Iran, traversing through the 700 km stretch of Pakistani territory, before entering India. There was also optimism that this 'peace pipeline' diplomacy might augment regional cooperation in the form of India–Pakistan collaboration, along with India–Iran and Iran–Pakistan collaborations, which could potentially influence bilateral relationships between the countries involved, on the key conflicts of Afghanistan and Kashmir, and on overall national security.

The proposed pipeline would be expected to transport 90 million standard cubic metres of gas every day from Iran's South Pars fields to India from 2009–10 onwards, while Pakistan would receive 60 million standard cubic metres. Moreover, Pakistan could earn as much as $500 million in annual royalties from a transit fee, and save $200 million by purchasing cheaper gas from this pipeline project. However, the debate on the pipeline in both the countries suggests that the proposed pipeline might eventually prove to be a pipe dream because of the persistence of instability in Afghanistan and the possibility of international sanctions on Iran. Moreover, active US opposition to this pipeline project has further complicated matters.

Regional politics also plays a major role in defining the game. As international gas pipelines have to transit through many countries, their construction depends on multi-country agreements for the smooth and continuing supply of gas. Disagreements between India and Bangladesh have arisen due to India's accusation that Bangladesh is fuelling separatist movements in India's north-east, against the backdrop of rising Islamic fundamentalism and anti-India sentiment in Bangladesh under the Bangladesh National Party-led coalition government, illegal immigration from Bangladesh, and Bangladesh in turn accusing India of attempting to re-route the Ganges and Brahmaputra river systems that traverse both states. These disagreements have slowed the progress of discussions on a natural gas pipeline from Myanmar to India, which will have to pass through Bangladeshi territory, forcing India to look into the expensive option of creating a deep-sea pipeline through the Bay of Bengal that would bypass Bangladesh.[74] Here again, SAARC can play a key role in defusing tensions between nations and help them negotiate frameworks within which the governments concerned could agree on the measures relating to risks such as political tensions, terrorism, and natural disasters.

What is commendable about SAARC is that, notwithstanding periodic intra-regional wars as well as animosities between the member states, it has survived to this day. This is unlike some other such organizations in Africa and Latin America which soon succumbed to local crisis. Undoubtedly, the South Asian region has acquired growing relevance in world politics. As a consequence, many countries—Asian and non-Asian—including Afghanistan, Iran, China, USA, the EU, Japan, and South Korea, want to be associated with SAARC. It is true that SAARC, notwithstanding its 24 years of existence, has not been able to achieve much in terms of economic integration and inter-regional trade, but it is recognized as a market of the future given its huge material and human potential.

The South Asian region is also recognized as an emerging global economic force, having an aggregate gross domestic product (GDP) growth of 8 per cent in 2008.[75] South Asia's recent economic performance shows that the region is being transformed into a dynamic and vibrant economic grouping. At the 14th SAARC Summit in 2007 Afghanistan was the eighth country to join SAARC, being formally admitted into it at the Thirteenth Summit held in Dhaka. Both India and Pakistan backed Afghanistan's membership of the organization, albeit from different perspectives. Pakistan supported it in anticipation of controlling trade and other economic activities, while India's backing stemmed from its policy of supporting the post-Taliban government in Kabul and probably from its view of Afghanistan as a key link to energy-rich Central Asia.

Moreover, the inclusion of Afghanistan as a new member of SAARC has far-reaching consequences. Afghanistan, at a rudimentary stage of nation-building, has many expectations as a member. Surrounded by uneasy neighbours, Afghanistan desperately wants to end its isolation, give a boost to its moribund economy, integrate itself with the region, and benefit from its markets and resources. As a member, Afghanistan stands to benefit from various SAARC development programmes as well as from any collective anti-terrorism measures, thereby promoting its own security.

The 14th Summit of SAARC had the unique distinction of being attended for the first time by five observer states—USA, China, Japan, South Korea, Iran—and the EU. The presence of six major economies and resource-rich Iran from outside the region in fact extended the appeal of SAARC to the larger international community. Their presence symbolized the enhanced interest of the international community in its functioning. Although it could lead to some power play, as big powers always have their own agenda, there is general agreement among political observers and the inner circles of SAARC that the association of economic superpowers with SAARC would have some positive impact on South Asia.[76] It has been assumed that a number of observer countries are likely to play a more proactive role in economically engaging the region and may exert pressure on SAARC for more cooperation and integration.

* * *

To conclude, it may be said that integration and supra-nationality, in the sense in which the terms are used in the EU, were never a designated goal of SAARC. It did not intend to make regionalism a 'state-led project'. Rather, the goal was to establish a functional network of economic, cultural, and political contacts in the sphere of low politics. Thus, in order to broaden the scope of cooperation, regional organizations such as SAARC can apply the Nordic model, where cooperation has traditionally found a place in the sphere of low politics. It is a proven model that has functioned successfully between the Scandinavian countries since the Second World War. These countries have acted as a somewhat homogeneous region in some issue areas in world politics. Intergovernmental cooperation and NGOs have been the essence of the Nordic cooperation network. This has entailed a preference for a gradual, incremental approach to cooperation over legalistic and fast-track modalities of institution-building. Moreover, the Nordic approach places a premium on second-track dialogues in which government officials participate in their private capacity. In this way, it is possible to settle many sensitive issues informally between member countries.

In the South Asian region, the distribution of power is hugely uneven and in a state of flux. There are a variety of territorial disputes, jurisdictional conflicts, and ethnic and religious animosities in the region. Not only do the countries in the region lack experience in collective problem-solving, but are also suspicious of one another and rarely encourage their citizens to mutually engage across national borders without their direct control or monitoring. Given the animosities among South Asian states, it is highly unlikely that governments will soon develop a common political and security agenda.

SAARC can play a key role in defusing tensions between nations and help them negotiate frameworks within which the governments concerned can agree on the measures relating to a reduction of political and other tensions in the region.

There are also less contentious issues that have the potential to cause a range of wider security threats, such as refugee inflows, illegal immigration by sea, small arms proliferation, and drug trafficking. Such issues can be amicably settled among SAARC's member states through informal dialogue and negotiation. For example, the potentially devastating issue of illegal migrants from Bangladesh to India is on the minds of many government officials in both the countries. However, to date, the issue has not been raised at any international forum, reflecting the sensitive nature of this problem, nor has there been any informal dialogue between SAARC member states on this issue. Promoting cooperation on less contentious issues might build the trust necessary for productive discussions on security matters at a later stage. It is here that SAARC can help in building a sense of community among the member states in the region.

As both India and Pakistan are de facto nuclear weapons states, it is imperative to have inter-governmental cooperation which focuses on establishing trust and confidence-building measures, including border, maritime, air, and nuclear risk-reduction measures, a crisis prevention centre, and transparency amongst SAARC member states to promote strategic reassurance in the region. While discussing the trust factor in the Indo-Pakistan context during the SAARC Summit held in Dhaka in 2006, Pakistan's Prime Minister Shaukat Aziz mentioned that the region suffers from a 'trust deficit'. Indian Prime Minister Manmohan Singh went further to say that the task is to convert it into a 'trust surplus' area.

The need of the hour is, therefore, to use the SAARC platform to promote non-traditional security issues such as economic and human security, as is the case among Southeast Asian nations. This approach of building from the bottom and focusing on non-security forms of cooperation, rather than a premature and probably unstable regional security arrangement, is necessary to build the trust that is essential to resolve traditional security issues, so that the governments and the peoples of South Asian nations see each other as members of a single community, with similar goals of national security and regional development through mutual cooperation. The road to the high politics of security cooperation lies through the low politics of economic and other non-security cooperation.

Notes

1. Robert O. Keohane, *After Hegemony: Cooperation and Discord in the World Political Economy* (Princeton, NJ: Princeton University Press, 1984). See also for further reading, Barry Buzan, Charles Jones, and Richard Little, *The Logic of Anarchy: Neorealism to Structural Realism* (New York: Columbia University Press, 1993).

2. Keohane, *After Hegemony*.

3. Robert O. Keohane, 'Institutionalist Theory and Realist Challenge after the Cold War', in David Baldwin (ed.), *Neorealism and Neoliberalism: The Contemporary Debate* (New York: Columbia University Press, 1993), p. 274.

4. Keohane, *After Hegemony*, p. 13.

5. Robert O. Keohane and Joseph Nye (eds), *Power and Independence: World Politics in Transition* (Boston: Little Brown & Co., 1977).

6. Robert O. Keohane and Joseph S. Nye, *Power and Interdependence: World Politics in Transition*, 2nd Edn (Illinois, Boston, & London: Scott, Foresman & Co., 1989).

7. See John Ruggie, 'Territoriality and Beyond: Problematizing Modernity in International Relations', *International Organization*, 47 (1) (Winter 1993), pp. 171–2.

8. Barry Buzan, *Peoples, States and Fear* (London: Harvester Wheatsheaf, 1991), p. 208.

9. Andrew Hurrell, 'Regionalism in Theoretical Perspectives', in Louise Fawcett and Andrew Hurrell (eds), *Regionalism in World Politics: Regional Organization and International Order* (Oxford: Oxford University Press, 1995), pp. 47–9.

10. See, in this context, Bjorn Hettne, 'Globalization and the New Regionalism: The Second Great Transformation', in Bjorn Hettne, Andras Inotai, and Osvaldo Sunkel (eds), *Globalism and the New Regionalism* (London: Macmillan, 1999), p. 123.

11. Ibid.

12. Ibid.

13. Keohane and Nye, *Power and Interdependence*, 2nd Edn, pp. 247–8.

14. David Mitrany, *A Working Peace System* (Oxford: Oxford University Press, 1944).

15. Ernst B. Haas, *The Uniting of Europe: Political, Social and Economic Forces 1950–57* (Stanford, CA: Stanford University Press, 1958); Karl W. Deutsch, Sidney Burrell, and Robert A. Kann, *Political Community and the North Atlantic Area: International Organization in the Light of Historical Experience* (Princeton, NJ: Princeton University Press, 1957).

16. Deutsch *et al.*, *Political Community and the North Atlantic Area*.

17. Ibid.

18. Ernst Haas, 'The Study of Regional Integration: Reflections on the Joy and Anguish of Pre-theorizing', *International Organization*, XXIV (4), 1970, pp. 607–46, especially pp. 642–3.

19. Charles Pentland, *International Theory and European Integration* (New York, NY: The Free Press, 1973), p. 147.

20. See, in this context, Pentland, *International Theory and European Integration*.

21. Haas, 'The Study of Regional Integration', p. 617.

22. Ibid.

23. Keohane, 'Institutional Theory and the Realist Challenge after the Cold War', p. 386.

24. Leon N. Lindberg, *The Political Dynamics of European Economic Integration* (Stanford: Stanford University Press, 1963), p. 9.

25. See, in this context, Ernst Haas, 'The Uniting of Europe and the Uniting of Latin America', *Journal of Common Market Studies*, 5(4), 1967, pp. 327–8; see also Stanley Hoffman, 'Discord in Community: The North Atlantic Areas as a Partial International System', in Francis O. Wilcox and H. Field Haviland (eds), *The Atlantic Community* (New York: Praeger, 1963), p. 13.

26. Ibid.

27. Charles Pentland, *International Theory and European Integration* (New York: The Free Press, 1973), p. 130.

28. Lindberg, *The Political Dynamics of European Economic Integration*, p. 10.

29. Ernst Haas, 'The Challenge of Regionalism', *International Organization*, 12 (4), 1958, pp. 441–58.

30. Deutsch *et al.*, *Political Community and the North Atlantic Area*, and E. Adler and M. Barnett (eds), *Security Communities* (Cambridge: Cambridge University Press, 1998).

31. Deutsch *et al.*, *Political Community and the North Atlantic Area*, p. 5.

32. Buzan, *Peoples, States and Fear*, p. 192.

33. See Barry Buzan, 'The Post-Cold War Asia-Pacific Security Order: Conflict or Cooperation?', in Andrew Mack and John Ravenhill (eds), *Pacific Cooperation Building: Economic and Security Regimes in the Asia Pacific Region* (Boulder, CO: Westview, 1995).

34. Buzan, *Peoples, States and Fear*, p. 192.

35. Deutsch *et al.*, *Political Community and the North Atlantic Area*, p. 36.

36. Richard Merritt and Bruce M. Russett, 'Karl Deutsch and the Scientific Analysis of World Politics', in Richard Merritt and Bruce M. Russett (eds), *From National Development to Global Community: Essays in Honor of Karl Deutsch* (London & Boston: George Allen & Unwin, 1981), p. 8.

37. See Ben Resmond, *Theories of European Integration* (New York: Palgrave, 2000), p. 12.

38. Ronald Yalem, 'Regional Security Communities', in George W. Keeton and George Schwarzenberger (eds), *The Year Book of International Affairs* (London: Steven & Sons, 1979), p. 217.

39. Cf. William Wallace and Julie Smith, 'Democracy or Technocracy? European Integration and the Problem of Popular Consent', *West European Politics*, Special Issue on the Crisis of Representation in Europe, Jack Hayward (ed.), 18 (3), July 1995, p. 153.

40. Deutsch *et al.*, *Political Community and the North Atlantic Area*; Adler and Bernett (eds), *Security Communities*.

41. See Joseph Nye, *Understanding International Conflicts: An Introduction of Theory and History* (New York: Longman, 2000).

42. Carl Johan Åsberg and P. Wallensteen, 'New Threats and New Security: The Post-Cold War Debate Revisited', in P. Wallensteen (ed.) *Preventing Violent Conflicts: Past Record and Future Challenges* (Uppsala: Uppsala University, Department of Peace and Conflict Research, 1998), pp. 167–202.

43. J. Baylis and N.J. Renggers, *Dilemmas of World Politics: International Issues in a Changing World* (Oxford: Clarendon Press, 1992), pp. 45–6.

44. Ernst Haas, 'The Study of Regional Integration: Reflections of Joy and Anguish of Pretheorizing', *International Organization*, XXIV (4), 1970, p. 626.

45. Nils Andren, 'Nordic Integration: Aspects and Problems', *Cooperation and Conflict*, II, 1967, p. 6.

46. Deutsch *et al.*, *Political Community and the North Atlantic Area*, p. 5.

47. Robert O. Keohane, 'Theory of World Politics: Structural Realism and Beyond', in Robert O. Keohane (ed.), *Neorealism and its Critics* (New York: Columbia University Press, 1986), p. 197.

48. Adler and Barnett (eds), *Security Communities*, p. 31.

49. Ibid., p. 7.

50. Andren, 'Nordic Integration: Aspects and Problems', pp. 1–25.

51. Ibid., p. 5.

52. Shrikant Paranjape, 'Development of Order in South Asia: Towards a South Asian Association for Regional Cooperation', *Contemporary South Asia*, 11 (3), 2002; and David Myers, 'Threat Perceptions and Strategic Responses of the Regional Hegemon: A Conceptual Overview', in David Myers (ed.), *Regional Hegemony: Threat Perceptions and Regional Responses* (Boulder, CO: Westview Press, 1991), pp. 1–29.

53. Bjorn Hettne, Intoi Andras, and Osvaldo Sunkel (eds), *Globalism and the New Regionalism* (London: Macmillan, 1999).

54. Muchkund Dubey, Lok Raj Baral, and Sobhan Rehman (eds), *South Asian Growth Triangle: Framework for Multilateral Cooperation* (New Delhi: Macmillan, 1999). See also C. Raja Mohan, *Crossing the Rubicon: The Shaping of India's New Foreign Policy* (New Delhi: Penguin, 2003).

55. *Annual Report*, Ministry of Commerce, Government of India, various issues.

56. See Government of Bangladesh, 'SAARC Document, A Paper on the Proposal for Regional Cooperation in South Asia', November 1980.

57. SAARC Secretariat, 'Charter of the South Asian Association for Regional Cooperation', Kathmandu. See also 'Declaration of SAARC', issued by the First Political Meeting of the Foreign Ministers, 1–3 August 1983, New Delhi, India.

58. A.K.M. Abdus Sabur, 'Security Scenario in South Asia', paper presented at the seminar on South Asian Security and Sino-Bangladesh Relations,

organized by Bangladesh Institute of International and Strategic Studies (BIISS) on 2 March 2005.

59. Bary Buzan, 'South Asia Moving Towards Transformation: Emergence of India as a Great Power,' *International Studies*, 39 (1) January–March, 2002.

60. Imtiaz Ahmed, Ajaya Dixit, and Ashish Nandy, *Water, Power and People: A South Asian Manifesto on the Politics and Knowledge of Water* (Colombo: Regional Centre for Strategic Studies, 1997).

61. See Lok Raj Baral, 'Indo-Nepal Relations: Continuity and Change', *Asian Survey*, 32 (9), September 1992, pp. 815–29.

62. Umashankar Phadnis, 'India: Geo-political Strategic Concerns', *World Focus*, January 1989, pp. 10–17.

63. S. Malcom Adiseshiah, 'The Economic Rationale of the SAARC', *Asia Journal*, 1, 1987. Also see S.N. Raghavan, *Regional Economic Cooperation Among SAARC Countries* (New Delhi: Allied Publishers, 1995).

64. Former Indian Prime Minister Inder Kumar Gujral's regional policy derives from the simple recognition that India could hold sway in South Asia through persuasion not coercion.

There are two sides to what is sometimes referred to as the Gujral Doctrine. One is the enhancement of India's dominance of South Asia through generosity rather than coercion. The other is to counteract India's alienation from the West on a number of international issues by building alternate circles of influence such as the Indian Ocean rim organization or cozying up to Southeast and West Asia.

65. SAARC Secretariat, Kathmandu, SAARC Agreement on Preferential Trading Arrangement (SAPTA 1993), Article 3.

66. Bangladesh, Bhutan, the Maldives, and Nepal are considered LDC member states within SAARC.

67. Saman Kelegama, 'Sri Lankan Exports to India: Impact of Free Trade Agreement', *Economic and Political Weekly*, 38 (30), 2003.

68. Ahmed *et al.*, *Water, Power, and People*.

69. Sankar Ghosh and Somen Mukherji, *Emerging South Asian Order: Hopes and Concerns* (Calcutta: Media South Asia, 1995), p. 197.

70. Adiseshiah, 'The Economic Rationale of the SAARC'. Also see Raghavan, *Regional Economic Cooperation Among SAARC Countries*.

71. Kargil Review Committee Report, *From Surprise to Reckoning* (New Delhi: Sage Publications, 2000), fn. 67.

72. Mircea Malitza, 'Ten Thousand Cultures, A Single Civilization', *International Security*, 21 (1), Summer 1996, cited in E. Sridharan, 'Improving Indo-Pakistan Relations: International Relations Theory, Nuclear Deterrence and Prospects for Economic Cooperation', *Contemporary South Asia*, 14 (3), September 2005, pp. 325–6.

73. Sridharan, 'Improving Indo-Pakistan Relations'.

74. In this connection, see Aparajita Biswas, 'Non Traditional Security Issues: Recent Trends in the Hydrocarbon Sector in the Indian Ocean Region',

in Sanjay Chaturvedi and Dennis Rumley (eds), *Energy Security and the Indian Ocean Region* (New Delhi: South Asian Publishers, 2005), pp. 75–87.

75. See *Asian Development Bank Report*, Philippines: Department of External Affairs, Asian Development Bank, 2008.

76. Rashid Ahmad Khan, 'The Role of Observer in SAARC', *IPRI Journal*, IX (2), Summer 2009, pp. 1–16, see http://ipripak.org/journal/summer2009/Article1.pdf, 13 Hindu, accessed on 1 April 2008.

Part II

DOMESTIC POLITICS AND ITS FOREIGN POLICY IMPLICATIONS

4   The Evolution of Civil–Military Relations in South Asia

Ayesha Siddiqa

Civil–military relations are usually analysed along a linear trajectory and from the point of view of the military's command and control apparatus and its decision-making processes. So long as decisions are being processed by civilian authorities, the balance of civil–military relations is said to favour the former. Such a formulation has its genesis in Samuel P. Huntington's definition of the military profession, which I will outline shortly. This is, however, an imperfect analysis and does not capture the vertical and horizontal advances in civil–military relations in a given state.

This chapter aims at evaluating civil–military relations in Pakistan, Bangladesh, Sri Lanka, and India from the point of: view of (i) command and control of the armed forces, (ii) the evolution of the political environments in the four countries, and (iii) the relationship between the states and their respective societies. A more dynamic framework will capture the way in which the relationship has evolved over the years since all these countries gained independence.

THE THEORETICAL FRAMEWORK

The term 'civil–military relations', as normally used in understanding the relationship between the military, the state, and the society, falls short of explaining or understanding the way in which militaries have evolved in terms of politics and policy-making, and the organization's relationship with the larger society. The term is restrictive because of the limited imagination of the political and strategic communities in most states in viewing the issue in the wider context of the relationship between military force and political power. Such analytical limitations lead to a restricted understanding of the term and in turn a general tendency to view civil–military relations in terms of civilian control of the armed forces or vice versa.

While conducting research on the subject, the initial responses of several interviewees were guarded, and the questions often evoked answers based on predetermined notions. A number of people interviewed usually got entangled in comparisons, suggesting that in their countries (this particularly refers to India, Bangladesh, and Sri Lanka) the militaries were under civilian control. There was a general tendency to compare their societies with that of Pakistan or to establish that they were not praetorian. Clearly, there was recognition of democracy as a superior value which made states and societies that were democratic or had civilian control of their militaries superior to those where the military dominated politics. Viewed as such, the term 'civil–military' was value-laden.

These preconceived notions of civil–military relations emanate from the existing literature on the subject that tends to define the term from the standpoint of military professionalism. A professional force is a corporate entity which allows civilian authorities to exercise control over the organization. Samuel P. Huntington's work entitled the *Soldier and the State* has played a key role in defining the nature of the relations between militaries and civilian leaderships, elaborated in the following.[1] A professional military is subservient to civilian control as opposed to praetorian armed forces that control the political and administrative functioning of the state. In fact, Huntington identifies the military's subservience to civilian authority as one of the prerequisites for its organizational professionalism. Other authors, such as Amos Perlmutter, further elaborate upon the concept, firmly linking the military's subservience to political masters as a feature of a liberal or democratic political environment.[2] Although subsequent works by Alfred Stepan and Morris Janowitz[3] sought to play around with a re-explanation of military professionalism, Huntington's definition continues to be significant in shaping arguments about civil–military relations.

One of the problems with Huntington's definition is that it does not completely capture the relevance of military force for public policy or the organization's relationship with the state and the civil society. The military is one of the key institutions of the state, and the way in which it operates depends upon how the organization is perceived by the policymakers and/or the operational space which the organization is allowed in the political system. In other words, the specifics of control of the armed forces form just one aspect of the civil–military relationship. This relationship is ever evolving, depending upon the politics of the state, which is in turn determined by the interests of the various actors and the relationships among the stakeholders. However, there are three factors that determine the extent of the influence that a defence establishment eventually exercises. First, the nature of the political system and the relative strength of others involved is a key determinant. In a state where political forces are weak, the militaries claim greater political space. Second, the character of the military has a bearing on its ability to claim greater political space. Third, political and geopolitical objectives determine the degree of influence exercised by a military. Therefore, civil–military relations are not purely an issue of control, but also about how military force is relevant to the political goals of the stakeholders. The military is essentially a policy tool, and how it is utilized by the ruling class depends upon the nature of a country's politics. The way in which the military is deployed, in turn, determines the tenor of the relationship between it and the general public.

The argument in this chapter is linked to two paradigms. First, civil–military relations must also be evaluated from the perspective of the degree of coercion exercised by the armed forces in their interaction with civil society and the common people, and not merely as a matter of civilian control or otherwise. One of the variables for evaluating civil–military relations is to analyse the role of the armed forces and the organization's relations with the people during an intra-state conflict. States employ armed forces as a tool of coercion to implement policies. I have borrowed from Charles Tilly's framework of the state as a 'racketeer', elaborated later, that uses various methods, including coercion, to extract resources from its people. The strength of a state is in fact determined by its ability to extract resources or implement its policies. According to Tilly, the state undertakes seven core functions: (i) state-making, (ii) war-making, (iii) protection, (iv) extraction, (v) adjudication, (vi) distribution, and (vii) production.[4]

However, the state is not a neutral entity but a compound of the interests of the stakeholders. Sometimes the military is used coercively in pursuit of vested interests; in other instances the defence establishment plays a key role in defining these interests. Internal conflict is thus a consequence of the relationship among the various stakeholders, especially those playing a dominant role in the state as against those not so positioned. Consequently, how a military is perceived depends upon which group exercises coercion and to what degree. Those at the receiving end of coercion will tend to have a different perception of the military than those who use it as a tool. Internal conflict or coercion is extremely relevant to the analysis of post-colonial state structures such as those in South Asia, where the emphasis has been on maintaining a unitary state, often in pre-industrial, multi-ethnic, and multi-racial societies. The issue then is not just one of control but of the use of the armed forces as a tool of coercion by the state. The military is one of the many actors vying for greater influence over the state or within the political system, and a share of the resources. Ultimately, it is the strength of the political system that determines the significance—greater or lesser—of the armed forces in relation to the others.

Second, civil–military relations evolve according to the relevance that the armed forces have for policy-making, especially a state's external policy. This argument can be better understood by looking at Frederic Lane's concepts of tribute and rent.[5] The term tribute refers to the price that the armed forces extract to enhance a state's capacity to extract resources vis-à-vis other states. Rent refers to the differential between cost of security and the dividends. What is significant in Lane's theoretical formulation is the idea of the military using coercion to provide certain advantages to its clientele. Thus, civil–military relations are bound to undergo certain adjustments and modifications, depending upon the relevance of military force for the stakeholders. A military's significance in decision-making will increase or decrease depending upon the role it is required to play in underwriting a state's geopolitical agenda.

A theoretical framework that explores the depth of this linkage was necessary for analysing such diverse cases as India, Pakistan, Bangladesh, and Sri Lanka. From a traditional command-and-control standpoint, Pakistan and India represent two ends of the spectrum, with Bangladesh and Sri Lanka falling in between. While these four countries share a common heritage of colonialism, civil–military relations have developed in accordance with the particularities of their political systems. Intra-state conflict has also provided a common thread in all the cases, impacting upon civil–military relations. In order to assess the military's role and significance vis-à-vis other stakeholders, this study will analyse the following dimensions:

1. Command and control of the armed forces;
2. The military's role in politics;
3. Structure of the higher defence organization;

4. Impact of the military's external role on the organization's significance in policy-making; and

5. Conduct and impact of intra-state conflict on civil–military relations.

The following sections present case studies of the four states. The purpose is to analyse what positions and directions the states, their polities, societies, and militaries have taken vis-à-vis each other since the countries gained independence from a common colonial master and the implications of this for the role of the military. The other emphasis is on the different historical factors that have driven these states towards their respective civil–military equations.

PAKISTAN

Pakistan is a case of an extreme form of military domination of the state and society. Over the years, the armed forces have established their hegemony by penetrating the society, economy, and politics, and exercised intellectual/philosophical dominance by controlling the strategic and foreign policy debate. Politically, the military exercised indirect control for 30 years in the 63 years since independence, and directly for 17 years.[6] Economically, the military dominates the three major segments of the economy—agriculture, services, and manufacturing. The armed forces run the two largest business conglomerates and operate in the formal, informal, and illegal sectors of the economy. Finally, their philosophical or intellectual presence is indicated by their involvement in education and in all major deliberative forums in the country. Retired and serving military personnel have been inducted into all strategic institutions and the military regimes have gradually and systematically created a constituency favouring the armed forces amongst the civilian academics and journalists by offering them financial rewards or career opportunities. Furthermore, intellectual dominance is exercised by projecting the country's image as a threatened state that has to be protected by investing a major share of national resources in military security. Hence, at this particular juncture, the military is the state.[7]

Over the 63 years since independence, the military not only managed to remain at the helm of affairs, but also emerged as an independent class distinguished by its own norms, rules, principles, and values.

The military's dominance dates back to the days after Pakistan's independence in 1947. The inability of the civilian leadership to establish firm control over the armed forces and the policy of initiating a war with India soon after independence transformed the larger socio-political agenda of the state. The first war of 1947–8 established the primacy of military security. Moreover, the inability of the successive political governments during the initial years to pursue the development agenda or offer a political and socio-economic vision for the nation allowed territorial security to become the state's prime agenda. The country's policy-making elite tends to define the threat to national security principally in terms of the peril perceived from New Delhi. India's alleged hegemonic policies and belligerent attitude are considered the greatest threats to the survival of the state. Over the past 60 years and more, the dominant school of thought that has influenced policy-making believes that the Indian leadership has never been comfortable with an independent homeland for the Muslims and would lose no opportunity to destroy or invade Pakistan. Policymakers are equally uncomfortable with India's urge to gain regional or global prominence. Any reference to India acquiring a prominent role, especially due to a comparatively greater military capacity, is seen as a potential threat and as inherently antithetical to Pakistan's security interests.

After the war of 1947–8, the government allocated about 70 per cent of the estimated budget for defence in the very first year.[8] This budgetary allocation symbolized the prioritization of military security as the national agenda. According to Hussain Haqqani, a research fellow at the Carnegie Endowment for International Peace, after the first war in 1947–8, '"Islamic Pakistan" was defining itself through the prism of resistance to "Hindu India".'[9]

The India threat had an immediate effect in making the military prominent in comparison to all other domestic actors. This development was accompanied by lax control of the armed forces by the civilian leadership. In fact, Pakistan's founding father, Mohammad Ali Jinnah, was unable to assume firm control of the armed forces during the early days. Jinnah could not even enforce his decision to deploy troops in Kashmir. General Gracey, Pakistan army's commander-in-chief, expressed reluctance to obey Jinnah during the 1947–8 war with India for which he was not admonished. However, Pakistani historian Ayesha Jalal reveals that the military did not shirk its responsibilities but that Jinnah was persuaded by General Auchinleck, the joint commander-in-chief for India and Pakistan, to reverse his earlier decision to deploy troops in Kashmir.[10] Adopting a contrary view, Stephen P. Cohen holds the founding father of Pakistan responsible for lax control over the army by leaving ultimate military strategic decision-making to General Gracey.[11] In any event, the war opened a Pandora's Box by defining Pakistan as a state that viewed its existence through the lens of its hostile relations with India. Brig. (retd) A.R. Siddiqui is of the view that 'the use of Pakhtoon tribals to take control of the Kashmir valley led to the war,' thus sealing the fate of Kashmir and turning Pakistan into a military-dominated state'.[12]

Subsequently, the civilian leadership, particularly the civil bureau-cracy, dominated the post-colonial state of Pakistan. This condition was identified by Pakistani political scientist Hamza Alavi as the crisis of an 'overdeveloped' state. The term signifies the dominance of the state by its civil and military bureaucracy. The bureaucracy is trained to protect the state from external as well as internal threats. According to Alavi, 'The [civil and military] bureaucrats were brought up on the myth of "guardianship", the idea that it was their mission to defend the interests of the people as against the supposed partnership of and personal ambitions of "professional" politicians'.[13] Thus, the military's role in the state was not restricted to coercion but also extended to the legitimation of regimes, a task the organization was able to perform, given its authority and standing in the state and society.[14]

The civil bureaucracy viewed the political chaos prior to the imposition of martial law in the country for the first time in 1958 as advantageous to its wresting control of the state. The coup itself was a consequence of the battle between the political forces and the civil bureaucracy. In the post-colonial state of Pakistan, the executive or the bureaucracy can be understood as a 'group of bearers of office authority [that] ... reduces the political parties to the role of mere brokers, who manipulate public relations in their favour and thus function as a legitimacy factor'.[15] The power equation between the executive and the legislature during the early days of the country's independence was inherited from the British rulers. The colonial power controlled India by strengthening the state bureaucracy.[16] This pattern persisted in the ensuing years and the civil–military bureaucracy developed an interest in controlling the state and its politics.

The civil bureaucracy in Pakistan was as powerful as it was in India. However, the principal difference between the two was in their approach towards military power and political control. While the Indian civil bureaucracy recognized and accepted the dominance of the politicians and established control over the armed forces by strengthening the Ministry of Defence (MoD), Pakistan's civil bureaucracy chose to partner with the military to further their dominance over the political leadership. The civil bureaucracy, represented by bureaucrat-turned-politician Ghulam Mohammad, the governor-general in the early 1950s, viewed the military as a junior partner capable of keeping the raucous politicians at bay. The governor-general trusted the army chief more than the civilian prime ministers.

Iskander Mirza, who succeeded Ghulam Mohammad in 1955 and was also a former bureaucrat, relied equally on the army. A close friend of Ayub Khan, Mirza increasingly involved the military in the functioning of the state.[17] He asked General Ayub Khan to take over the government by replacing Prime Minister Bogra, with whom the former had had a falling-out in 1954.[18] However, this did not materialize. According to Lt General (retd) Chishti, the civilian government's decision not to retire Ayub Khan in 1954 and to give him a role in the cabinet weakened the civilian institution.[19] Such favours to the army chief smacked of a conspiratorial partnership between Ayub Khan and the governor-general, and were vital for the latter's survival and that of the civil bureaucracy-dominated state.

Saeed Shafqat, a Pakistani expert on civil–military relations, claims that the Ayub–Mirza alliance (1955–8) was the civil bureaucracy's bid to forge a superordinate–subordinate relationship with the armed forces.[20] The office of the governor-general was abolished after the introduction of the first constitution in 1956, after which Mirza insisted on becoming a powerful president. To ensure his army friend's allegiance, Mirza twice gave Ayub Khan extension as commander-in-chief, first in 1955 and again in 1958.[21] These concessions, however, would prove exceedingly costly to the civilian leadership. In 1958, the military could no longer be treated as a junior partner and the superordinate–subordinate relationship was reversed. Although Mirza imposed martial law on 7 October 1958, Ayub finally decided to bring the military to the forefront through a counter-coup on 27 October 1958.

Notwithstanding the fact that the post-independence leadership was relatively weak, the politicians were unable to counter the manipulative strength of the civil and military bureaucracy. While General Ayub Khan entered into a partnership with the civil bureaucracy, especially the Civil Service of Pakistan (CSP) cadre (denoting the administrative services), the political leadership failed to muster the strength to fight military authoritarianism. Consequently, the military continued its rule until 1971 when it was forced to return to the barracks after losing a war with India. According to Shafqat, 'It was not Bhutto's election victory but the tragic conditions caused due to defeat in the war that facilitated the transfer of power from the army to him.'[22] Although Bhutto had won elections in the western wing of the country, he was brought to power through the military leadership's manipulation which ultimately led to the independence of its eastern part (as Bangladesh) in 1971. Compared to Sheikh Mujibur Rehman and his Awami League, Bhutto and his Pakistan Peoples Party (PPP) were a preferred option for the military. The military did not intend to relinquish power once it took control of the state in 1958. The return of democracy and the promulgation of the 1962 constitution under Ayub Khan were merely a re-engineering of the state's political structure to ensure that he continued to control the government. Ayub Khan's ouster by army chief General Yahya Khan in 1969 denoted a change manipulated by the army rather than any substantive change in the tone of politics.

By the end of the 1960s and the early 1970s, Pakistan's politics had acquired an authoritarian character that was partly reflected in Bhutto's decision to assume the reins of the government as the chief martial law administrator in 1971. It was also the very nature of this politics that later thwarted Bhutto's efforts to transform civil–military relations in favour of civilian governments. Despite the restructuring of the 'Higher Defence Organization', the military gradually acquired strength during the Bhutto regime. The first popularly elected prime minister of Pakistan adopted the flawed policy of bringing the military back into politics, a development that backfired and resulted in the second military takeover in July 1977. The tenor of Bhutto's policies was determined by his dependence on military force and an authoritarian ethos. This was demonstrated by his handling of the political crisis in Baluchistan and the establishment of a paramilitary force placed directly under his control. The prime minister sought to reduce the friction between the Centre and the province of Baluchistan, which had escalated to an insurgency, by deploying the army. The military operation in Baluchistan in 1973 led to the killing of about 6,000 Baluch people.[23] He also established the Federal Security Force (FSF) in May 1973 as a tool for coercion. This was also a reflection of the PPP leadership's failure to institutionalize party democracy. The creation of the FSF, which operated like Bhutto's private Savak (the Shah of Iran's intelligence agency) signalled to other political leaders the significance of military force in the political arena.

During the regime of General Ziaul Haq (1977–88), coercive methods were used to control both the state and society. The regime's coercive measures included: (i) sentencing to death an elected prime minister, Bhutto, through a sham legal trial in 1979; (ii) imposing media censorship; (iii) suspending fundamental rights granted by the constitution introduced by Bhutto in 1973; (iv) banning labour and student unions; and (v) cracking down on all public protest. According to a prominent Pakistani journalist, Mushahid Hussain, who later under Musharraf's regime morphed into the military's client, General Zia followed the Turkish model of banning students' unions.[24] The military dictator, in fact, visited Turkey in 1984 with some education sector administrators to learn how Ankara had dealt with politically orchestrated campus violence.[25]

The regime also followed the Turkish model in dealing with labour unions. The PPP and its support base, consisting largely of the urban and rural poor, primarily the urban proletariat, had to be marginalized and forced into submission to make way for the interests of the military and other classes. The media was dealt with even more harshly. The military government amended Section 499 of the Pakistan Penal Code with the objective of prosecuting newspaper editors for publishing stories against the interests of the regime.[26] For instance, in 1978, for the first time in the country's history, journalists were whipped under sentences passed by military courts.[27]

The regime's coercive tactics were reflected in the way in which it tried to establish its control by dictating the norms and ethos of society at large. The army co-opted the religious right and used religious ideology to muster support among the general public. The alliance with the religious parties and propagation of Islamic culture were intended to establish the military's hegemony over civil society.[28] The creation of the office of the nazim-e-salaat (controller of prayers) and the introduction of Sharia law and Islamic banking in the mid-1980s were some of the tools used to combat the secular image of Bhutto's party. The nazim-e-salaat was deputed in every neighbourhood to ensure that all males attended the prayer congregation. Those who failed to do so were harassed through propaganda and the use of force. These measures gave the military dictator symbolic legitimacy.[29] Using state propaganda, Bhutto was condemned for his drinking habit. Thus, the army was shown to have taken control of governance to cleanse the state of a debauched leadership that was pushing society away from its Islamic moorings. Driving society towards social conservatism required the military to cosy up not only to the religious right, but also the socially and politically conservative elements.

The army under Zia skilfully used the intelligence agencies to manipulate political parties. The military's primary intelligence agency, the Inter-Services Intelligence (ISI), which was strengthened through the 1980s by its close involvement in the Afghan war, was also involved in the formation of the Islami Jamhoori Ittihad (IJI) party in 1988 and the Muhajir Qaumi Movement (MQM) in 1984 to counter Bhutto's PPP.[30] The regime's adroit use of religious ideology and ethnic identities was also intended to perpetuate political factionalism. Socio-political fragmentation would naturally result in strengthening the myth of the military as a national saviour.[31] The MQM and the IJI were meant to counter the late Bhutto's continuing popularity in his home province, Sindh, and other parts of the country. The MQM was known for the violence it unleashed in the urban centres of Sindh in the late 1980s and 1990s.[32]

Notwithstanding the reintroduction of democracy in 1985, General Zia did not betray any signs of withdrawing the army leadership from politics. Under him, the government informally split into two segments: (i) the civilian section headed by a prime minister handpicked by General Zia, and (ii) the president who was the central figure in the country's power politics. The introduction of the Eighth Amendment to the 1973 Constitution made the president the supreme commander of the armed forces and empowered him to sack any political government, a power that was exercised by Zia in 1987 when he dismissed Prime Minister Junejo's government on charges of corruption.

This system of parallel governments was used repeatedly during the 1990s after General Zia's death in a mysterious plane crash in August 1988. It was intended to safeguard the military's interests and to keep a firm check on political governments. This constitutional provision was invoked thrice during the 1990s until it was annulled in 1995–6 by Prime Minister Nawaz Sharif. The constitutional change, however, proved to be a double-edged sword because, in the absence of this provision, which in the mind of the military top brass worked as a political 'fire-break', the army General Headquarters (GHQ) had no option but than to intervene directly in 1999 to remove Nawaz Sharif. The prime minister was seen as having challenged the primacy of the armed forces when he used his power to remove the army chief, General Pervez Musharraf.

General Musharraf reset the norms of civil–military relations by restoring the controversial amendment to the constitution and establishing the National Security Council (NSC) in 2004, which gave the military a constitutional role in the politics and governance of the state. The NSC was established by an amendment to the 1973 constitution. Although established as an advisory body, the council gave a formal role to the military in the country's decision-making. The stated purpose was to ensure that democracy would not get derailed in future. However, akin to the Turkish NSC, the Pakistani council gave the military the status of an equal partner in policymaking.

Management of Defence

This narration of Pakistan's political history was directed towards explaining how the military dominance of politics has affected the command and control of the armed forces. The current system of defence management dates back to the 1970s when Zulfiqar Ali Bhutto introduced a new method of managing the defence sector. The pre-1973 defence management system was inherited from the pre-independence days in which all three services were headed by their respective commanders-in-chief, with hardly any coordination between the services. This approach not only led to a lack of coordination during the two wars of 1965 and 1971, but it also made the commanders-in-chief politically powerful. The defence management system designed under Bhutto, therefore, aimed at bringing the military under firm civilian control (Figure 4.1).

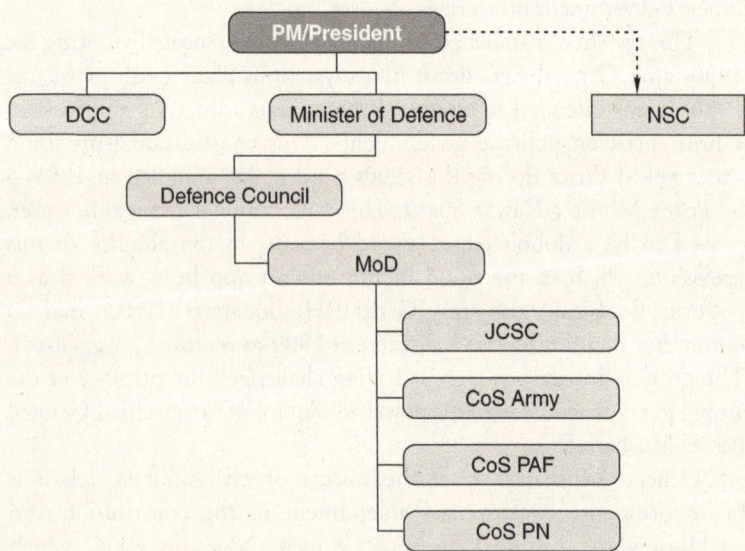

FIGURE 4.1   Pakistan: System of Defence Management
Source: Author's own formulation.

According to Figure 4.1, the prime minister was the supreme commander and controlled the armed forces with the help of the MoD. The commanders-in-chief were re-designated as chiefs-of-staff and were accountable to the MoD. In addition, a new institution of the chairman, joint chiefs of staff committee (JCSC), was established to serve as the interface between the military and the MoD. The JCSC was responsible for joint planning and coordination. The minister of defence was a member of the cabinet, which was the primary body for defence decision-making. The Defence Committee of the Cabinet (DCC) took decisions on defence-related issues. Moreover, the minister headed a defence council which was meant to oversee implementation of decisions undertaken by the DCC. In this system, the prime minister was the supreme commander of the armed forces, a power which was transferred to the president during the 1980s as a result of the eighth amendment to the 1973 Constitution.

Unfortunately, the entire structure collapsed prematurely due to the imposition of martial law for the second time in July 1977. Army chief General Ziaul Haq, who captured political control by overthrowing Zulfiqar Ali Bhutto, was not interested in strengthening structures that challenged his authority. The JCSC was therefore a lame duck from the time of its inception. Ziaul Haq also changed the mechanism for the command and control of the armed forces by making the president, rather than the prime minister, the supreme commander. One of the explanations for JCSC's inability to strengthen itself institutionally lay in the fact that its creation coincided with the imposition of Ziaul Haq's martial law. As the chief martial law administrator (CMLA) and president, General Zia could not make himself available for the JCSC meetings. He was represented during the committee meetings by the service's chief of staff, Lt General K.M. Arif. This development completely undermined the concept of the equality of the three services because the person representing the army was junior to the air force and naval chiefs. Therefore, correcting organizational balance through the JCSC was a non-starter from the very outset.

The inequitable distribution of power within the military organization and the government at large did not help alter the civil–military relations balance in favour of the former. The army's power within the defence establishment was apparent from the fact that even without bringing the two other services on board, it launched a full-fledged military operation against India, which eventually escalated into a medium-intensity war, the Kargil conflict (1999). In fact, as the then air chief P.Q. Mehdi disclosed, the Pakistan Air Force (PAF) was gently snubbed and told to mind its own business when it made inquiries regarding some movements it had detected in the north.[33]

Over the years, the army also managed to dominate the JCSC and neutralize the effectiveness of the organization by eliminating the concept of joint control. The military government of General Pervez Musharraf installed in October 1999 flouted the principle of appointing the chairman of the JCSC from within the three services on a rotational basis based on the principle of seniority. The principle of appointing the most senior military commander was initially not honoured by Prime Minister Nawaz Sharif. He appointed Musharraf, who was the army chief, as chairman of JCSC, despite the fact that it was naval chief Fasih Bokhari's turn to be appointed. This appointment, as the former naval chief claimed, was to appease Musharraf and forestall him from taking any adverse action against Sharif. There had been a falling out between the prime minister and the army chief over the Kargil issue, and both were playing a game of cat and mouse.[34] The idea was to protect oneself and be able to remove one's opponent.

Eventually, it was General Musharraf who supervened. The army chief retained his service's control over the JCSC after the change in government, established by appointing a senior army officer as the chairman. Post-1999, the office of the chairman JCSC was used to reward or sideline senior army officers. For instance, General M. Aziz, who was considered a threat to Musharraf, was appointed chairman on 21 March 2003. In any case, the army's top management viewed the JCSC as redundant. There was talk of scrapping the institution before the coup took place in 1999. While army officers complained about the inability of the JCSC to deliver results, they overlooked the fact that it was the political manoeuvring of the largest service that had made the committee powerless. When it came to strategic military planning, it was the army that called the shots.

Other reasons why Bhutto's policy changes did not take off were his political flaws. According to the late General Gul Hassan Khan,[35] Bhutto tried to partner with the military in order to survive, by giving it a role in the administration by imposing martial law in major cities such as Karachi, Lahore, and Hyderabad in 1977 to curb political unrest and mass demonstrations. The army was asked to fire at the demonstrators. This was tantamount to politicizing the army, which refused to permit Bhutto's excesses once it was felt that the regime's policies would divide the military institution from within. Three army brigadiers reportedly resigned because their troops refused to engage in killing the anti-Bhutto demonstrators. Obviously Bhutto had failed to convince the military that the opposition movement was a conspiracy against the state. The episode of the brigadiers' resignations worried senior generals about Bhutto's politicization of the military and the damage inflicted on its organizational norms and ethos. The prime minister had got into the habit of discussing the political situation with the top generals. In addition, General Gul says about Bhutto's politicization of the army:

His recognized link with the Army was the Chief of Staff, but every Tom, Dick, and Harry who was a corps commander, and at times even PSOs, was commanded to attend these [Bhutto's] deliberations. This was a fatal blunder on Bhutto's part: he was, for his own ends, politicizing the Army and, worse still, unconsciously furnishing the generals with an opportunity to witness the insecurity that had gripped him.[36]

From a command and control perspective, civilian governments have never been able to muster effective control over the armed forces. This is a situation attributable to the peculiar nature of Pakistan's sociology and politics and will be discussed in the following section.

The Military–State–Society Relationship

Pakistan's military is a coercive arm of the state not just in terms of its security policy, but also in domestic policy. The military has always been deployed to perform a policing function domestically. The military was coercively deployed in East Pakistan (1971), Baluchistan (1973; 2005 onwards), rural Sindh (1985), and urban Sindh (1990s).

Although most of such deployment took place under military rule, what is more significant is that the army was used in Baluchistan in 1973 under the popular representative government of Zulfiqar Ali Bhutto, and under Benazir Bhutto's government during the mid-1990s in Karachi and elsewhere in urban Sindh. This pattern is indicative of the authoritarian nature of the country's politics and a sense among the ruling elite that any popular uprising must be crushed by force to keep intact a centralized state. Over the years, the state has grown to represent the combined interest of the dominant classes. The state, as argued by Hamza Alavi, plays a central role in the interests of the three dominant classes: the feudal landed class, the indigenous bourgeoisie, and the metropolitan bourgeoisie. These three groups constitute the ruling power bloc that competes in the framework of peripheral capitalism.[37] While some form of the capitalist mode of production and distribution was introduced in the form of post-colonial capital, the pre-capitalist system remains intact.[38] The military's stakes are intertwined with those of the three groups, making it imperative for them to protect each other's interests. The dependence of the dominant classes on the military does not allow the civilian institutions to control the military in the same way as the military infiltrates civilian institutions.

Pakistan's socio-political system has evolved to allow the ruling elite to co-habit with the military, which has also evolved into an independent class. The armed forces have both financial and political autonomy that empowers them to establish their hegemony over the state and society. The military also has deep economic interests, exemplified by its 6–7 per cent stake in total private sector assets.[39] This economic role is not benign, but rather provides for a commonality of interests among the ruling elite, of which the military forms a part. The domination of the state and financial resources are two core objectives of the ruling class.

The conflict in Baluchistan under the Bhutto and Musharraf regimes is an example of how elite interests have impacted the state's policy-making and relations between the Centre and the provinces. Under Bhutto, the conflict in Baluchistan erupted into competition between the ruling elite in Islamabad and the indigenous elite of Baluchistan. In this case, the military was deployed to accommodate the power interest of the Bhutto regime. Although a civilian leader, Zulfiqar Ali Bhutto had chosen to deploy the armed forces to eliminate all elements that challenged his power. The military deployment under Musharraf denotes a role reversal in which the military decided to use force to protect its own interests along with those of its civilian cronies. The resource-rich province offered economic possibilities for the dominant classes, and therefore it was imperative to grant excessive power to the indigenous elite. The military's political clout and its ability to determine state–society relations will remain unchallenged unless national political forces muster sufficient political capital to effect mass mobilization and bring about effective political change.

Sri Lanka

Sri Lankans are proud of having adhered to democratic norms and maintaining civilian control over the defence establishment. On paper, the military takes its orders from the civilian leadership. The armed forces serve as a tool used by politicians to further their political interests. The political leadership's dependence on military force, however, has not had the same results as in Pakistan. The command and control structure is dominated by civilians. However, the military is extremely important in the state's politics. The symbiotic relationship between military force and political power that we find in Pakistan's case is apparent in Sri Lanka too. The structure of the military's management and the links between political forces and the military in Sri Lanka are also products of the circumstances in which the country was born.

In reviewing the military's role in Sri Lanka, a distinction must be drawn between the Colombo-managed system and that in the north-east. This is not to suggest that the military is less relevant to the sociology and politics of the north-east. In fact, in the country's north-east the political and military structures are tightly combined. This section of the chapter will look at both the structures and see how the relevance of the armed forces and military power have grown over the years, thus giving greater prominence to the military.

The Politics of Managing the Armed Forces without a Professional Military

A discussion on Sri Lanka's management of defence is a complex issue because the debate cannot be limited to the Colombo-controlled armed forces. The Liberation Tigers of Tamil Eelam (LTTE) exercised control over the northern and eastern parts of the country (until 2004 when the Karuna faction in the east defected; later the LTTE was militarily defeated and its leadership eliminated in May 2009). Over the years, it managed to develop its own military and administrative infrastructure, which must be brought into the discussion. Therefore, this section of the chapter will analyse the military's role in politics and policymaking in two distinct parts of the country prior to the defeat of the Tamil Tigers.

The Armed Forces of the Government of Sri Lanka

The military in Sri Lanka is central to the imagination of the dominant political class. The armed forces were deployed on various occasions to deal with issues of internal security. In fact, the internal political problems of the state have created a self-serving justification for the presence and growth of military power in the country. A glance at Sri Lanka's chaotic political history raises the fundamental question of why the armed forces have not usurped power. The answer lies in the fact that the Sri Lankan military did not evolve as a professional force. It continues to operate more like a police force whose task is that of coercing groups challenging the unitary character of the state or demanding a more egalitarian distribution of power and resources. The military has adhered to the role of coercion on behalf of the ruling class/ethnic group and seeks advantages for itself within this framework. In addition to the specific structure of the armed forces, the military was kept away from controlling governance by encouraging factionalism within the ranks and the officer cadre.

Maintained under the British primarily for ceremonial purpose, the 6,000-man army at the time of independence grew into an approximately 150,000-man force. The total number of the armed forces was around 350,000 in 2009.[40] The increase in numbers is, however, not proportionate to any well-defined and clearly spelt out strategy. Although the retired and serving officers get extremely perturbed at the mention of a ceremonial role, the fact is that the military was assigned tasks in an extremely arbitrary fashion. Its expansion was driven by political concerns to fight intra-state conflict and to enforce the state's writ over the society.

The structure of the armed forces was dictated by the political agenda of the ruling elite. The political and religious leadership used the armed forces as a coercive tool to implement orders and enforce rules and regulations suited to the interests of the elite. A professional armed force was therefore not in the interest of the ruling class. Thus, the ceremonial military was deployed since 1956 to perform internal security functions and enforce policies without any thought given to the management of this organization. After 1956, when the army was used to quell a strike, it was deployed both in the country's south and the north-east to suppress any political dissent. The military was used to quell the unrest in the Sinhalese-dominated south, where the youth had rebelled against the central government in 1971. Unlike the north-east, the southern rebels were driven by a Marxist–socialist ideology, demanding greater job opportunities and economic uplift. Given that the ruling elite did not have a clear development or political agenda, they did not employ political methods to handle the unrest. Sri Lanka was clearly another example in South Asia of ethnic identity not being a cementing factor in forming a state, or maintaining stability in the country. The military massacred about 60,000 youth during the political unrest in the south in 1971. Since 1982–3, the defence forces were also used against the Tamil uprising in the north-east.[41]

The framework for the management of the armed forces is based on the 1972 constitution that upholds the principle of a unitary state. The subsequent 1978 constitution also defined the character of the political system as presidential. An excessively powerful president was intended to ensure the integrity of a unitary state controlled by the Sinhalese–Buddhist majority community. As a strong president was intended to ensure the stability of the state, the incumbent was appointed the supreme commander of the armed forces and the source of all political power. Traditionally, the Sri Lankan president has always retained the defence portfolio and is superior to any institution governing the military. Figure 4.2 shows that the president is at the head of the decision-making hierarchy.

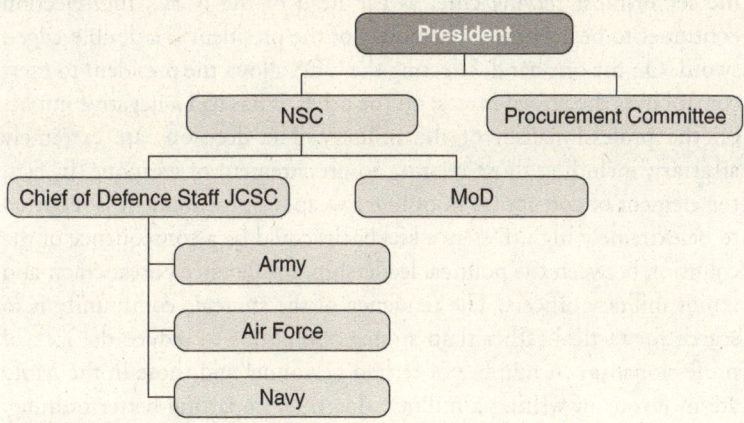

FIGURE 4.2   Sri Lanka: Military's Command and Control
Source: Author's own formulation.

The Sri Lankan defence policymaking system does not have the concept of an independent minister of defence. Traditionally, the portfolio is with the president. The only exception was in 2002 when the elected government was allowed to have a defence minister, but the president, Chandrika Kumaratunga, reversed the decision and re-acquired the portfolio. She was apparently dissatisfied with the performance of the minister concerned. It is nonetheless true that in the politically predatory system that prevails in Sri Lanka, it is vital for those at the helm of state affairs, which in this case is the president, to control the principal instrument of violence—the armed forces.

According to Figure 4.2, the president is superior to all institutional arrangements that manage the defence sector. The president is also the head of the NSC. Other members include the prime minister, the service chiefs, and the police advisor. The council meets as often as twice a week, especially when there are important issues. There is also a JCSC headed by a general. The chairman of the committee is selected by the president, as are the three service chiefs. In addition, there is the procurement committee constituted by the NSC. This committee can be asked by the president to review weapons procurement decisions.

The excessive power in the hands of the president is a deliberate design to maintain a certain balance of power within the state. Successive presidents have retained the power to select and appoint the head of the JCSC, also known as the chief of the defence staff (CDS). Although the three service chiefs had agreed in 2003 on a formula to appoint the senior-most serving chief as the head of the JCSC, the selection continues to be arbitrary. The power of the president is a double-edged sword. On the one hand, selecting the CDS allows the president to exert control over the armed forces; on the other, it has had a negative impact on the professionalism of the military. The decisions are extremely arbitrary, including those relating to procurement of weapons. In fact, the element of corruption in military weapons procurement is reported to be extremely high. Defence kickbacks could be a consequence of the collusion between the political leadership, the defence bureaucracy, and senior military officers. The tendency of the strategic community is to search for tactical rather than strategic solutions to reduce the lack of professionalism. A number of retired personnel and those in the MoD are in favour of writing a military doctrine, imparting better training, and introducing new concepts. There are even those who speak of deterrence without specifying the manner in which the concept will apply to Sri Lanka.

However, the discussion about professionalizing the defence forces stops short of highlighting the need for strategic changes, such as correcting the balance of power in terms of politics and policymaking in the country. There does not appear to be the possibility of a president voluntarily agreeing to the curtailment of his/her power. Former president Chandrika Kumaratunga had won the elections in 1994 on the basis of her election agenda to talk peace with the Tamils, which meant opening up to a federal solution, and reducing the excessive powers of the president. However, when it came to taking concrete action, she reneged on her promises.

The management of the armed forces is a reflection of the overall political nature of the state. The Sri Lankan state, as written into the

1972 constitution, is dominated by the socio-political ethos of the Sinhalese Buddhist majority. The issue of the excessive power in the hands of the president is interlinked with the larger political problem of a unitary state dominated by the Sinhalese Buddhists.[42] As there is a lack of consensus on changing the character of the state and devolving power to empower the Tamil minority, there is very little movement to reduce the powers of the president. The entire issue of restructuring defence is, therefore, part of the larger problem of the excessive power in the hands of the president and alteration in the unitary character of the state.

The dominance of the Sinhalese majority is also a feature of the armed forces. Since the creation of the military from 1949–51, the ethnic composition of the armed forces also changed. Rather than being representative of all ethnic groups, the military became an exclusively Sinhalese force. This led to an attempted coup in 1962. A group of civil servants led by Douglas Liyanage, in collusion with some members of the armed forces and the Catholic community, sought to seize power in protest against the socialist political structure and Sinhalization of the state. These officers were trained in elite English-medium schools and were members of the middle class. The failure of the coup had its repercussions, beginning with the change in the ethnic and class composition of the armed forces. After 1962, minority ethnic groups were pushed out of the military. Also, the class composition began to change. Today, about 95 per cent of the military personnel are from among lower middle-class Sinhalese.[43] These people, like the rest of the Sinhalese community, desire a unified state for the Sinhalese and have little sympathy for any federal arrangement proposed by the Tamil community or the LTTE.

The Politics of Power

As far as civil–military relations in Sri Lanka are concerned, it is primarily the first paradigm that applies. The military is embedded in policymaking as a tool of repression and coercion. Since the creation of the state in 1948, there have been two noticeable characteristics of the country's politics. First, there was a gradual abandonment of the principles of secularism and multi-ethnicity. Although the state's formation is not declared to be on religious grounds, Buddhism was granted a special place in the 1972 constitution. Moreover, successive leaders have surrendered to the power of Buddhist monks and Sinhalese nationalists. Consequently, the Sinhalese ethnicity of the Sri Lankan state is extremely pronounced.

The ethnic nature of politics becomes most apparent in the way that the conflict with the Tamil minority is being handled. The smouldering problem between the Sinhalese and Tamils erupted in July 1983. The killing of a few police officials in the north provoked a backlash against the Tamil population in the capital and the southern part of the country. This was the beginning of a war that shook the Sri Lankan state and challenged its stability. The military was used in a coercive role to curb even unarmed protestors. In the north-east, the Sinhalese military has an image of a fascist force against which the common people need security. However, other ethnic groups, such as the Muslims in the east or the Sinhalese in Colombo or areas other than the south, view the armed forces more positively. The relationship of civil society and the general public with the armed forces largely depends on the ethnicity and political stance of the group concerned.

The armed conflict in Sri Lanka appeared to be unending until the LTTE was finally defeated in 2009. The political leadership, especially in the south, had not reached, as one commentator claimed, a psychological stalemate. There was a lack of enthusiasm to consider or debate federalism as an option. This stalemate continued notwithstanding the fact that Colombo was forced to review its hard-line position in 2002 and sign a ceasefire agreement (CFA) with the LTTE. This was after the Tamil Tigers managed to destroy both civil and military aircraft at the country's only international airport. This affected the tourist trade and had an adverse impact on the economy, forcing the Sinhalese leaders to consider talking to the LTTE. The majority of the Sinhalese leaders tended to look at the conflict largely as a terrorist issue that ought to be resolved through force. A number of former officials and analysts interviewed in Colombo appeared pessimistic about the political developments. Political experts, such as Jayadeva Uyangoda, were indeed of the view that the LTTE had demonstrated a comparatively greater political vision through its 2003 interim self-governance proposal than the government of Sri Lanka (GOSL).[44] Although the Sinhalese leaders sought restoration of peace and order in the country, there was hardly any clarity regarding the concept of federalism. The current President Mahinda Rajapakse had spoken in March 2006 of the political arrangement (devolution) prevalent in the UK.[45] Nevertheless, such an approach was unacceptable to the Tamils who continued to speak of greater autonomy.

Under the circumstances, the military appeared to exploit the Sinhalese fear of a federal structure politically dividing the country into two self-governed divisions. There was indeed much hyperbole in defence circles regarding the conventional capabilities of the Tamils. The fact that the LTTE had its own navy and had developed limited airpower was debated as a reason for the Sri Lankan armed forces to strengthen their capability. Interestingly, some people like General R. D'Silva also speak of the threat posed by India to justify the development of a larger deterrence capacity. D'Silva suggested a naval expansion. A stronger navy, in the general's view, was necessary to counter the threat posed by the Sea Tigers, particularly to counter the smuggling of illicit weapons.[46] D'Silva is among a number of retired senior military officers who have formed an association of retired flag officers. Their purpose is to influence the government's policy on national security and lobby for defence restructuring with the objective of making the defence establishment more professional. Indeed, D'Silva's paper on the war in the north-east fixes responsibility for the political losses in the conflict zone on tactical military failures.[47] However, his approach is tactical too. It examines the issue of war and conflict largely in military terms. The influence of this approach has resonated in other circles too. In 2003, the government appointed a group to restructure the armed forces with the intention of professionalizing them. The idea was to have a more efficient force that could effectively achieve the GOSL's military objectives.[48]

Others, such as Sanjay Colonne, an advisor appointed by President Chandrika Kumaratunge to the MoD, spoke about deterrence in terms of defending the exclusive economic zone (EEZ). Trained in Singapore, Colonne appeared impressed by that country and believed that Sri Lanka should have a strong line of defence as Singapore has.[49] In fact, a number of people from the strategic community who were interviewed seemed inclined to strengthen military security. A senior serving officer from the Special Task Force (STF) was of the view that the military was strong enough to take on the LTTE in a war. Government officials and the strategic community spoke of a military threat and military solutions rather than a larger political problem.

The search for professionalism is taking the strategic community towards an expansion of the military's role with greater reference to external threats. For example, in the course of the interviews conducted during research for this essay, there were frequent references to India's bid to divide Sri Lanka into two independent states. Retired senior bureaucrats, such as K. Godage and several others, believe that New Delhi would have been able to achieve such objectives had it not been for the weapons supply to Sri Lanka from Pakistan and China.[50] Such elements seek military professionalism as the key to securing the Sri Lankan state. However, there is little thought given to the fact that in the absence of political solutions and a stronger political consensus, a professional military could evolve into a threat to the state. Moreover, the enunciation of an external threat is based on finding an external role for the armed forces. The underlying assumption is that an external threat–oriented military will expand the state's role in regional geopolitics. However, the Frederic Lane paradigm does not apply to Sri Lanka. Given the state of internal insecurity and the size and professionalism of its military, the defence forces cannot be used for taking on external threat and external colonization, which, as Lane argued, may provide financial benefit to the state and major internal economic stakeholders.

The Liberation Tigers of Tamil Eelam

A discussion on Sri Lanka will be incomplete without talking about the parallel military structure and relevant civil–military relations in what were once the Tamil-controlled north-eastern regions. Although the LTTE does not remain the force it was after the killing of Velupillai Prabhakaran in May 2009, the years of LTTE control demand analysis, principally to understand the power–political culture that prevailed for two decades. It will certainly take years of democratic rule and good governance for the area to emerge from the psyche created by the LTTE's control. Also, the continued unsympathetic approach of the Sinhala-controlled government may not help bring about a change. According to recent reports, the Sri Lankan army chief was summoned in 2009 by the US Federal Bureau of Investigation (FBI) for questioning regarding his links to the killing of innocent Tamils during war with the LTTE.[51]

The Organization of Violence

The LTTE, which was the prime military and political organization in the north-east, is worth studying as it dominated politics and also had military control over the region It was a guerrilla force that had, over the years, also developed limited conventional capabilities. The best overview of the military structure of the LTTE is provided in M.R. Narayan Swamy's biography of LTTE leader Prabhakaran, and D.R. Karthikeyan and Radhavinod Raju's account of the investigation of the Rajiv Gandhi assassination. Figure 4.3 will show that the Tamil

Tigers were organized like a force with eight area commanders and intelligence and procurement wings.[52]

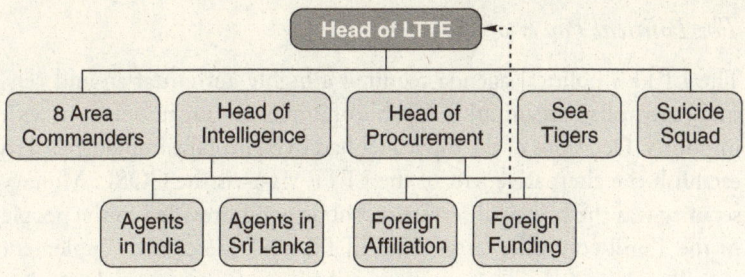

FIGURE 4.3   LTTE: Command and Control

Source: Author's own formulation.

The intelligence unit operated within the LTTE-controlled areas as well as in other countries such as India. The assassination of Rajiv Gandhi was in fact carried out through a carefully planned and dedicated intelligence operation by operatives based in India.[53] The mission was the handiwork of members of a separate group called the 'Black Tigers', a special group trained for suicide attack missions. It had special status and was one of the most coveted wings of the LTTE. In addition, there were the Sea Tigers and a small air force with a limited capacity.

The military structure of the LTTE was extremely centralized and subservient to Prabhakaran's personal control. The LTTE leader was said to have once controlled a force of about 7,000 people.[54] The leader kept the force unified using fear and coercion. Reportedly, there were many instances in which those who did not obey Prabhakaran were eliminated. The LTTE appears to have been an extremely disciplined force. People who left were careful to remain silent, and in any event would have been unable to leave without a valid reason.

In many respects, the force seemed initially less factionalized than the armed forces of the GOSL. This was due to the clarity of mission and centralized control. However, there was a rift when the eastern commander, Colonel Karuna, defected in March 2004 and challenged Prabhakaran's authority. The disagreement was on the division of spoils between the north and the east. This defection played a major role in Prabhakaran's ultimate downfall. Furthermore, the alienation of the Muslim population living in the eastern region also resulted in divisions that did not benefit the LTTE militarily or politically. Centralized control and coercion was a costly approach in the long-run, resulting in the Tamil Tigers losing potential allies.

The Political Power of Violence

The LTTE's political agenda required a highly authoritarian and centrally controlled organization capable of implementing its decisions with impunity. Decisions of the top leader had to be brutally implemented to establish the alternative writ of the LTTE vis-à-vis the GOSL. Military security was the principal service or public good provided to the people in the Tamil-controlled areas. The LTTE used coercion to implement its will and control over a certain area. Military force was used to extort money and levy taxes. Over the years, this was the only service that the organization was able to provide. Analysts are of the view that the destruction caused by the tsunami of 26 December 2004 exposed Prabhakaran's inability to provide any other service to his people.[55] Such an inability, of course, bred resentment. The LTTE leadership tried to address the problem by negotiating for greater autonomy in the north and east. Such short-term concessions were intended to deal with internal political problems. Prabhakaran actually used a two-track approach to cope with the internal problems of power politics. While offering a few carrots to the dissenters, his central emphasis was on building his military strength to a degree that would impress both the GOSL and internal stakeholders. Developing air power, for instance, consolidated Prabhakaran's position versus both the external enemy and internal power challengers. The ability to acquire air power, though limited and symbolic, established his reputation as a leader who had vision and could muster the resources necessary to improve the only service provided by the LTTE—security. As he had succeeded in organizing a successful militant force and resisted the Sri Lankan state, the political structure had necessarily to be highly centralized. In an interview, the LTTE leader spoke about an Eelam where politics would be run through a single party.[56] The proposed political structure[57] was one of a fascist state with centralized control. In this context, the design or the outcome of the design would not be more than marginally different from that of the GOSL.

Prabhakaran's violent death and the defeat of the LTTE in May 2009 proved that centrally controlled power structures are bound to eventually crack because of their lack of adaptability. The comparative cases of the Taliban in Afghanistan and Pakistan's tribal areas also demonstrate that cracks are bound to appear in centralized structures, resulting in a break-up of the group or death of its leader. However, the lingering influence of centralized ultranationalist/fascist politics on political behaviour is something that will continue to haunt Sri Lanka, especially the Tamil-dominated areas.

BANGLADESH

The year 2007 saw the Bangladeshi military gently creep into politics by playing an indirect role. This was after the Bangladeshis were generally of the view that the armed forces, humiliated in 1990, would not return to politics. However, what no one anticipated was a situation in which the ruling elite would want the military to play a role in defence of democracy and to save the country from the constant and endless bickering of the two principal political parties, the Awami League (AL) and the Bangladesh National Party (BNP). For the majority, this was thought to be impossible because the Bangladeshi military was comfortably preoccupied with United Nations peace-keeping missions.

While shunning the idea of future military intervention or even the army's indirect involvement in politics, Bangladeshis would proudly underscore their difference from Pakistan, a praetorian state to which the Bangladeshis once belonged and which has seen repeated military intervention. What was even more intriguing was the fact that the military's latest intervention in politics was based on a civil–military partnership in which the upcoming middle class was trying to oust the traditional ruling elite through the use of force rather than political means. The gradually increasing conservatism and radicalization of the society, especially at the level of the lower and lower-middle classes, growing disenchantment with India and the larger neighbour's attempts at arm-twisting, improved links with Pakistan, and the influence of militant organizations that have begun operating in Bangladesh too, are some of the factors that have increased militarism in the society and consequently increased the military's overall influence. There was even a failed coup attempt in 1996. The military failed then because of its structure. As it had still not evolved into a fully developed hierarchical entity like Pakistan's, the coup-makers had little chance. Those marching towards Dhaka had not taken into confidence the troops securing the capital city.

For many Bangladeshis, 6 December 1990 marks a political watershed. The ruling army agreed to withdraw to barracks in the face of a popular uprising. Military dictator General Hossain Muhammad Ershad's resignation as Bangladesh's president in 1990 paved the way for the re-establishment of democracy. Since then, the military has not attempted a return to power and the process of change in civilian governments has been smooth. From the perspective of a transitional democracy, Bangladesh can seemingly boast of a good track record of pushing the military out of politics. Notwithstanding its chaotic politics, the armed forces are firmly under the control of the civilian government. However, the apparent strengthening of democracy in the country also indicates a fundamental shift in civil–military relations. The military seems to have conceded civilian supremacy in exchange for the political governments ensuring the security of the organization's corporate interests. Today, the military in Bangladesh has greater prominence in terms of its share of the economic resources of the state and its place in power politics. The military's status as an equal partner in running the state is owed to the particular nature of civil–military relations, which can be explained by looking at the history of the evolution of the Bangladeshi state.

The following sections will analyse the current system of the military's command and control and the evolution of civil–military relations in the country.

Management of the Defence Sector

The Bangladeshi military appears to be firmly under the control of the civilian government, especially the Prime Minister's Office (PMO). The three branches of the armed forces—army, navy, and air force—and the intelligence agencies are controlled by the PMO (Figure 4.4). The PMO, which is currently the central controlling nerve of the armed forces, has a principal staff officer (PSO) (of the rank of a major general) and the Armed Forces Division (AFD) representing the three services of the military. The presence of these officers in the PMO and in critical positions means considerable military influence. The PSO assists the prime minister in defence decision-making, including weapons procurement. The AFD represents an interface between the PMO and the armed forces. In the AFD, the army is represented by an officer of the rank of a brigadier, the navy by a commodore, and the air force by an air commodore. Besides the PSO and the AFD, the PMO also controls the National Security Intelligence (NSI), which is the primary intelligence organization of the state. The other intelligence establishment, the Directorate-General of Forces Intelligence (DGFI), is controlled by the MoD. As the prime minister is also the defence minister, the office-bearer is under the PMO.

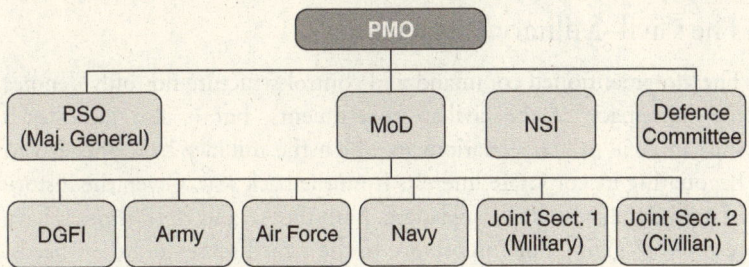

FIGURE 4.4   Bangladesh: Military's Command and Control
Source: Author's own formulation.

The significance of the PMO in defence decision-making is owed to the political changes which took place during the 1990s when Bangladesh changed its system from the presidential to the parliamentary form of democracy. According to Bangladeshi political analyst Amena Mohsin, the leaders of the AL and the BNP—Sheikh Hasina Wazed and Begum Khaleda Zia respectively—adopted a hands-on role for the armed forces by shifting the control from the president's office to that of the prime minister.[58] Originally, the AFD, which was established in 1977 under the regime of General Zia-ur-Rehman, President, as the commander-in-chief's headquarters and later turned into the president's headquarters during the military government, was brought under the control of the PMO.[59]

After 1996, successive prime ministers have also strengthened their control over the military by keeping the MoD weak and instead boosting the power of the PMO. The principal strength of the MoD is the two joint secretaries, one civilian and one military. While the civilian joint secretary is responsible for military land and budget, the second joint secretary is responsible for training and expenditure. Clearly, the MoD is confined to mundane matters such as pay and pension, retirement, and other budgetary issues. It is also responsible for related departments such as the survey of Bangladesh, military electricity supply (MES), and the meteorological department. According to Major General Mehbub-ur-Rehman, the former chief of the army staff (May 1996–December 1997), who had served as chairman of the Standing Committee of Parliament on Ministry of Defence, the core issues relating to defence are discussed by the defence committee headed by the prime minister.[60] The committee comprises of ten members and its meetings are held in camera.

The Civil–Military Partnership

The aforementioned command and control structure not only denotes the supremacy of the civilian governments, but it also indicates a shift in civil–military relations in which the military has conceded to negotiating its corporate interests from the back seat. Given the history of military takeovers in Bangladesh, both the AL and BNP regimes have resorted to giving due importance to the armed forces and their needs. Consequently, the defence budget has been sustained at a higher level. According to Amena Mohsin's study, the BNP and AL governments, on an average, have allocated 16 per cent and 19 per cent of government expenditure to defence, respectively. In addition, new institutions such as the National Defence College have also been established to train senior military officers.[61]

This, however, is not the full extent of the civilian regimes supporting the military's corporate interests. Since the 1980s, the military has also expanded its reach in the economy. According to the economic and political affairs officer representing the European Union, Zillul Hye Razi, the military is prominent in certain key sectors of the economy.[62] The armed forces welfare foundation is now in the hotel business with stakes in the Radisson Hotel in Dhaka. Besides, the Sena Kalyan Sangstha, the military's welfare foundation, runs a flour mill, an ice cream factory, a hosiery mill, a fabric manufacturing factory, a textile factory, a CNG project, a bread and confectionery factory, an electrical products manufacturing unit, and a television manufacturing plant, and has stakes in real estate.[63] Although the welfare foundation was an inheritance from the Pakistan days when the Fauji Foundation had established businesses in the Eastern wing of united Pakistan, the actual boost to the military's role in the corporate sector came under the regime of General H.M. Ershad, who encouraged the military's profit-making ventures to acquire financial autonomy for the armed forces.[64] Today, the military is not a significant player in the commercial sector, but its presence in business has been gradually increasing and seems to have grown as a result of the flow of revenue made possible by the UN peace-keeping missions. In fact, the UN peacekeeping missions are an essential part of the Bangladeshi military's corporate interests.

According to one estimate, about 40,000 troops have served on UN peace-keeping missions and there are about 11,000 troops serving on such missions at any given time.[65] Part of the earnings from the UN peace-keeping missions is diverted towards the projects of the welfare foundation. Some observers believe that as long as the military gets its extra funds from the UN peace-keeping missions, the institution will not be tempted to look inside the country for additional resources. However, several interviewees in Bangladesh did not speak of the impact of allowing the military to penetrate the corporate sector. Not much thought is given to this, especially in dealing with a situation when the earnings from the UN dry up.

The comment regarding the impossibility of the military trying to take over the state to further its corporate interests indicates a certain quid pro quo between the civilian governments and the military leadership.[66] Providing the military extra-budgetary resources is essential to keep it happy, especially given the fact that the Bangladeshi military has enjoyed direct power for a number of years between 1975 and 1990. Even the apparently ideologically more progressive parties such as the AL tend to accommodate the military's corporate interests, such as giving control of Khulna Shipyard to the navy and the Machine Tool Factory to the army.[67] Such a move also represents the confidence of the political leadership and the society in the discipline and order that the armed forces have to run and revive sick industrial units. However, the fact remains that the military in Bangladesh has penetrated the society, economy, and politics, both directly and indirectly. The indirect penetration, which takes the form of a greater number of retired military personnel joining political parties and running for elections to parliament or being absorbed in the private sector, bolsters the military's overall influence. According to Bangladeshi security and political analyst, Abdur Rob Khan, both political parties try to placate the armed forces by giving the latter a greater institutional role and accommodating its retired members.[68] It is necessary to keep the military satisfied because the armed forces are a conservative institution that inherited a number of traditions from their parent institution, the Pakistan military. A large proportion of the Bangladeshi armed forces consisted of personnel who were repatriated from Pakistan after Bangladesh's independence in 1971. At the time of the partition and afterwards, the Bangladeshi military consisted of 55,000 personnel, of which 28,000 were repatriated from Pakistan (including 1,100 officers).[69] These personnel had not gone through the experience of the liberation war and had a different mindset from the freedom fighters who were part of the Mukti Bahini. As the prominent Bangladeshi political scientist Talukder Maniruzzaman points out about the Pakistani military, 'The armed forces' leadership [during the united Pakistan days] was an elite group, with high salaries and entrenched privileges.'[70] As it appears from the country's history, the repatriated officers of the Bangladesh armed forces aligned with the politically conservative elements to strengthen control over the state and the society. This is obvious from the first military takeover in 1975. Bangladeshi military commanders from the days of the struggle for independence, such as Colonel (retd) Usman Chaudhry, were of the view that General Zia-ur-Rehman was brought into power to fight the influence of the leftist elements in the armed forces and the country.[71] The leftist party, Jatiyo Samajtantrik Dal (JSD), was popular amongst the soldiers and freedom fighters, and it supported the idea of a people's army. Maniruzzaman was of the view that the repatriated officers, in particular, were looking for an officer such as Zia-ur-Rehman who could take over the army and the country and thwart the efforts of the JSD, a party which was unhappy with Sheikh Mujib's rule and his controversial policies, such as using military force against the Naxalite (extreme left) forces.[72]

However, the JSD was not necessarily behind Sheikh Mujib's assassination. It was one of the three principal political factions in the country and was known for its leftist political agenda and popular slogans such as 'sepoys are brothers'.[73] The other two factions were: (i) the freedom fighters and (ii) those responsible for killing Mujib in August 1975. The assassination took the JSD completely by surprise and pushed the country towards chaos. The conservative elements saw this as an opportunity to take control of the affairs of the state. One of the army generals, Major General Khaled Musharraf saw this as an opportunity to take control of the presidency on 3 November 1975 and imprison the army chief, Major General Zia-ur-Rehman, who was later rescued by the JSD supporters in the army and installed in power after some infighting in the army.[74]

Zia's takeover at the end of 1975 did not, however, represent the success of JSD ideology. The army chief-turned-president gradually brought conservatism into the social and political discourse, which included encouraging the religious parties which were held responsible for the massacre of Bengalis during the liberation war. Zia-ur-Rehman introduced the fifth amendment to the 1972 constitution which allowed religious parties, such as the Jamaat-i-Islami, to operate. The members of the Jamaat were among the many who were politically ostracized after the passage of the 'Collaborators Act' by Sheikh Mujib in 1973 with the objective of punishing those who had colluded with the Pakistan army. It is also a fact, as highlighted by social and political activist Sultana Kemal, that several collaborators went scot-free notwithstanding the passage of the aforementioned law.[75]

Was this leniency towards collaborators accidental or deliberate? A deeper look into the history of Bangladeshi politics shows that the political leadership, including founding father Sheikh Mujib, did not make much of an effort to push back the regressive forces. State policies during Sheikh Mujib's rule did not indicate a break from the pre-independence days. The regime used military force to curb leftist movements in certain parts of the country. Political power was concentrated in the hands of one man, Sheikh Mujib,[76] and there was rampant corruption. In fact, Mujib tried to consolidate power by establishing a paramilitary force, which was provided with greater funds for institutional development than the armed forces, and proposing a single-party system. These policies showed that Mujib was basically a successful political activist and agitator with no clear vision about how to bring about a fundamental change in the tenor of politics. Therefore, the socio-political and economic conditions deteriorated. The move towards establishing a paramilitary force without restructuring the military was a major error that was instrumental in creating unrest amongst the armed forces, eventually leading to some military officers conspiring to kill the founding father of Bangladesh.

During the course of this research, an interesting document was found. This was the minutes of the meeting of the formation commander's conference held at the Bangladesh forces headquarters on 2 January 1972 in which the commander-in-chief of the armed forces discussed the prime minister's directions to the army GHQ to form a national militia. The idea was to have a people's army as a second line of defence to support a small standing military. The plans were, however, never implemented largely because, as claimed by Major General (retd) Shafeeullah, Mujib tended to leave defence issues to the military.[77] Moreover, the military was allowed to become dissatisfied by the growing significance of the paramilitary force, the Rakhi Bahini. While subscribing to the aforementioned view, Major General (retd) Azizur Rehman added that there was a fear among the officers that the army would possibly be disbanded and replaced by the Rakhi Bahini which had grown in power and influence and was notorious for its involvement in smuggling and other illegal acts.[78] Although political activist and an old colleague of Sheikh Mujib, Kemal Hossain was of the view that the rise of Rakhi Bahini's power was due to the reluctance of the armed forces to accommodate the freedom fighters or the irregulars,[79] the truth is that there was deep discontent amongst the armed forces. In addition, the high-handedness of Mujib's relatives, who used their association with the nation's top leader for private gain, further aggravated the situation.

General Zia-ur-Rehman's takeover in 1975 after Sheikh Mujib's assassination strengthened the politically regressive forces. Zia, in fact, aimed at strengthening his own political position and authority by aligning with elements that did not want a socialist political system in the country. Encouraging the religious parties was also a move towards consolidating power and for a coalition of political forces to counter the popularity of the AL. As in the case of Pakistani military dictators, it was necessary for Zia-ur-Rehman to seek out partners who could help him challenge the political legitimacy of the AL and counter the memories of Sheikh Mujib.

The partnership-building was both formal and informal. While informal refers to encouraging religious forces and other anti-liberation forces, formal coalition building relates to seeking alignments through the establishment of political parties such as the BNP. The party was created in 1978 with Zia-ur-Rehman as its chairman. The BNP was the 'King's' party which sought out political leaders to gain political legitimacy. In return, these politicians enjoyed all the benefits of aligning with the ruling party. Such a party-building approach suffered from the same drawbacks as any other military regime–supported dispensation. One of the problems, for example, was factionalism.[80]

While building coalitions, General Zia also sought support from the anti-liberation forces and pushed back elements that proposed a change in the political system. The freedom fighters, in particular, were a different breed of people who sought just such a radical change in politics. Therefore, according to Shafeeullah, by 1981, 70 per cent of the freedom fighters in the army were killed. This was possible due to the rampant factionalism and political divisions in the armed forces which were clearly divided between the repatriated officers and the freedom fighters. The 17 attempted coups that took place in the military between 1975 and 1981 provided an opportunity for the regressive forces to rid themselves of the freedom fighters.[81]

Such divisions in the army were not anomalous, and represented the nature of the armed forces. The presence of freedom fighters, who were directly involved in the liberation war and were therefore responsible for the creation of Bangladesh, gave the military a revolutionary character. Revolutionary militaries, as is obvious from the literature on the armed forces, are given to factionalism and are vulnerable to coup attempts. The Bangladeshi military during the 1970s and the 1980s was certainly not a professional force but an amalgam of revolutionary personnel and professionally trained personnel but with a praetorian mindset.

The first successful coup attempt came in 1981 when General Ershad replaced Zia-ur-Rehman after the later was assassinated. Observers believe that certain forces in the country did not want to see Zia bring about changes in the political system that would consolidate civilian rule in the country.[82]

The Ershad years are known for further factionalism in society, greater authoritarianism, and institutionalization of the military's role in politics and society. Although the military had to retreat in 1990 in the face of popular unrest, these were the years that created conditions that made it imperative for civilian regimes to seriously negotiate with the military and grant the organization certain advantages. Besides, the failed coup attempt by some military commanders in 1996 made the civilian leadership even more conscious of the importance of keeping the armed forces happy. The coup attempt was a reaction to President Abdur Rahman Biswas's removal of the army chief, Lt General Naseem, and two other senior generals, Major General G.H. Morshed Khan and Brigadier Miran Hamidur Rahman. The president had taken this decision by invoking the power conferred on him through the 13th Amendment to the constitution. Although this amendment, which empowered the president to appoint a caretaker government, was challenged by a number of political parties, the fact remains that the president was authorized to sack the army chief. The key player in the attempted coup was Major General Hilal Morshid who conspired with some other commanders to move forces to Dhaka. However, his action led to friction in the armed forces which were divided about the idea of overthrowing a civilian president, and this also resulted in the failure of the coup attempt. This failure, according to Mohsin's study, is owed to the fact that the Dhaka-based 46th brigade of the army, which is outside the regular chain of command of the military, was not privy to the plan. This peculiar command and control structure was the handiwork of General Zia-ur-Rahman who had faced 17 coup attempts during his rule as president.[83] The sacked army chief, Lt General Naseem claimed that he did not perpetrate an act of rebellion against the civilian government, which makes experts such as Rehman Sobhan claim less than credibly that the 1996 incident was not a coup attempt.[84]

The truth is that the 15 years of direct political control by the military was crucial in building the organization's overall influence in the state and society. According to a Bangladeshi parliamentarian, Farooq Chaudhury, the military has created a niche for itself in the corridors of power. The increase in the number of military officers in both political parties is a case in point. The Bangladeshi military resembles the Pakistani military in terms of the growth of its social, political, and economic influence. The military's active role in politics is also natural because the armed forces have a legacy as a revolutionary force that is less professional in fully accepting the supremacy of the civilian authorities. Therefore, revolutionary militaries are prone to attempt coups and to greater friction with the civil power.

The military's influence in decision-making is evident in more than just its share of economic resources. Observers such as Shamsul Arefin, a retired military officer and chairman of Bangladesh Research and Publication Ltd, were of the view that the military has systematically injected anti-Indianism in policy-making to justify its presence.[85] Although the anti-Indianism, as is obvious from Maniruzzaman's work, is part of the military's institutional memory and ethos,[86] such sentiment has become more pronounced, and security analysts speak about the need to stand up to the threat from India. The scepticism and suspicion of the Indians dates back to the liberation war. It is believed that despite helping Bengalis get their independence, the Indians did not give a fair deal to the Bangladeshis, and there were even reports of Indian forces engaging in looting and extortion. Such perceptions seem to have increasingly clouded the thinking of policymakers in Dhaka to the extent that even the AL has to be careful in pursing policies vis-à-vis India. The division of water resources and the increasing Islamist religious influence in Bangladesh are issues that are increasing the gap between Dhaka and New Delhi. The clash between the Indian and Bangladeshi border security forces has resulted in some violent incidents which add to the belligerence of the general public in Bangladesh.

The military is one of the beneficiaries of such hostile relations. The need to confront a large and apparently unfriendly neighbour adds to the logic of a greater military build-up. The internal security situation, especially in Chittagong Hill Tracts (CHT), adds to the external threat that the military is called upon to address. According to Amena Mohsin, the military, which was sent to fight an insurgency in this area, eventually established its dominance by controlling the economic, political, and social lives of the CHT people.[87] Such pervasive control was most pronounced under the military regimes. However, negotiations with the United People's Party of the CHT were renewed after 1991 and a settlement reached after democracy was restored. Reportedly, the military was also satisfied with the accord and not resistant to any settlement because it had acquired a central position in the country's politics[88] and had an alternative means to sustain its financial autonomy through the UN peace-keeping missions.

The term which best describes the connection between the two poles in Bangladesh, civil and military, is civil–military partnership. This relationship has emerged due to the civilian leadership's recognition of the military's role in the country's society and politics, and the understanding that the best way for providing an exit to the military from politics was by ensuring an environment where the organization's corporate interests were guaranteed by civilian governments. In spite of the fact that the military is today back in the barracks, it is not peripheral to the politics of the state. It is believed that the former ruling party, the BNP, viewed the armed forces as a resource on which it could rely in a crisis in which the party's power was challenged.[89]

It is also worth considering that over the years the society seems to have drifted towards a greater division between secular–nationalist and religious forces. This division adds to the existing political division between the BNP and the AL. In fact, the country is known for a sharp ideological divide between the supporters of the two parties at all levels of society. Unless better means are evolved to manage a dialogue between the different segments of society, a situation might be created where the military finds it opportune to interfere in politics all over again. After all, the Bangladeshi military today has greater penetration in the society, polity, and economy than it ever had.

INDIA

Out of the four countries discussed in this chapter, India is the only one which can boast of an excellent track record of civil–military relations. India's armed forces are professionally trained and completely under the control of the civilian governments, in conformity with Huntington's specifications. However, command and control is one aspect of civil–military relations. There is another dimension which relates to the military's interaction with the larger Indian society. The fact is that the perception of the military, so far as the society is concerned, is divided. For some, the Indian armed forces are a tool of coercion used by the Central government to forcibly implement its policies, and for others it is a means of protection.

The Indian military is increasingly involved in internal security, which adds to the varied views. In addition, a number of exogenous and endogenous factors have shaped the military's organizational capabilities and its relations with both the state and the society. Such changes, as will be argued in this section, relate to changes in the perceptions of the civilian political leadership regarding the objectives of the state. The primary goal of establishing India as a powerful regional and global actor has resulted in technological and other changes that impact upon the role of the armed forces and its relations with civil society and civilians at large. In a nutshell, the Indian military's relative clout has increased, which reflects in certain critical decisions. Therefore, while the military continues to operate in an environment where it is constantly challenged by other stakeholders, it has, as an institution, found formal and informal methods to extend its overall influence. Much of this change is linked with India's growing desire to establish itself as a global power. The upcoming and affluent middle class and the Indian diaspora have a relatively aggressive stance so far as national power is concerned, which adds to the military's relative influence.

The Management of the Defence Forces

The Indian military is firmly under civilian control and is managed through a committee system which was designed by Lord Ismay, soon after Partition. As is obvious from Figure 4.5, the primary control of the defence establishment rests with the defence minister who exercises authority over the armed forces on behalf of the government.

Although the president is constitutionally the supreme commander of the armed forces, he/she acts upon the advice of the prime minister, who is in turn guided by the defence minister. In addition, there are 17 committees dealing with defence matters.

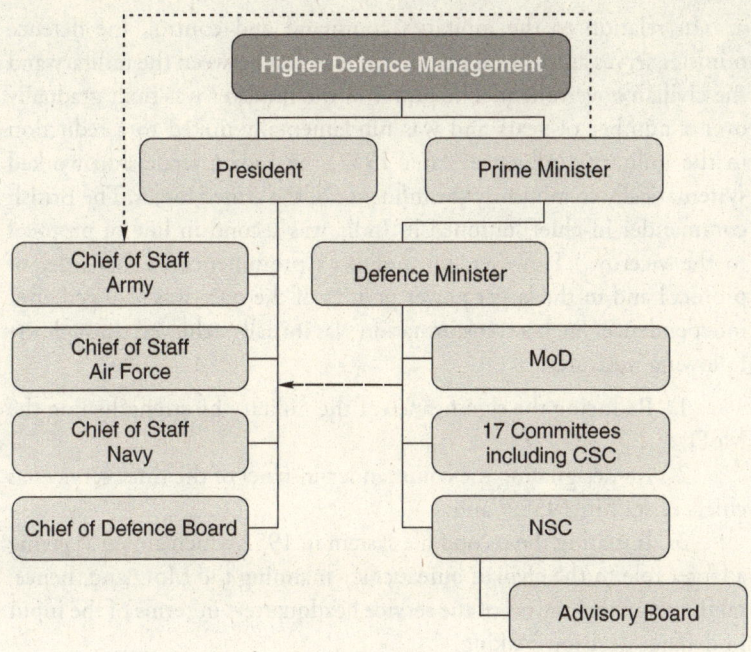

FIGURE 4.5   Indian Defence Establishment: Command and Control
Source: Author's own formulation.

In 1998, however, the Indian government of Prime Minister A.B. Vajpayee established the NSC, designated as the apex body looking into political, economic, energy-related, and security issues. The NSC was to be assisted by an advisory board, a strategic policy group, and a joint intelligence committee. The advisory board, which is comprised of retired military and civilian experts and is mandated to carry out in-depth analysis and provide inputs to the NSC, is the most functional sub-organization out of the three proposed to assist the NSC. The council comprises of a national security advisor; the ministers of defence, external affairs, home, and finance; and the deputy chairman of the Planning Commission. According to former Indian intelligence officer B. Raman, an important aspect of the NSC's responsibilities relates to determining the optimum strength of the military and the defence bureaucracy.[90] These changes were made to strengthen strategic, especially defence, planning. The NSC was a result of the Arun Singh Committee report in 1992, which had advocated greater efficiency in defence management. Subsequently, there was also a Group of Minister's (GoM) report in 2000 which influenced its shape.

In relation to the military's command and control, the defence minister serves as the focal point of interaction between the military and the civilian government. The power of the minister was built gradually over a number of years and was fundamentally linked to a reduction in the military's influence. After 1947, the Indian leadership worked systematically to minimize the influence of the armed forces. The British commander-in-chief stationed in India was second in line of protocol to the viceroy.[91] However, the military's prominence in the order of protocol and in the larger power politics of the state was changed after independence. Such a transformation was initially achieved through the following measures:

1. Reducing the significance of the military by strengthening the MoD;

2. Re-designating the commander-in-chief of the three services as chiefs of staff in 1955;[92] and

3. Initiating the second file system in 1952 which aimed at giving a larger role to the civilian bureaucracy manning the MoD and, hence, taking away the powers of the service headquarters in terms of the input in defence decision-making.

Today, the popular notion amongst the armed forces in India and the security community is that military personnel have no input in defence decision-making, which, in their minds, is a lacuna in national security policymaking. This particular power balance dates back to the days of Prime Minister Jawaharlal Nehru. Concerned with the growing power of the military in Pakistan, Nehru allegedly wanted to keep the Indian military in check, an objective which was achieved by empowering the civilian bureaucracy and the civilian minister of defence. Krishna Menon was a visionary who, unfortunately, chose to override the military perspective on war preparedness to make room for his larger plans for national security. Menon wanted to strengthen India militarily by developing an indigenous weapons production capability and the overall capabilities of the armed forces. This plan also had a political angle—soliciting peace with China in order to buy time, which could then be used to strengthen the military. In undertaking such strategic planning, Menon completely disregarded tactical planning for the immediate threat that was posed by Beijing in terms of pursuing its plans to occupy territory bordering on China. Therefore, the MoD or the defence minister did not give much credence to intelligence reports or the top military leadership's concerns regarding Chinese movement on the border. Thereafter, the war fought with China in 1962 was lost and proved to be a great embarrassment for the Indian political leadership. A prominent strategic analyst, K. Subrahmanyam explains the 1962 conflict as a situation in which 'the Indian army didn't have any capability and that war was fought by a wrong general who didn't fight a war. The cabinet committee didn't function as it should have nor did the Parliament understand the [strategic] concepts'.[93]

The defeat in 1962 exposed the fundamental lacunae in the overall national decision-making. Apart from not adhering to the advice of the military leadership, the defence minister made the blunder of appointing a general who did not have the experience or capability to fight and win a war. The post-war analysis made the government realize its mistake of politicizing the armed forces. According to a senior retired defence bureaucrat, N.N. Vohra, Krishna Menon began to function on the basis of personal likes and dislikes.[94] He gave importance to Lt General B.M. Kaul whose Eastern Command did not do well. People such as Major General (retd) Dipankar Banerjee believe that the 1962 crisis made people realize that army should not be interfered with, and thus a bargain was struck between the civilians and military in the early days according to which civilians would not meddle in matters military.[95] The realization of giving importance to the opinion of the military leadership was definitely appreciated, causing former Defence Minister Swaran Singh to suggest in 1963 that it was useful to have serving military officers in the MoD, three in defence and three in defence production, but the army never posted anyone there.[96] This was perhaps the result of the organizational ethos inculcated by the earlier military leadership such as General K.M. Cariappa. The Indian army chief did not allow any association with political parties or discussion of politics.[97] Since strategy involves the higher politics of decision-making, it might have been considered a viable option to keep the military away from playing any role in decision-making, including the bureaucracy.

However, there are others in India who believed that keeping the military out of politics and policymaking was a deliberate decision made by the political leadership in collusion with the civil bureaucracy. According to Lt General (retd) V.R. Raghavan, the fact that General J.N. Chowdhury moved a brigade to Delhi soon after Nehru's death raised concerns amongst politicians regarding the military's intentions.[98] Others, such as a prominent analyst C. Raja Mohan, hold the bureaucracy responsible for minimizing the military's role in defence decision-making. In Raja Mohan's view, the Indian state is a bureaucratic state dominated by the civil bureaucracy in which the army was pushed out from its functions and kept to ceremonial roles. The key linchpin in the Indian power hierarchy is the joint secretary.[99] Such a view was also subscribed to by strategic experts such as Varun Sahni who further added to the earlier comment by saying that the Indian Administrative Service (IAS) officers dominate the government. These are not specialists but generalists who have no clear idea about defence matters but by tradition are well-entrenched in policymaking. He went on to add that the power of the IAS officers in defence-related issues and the government in general has increased due to the growing dependence of the politicians on the defence ministry's bureaucracy. The politicians are ignorant of military matters and in the habit of abdicating defence decision-making to civilian bureaucrats.[100] The weakness of the politicians does not allow them to detect the structural flaw in the defence bureaucracy that the IAS officers do not have the expertise to deal with defence-related matters. Manvendra Singh, a former journalist and Member of Parliament (MP), provided figures to highlight the problem. Singh was of the view that only 10–15 per cent of the MoD bureaucrats eventually get absorbed in the ministry, which signifies the level of competence and expertise of the MoD officialdom.[101]

Emerging Civil–Military Partnership

Does the aforementioned situation indicate a static relationship between the civilian government and the armed forces? Indubitably, the military is under the firm control of the civilian establishment and the political leadership. Barring a limited number of incidents, which denote an underlying tension between the civilian government and the military, there is no significant evidence available to suggest any rupture in the traditional command and control system. The removal of Admiral Vishnu Bhagwat in December 1998 by the BJP-led government for publicly challenging the government is one such incident. Most of the senior retired military officers interviewed were critical of Bhagwat's decision to challenge the writ of the government, including that of the MoD's bureaucracy. The rift between the former Indian naval chief and the government had erupted after Bhagwat refused to accept the latter's decision regarding the appointment of a senior officer in the naval headquarters. According to Bhagwat,[102] the MoD and the political administration were obliged to adhere to his advice and not make a political appointment at a senior-level position. However, the admiral pushed the envelope by accusing the government of bias against him on communal grounds (Bhagwat's wife was a Muslim). Rear Admiral (retd) Raja Menon, one of the India's top strategic analysts, said that Bhagwat was not wrong in contesting his right to appoint a senior officer he considered suitable rather than the MoD thrusting an officer on him. Menon further added that the rift between the former naval chief and the government actually revolved around the questionable double-file system which had been strengthened during the 1980s by the MoD to increase the ministry's hold over the armed forces. This particular system discourages the service headquarters' voice from reaching the political decision-makers.[103] Menon, in fact, was the only one other than C. Raja Mohan who defended Bhagwat's position. Others, such as Lt General V.R. Raghavan (retd), were of the view that Bhagwat had overstepped his authority and had challenged the norm of civil–military relations.[104]

The incident is crucial because it contributed to subtly redefining the relationship between the civil bureaucracy and the military. Admiral (retd) K.K. Nayyar, who was one of the members of the Arun Singh Committee, is of the view that the senior military leadership has greater power to appoint and promote its officers. Unlike in the past, when even the promotions of lieutenant colonel and above were decided by the MoD, the present-day military leadership has the freedom to promote officers of the rank of brigadier and above. Moreover, all revenue expenditure has been under the service chiefs.[105] Lt General (retd) V.R. Raghavan added that currently the consultative process has changed tremendously. The three-star generals have a whole range of powers, including that of expenditure, allotted to them. Giving the power to spend is not about legality but about trust. Today, military personnel lead weapons procurement delegations abroad, something that was earlier undertaken by bureaucrats: military personnel are in a better position to knock down the price. The government views the military as a source of stability, a development that is different from the conditions prevalent during the 1960s and the 1970s, and does not intend to marginalize or downgrade it.[106]

The Bhagwat episode is, however, not the sole reason for the apparent change. There is a realization that the relationship between the civilian members of the government and the military cannot remain static. Although the government traditionally respected the space given to the armed forces and did not really interfere with operational planning, the military today has greater significance, a condition which can be viewed as the development of a civil–military partnership. Such a relationship naturally assigns greater importance to the armed forces, but in the main to pursue the political and larger geopolitical objectives of the political leadership. The following issues have been crucial in redefining civil–military relations in India:

1. Internal security and war against terrorism;
2. India's expanding geostrategic role;
3. Nuclear deterrence; and
4. Alliance with external powers such as USA.

The next section briefly looks at these issues to understand the dynamics of civil–military relations in India.

Internal Security and War on Terror

The Indian army plays a key role in internal security, which is understandable considering that the country faces numerous insurgencies. This is contrary to the perception that the military's leadership is averse to the involvement of armed forces in internal security. However, such a notion must be carefully analysed. A number of retired senior army officers interviewed expressed contradictory opinions. On the one hand, they believed that a professional military must focus on external threat and that it should not be deployed in internal security issues. On the other hand, it is proudly claimed that the armed forces are the only entity that has the capacity to fight insurgency and the only institution capable of 'pulling the government's chestnuts out of the fire'.[107] This remark was made in view of the role played by the army in troubled areas such as Assam, Kashmir, and the north-east. Lt General (retd) B.K.N. Chhibber, for instance, claimed that it was the army which saved the situation in Punjab during the height of the insurgency during the 1980s.[108] Although this view is debatable, the fact is that army officers believe that they have a positive role to play in a political environment ridden with corruption and instability. A retired senior army officer was of the view that the general public had lost faith in the political system due to rampant corruption. Therefore, he claimed, 'all Indian army officers are asked to take over but do not do so due to their respect for professionalism'.[109]

Referring to the counter-insurgency operation in Punjab, which is the only such successful operation in the country's history, Lt General (retd) B.N. Sharma was of the view that the problem was solved due to the military's prowess. He states:

In Punjab, we went after the village heads and threatened them. We told them that if they don't cooperate then we will kill them since we were the biggest executioners. We also put the night curfew and threatened that anyone caught would be handed over to the police and we followed up on arrest.[110]

However, others debate this claim. Former director-general of Punjab Police, K.P.S. Gill, the officer responsible for defeating terrorism in Punjab, claimed that it was actually the police that had pulled the military's chestnuts out of the fire after the army had undertaken a botched operation 'Blue Star' in 1984 involving a raid on the Golden Temple in Amritsar.[111] In fact, the dissenting opinion was that the army did not know how to operate in Punjab. As the army denotes coercion more than any other force, it pushed the Punjabi youth into 'the lap of Pakistani intelligence agencies'.[112] Moreover, the army had to use additional coercive force given its inability to access local intelligence.[113] Ajai Sahni added that the police have greater ability in intelligence gathering. This capability came in handy while conducting counter-insurgency operations during the late 1980s, a plan that was carried out jointly by the police and the army. While the police engaged in house-to-house searches and interrogated people, the army was given a supportive role of cordoning off areas where the search was to be conducted.[114]

Despite this success, the counter-insurgency model of Punjab was not used in other troubled areas such as the north-east and Kashmir. Was it due to the perception held by most military officers that the police are corrupt and cannot provide security? Or is it because, as Ajai Sahni, a commentator on strategic issues said that, policies and postings in India are not based on experience?[115] Experienced police officers such as former director-general of the Central Reserve Police Force, Ram Mohan, challenged the latter assertion. Ram Mohan, who served in Kashmir and the north-east, was of the view that in Kashmir in 1989, 95 per cent of the police was loyal but was pushed away by the policies of the state government, which saw a solution to the insurgency in Kashmir primarily as a cross-border problem that had to be solved by the use of maximum force.[116] He stated that using the military and paramilitary in internal security operations is counter-productive because these forces are far more coercive than the police. But Indian policymakers or army generals do not subscribe to this view. There are three possible explanations.

First, according to Major General (retd) Ashok Mehta, internal security operations involve resources and the police, military, and paramilitary justify allocation of greater financial resources on the basis of their involvement in counter-insurgency operations.[117] Second, the army views counter-insurgency operations, especially after 9/11, as a means to enhance its role. Considering the debate in India's strategic community regarding the need for a revolution in military affairs (RMA), which would require right-sizing the armed forces, the smaller services, the Indian Air Force (IAF) and the Indian Navy (IN) question the large size of the army. It is believed that the armed forces have to be lean and must be strengthened technologically.[118] Such a debate makes the army highly nervous and results in army officers arguing that the army cannot be down-sized because of the role it must play in fighting terrorism.[119]

Third, the military and its coercive capacity are central to the authoritarian dynamics of India's politics. Since, as Ashis Nandy pointed out, the Indian state is ruthless,[120] coercion is a tool that the political elite use to engage with society. Despite the strong tradition of electoral democracy in India, the fact is that India is essentially a post-colonial state in which the civil bureaucracy and the political elite dominate decision-making to guarantee their interests. Political scientists Veena Kukreja and M.P. Singh believe that there is internal violence in the sub-regions that are not part of the 'Brahmanical social order'.[121] Violence has increased in all areas, starting from the Indo-Nepalese border, to Bihar, Jharkand, Orissa, Madhya Pradesh, Chhattisgarh, and Andhra Pradesh. It is a corridor of violence where the people's exclusion from the benefits of economic growth and heavy pressure of growing population have resulted in resistance against the state. The north-east, in particular, faces the continuation of a historical problem of lack of integration of the territory by the British with the British Indian empire. Efforts made for integration after independence failed due to popular dissent. The violence in different states represents the typical problems of socio-economic underdevelopment, inequitable distribution of resources, and the inability of the political system to facilitate negotiation between the state and society or amongst various societal actors. Thus, there are people who see the military or the law enforcement agencies as representing the aggressive posture of the state. On the other hand, there are groups like the Mizos who view the Indian army as a lesser evil.[122] There is no clear distinction between the pro- and anti-army elements. It is the nature of politics which defines the relationship between communities and the state and society, which, in turn, determines the perception of the people towards the armed forces.

However, it is not fair to say that everyone views the military as a benign force or a source of social integration.

The army's counter-insurgency role is significant in increasing the interaction between the civilian leadership (including the bureaucracy) and the armed forces. Legislations such as the Armed Forces Special Powers Act (AFSPA) are instruments that have increased the military's involvement in administration and governance in areas experiencing internal violence.

India's Role in Geopolitics and the Military

The aforementioned role of the military in internal security is bound to increase, especially after 9/11. India's partnership with USA means a further increase in the military's significance for accomplishing the objectives of the war on terror. The Indian military is central to the growing relationship between New Delhi and Washington. It is not only limited to fighting terrorism but extends to larger military cooperation. In fact, India's ambition to expand its diplomatic outreach to adjoining regions requires the use of the country's overall resources, including its military, and also encompassing naval visits and policing the Indian Ocean.

India's desire to attain a prominent role in the hierarchy of nations or global politics is no secret. This is an ambition which has gained greater support in the strategic community and, consequently, greater prominence too. The ability to deploy the country's financial, human, and military resources is essential for New Delhi to carve out a niche for itself in global geopolitics. India's significance is gradually being recognized by other important global actors including the sole superpower, USA. The recent India–US nuclear deal, which ensures the transfer of civilian nuclear technology to New Delhi, would not only enhance India's technological capabilities but also have ramifications for the country's nuclear weapons programme. Implicit in the agreement is an informal and tacit acceptance of India's military programme. Furthermore, the US–India cooperation is based on Washington's need to partner with New Delhi to counter China's growing military power. The growing significance of India's military–strategic role will necessitate a re-evaluation of the civilian government's relationship with its armed forces. For one, it will be imperative to redefine the military's role in issues relating to national security. The government seems to have already become more mindful of the military's opinion on key issues. For instance, a decision regarding withdrawal of troops from the Siachen glacier depends upon the army agreeing to the plan. Although keenly negotiating an end to years of military engagement with Pakistan, the current Congress government appears to be taking the advice from its army headquarters seriously. The army, on the other hand, has strongly advised against demilitarization of the glacier without authentication of present troop positions.[123] There are three explanations for the civilian government's attention to the military's opinions.

First, policymakers do not want to make the same mistake as they did in 1962, when ignoring military advice cost them a war with China. Second, the nature of coalition politics is such that no one wants to take decisions which might bring the ruling dispensation negative publicity. Such an emphasis on electoral implications creates a lot of space for the military to manoeuvre, especially on issues relating to national security. Finally, as pointed out by Varun Sahni, politicians have become increasingly illiterate about defence matters and tend to leave these issues to the bureaucracy, both military and civil.[124]

The Military in Nuclear Decision-Making

From a purely command and control perspective, the battle between the civil and military bureaucracy in India continues. While the significance of the military or national security grows in the overall strategic planning of the state, the political government would like to operate through the civil bureaucracy, and this has resulted in a conflict between the two bureaucracies on two issues in particular: (i) the military's role in nuclear decision-making, and (ii) restructuring of the armed forces and establishing the institution of a chief of defence staff of the armed forces.

The military's involvement in nuclear decision-making is one issue on which armed forces personnel express many reservations. The civilian government prefers to keep the military away from the nuclear button to avoid any inadvertent escalation of conflict. However, the perception in military circles is that the organization's role in national security decision-making must be increased.

The following section will review some of the arguments made by the military civil bureaucracies in this regard.

Restructuring the Armed Forces

Traditionally, the civil bureaucracy played the role of the primary source for implementing decisions or making policies. However, it was realized, especially during the 1990s, that the military's role in national security decision-making had to be redefined by introducing new structures, such as the organization of the chief of defence staff (CDS). The new organization was intended to reduce the overall inefficiencies in the armed forces and bring about a joint planning culture. This was one of the principal conclusions of the Arun Singh Committee report of 1992. This report was followed by the GoM's report in 2000 which was a product of four independent reports, all of which recommended a joint-service culture and establishment of a CDS. The Integrated Defence Staff was finally established in late 2001 by the government of Prime Minister A.B. Vajpayee.

However, the CDS, which is supposed to head the Integrated Forces Defence Staff (IFDS), remains a lame duck. According to Air Marshal (retd) Vinod Patney, all that the new structure has achieved is to collate the plans of the three services.[125] One of the reasons, as explained by senior bureaucrat N.N. Vohra, is that the military, especially the IAF, had reservations about the integration plan. Some retired IAF officers had, in fact, approached the prime minister asking him not to activate the CDS plan.[126] By then, the BJP government had implemented about 80 per cent of the recommendations incorporated in the Arun Singh Committee report, and the CDS was one of the big-ticket items that remained unimplemented.

The IAF's reservations pertain to inter-services rivalry and the fear of the army dominating the integrated force structure. Air Vice-Marshal (retd) Kapil Kak was of the view that the CDS system will not work in India because 'we have three services with independent cultures. The CDS is supposed to provide single-point advice, and why should the government listen to one person's advice? The synergy between the three services is lacking.'[127] However, the IAF is not alone in opposing the CDS proposal. The army too has its reservations. Senior analysts, such as Lt General (retd) V.R. Raghavan also had problems with the concept. He was of the view that CDS would not work in India because direct control of the services by their chiefs is critical. The CDS, he further opined, should look at strategic forces and no more.[128]

Air Commodore (retd) Jasjit Singh, however, believes that the real issue is not a matter of bringing about the right balance amongst the armed forces, but restructuring the entire defence establishment with the objective of integrating the armed forces with the MoD where the former barely have any representation.[129] This idea will certainly be debated by the MoD bureaucracy. However, the crux of the matter is that an India with a growing strategic significance will need to concede some space to the armed forces in national security decision-making. A new security structure which concedes a larger role to the military will be a structural parallel to the emerging civil–military partnership in India.

* * *

The South Asian region offers interesting variation in terms of civil–military relations. The region comprises of countries such as India where the civil–military relations balance strongly favours the civilian stakeholders, and Pakistan where this set of relations is completely tilted in favour of the armed forces. The key argument of this chapter is that it is unfair to review civil–military relations in the region, or for that matter any region, purely from the perspective of command and control of the armed forces. Such a perspective is relevant but it does not have an inherent capacity to deal with the changes that have taken place in the relationship between the military and other institutions of the state.

In today's South Asia, the armed forces have become increasingly relevant to the politics of the state. The command and control structure in a given state is highly relevant because it serves as a basic starting point in analysing relations between the military, the state, and society at large. However, what gives a fillip to enhancing the military's role and its influence over state and society is the additional role given to the armed forces. From this perspective, civil–military relations cannot be viewed as a simple command and control matter.

In countries such as Pakistan, the military's role in politics and policy-making has increased because of the organization's ability to penetrate the society, the economy, and its politics. In other countries, such as Bangladesh and Sri Lanka, the military's role has increased because of the institution's relevance for the political leadership and in the larger policymaking of these states. So, while the civil society in these two countries might imagine that the military remains under civilian domination, the fact is that the armed forces have gained greater significance as a consequence of the political leadership's intention to use them to achieve its political objectives. What is not realized is that giving the military a greater role in domestic issues is bound to enhance the overall power of the institution.

Then there are countries like India where the military is under civilian control. However, even there the relationship has gradually evolved into a civil–military partnership. While the military and its officer cadre remain firmly under civilian control, the Central government tends to use the armed forces as a tool to implement policies. This has an impact on the overall relationship between the military and society, which does not simply view the institution as a benevolent policymaking tool. From this perspective, the military has inadvertently become a partner of the civilian leadership. This partnership is likely to strengthen as the political leadership's dependence on the military as a tool for redefining India's role in global geopolitics increases.

Revisiting the central argument of this chapter, civil–military relations cannot be viewed simply from the perspective of command and control, especially in post-colonial societies where force or authoritarianism is part of the larger political culture. It is meaningless to base the relationship between the military and the civilian institutions purely from the perspective of the links between the armed forces and the state. There is the society as well, which forms its perspectives about state institutions depending upon its interaction with the various segments or branches of the state. In political environments where force is relevant for politics, civil–military relations cannot remain static and must not be viewed through the narrow prism of command and control.

Notes

1. Samuel P. Huntington, *Soldier and the State: The Theory and Politics of Civil–Military Relations,* new edn. (Cambridge, Mass: Belknap Press, 2005).

2. Amos Perlmutter and Valerie Plave Bennett (eds), *The Political Influence of the Military* (New Haven: Yale University Press, 1980), pp. 13–14.

3. Alfred Stepan, *The Military in Politics Changing Patterns in Brazil* (New Jersey: Princeton University Press, 1971), pp. 9–20; Morris Janowitz, *Military Institutions and Coercion in Developing Nations: The Military in the Political Development of New Nations* (Chicago: University of Chicago Press, 1988 [Midway Reprint]).

4. Charles Tilly, *Coercion, Capital and European States* (Oxford: Blackwell Publishing, 1992), pp. 96–7.

5. Frederic C. Lane, *Profits from Power* (Albany: State University of New York Press, 1979), pp. 12–65.

6. The 47 years include: (i) the Ayub and Yahya regimes, 1958–72; (ii) the Zia regime, 1977–88; and (iii) the Musharraf regime, 1999–2008. The 30 years of indirect control include 15 years of military presidents, 11 years rule as part of a power troika and four years of increased military power from 1954 to 1958. The years 1954–7 and 1971–7 were civilian rule. See Mohammad Waseem,

'Civil-Military Relations in Pakistan', in Rajshree Jetly (ed.), *Pakistan in Regional and Global Politics* (New Delhi: Routledge, 2009), p. 185.

7.   Discussant comments by Hasan-Askari Rizvi at the Conference of the University of Pennsylvania Institute for the Advanced Study of India, New Delhi, 27 March 2006.

8.   Abdurrahman Siddiqi, *The Military in Pakistan: Image and Reality* (Lahore: Vanguard Books, 1996), p. 70.

9.   Hussain Haqqani, *Pakistan Between Mosque and Military* (Washington, DC: Carnegie Endowment for International Peace, 2005), p. 15.

10.   Ayesha Jalal, *The State of Martial Rule*, Pakistan Edn (Lahore: Vanguard Books, 1991), p. 44.

11.   Stephen P. Cohen, *The Idea of Pakistan* (Washington, DC: Brookings Institution Press, 2004), p. 102.

12.   Interview with Brigadier (retd) A.R. Siddiqui, Karachi, 20 July 2004.

13.   Hamza Alavi, 'Class and State', in Hassan Gardezi and Jamil Rashid (eds), *Pakistan: The Roots of Dictatorship* (London: Zed Press, 1983), p. 66.

14.   Ibid., p. 71.

15.   Ibid.; Siddiqi, *Military in Pakistan*, p. 70; Mohammad Waseem, *Politics and the State in Pakistan*, 2nd Edn (National Institute of Historical and Cultural Research, Islamabad, 1994), p. 133.

16.   Waseem, *Politics and the State in Pakistan*, pp. 51–131.

17.   Hasan-Askari Rizvi, *Military, State and Society in Pakistan* (London: Palgrave Macmillan, 2000), p. 80.

18.   Hassan Abbas, *Pakistan's Drift into Extremism: Allah, the Army and America's War on Terror* (London: M.E. Sharpe, 2005), p. 28.

19.   Interview with Lt General (retd) Faiz Ali Chishti, Rawalpindi, 6 November 2003.

20.   Saeed Shafqat, *Civil-Military Relations in Pakistan: From Zulfikar Ali Bhutto to Benazir Bhutto* (Boulder, CO: Westview Press, 1997), p. 9.

21.   Abbas, *Pakistan's Drift into Extremism*, p. 35.

22.   Shafqat, *Civil–Military Relations*, p. 79.

23.   Discussion with the Baluch leader and former Senator Sanaullah Baluch, Islamabad, 8 July 2006.

24.   Mushahid Hussain, *Pakistan's Politics: The Zia Years* (Lahore: Progressive Publishers, 1990), p. 22.

25.   Ibid., p. 22.

26.   Ibid., p. 32.

27.   Ibid.

28.   Seyyed Vali Reza Nasr, *Islamic Leviathan* (New York: Oxford University Press, 2001), p. 7.

29.   Nasr, *Islamic Leviathan*, p. 144.

30.   Interview with Hameed Gul, Islamabad, 15 May 1994. Also see Haqqani, *Pakistan between Mosque and Military*, p. 201.

31. Khalid Mahmud Arif, *Working with Zia* (Karachi: Oxford University Press, 1995), p. 143. Arif cites Major General Sher Ali Khan advising General Yahya Khan in 1969 about the art and impact of creating a myth about the military's image as a saviour. This advice was followed by all subsequent military dictators.

32. Oskar Verkaaik, *Migrants and Militants: Fun and Urban Violence in Pakistan* (New Delhi: Manas Publications, 2005), pp. 61–87, 111–17.

33. Discussion with P.Q. Mehdi, Islamabad, 2003.

34. Interview with Admiral (retd) Fasih Bokhari, Islamabad, 2004.

35. Interview with General (retd) Gul Hassan Khan, Rawalpindi, 7 November 1993.

36. Interviews with General (retd) Gul Hassan Khan and Brig. (retd) Ishtiaque Ali Khan, Islamabad, 4 June 2007. Ishtiaque was one of the brigadiers who resigned.

37. Hamza Alavi, 'The Structure of Peripheral Capitalism', in Hamza Alavi and Teodor Shanin (eds), *Sociology of Developing Societies* (New York: Monthly Review Press, 1982), pp. 172–91.

38. Hamza Alavi, 'State and Class Under Peripheral Capitalism', in Alavi and Shanin (eds), *Sociology of Developing Societies*, pp. 296–9.

39. Ayesha Siddiqa, *Military Inc: Inside Pakistan's Military Economy* (London: Pluto Press, 2007).

40. See http://www.defensenews.com/story.php?i=4607909, accessed on 7 July 2006.

41. Gleaned from confidential interviews with human rights activists.

42. Ibid.

43. Interview with former defence secretary, Austin Fernando, Colombo, 15 February 2006.

44. Interview with Jayadeva Uyangoda, Colombo, 2006.

45. http://www.asiantribune.com/news/2006/03/09/president-mahinda-rajapakse's-uk-style-devolution-analyzed, accessed on 9 March 2006.

46. Interview with General D'Silva, Colombo, 10 February 2006.

47. This was a private paper which was not permitted to be cited.

48. Interview with Sanjay Colonne, Colombo, 14 February 2006.

49. Ibid.

50. Interview with K. Godage, Colombo, February 2006.

51. http://www.thehindu.com/thehindu/fline/fl2624/stories/20091204262412800.htm, accessed on 7 July 2006.

52. M.R. Narayan Swamy, *Inside an Elusive Mind* (Colombo: Vijitha Yapa, 2003), pp. 200–1.

53. D.R. Karthikeyan and Radhavinod Raju, *The Rajiv Gandhi Assassination* (New Delhi: New Dawn Press, Inc., 2004).

54. Swamy, *Inside an Elusive Mind*, pp. 202–3.

55. Interviews with former defence secretary, Austin Fernando, Colombo, 15 February 2006, and Sanjay Colonne, Colombo, 14 February 2006.

56. Swamy, *Inside an Elusive Mind*, p. 138.

57. Ibid.

58. Amena Mohsin, 'Bangladesh: An Uneasy Accommodation', in Muthiah Alagappa (ed.), *Coercion and Governance: The Declining Political Role of the Military in Asia* (Stanford: Stanford University Press, 2001), pp. 218–19.

59. Interview with General (retd) Amin Ahmed Chaudhry, Dhaka, 7 February 2006.

60. Interview with former chief of the army staff, Major General (retd) Mehbub-ur-Rehman, Dhaka, 3 February 2006.

61. Mohsin, 'Bangladesh', p. 221.

62. Interview with Zillul Hye Razi, Dhaka, 29 January 2006.

63. http://www.senakalyan.org, accessed on 22 September 2010.

64. Interview with General (retd) Amin Ahmed Chaudhry, Dhaka, 7 February 2006.

65. Interview with a retired brigadier, Dhaka, 5 February 2006.

66. Interview with Rehman Sobhan, Dhaka, 2 February 2006.

67. Interview with an Awami League Member of Parliament, Faruk Khan, Dhaka, 30 January 2006.

68. Interview with the director, Bangladesh Institute of Strategic Studies, Abdur Rob Khan, Dhaka, 30 January 2006.

69. Talukder Maniruzzaman, *The Bangladesh Revolution and its Aftermath* (Dhaka: University Press Ltd, 1988), p. 173.

70. Ibid., p. 75.

71. Interview with Colonel (retd) Usman Chaudhry, Dhaka, 29 January 2006.

72. Interview with Talukder Maniruzzaman, 4 February 2006.

73. Interview with Major General (retd) S.M. Ibraheem, Dhaka, 9 January 2006.

74. Ibid.

75. Interview with Sultana Kemal, Dhaka, 3 February 2006.

76. Rounaq Jahan, *Bangladesh: Politics Problems and Issues*, Expanded Edn (Dhaka: University Press Ltd, 2005), pp. 157–8.

77. Interview with Major General (retd) K.M. Shafeeullah, Dhaka, 29 January 2006.

78. Interview with Major General (retd) Azizur Rehman, Dhaka, 4 January 2006.

79. Interview with Kemal Hossain, Dhaka, 4 February 2006.

80. Jahan, *Bangladesh*, pp. 243–4.

81. Interview with Major General (retd) K.M. Shafeeullah, Dhaka, 29 January 2006.

82. Interview with a former military personnel and chairman, Bangladesh Research and Publications Ltd, Shamsul Arefin, Dhaka, 1 February 2006.

83. Mohsin, 'Bangladesh', pp. 223–4.

84. Interview with Rehman Sobhan, Dhaka, 2 February 2006.

85. Interview with Shamsul Arefin, Dhaka, 1 February 2006.

86. Maniruzzaman, *The Bangladesh Revolution*, p. 174.

87. Mohsin, 'Bangladesh', p. 220; the Chittagong hill tracts insurgency years were 1975 to the peace accord of 1997, peaking in the 1980s.

88. Ibid., pp. 220–1.

89. Interview with advocate of the Bangladesh Supreme Court, A.K. Faez-ul-Haq, Dhaka, 31 January 2006.

90. http://www.subcontinent.com/sapra/research/nationalsecurity/img_1998_11_24.html, accessed on 22 September 2010.

91. Interview with Lt General (retd) V.R. Raghavan, New Delhi, 20 December 2005.

92. Interview with Air Vice-Marshal (retd) Kapil Kak, New Delhi, 24 December 2005.

93. Interview with K. Subramanyam, New Delhi, 14 December 2005.

94. Interview with N.N. Vohra, New Delhi, 13 December 2005.

95. Interview with Major General (retd) Dipankar Banerjee, New Delhi, 14 December 2005.

96. Interview with Air Commodore (retd) Jasjit Singh, New Delhi, 8 January 2006.

97. Interview with Lt General (retd) V.R. Raghavan, New Delhi, 20 December 2005.

98. Ibid.

99. Interview with C. Raja Mohan, New Delhi, 17 December 2005.

100. Interview with Varun Sahni, New Delhi, 7 January 2006.

101. Interview with Manvendra Singh, New Delhi, 20 December 2005.

102. Reported in newspapers of the time.

103. Interview with Rear Admiral (retd) Raja Menon, New Delhi, 1 January 2006.

104. Interview with Lt General (retd) V.R. Raghavan, New Delhi, 20 December 2005.

105. Interview with Vice-Admiral (retd) K.K. Nayyar, New Delhi, 27 December 2005.

106. Interview with Lt General (retd) V.R. Raghavan, New Delhi, 20 December 2005.

107. Interview with Lt General (retd) Vijay Oberoi, New Delhi, 22 December 2005.

108. Interview with Lt General (retd) B.K.N. Chhibber, New Delhi, 10 January 2006.

109. Interview with Lt General (retd) B.N. Sharma, New Delhi, 19 December 2005.

110. Ibid.

111. Interview with former Director-General of the Punjab Police, K.P.S. Gill, New Delhi, 23 December 2005.

112. Ibid.

113. Ibid.

114. Interview with Ajai Sahni, New Delhi, 22 December 2005.

115. Ibid.

116. Interview with former Director-General of the Central Reserve Police Force, E.N. Rammohan, New Delhi, 7 January 2006.

117. Interview with Major General (retd) Ashok Mehta, New Delhi, 11 January 2006.

118. Interview with Air Commodore (retd) Jasjit Singh and Air Marshal (retd) Vinod Patney, New Delhi, 8 January 2006 and 24 December 2005.

119. Interview with Lt General (retd) V.N. Sharma, New Delhi, 19 December 2005.

120. Interview with Ashis Nandy, New Delhi, 12 January 2006.

121. Interview with M.P. Singh and Veena Kukreja, New Delhi, 17 December 2005.

122. Interview with Thingkanlal Nighte, New Delhi, 17 February 2005.

123. 'Resolution of Siachin is a Matter of Days', *The Times of India*, 13 November 2006.

124. Interview with Varun Sahni, New Delhi, 7 January 2006.

125. Interview with Air Marshal (retd) Vinod Patney, New Delhi, 24 December 2005.

126. Interview with N.N. Vohra, New Delhi, 13 December 2005.

127. Interview with Air Vice-Marshal (retd) Kapil Kak, New Delhi, 24 December 2005.

128. Interview with Lt General (retd) V.R. Raghavan, New Delhi, 20 December 2005.

129. Interview with Air Commodore (retd) Jasjit Singh, New Delhi, 8 January 2006.

5 Re-designing the Architecture of the State?

Sri Lanka's Transition from Civil War to Post-Civil War State

*Jayadeva Uyangoda**

In this chapter I explore the conceptual possibilities for re-working the Sri Lankan state in conjunction with a negotiated political settlement to the ethnic conflict that addresses ethnic minority grievances. I look at the possibilities for a substantially reformed post-conflict state from the point of view of the minority communities, because it is the minority politics that has given rise to, and made possible, a state-reform discourse in Sri Lanka. This chapter grapples with three paradoxical conditions of possibilities for state reform in the context of Sri Lanka's ethno-political war. The first is that while the politics within the ethnic majority community is embedded in resistance to state reform, the long-term interests of the majority community can only be served through reforms that can effectively address the possibility of secession. The second is that although ethnic conflicts do not have ethnic solutions at the expense of democratic solutions, democratic solutions cannot be divorced from minority claims to state power conceived essentially in ethnic terms. The third is that a federalist state reform project may address demands for

---

* This chapter was written well before the war with the LTTE ended and the facts presented may not be representative of recent developments. Nevertheless, the ethnic conflict serves to play itself out in subtle, non-military ways despite the end of the war.

accessing state power made by a large ethnic minority, but it may run a double risk: resistance from the majority community and the exclusion of smaller minorities. Taken together, they constitute a problem that requires a major alteration of the architecture not only of the existing Sri Lankan state, but also of the alternative state visions that have so far emerged. Thus, the central burden of the chapter is on developing a perspective on refashioning the existing state and the alternatives that actually exist. I use such expressions as reworking, remaking, re-forming, restructuring, reconstructing, and reconstituting to denote this specific idea of refashioning the state not just in terms of institutions, but essentially in relation to its ethnic foundations as well as their associational bases.

THE STATE AND THE ETHNIC CONFLICT

The question of the state has been at the centre of Sri Lanka's ethnic conflict as well as attempts to find a political settlement to it. Similarly, exploration of a political settlement to the country's Sinhalese–Tamil ethnic conflict has been a recurrent theme in Sri Lanka's political debate in recent years. Quite understandably, there has been no unanimity among the political actors in Sri Lanka or the international custodians of Sri Lanka's peace process about the nature of the post-conflict political order. From the perspective of the ethnic conflict, there are at present three major approaches to the question of the state. The first approach, shared by the Sinhalese nationalist forces, seeks to restore the unitarist foundations of the Sri Lankan state while granting a district-based, or even village-based, system of administrative decentralization to the Tamil and Muslim minorities. India's panchayati raj system is their latest fascination. The second approach, shared by some of Sri Lanka's ruling elites, civil society groups involved in the peace process, as well as the international political actors, stands for a federalist solution of the conventional type. Indian federalism, which has established the model of a strong centre and subordinate regional units, approximates their master model. The third approach has emerged from the Liberation Tigers of Tamil Eelam (LTTE). Its maximalist goal is a separate state while the minimalist goal presupposes an extensive framework of regional autonomy in a confederalist-type arrangement.

The extensive public debate that has taken place around the theme of a 'political solution' has not yet produced a common ground among these competing perspectives. Often, negotiations between the government and the LTTE have led to conditions of political impasse, with no agreement on the framework of a possible settlement. Thus, the public debate on a political settlement and the post-conflict state forms has often taken place outside the negotiation process.

Meanwhile, there have been instances in the negotiation process that have suggested conceptual outlines of a possible political settlement with suggestions for new state forms. The first was the so-called Thimpu Principles, formulated by Tamil militant groups at the talks held in Thimpu, the capital of Bhutan, in August 1984. The Thimpu Principles advocated the recognition of (i) the Tamils in Sri Lanka as a 'distinct nationality', (ii) an identified Tamil homeland and the guarantee of its territorial integrity, and (iii) the 'inalienable right of self-determination' of the Tamil people.[1] The Sri Lankan government declined to accept these principles because they suggested a power-sharing arrangement on the basis of the Tamils being recognized as a nationality, with a right to regional autonomy within a distinct territory on the principle of internal self-determination. The Indo-Lanka Accord of July 1987 to some extent accommodated these principles when it proposed a system of devolution for a merged Northern and Eastern provinces, treating them as constituting 'areas of historical habitation of Sri Lankan Tamil-speaking peoples'. The Provincial Councils system, introduced in Sri Lanka in 1987 in order to give effect to the Indo-Lanka Accord, was also the first important attempt to reform the Sri Lankan state structure in response to the ethnic conflict. However, the devolution of power in 1987 failed to terminate the conflict, although a number of Tamil militant groups who were earlier engaged in the insurgency accepted the Provincial Councils and returned to parliamentary politics. The LTTE, while rejecting both the Indo-Lanka Accord and the Provincial Councils system, continued the war for secession, occasionally suggesting that they would consider a proposal for regional autonomy if it satisfied 'Tamil aspirations'.[2]

The second instance was in December 2002, when the United National Front (UNF) government and the LTTE agreed in Oslo to explore a 'federal solution'. Almost echoing the Thimpu Principles as well as some key clauses of the Indo-Lanka Accord of July 1987, the two sides agreed in Oslo 'to explore a solution founded on the principle of internal self-determination in areas of historical habitation of the Tamil-speaking peoples, based on a federal structure within a united Sri Lanka'.[3] However, this exploration never took place. The talks between the UNF government and the LTTE reached an impasse in early 2003. Then the LTTE formulated and submitted to the government a new set of proposals for what the LTTE called an Interim Self-Governing Authority. These proposals suggested a model of power-sharing with greater autonomy and competence to the Northern and Eastern provinces than under a conventional federal model. The fact that the LTTE's proposals for even an 'interim' administrative arrangement assumed a confederal character had a debilitating impact on the public debate on a political settlement. Not surprisingly, they strengthened the unitarist and counter-reformist political forces in the Sinhalese polity. Against that backdrop, the official government position on a possible political solution became 'maximum devolution within a unitary state'. In this oxymoronic formulation lies an uneasy accommodation between reformist and anti-reformist forces in the ruling United People's Freedom Alliance.

Thus, Sri Lanka's political debate on a political settlement has made advances and suffered setbacks. Even so, the idea that political reforms are necessary and inevitable is shared by most of the country's political forces. The disagreements are essentially about the extent and depth of reforms. From the Tamil side, the argument is for what one may call 'thick regional autonomy' whereas the political forces in Sinhalese society which are committed to a negotiated settlement favour 'thin autonomy'. It is not yet clear how these fundamental differences can be resolved.

Since early 2006, there seems to have emerged in both sides a great temptation to allow a new phase of war to resolve this contradiction. Nonetheless, political reforms presuppose some structural alterations to the way in which political power is currently organized in Sri Lanka. The contestation is about minimalist and maximalist projects of such structural alterations. In view of the energy and vitality that the ethnic war seems to possess in reproducing itself, one may even argue that the real challenge is nothing short of re-designing the architecture of Sri Lanka's post-colonial state. It is a process that carries within it immense difficulties as well as possibilities to effect a transformatory political change. This chapter will examine these complexities as well as possibilities for reworking the architecture of the Sri Lankan state, linking the reform process to a programme of re-envisioning the state as providing mediatory space for inter-group negotiations, community interest-bargaining, and solidarity.

The Existing State: Competing State-Remaking Projects

Why should the present Sri Lankan state be re-formed and remade? One way to answer this question in the context of the protracted ethnic conflict is to admit that the constitutional foundations and the current structural form of the Sri Lankan state are quite anachronistic given the political struggles that are being waged by the ethnic minority communities. Political struggles for state power have surpassed and outgrown the existing Sri Lankan state. The state in its unitarist and centralized form not only lags far behind these struggles for state power, but is also an obstacle to any democratic reconfiguration of majority–minority relations. Moreover, it blocks the possible paths to ethnic conflict transformation and resolution. To put it somewhat dramatically, the state faces either a process of dissolution or re-forming. This chapter explores the conceptual possibilities for state re-forming in Sri Lanka.

Sri Lanka's post-colonial state has been the continuation in form and content of the centralized, unitary state constructed under the British colonial rule. At independence, there was no rupture with the past, except that the post-colonial state came to be managed by the indigenous ruling elites. The constitutional foundations of the state were initially set out in the Soulbury Constitution of 1947 which provided for a unitary and centralized state. The structure of governance it established was designed in the British parliamentary tradition. Thus, Sri Lanka inherited from the British a bicameral legislature and a cabinet system of government with the prime minister as the head of the political executive. Local government, designed in line with the British system, provided the only institutional mechanism for limited decentralization in the very limited domain of service delivery. It needs to be noted that those who designed the constitutional foundations of the post-colonial Sri Lankan state either shared the assumption that Sri Lanka was an ethnically homogenous polity or did not realize the need to design political institutions to suit a multi-ethnic society.

The framers of the Soulbury Constitution were nonetheless aware of what was known at the time as the 'communal problem'. It had evolved to express itself as an intense competition for representation and a share of governmental power between the majority Sinhalese and the minority Tamil and Muslim communities. However, federalism or regional autonomy was not on the political agenda of ethnic minorities or the British framers of the constitution prior to independence.

Therefore, the Soulbury Constitution provided for a few measures concerning minorities that were described in the constitutional discourse of the time as 'minority safeguards'. One such key 'minority safeguard' was the limit imposed on the independent parliament in its legislative powers. Section 29 of the Soulbury Constitution limited the legislative sovereignty of Sri Lanka's parliament in relation to religious or inter-community matters. Thus, no law enacted by the Sri Lankan parliament had the authority to prohibit or restrict the free exercise of any religion, or make persons of any community or religion liable to discriminatory restrictions or disabilities. This was a constitutional device meant to prevent the legislators of the majority community, who would invariably enjoy an entrenched numerical majority in parliament, from abusing the legislature for the denial of minority rights.

However, the constitutional and political thinking that evolved within Sinhalese nationalism in the post-independence years did not find the 'minority safeguard' provisions particularly palatable. In fact, the Sinhalese nationalist constitutionalists viewed them as an impediment on the political independence and sovereignty of the state. This was indeed a part of the political vision of post-colonial Sinhalese nationalism that conceptualized the state to be the supreme instrument in the service of the interests of the majority community. That larger political vision was in turn constructed on the assumption that European colonialism had favoured ethnic and religious minorities at the expense of the Sinhalese–Buddhist majority who were the legitimate 'sons of the soil'. Thus, soon after independence, a powerful argument developed in favour of transforming the Sri Lankan state into a 'genuinely independent' entity, in the sense of constitutionally ensuring that the political power of the majority community remained secure and entrenched. Thus, the constitutional reform debate in the 1950s onwards was about how to remake the post-colonial state in strictly ethnic-majoritarian terms. There was a particular conceptualization of political independence, as constructed by Sinhalese nationalists as well as left-wing political thinkers in Sri Lanka. It was centred on the notion of 'national sovereignty'. The 'really independent' and 'sovereign' state was to have the following characteristics: (i) territorial unity of the state with no political or administrative decentralization; (ii) a centralized parliament with no limitations on its legislative competence and without any parallel or subordinate law-making bodies; and (iii) state institutions embodying and serving the interests of the Sinhalese–Buddhist majority community.[4]

Political leaders and legal thinkers from both Sinhalese nationalist and left persuasions worked together to achieve this goal. The First Republican Constitution of 1972 was the outcome of this movement. It made the Sri Lankan state explicitly unitary and centralized/abolished all the minority safeguard provisions of the previous constitution, and changed the composition of parliament by making it a unicameral legislature with untrammelled law-making powers. In a major statement of majoritarian nationalist assertion, the framers of the 1972 Constitution made Buddhism 'the foremost religion' of the country, committing the state to 'foster and protect' it. In effect, the 1972 Constitution constitutionalized all the major demands of Sinhalese–Buddhist nationalism and formalized the exclusion of the minorities from the domain of state power. The constitutional reform of 1978 did not alter this aspect of the state at all. The new constitution enacted in 1978 continued, with no change whatsoever, the same Sinhalese-majoritarian control of the state established in the 1972 Constitution.

Meanwhile, there was a recurrent argument in favour of reforming the post-colonial Sri Lankan state in a framework of power-sharing among ethnic communities, but it did not enjoy political support within the majority community. This was the demand for federalist remaking of the Sri Lankan state, as articulated by Tamil nationalists. They began the federalist campaign within the first five years of the political independence of 1948 in response to the citizenship and franchise legislation initiated by the Sinhalese political leadership. These were legislations that were openly and blatantly discriminatory vis-à-vis the minority Tamil community. The Tamil federalist demand, advanced by the Federal party formed in 1951, was based on the belief that regional autonomy for the Tamil majority Northern and Eastern provinces would safeguard the Tamil rights within a state claimed and owned by the ethnic majority. Precisely because of the fact that this federalist demand came from the minority Tamil perspective, it did not receive any political legitimacy, or even sympathy, within the mainstream political debate in Sri Lanka. The Sinhalese nationalist response to the Tamil demand for federalism was that federalism would be totally detrimental to the independence, sovereignty, and territorial unity of the state of Sri Lanka. Resistance to federalism, in this argument, was a patriotic duty. The left parties too opposed the federalist campaign of Tamil nationalism on the basis that it was a reactionary demand intended to divide the working classes along communal identity politics.[5] When the Tamil parties proposed a federal framework during the constitutional reform debate in 1972, the leaders of the United Front regime summarily dismissed the Tamil demand, without even discussing it in the Constituent Assembly. The same disregard for Tamil claim to regional autonomy was re-enacted in 1978 when the Second Republican Constitution was adopted.

A deviation from the entrenched constitutionalist unitarism occurred in 1987 with external, Indian in this case, intervention. When the civil war was escalating, the Indian government worked with the government of Sri Lanka to formulate the constitutional framework for a political settlement. After initial reluctance and resistance, the Sri Lankan government agreed with India to create a new political structure for power-sharing through devolution. The Indo-Lanka Accord of July 1987 and the subsequent 13th Amendment to Sri Lanka's 1978 Constitution created a system of provincial councils. These were designed in the Indian mould of federalism with much less powers to the councils. Even then, the creation of provincial councils through a constitutional amendment was a significant step in the direction of reforming the Sri Lankan state.

However, the provincial councils did not bring Sri Lanka's ethnic conflict to an end. The LTTE continued its war for secession. No government succeeded until May 2009 in militarily defeating the LTTE, nor had the LTTE succeeded in achieving its secessionist objective either. What became clear in this protracted conflict was that a military solution was not the best strategy to resolve the ethnic conflict politically and in a lasting manner. A negotiated political settlement could have provided a stronger foundation for a lasting political settlement to the conflict. While negotiations did take place to find a political settlement, the central issue that was debated and deliberated upon was, as it has been in the case with the war, is state power. Sri Lanka's ethnic conflict, as well as its possible termination, is embedded in the vital question of state power. That is not to deny the importance of 'underlying causes'[6] or 'structural' factors[7] in generating Sri Lanka's ethnic conflict. Group discrimination, limited access to public resources, and cultural marginalization were indeed the key components of the minority experience that eventually resulted in the ethnic conflict and the secessionist war. However, the protracted war has transformed the core dynamic of the conflict by replacing the discourse of grievances with a discourse of state power. This shift has been paralleled with a tendency in which the consequences of the war and violence, rather than the original 'root causes', had acquired a greater capacity to propel the conflict forward. One can even argue with a great measure of confidence that the war that has characterized the conflict for over two and half decades had pushed the 'underlying causes' and 'structural factors' into the background and brought the question of state power to the centre of the conflict as well as the agenda for peace. The protagonists of the ethnic conflict were locked in this intractable problem of state power. They had made issues of economic development, humanitarian assistance, and social reconstruction secondary to how these issues would impinge on the existing or emerging dynamics of state power.One can scarcely disagree with Holsti's assertion that wars of the late twentieth century had not been about foreign policy, security, honour, or status. Rather, they have been about 'statehood, governance and the role and status of nations and communities within states'.[8]

Remaking the State

It is reasonable to assert that a sustainable political settlement to Sri Lanka's ethnic conflict seems to presuppose some form of remaking of the existing state. After over 20 years of civil war, Sri Lanka's political order cannot remain unreformed, except in a condition of perpetual conflict, violence, and lack of peace. A question that arises in the context of Sri Lanka is whether it is possible at all to reintegrate a secessionist ethnic community into the state without radically altering the way in which the state power is organized. 'No' would be a reasonable response to this question. A credible counterweight to secession is a substantial measure of political reforms that promise and practise right to internal self-determination of the minority communities.

If substantial political reforms are a precondition for making secession redundant, then there should be political space for such reforms to be imagined, debated, concretized, and implemented. How then and where can the space for state-remaking initiatives be found in the midst of an ongoing civil war? Finding such space itself requires a process of political transformation, because, as Sri Lanka's experience demonstrates, in an ethnically polarized society, arguments and visions for re-form command less legitimacy and support than agendas for unilateral gains to be achieved through military means. Even then, political transformation is contingent on the presence in society of a process towards a political settlement of the conflict which is also shared by the principal parties to the civil war. In this perspective, there is a link between the will to terminate the civil war, a commitment to the political management of the ethnic conflict, and a belief in the possibilities for the institution of state-remaking reforms.

Envisioning of a sustainable initiative for reforming the state in order to constructively deal with the ethnic conflict in Sri Lanka would have necessitated three interrelated and overlapping tasks. The first is the termination, or substantial de-escalation, of the war through negotiations between the government and the LTTE, who were the two principal parties to the war. Weakening the link between ethnic conflict and war should have been the most important strategic goal to be achieved in this initial phase. Negotiated termination and sustained de-escalation of the war would have provided continuing space for the emergence of political and social conditions that would effectively delink the ethnic conflict from war and violence. This may be termed as a phase of transitional 'negative peace'.

The second was reforming the state through a constitutional covenant worked out on the basis of a consensus among all or most of the island's national-ethnic communities in order to determine the nature of power-sharing in the future state. This idea of a constitutional covenant would have had two crucial consequences. First, it could have provided a means of eliciting popular sanctity for the new constitution as a federalizing charter to broad-base the ethnic foundations of the post-conflict state. Second, it would have enabled regional/local minority communities, that is, numerically small identity groups, to participate in the new polity not as 'minorities' in the liberal constitutionalist sense, but as moral equals whose consent is worthy of being counted in the post-conflict political compact. In this second phase, constitutional foundations of the post-conflict state could have been defined while creatively synthesizing the territorial and non-territorial forms of power sharing.

The third phase was to be one of transition from 'negative peace' to 'positive peace'. It could have entailed a relatively long period of post-settlement reconstruction of the state and political communities in which the terms of the peace settlement and the new constitution were effectively implemented. Linking the three phases together are tasks of political reconstruction, specific to each phase, yet facilitating transition from civil war to negative peace and then from negative peace to positive, sustainable peace. In this proposition, negative would mean peace as the absence of war as well as violence, agreed upon by the parties to the civil war as a prelude to negotiations seeking war termination. Incidentally, in ceasefire conditions, violence can continue without war, jeopardizing the entire ceasefire process. Positive peace is defined as a sustainable condition of democracy and pluralism, strengthened by the absence of legitimate reasons for returning to civil war as a means resolving social and ethnic grievances.

In introducing the above three tasks of Sri Lanka's post-conflict state remaking efforts in the period during the war, one can also posit them as a critique of the dominant paradigm of conflict resolution shared by the government leaders as well as liberal constitutionalists. A key assumption in the mainstream approach to negotiation, which existed in Sri Lanka's 1994–5 attempt at negotiation as well as the 2002–3 peace process, is that once a ceasefire agreement is in place and the negotiations on track, a formal legal process should take over the trajectories of politics in order to extend, with some minimal alterations, the existing state of the Sinhalese south to the Northern and Eastern provinces. Excessive faith in unilateralist constitution-drafting as well as the pre-eminence accorded to constitutional lawyers in designing the future Sri Lankan state is only an outward manifestation of an issue that continues to characterize Sri Lanka's current political debates on conflict resolution. It refers to the inability of the Sinhalese political elites to grasp the point that nearly 30 years of ethnic war has itself been an integral component in Sri Lanka's post-colonial process of state formation. I argue that in order to grasp the dimensions of this process of state formation under conditions of a protracted conflict, it is quite useful to acknowledge that while the secessionist war has radically undermined the foundations of the post-colonial unitary state in Sri Lanka, it has also given rise to new and conflicting directions, as well as new political dynamics, of state formation.

The concept of state formation is defined here to mean the continuing processes that shape the conceptualization, organization, as well as structures of state power in response to social conflict, class struggle, ideological battles, group mobilization, and even external intervention. The directions of state formation have been conditioned by a host of disjunctures in the politics of post-colonial Sri Lanka. The primary disjuncture has developed in the mutually antagonistic processes of state formation in Sinhalese and Tamil societies. The spread of ethnic conflict and then the ethnic war exacerbated this process of disjuncture. It manifested itself in a variety of ways. The primary among them is the presence of the Sri Lankan state in the Northern and Eastern provinces since 1983, that is, since the civil war began, exclusively as a coercive military entity that engaged in war and occupation of what the

Tamil nationalists view as the 'homeland' of Sri Lankan Tamils. In the context of the war, the Sri Lankan state's democratic institutions and practices have been largely withdrawn from the Northern Province and most of the Eastern Province for over two decades. In the circumstances of the civil war, the Tamil society in Sri Lanka's North and East has also produced its own semi-state structures.[9] Built on the LTTE's guerilla and counter-state military institutions, the emerging, alternative state in the North and East has been primarily constituted by institutions as well as practices of primitive accumulation of state power through warfare. The regular deployment of extreme violence and coercion against the populace, the existence of extensive networks of espionage, control, discipline, and punishment, the deployment of 'annihilatory violence',[10] and the existence of vast networks of extortion, protection rackets, and economic control have been some of the dynamics that have shaped the nature of the emerging Tamil 'ethnic' state under the conditions of the secessionist war. These were indeed practices associated with all Tamil militant groups, the military institutions of the Sri Lankan state, as well as the Indian army that occupied these areas for three years in the late 1980s.

Meanwhile, whenever the LTTE established control over civilian populations in the North and East, it also established institutions of governance and administration in order to maintain public order, taxation, social welfare, policing, and crime control, administration of justice and imprisoning convicts and political opponents, and providing health and educational facilities. These were primitive institutions of an emerging state that appeared to function at a rudimentary and underdeveloped level, yet with deadly efficiency in ensuring social control, mass domestication, and social obedience. The LTTE held the view that this parallel state, however incomplete or deformed it may appear, represented the key 'historical achievement' of the Sri Lankan Tamil nation. In the LTTE's understanding, it was a state that has grown out of the Tamil nationalist struggle for sovereignty. In the LTTE's thinking, its dismantling and subsequent replacement with the institutions of the Sri Lankan state would amount to dissolving the most important gains of the 20 years of nationalist struggle of Sri Lankan Tamils.[11]

From the LTTE's perspective, any settlement to the conflict would have to grant legitimacy and acceptance to these institutions and structures of state power in the North and East. When being a militarily unvanquished minority nationalist movement, the LTTE could scarcely be expected to welcome the extension of the Sri Lankan state to what the Tamils considered to be their 'homeland'. Even the LTTE's most conciliatory option presupposed the relative retreat of the Sri Lankan state from the North and East. In this backdrop, a credible political settlement to the civil war in Sri Lanka needed to be worked out within a framework that would have enabled the discovery of common ground between the existing state and the emerging regional state. Although it can be argued that a way out may be found in the concept of 'shared sovereignty', the Sinhalese political class, which includes the dominant ruling elites of the United National Party and the Sri Lanka Freedom Party as well as the secondary ruling elites of the Janatha Vimukthi Peramuna (People's Liberation Front), was not willing to concede such a radical position concerning state power.

The preceding discussion has far-reaching implications for the way in which the idea of sovereignty would be understood in relation to the emerging, post-conflict Sri Lankan state. First, the Sinhalese nationalist concept of unified and undivided sovereignty cannot accommodate the Tamil nationalism's claim to sovereignty even within a framework of regional autonomy. Second, the Muslim communities, particularly those in the Eastern province, are most likely to resist the Tamil nationalist claim to regional autonomy as sovereignty. The Muslim political demands have been evolved during the ethnic war primarily in opposition to the theory and practice of Tamil secessionist politics that produced anti-Muslim ethnic cleansing, massacres, land-grabbing, and antagonisms grounded in fears of collaboration as well as betrayal. The continuing group violence, which has defined recent Tamil–Muslim relations in the Northern and Eastern provinces, has also been a dimension of alternative state formation in Sri Lanka's conflict zone. Linked to ethnic cleansing have been the expropriation of land and private property belonging to the rival ethnic community, planned destruction of multicultural settlements and the emergence in their place of mono-ethnic community life forms[12] that have been integral dimensions of the sociology and culture of this particular pattern of state formation. It defies, and is indeed antithetical to, multiculturalism and pluralism. It is a dimension of state formation developed under conditions of a violent and protracted ethnic conflict. It was obviously too much to expect this type of state formation process to provide much impetus for democratic state forms even in a post-conflict phase. It did not augur well for a negotiated political solution to the conflict either. Instead, what it actually propelled forward is a protraction of the war in which unilateral military outcomes enjoyed greater legitimacy and acceptability.

Thus, an agenda of democratization, if it were to be linked to a conflict transformation process, should not ignore the peculiarities of state formation in the Northern and Eastern provinces under the conditions of war. The difficult task of post-conflict democratic state formation entails delineating and differentiating democratic and pluralistic tendencies from authoritarian ones and creating political and social conditions for their consolidation. It suggests a transformative political agenda that can inclusively and creatively link democratic impulses developed in all ethnic formations in Sri Lanka. In the rest of the chapter I will discuss the conceptual possibility for such a transformation. Before moving into that discussion, I devote the next section to an examination of some comparative perspectives on the complex dimensions of ethnic conflict resolution in deeply divided societies engulfed in civil war.

PROTRACTED CONFLICTS AND THE QUESTION OF STATE POWER

In the recent literature on protracted social conflicts, there has emerged a considerable emphasis on the political reform dimensions necessary for their resolution. The assumption shared by scholars in the 1970s and 1980s that inter-state or intra-state conflicts were amenable to resolution through negotiation and mediation came to be re-examined in the 1990s against the backdrop of post-agreement difficulties in instances like Northern Ireland and Israel–Palestine. Failure of negotiation as well as the breakdown of settlement accords have been so frequent that in a recent study Darby acknowledges that '[o]f the thirty-eight formal peace accords signed between January 1988 and December 1998, thirty-one failed to last more than three years'.[13] In an examination of 41 civil wars between 1940 and 1990, Walter[14] has found that combatants of only 17 had initiated negotiations designed to end their fighting. While in eight of these 17 cases (47 per cent), the adversaries had signed and implemented successful peace agreements, in nine other cases (53 per cent), the parties returned to war. Walter makes two significant observations on this experience of civil war settlement. First, notwithstanding all the impediments to cooperation, the combatants involved in almost half of all peace negotiations did succeed in ending their conflict off the battlefield. Second, despite the high costs of fighting, including the possibility of elimination on the battlefield, over half the combatants involved in negotiations chose to return to war.[15] Sri Lanka provides further insights into the complexities in negotiation to end civil war through a repeated cycle of war, negotiation, mediation, accord-making, a return to war, and return to the negotiation table. Sometimes it has been difficult to draw a distinction between negotiation and war-making. At other times, negotiations resembled war being conducted by non-military means.

Among scholars who have attempted to grapple with the new challenges of ending protracted conflicts, William Zartman has empha-sized the crucial need for what he calls 'returning to normal politics'.[16] Internal conflicts begin, in Zartman's illuminating formulation, 'with the breakdown of normal politics',[17] with the inability of or unwillingness of the government to handle social grievances to the satisfaction of the aggrieved. Characterized by the dynamics of 'asymmetry', protracted internal civil wars have become the most difficult of conflicts to negotiate. Zartman points out that only a quarter to a third of modern civil wars have found their way to negotiation. About two-thirds of the internal conflicts have ended in the surrender or elimination of one of the parties involved. However, in protracted conflicts based on issues of deprivation, discrimination, and identity, the defeat of the rebellion merely drives the cause further underground—or even abroad, in contemporary conditions of globalization—only to re-emerge at a later stage. As Zartman says in fairly straightforward terms, 'It is the government's job to be responsive to the grievances of its people; it is the insurgent's purpose to draw attention to their grievances and gain redress. Negotiation is the natural meeting point of these needs, an extension of the "normal politics" that should characterize a "well-functioning polity".[18] However, as Zartman acknowledges, internal conflict works against its best outcome. The process of resolving internal conflicts through negotiation and assisted by mediation—a long, arduous, and complex process—presupposes a return to normal politics:

The eventual key to the effectiveness of mediators and negotiators is an outcome that returns the conflict to normal politics. In this respect, too, civil wars differ from many other conflicts. Internal conflict cannot be resolved by some wise judgment on an outstanding issue, such as the location of a boundary, the exchange of disarmament quotas, or the terms of a treaty. Rather, the outcome must provide for the integration of the insurgency into a new body politic and for mechanisms that allow the conflict to shift from violence back to politics.

Generally, *this involves creating a new political system in which the parties to the conflict feel they have a stake*, thus in a very positive sense co-opting all parties—government and rebels—in a new creation ... [A] stable outcome must be a joint creation with benefits for both sides to hold them to the agreement.[19]

In this discussion, I take further Zartman's insight of 'returning to normal politics' to argue that in protracted ethnic conflicts that involve the question of state power, often conceptualized in demands for autonomy or separation, normalization of politics should mean a reconstitution of the political order. It presupposes not a return to the old order, or some slightly altered version of it, but rather the creation of new political structures, or, to express it in different terms, reworking the associational bases of the state.

To explain the last point, let us ask the following question: Why should the associational bases of the state be reworked in post-conflict Sri Lanka? The answer to this question is not difficult to surmise, although it is not adequately acknowledged in Sri Lanka's conflict-resolution discourse. A majoritarian nation-state that has been confronting an intractable civil war could hardly restore its political viability without widening its ethnic associational bases. Actually, one way of understanding Sri Lanka's contemporary political crisis is to view the protracted ethnic conflict as a direct outcome of the continuing disjuncture between nation-building and state making.[20] Its defining characteristic has been the political incommensurability of two nations that have been struggling to exist in a single territorial state. Sinhalese and Tamil nations, unable to reconcile to each other in cooperation as one nation or two cooperative nations, have been locked in a civil war for nearly two decades. This incommensurability and mutual exclusivity of these two nation projects in a way represents a key political dimension of the intractability of Sri Lanka's ethnic conflict.

What are the possibilities for grappling with this problem of incommensurability of Sinhalese and Tamil nation projects? Negotiation for a political compromise could have offered the most productive way overcoming it. Even so, the leaders of the Sinhalese and Tamil communities will have to find a language of communication and a framework of conversation in order to discover concrete possibilities of compromise. In such a dialogue for compromise, the question of the state, and the mechanisms for sharing state power, are certain to figure as a central concern. This required the Sri Lankan government and the LTTE to invent something new, enabling the two hostile political entities—the existing state and the emerging counter-state—to coexist.

We can conjecture that only an advanced form of federalism could merge together two relatively independent and competing processes of state formation. Such a future for Sri Lanka can only be premised on the possibility that ethno-nationalist projects, in their majoritarian as well as minoritarian life forms, will hopefully be radically transformed to accommodate multiculturalism, pluralism, and competing trajectories of state formation.

This means that ethno-nationalist projects themselves require being democratic. There is, however, an apparently unresolvable puzzle in this context. Although ethno-nationalist insurgent projects highlight, in a larger-than-life fashion, ethnic grievances and injustices, they can rarely offer democratically emancipatory solutions or alternatives. There are a number of reasons for this fundamental inability of counter-state ethnic insurgencies to carry forward the democratic struggle. The first is closely linked to a foundational weakness in ethno-nationalism of minority politics. As the LTTE's version of Tamil nationalism has demonstrated in a paradigmatic sense, the insurgent state-making project is not likely to offer alternative visions for a democratic and pluralist state. It may even have the potential and desire to mimic the practices of the existing unitarist and majoritarian nation-state against which the minority nationalists have even rebelled. Thus, secession is essentially and fundamentally for separate sovereignty and not for deeper and greater democracy. The second is the general tendency among nationalist rebels to be authoritarian during the armed struggle against the state. The insurgent authoritarianism begins in the early years of the armed struggle when the rebels fight the state in a relationship of adverse asymmetry. Thus, engaged in an asymmetrical war with the state, the secessionist rebels usually develop a pervasive political culture of coercion and violence, treating democracy, human rights, and pluralism as unaffordable luxuries, relevant only to a post-liberation phase. As the experience of Sri Lanka's Tamil insurgent groups clearly indicates, and the LTTE has not been alone in this, the deployment of extreme violence within their own ethnic community has been accepted and legitimized as a liberationist privilege. Ruthless practices of annihilation, total denial of democracy and pluralism, and scorn for institutions of accountability have been legitimized as politically necessary dimensions of the 'liberation struggle'. These ethnic insurgents work on the premise that the deferment of democracy and human rights until the 'liberation' is achieved is both necessary and legitimate. This presupposes what Krishna[21] formulates as the 'logic of deferrence': the endless deferment of the very possibility of democratization in any concrete sense. This logic of deferment begins as a ploy for the self-preservation of rebels in a counter-state civil war but later develops into a foundational political practice.

A lesson that can be derived from this critique of Sri Lanka's Tamil minoritarian project is that ethnic conflicts demand democratic solutions and not a retreat to an ethnicized reconstitution of the political community. Democratization of the political community, pluralization of the state, and sharing of sovereignty are three programmatic goals around which non-ethnic solutions to ethnic problems could be envisioned and developed. Such solutions can be thought out as non-ethnic in two perspectives. First, they are not viewed through an ethnic zero-sum prism. In other words, they do not give rise to ethnic jealousies in terms of who gets what in what proportion. Second, they are pre-conditions for the political emancipation of all ethnic communities, grounding them as equal political communities. This is one way of liberating political emancipation from egoistic ethnic politics and reframing it as an egalitarian desire among all identity communities.

PLURALIZING THE ETHNIC BASES OF THE STATE

At this stage of the discussion, I shift the focus towards suggesting some conditions of possibility for a programme to recreate the associational bases of the Sri Lankan state for reasons of ethnic reconciliation, peace, pluralism, and democracy. This discussion is built around three assertions. The first, as I have already suggested in the previous section, is that ethnic conflicts do not seem to have what one might call 'ethnic solutions' that can deliver political emancipation to minority communities in multi-nation states. It implies that conflict resolution and political reforms in societies in the throes of ethnic conflict require democratic alternatives. They should be alternatives capable of accommodating the ethnic identity aspirations of all communities while protecting the political struggle for emancipation from being transformed into ethnically conceived programmes for hegemony.

The second is that pluralist reworking of the Sri Lankan state presupposes political re-association of the three principal ethnic communities of the island's society—the Sinhalese, Tamils, and Muslims—in active cooperation with regional, local, and other minorities. It suggests the extension of the entitlements of democratic group rights to regional and local minorities as well. The third assertion points towards the idea of state remaking. It considers that the state remaking project should be sufficiently politically open for the unitarist majority, the secessionist minority, as well as other ethnic and identity communities to discover a mutually enabling framework of political association in the form of an associational covenant. The covenant-based re-association should provide the ethnic communities a mutually agreed ground for sustainable cooperation and solidarity while discouraging inter-ethnic enmity, antagonism, violence, and war. This state-remaking proposal is further linked to the argument that covenantal re-association would enable all ethnic and identity communities who constitute the state to treat one another as political communities of equal worth, equal rights, and equal consequence.

To clarify the emphasis on 'regional and local minorities', it is important to recognize that the framing of political grievances and claims to democratic entitlements entirely on the basis of community identities has resulted in counter-democratic consequences in ethnic relations. Two such consequences may be highlighted. First, it has established and reinforced a discourse of majority–minority hierarchy, even naturalizing essentially non-egalitarian social and political practices. To be a 'minority' is to accept a 'natural' condition of second-class status of citizenship, tolerating its accompanying consequences of inequality, discrimination, and marginalization. Second, it has obliterated shifting power relations of communities in situations in which the majority–minority classification becomes meaningless under local circumstances. For example, a community that is a 'national majority' would find itself to be a 'regional minority' in a multi-ethnic local setting, as in the case of the Sinhalese community in Sri Lanka's Eastern province. Similarly, a community which is a 'national minority', like the Tamils in Sri Lanka, would find itself a majority in a regional context. In the unstable logic of group politics, there are not only majorities and minorities, but also many minorities: minorities even within the majority framed in such categories as region, caste, religion, language, and other identities. One radically subversive way of overcoming the majority–minority hierarchy and re-ground group relations in an egalitarian framework is to treat all communities as constituted by multiple minorities. I will discuss the constitutional implications of this position as well as constitutional options it offers in the section entitled 'Deep Federalization and Non-Territorial Power-Sharing'.

As the preceding discussion suggests, democratic alternatives to the ethnic conflict in Sri Lanka face a paradox. While ethnic conflict does not have ethnic solutions, democratic solutions cannot either obliterate or ignore the fact of ethnicity. So long as the ethnic war exists, with violence defining inter-group relations, ethnicized envisioning of political emancipation among communities has become not only a dimension of what one might call the existing political reality, but also constitutive of the ethnic conflict itself. The way out I suggest is to incorporate, instead of banishing, ethnicity into the political alternatives to war and conflict. This requires democratic solutions to be worked out as thin ethnic, as opposed to thick ethnic, solutions, but backed by shared normative goals that have non-ethnic or trans-ethnic foundations. In constitution-making, this offers the responsibility of fashioning a collective form of political life that 'respects otherness'[22] of all groups, grounded on what one may envision as 'just pluralism'.[23]

THREE MODELS FOR CONFLICT RESOLUTION AND CONSTITUTIONAL REFORM

In this section, I will briefly outline, with critical comments, three perspectives or conceptual models that seek to combine the goal of ethnic conflict resolution with a programme of power sharing and constitutional reform. The first is the 'consociational model' which has a powerful theoretical presence in legal and political science discussions on ethnic accommodation in plural societies. The second is the justice model which has primarily emerged in relation to South Africa, but finds resonance in the human rights approach to peace and democracy. Finally, the third is contractarianism which seeks to link contemporary concerns of ethnic peace and democratic accommodation in a value-based political covenant. These models may have considerable overlapping in terms of the issues they seek to address; yet they differ in their political conclusions and their implications for programme-oriented proposals for reform.

Consociational Constitutions for Ethnically Divided Societies

What kind of democracy would Sri Lanka find politically relevant in grappling with the task of restoring ethnic peace? How could Sri Lanka work towards pluralizing the post–civil war state in a deeply federal form while erasing the possibilities for majoritarian democracy to emerge at the national, regional, as well as local levels? Consociationalism offers options that are worth examining for Sri Lanka. It is based on the idea of a grand consensus among ethnic political elites. Arendt Lijphart began proposing 'consociational democratic' alternatives in the early 1970s for societies that were ethnically divided. As Lijphart observed in his comparative study of democracies[24], a key problem of democracy in plural societies was the emergence of majoritarian democracy. Particularly in societies that had parliamentary governments of the Westminster model, majoritarian democracy had led to the rule of ethnic majorities that had in turn made democracies unstable. Lijphart also argued that the majoritarian plural democracies lacked the most basic premise for the functioning of the democratic system: shifting majorities. Under these circumstances, majoritarian democracies tended to create 'permanent minorities'. Virtually as a rule they happened to be ethnic minorities with no say in government and with no hope of being in the governing majority. In this winner-takes-all system, ethnic minorities are usually excluded from political power, and the conflicts involving the minorities are easily channelled into extra-parliamentary and violent forms. To manage the conflicts that have arisen out of the contradictions of majoritarian democracy, Lijphart suggested a four-point formula[25] on which the governments could be re-arranged:

1. The creation of a grand ethnic coalition of all ethnic groups: This meant to facilitate coalitions not among political parties but among ethnic groups with the aim of managing ethnic conflicts.

2. Powers and the offices of the government should be proportionately shared and distributed among ethnic groups.

3. Each ethnic group in the coalition should have the power to veto public policy in order to safeguard its own ethnic interests.

4. The guarantee of ethnic autonomy, or segmented autonomy, in a system of federalism or devolution.

The consociational proposal has a fundamental premise concerning conflicts: It is extremely difficult to resolve conflicts in deeply divided societies where conflicts are often seen as intractable. Therefore, it is appropriate and meaningful for ethnically divided societies to accept and live with, rather than ignoring, the fact that ethnic divisions are a social reality. As deep ethnic cleavages are an inescapable reality, it is only prudent to design the system of government and public policy to deal with that reality. It then assumes that the task of conflict management should start from the top, with leaders of ethnic groups. Understanding and accommodation among leaders would provide the best starting point for a stable political order. It is much easier and even pragmatic for leaders, than for the followers, to accommodate each other's competing demands. In that sense, as the consociational model further assumes, it is wrong to suggest that democracy is unworkable in plural societies with ethnic cleavages. What needs to be done is to rework the systems of democratic representation and regime formation so that no significant subgroup or minority in society is left out without a say in government. This requires the building of political institutions for both democracy and conflict management. Federalism and proportional representation are meant to promote political institution-building. Other key elements of a consociational, federalized polity are the proportional electoral system, constitutionally mandated minority representation in the executive branch of the government, minority protection through the mechanism of minority veto, and segmented autonomy for ethnic groups in the internal matters of government.

Quite apart from the limited vision of conflict management implied in the consociational model, the idea of a 'grand ethnic coalition' could easily become a grand authoritarian alliance.[26] Consociationalist authoritarianism can come in a variety of forms. Malaysia is a case in point. It has an ethnic coalition as the ruling alliance and also a semi-federalist governmental structure. The ruling alliance is a corporatist entity with its own authoritarian version of Asian democracy. The primary characteristic of the Malaysian corporatism is the premise that only the ruling alliance has a legitimate claim to rule the country. Rather than accommodation, a consociational alliance may even re-ensure for the hegemonic ethnic majority its own dominant status while enabling, through segmented autonomy, territorialized minority rule to practise intolerant hegemony over local and social minorities. Without constitutional guarantees for individual rights as well as the rights of the local–peripheral minorities, the principle of segmented autonomy may run the risk of transforming minorities with territorialized power into authoritarian majorities in regional ethnic enclaves. The Muslim fear of Tamil hegemony in the Eastern province is based on this possibility inherent in the principle of segmented sovereignty. Without constitutional protection, local and cultural minorities which are not sufficiently resourceful to enter the grand ethnic coalition would suffer insecurity, discrimination, and even oppression. As Bellamy points out, consociationalism may prove a largely negative and doubly exclusionary strategy because 'it works by excluding new and potentially less manageable groups from attaining a political voice, and on the other hand by encouraging an increasingly exclusive identity amongst the various segments it does recognize'.[27]

Another difficulty with consociationalism is that it is an essentially utilitarian enterprise, assuming that political institutions can and should be manipulated for the maximum benefit of the largest possible number. This is a dangerous premise, both politically and philosophically. The consociational alliance and the sharing of power among leaders of ethnic communities are pragmatic enterprises, which may often lack lasting ethical, or normative, bases necessary for and by a democratic–plural polity. They are also devoid of explicit ethical–normative links between the ethnic leaders and larger society that is made of many ethnic communities. It runs the danger of valorizing and essentializing ethnicity in post-conflict conditions too. Similarly, the consociational approach does not say why the minority leaders should trust the majority leaders at all.

Finally, there has already emerged a proto-consociational model in Sri Lanka providing some valuable insights into the political validity of ethnic coalitions. Since 1994, the Sri Lankan government has been so organized that political parties representing all ethnic communities— Sinhalese, North-East Tamils, Plantation Tamils, and Muslims—have been members of a ruling coalition, sharing positions in the legislature as well as the cabinet. In the balance of power in parliament, ethnic minority parties wield considerable leverage, because no Sinhalese political party can form a government without entering into a coalition with Tamil and Muslim political parties to secure a parliamentary majority and survive. Even with that political leverage, the political capacity of minority parties to effect and shape public policy has been insignificant. In a competitive and corrupt political culture in which the articulation and mobilization of ethnic demands can easily turn into a means of accumulating political power and pecuniary gains, there is no compelling reason for ethnic parties in coalition regimes to define their behaviour and conduct in accordance with consociational goals.

Justice through the State Model

Conflict resolution in societies with institutionalized oppression, inequalities, and violence requires the creation of new political and constitutional structures that enshrine social and political justice as well as human rights. The constitutional model developed for South Africa by Justice Albie Sachs advocated 'a procedure for transforming South African society into a more just scheme of cooperation' so that in the new order social stability depends on 'a democratic social structure respecting individual human rights and distributing opportunities and social goods reasonably fairly among citizens'.[28] Sachs sought to combine political justice with social justice against a backdrop of devastating poverty, racial and social oppression, and inequality that had been major causes of conflict in South Africa. For Sachs, meaningful change required that these issues were addressed by the state. It was therefore necessary to construct a constitution that ensured a 'potent government with maximum ability for political action, a legal framework that secures the direction of change, while safeguarding basic rights of the individual against the state'.[29] Thus, democratic state-building was a major theme in Sachs' model of political change. The state should be transformed into a powerful instrument of social change and of safeguarding citizens' rights and liberties from illegitimate state intervention.

In apartheid South Africa, the historical experience of the state has been one in which the state was never allowed to carry out functions relating to social change. Rather, the state was the supreme instrument of social oppression and extreme inequalities. It was against this historical backdrop that Sachs sought a transformation of the post-apartheid South African state. His project was to transform the post-apartheid state into an agent of democratic change. Therefore, in Sachs' constitutional scheme, the state should be unitary and was expected to remain relatively centralized. This unitarist approach was based on a specific critique of federalism in South Africa, where the ethnic majority, the black nation, was seeking political power in the new democratic order. The old order was not one of 'majoritarian democracy' in the sense of Lijphart, but a minoritarian system of oppressive exclusion. Sachs' critique of federalism is that it was 'a way of depriving majority rule in South Africa of any meaning, by drawing boundaries around race and ethnicity'. Federalism was also thought to 'prevent the emergence of a national government, keep the black population divided, prevent any economic restructuring of the country, and free the economically prosperous areas of the country of any responsibility for helping develop the vast poverty-stricken areas'.[30] Sachs' proposal for the democratization for South Africa was to have a strong Bill of Rights in the constitution, setting up a government based on the principle of separation of powers, decentralization, and institutions of local democracy.[31]

Gloppen notes that Sachs' constitutional proposal for South Africa was guided by the twin concerns of distributive justice and the protection of individual rights and freedoms.[32] This is exactly where some Rawlsian influence on Sachs may also be seen. Sachs wanted to base his constitutional proposals on a set of normative principles, and in that justice was central. The primacy of justice should give legitimacy to the state, because the political order was seen as fair. Therefore, the political order should be seen to be fair by the majority of the South African population. Unless the basic rules of society were seen as just and fair by the majority, and indeed serve the majority—who had remained dispossessed under white minority rule—they were unlikely to generate the support and legitimacy necessary for stability. This position took Sachs along a course that is counter to the consociational scheme, which interestingly had an appeal to the South African white minority. Sachs called it 'multiracial apartheid' and described the consociational devices proposed by the whites as having 'two fundamental principles: there shall be no majority rule and there shall be no rapid moves to end the inequalities produced by apartheid'.[33]

The actual post-settlement constitutional reform process in South Africa offers extremely useful lessons concerning the working of constitutional models for societies in political transition. In the South African constitution-making process, there were sharp debates between contending schools of the justice and consociational models. The interim constitution of 1993, which was essentially a statement of constitutional principles, contained federal as well as consociational principles while reiterating the commitment to democracy, human rights, universal suffrage, equality before the law, non-discrimination, and affirmative action. However, in the second phase of constitution-making, which began in April 1994 with the constituent assembly, the consociational scheme, largely favoured by the National Party of the white minority, suffered setbacks while the African National Congress (ANC) justice model attracted greater support in the constituent assembly. The overall structure of the final constitution adopted in May 1996, according to Gloppen, resembles Albie Sachs' justice model. It provides for a basically centralist and majoritarian political structure, with no grand coalition requirements. It also proposes a strong reliance on the legal system, both in terms of balancing the powers of the government through judicial review and in terms of facilitating social change.[34]

Contractarian Model of Ethnic Justice and Fairness

Formulated by the present author a few years ago in relation to Sri Lanka, this approach is premised on the belief that ethnic conflict resolution in deeply divided societies necessitates a fresh reconfiguration of the bases of political association among different identity communities.[35] This approach also posits that ethnic conflict resolution requires a new social contract to provide the moral and political bases for the post-conflict state. It was developed as an attempt to appropriate Lockean contractarianism, particularly the liberal premise that the government was a trusteeship arrangement among equal citizens, through a revisionist Rawlsian concept of justice. The liberal notion of a contract serves in this model as a mode of conceptual imagination: a metaphor to signify the proposal for the restoration of the political–normative foundations of the state. In societies that have internal rebellions and separatist movements, there are sections of society that do not accept the moral authority of the state. They refuse political obligation to it and indeed project de-obligation as a legitimate response to the state. The willingness to disassociate from the state by communities is, paradoxically, one of the major problems of the modern state. Also, those dis-associationists often happen to be ethnic minorities. This background configures the political project of conflict resolution and political reform into a unified goal that goes beyond the social engineering objectives of the consociational enterprise.

The contractarian model's insistence on ethnic justice and ethnic fairness is justified on two grounds. First, it is important for any society to formulate a set of moral and normative standards, not pragmatic or utilitarian ones, against which the institutions and processes, which are created for conflict resolution, can be evaluated and their performance appraised. The second reason is linked to the political appeal of the claims to fairness and justice made by the minorities. The task of bringing secessionist minorities back to the state requires a moral basis so that the minorities can politically return as equals with equal worth. Thus, ethnic fairness and justice can very well provide the moral–normative framework for the terms of an egalitarian ethnic/social contract. In this contractarian imagination, the state is a political association whose membership is obtained by all individuals as well as all ethnic groups as moral equals and equally valuable agents. To restate this point in Rawlsian language, the state should be an association which is both fair and just so that each individual and ethnic group is to have an equal right to the most extensive basic liberty compatible with a similar liberty of others.

How should the concepts of ethnic justice and ethnic fairness be determined and by whom? To ask the same question in the communitarian language of Walzer,[36] what is the way of overcoming the blindness to otherness, thereby establishing a positive foundation for tolerance of difference and respect for otherness? The way out offered by this particular contractarian perspective assumes a two-phase approach: ignoring particularist ethnicity and a subsequent return to ethnicity as the foundation of pluralism. Initially, a thin ethnic approach is necessary to reconfigure all ethnic groups in the polity as moral equals and equally valuable. Therefore, they do not need to consider their ethnic identity as the sole and determining criterion in evaluating why they should be joining the association of the state through the new social contract. In other words, to be equals and equally valuable, the ethnic groups would disregard whether they are Sinhalese, Tamils, or Muslims. Each of them views itself as a political community seeking statehood in association with several other political communities. This is a relativizing strategy in the Habermasian sense. It proposes to different ethnic communities that they should set limits to their own claims by listening to and engaging with the claims of others. It helps them to evaluate their own particularistic identities, forms of existence, and group claims in relation to the claims made by others without 'sticking doggedly to the universalization of one's own identity' and without 'marginalizing that which deviates from one's own identity'.[37] In the contractarian exercise, groups enter the associational contract with the privilege of ignorance of each other's ethnic identity and become participants to the contract behind a veil of ethnic ignorance. Thus, the privilege of ignorance enables them to choose the principles of ethnic justice while being in a position to define 'fairness' untainted by ethnic interests or prejudices. This stage of ignoring ethnic identities to enter into the contract for political association is analogous to the 'state of nature' in classical contract theory and to the 'original position' in Rawls' theory of justice.

In determining ethnic justice and ethnic fairness, a Rawlsian 'bargaining' process is possible. For example, each ethnic group is to have an equal right to the most extensive total system of equal basic liberties compatible with a similar system of liberty for all. Similarly, if social and economic inequalities are to exist among ethnic communities, they are to be so arranged that the inequalities, to use the Rawlsian utilitarian language, are to serve the greatest benefit of the least advantaged, and attached to offices and positions open to all under conditions of fair equality of opportunity. Finally, all social goods—liberty and opportunity, income and wealth, and the bases of self-respect—are distributed equally unless an unequal distribution of any or all of these goods is to the advantage of the least advantaged. In this perspective of ethnic justice, the insistence is on two counts. First, a measure of egalitarianism among ethnic groups of unequal sizes and strength is determined on the basis of a principle of shared distribution of opportunities and disadvantages. Second, just institutions and practices should be the object of a unanimous agreement among affected communities. This approach to group justice seeks to re-politicize the reasons for ethnic communities to stay together in a state.

For Sri Lanka's immediate politics, there are three principal implications of this contractarian approach. First, the process for constitutional reforms and conflict resolution should be transformed into a process of negotiating 'a new social contract'; an engagement for a 'self-transformative process of identity reinterpretation'.[38] Second, the constitution should be a charter of ethnic fairness and justice. It should also be a 'peace treaty' among the ethnic and political communities in conflict. Third, sharing and devolving state power, its institutions of governance, just electoral processes, and public policy, the ultimate standard to measure their validity and performance, should be the consensus arrived at by all ethnic groups acting as equal political communities who can share both advantages and disadvantages of their being together in one state.

Covenantal Federalism for Sri Lanka

Taken together, the three models of conflict resolution and political reform discussed earlier offer some vital impetus for imagining afresh the way in which the political communities could be rebuilt in Sri Lanka as well as other societies in conflict. They all suggest, with varying degree of emphasis, that power sharing should be the kernel of any meaningful political agenda for reform. They also suggest, with different degrees of intensity, that power-sharing alone would not be adequate to resolve conflicts and reform political structures. From the liberal peace model's notion of 'agreement'—it may be interpreted as commitment to mutual promises made by parties to a peace deal—to the contractarian model's notion of de-ethnicized ethnic justice and fairness, there is an underlying assumption about the sustainability of peace agreements and political reform programmes. Treating a peace treaty as well as an extensively power-sharing constitution as components of a covenant, inviolable yet alterable, has an advantage you its sustainability. As all communities and individuals subscribe to the covenant, they have an ownership-holding relationship to political institutions. This will have greater capacity to make reforms feasible, lasting, and sustainable. Covenantal approach merely seeks to make all citizens stakeholders in peace and democratic reform. Indeed, the political reassociation of estranged ethnic communities within a reinvented nation-state can be best imagined through terms and categories available in the covenantal tradition of politics. Although the covenantal tradition has roots in South Asian intellectual history, it has been largely appropriated in recent years by individual politicians to legitimize their corporatist political goals.[39] My proposal is to ground the federalist–contractarian proposals on the covenantal foundation. It will then enable the idea of reworking the modern state's associational bases on vernacularized idiom. That will in turn foster indigenous discourses of democratic constitutionalism.

One of the greatest advantages of the covenant model is its premise of absolute egalitarianism among actors who join together to form the political association of the state. Daniel J. Elazar, the leading contemporary exponent of the covenantal model, writes:

The Covenantal model functions on an entirely different basis [from the Westminster-style parliamentarism], characterized schematically by a matrix, a group of equal cells framed by common institutions. Its founding comes about because equal individuals or individual entities join together through a covenant or political compact as equals to unite and establish common governing institutions without sacrificing their respective integrities. For the matrix model, the constitution is preeminent since it embodies the agreement that joins the entities or individuals together and establishes agreed upon rules of the game which all have to observe. Its politics that flows from that constitution is a politics of equals based on negotiation and bargaining and designed to be as open as possible, where all the actors will know what is happening. Administration is dependent upon the constitution of its authority and politics for its powers. This system is not hierarchical, even if hierarchies are sometimes organized within it. Nor does its have a single centre. Rather it is based upon multiple centres, each constitutionally protected. Its apotheosis is a federal system in which the constituent units are represented in the framing government and also preserve their own existence, authority, and powers in those areas which are not delegated to the framing institutions.[40]

This long quotation from Elazar is worth reproducing for its simple restatement of principles and virtues that a federalizing political community, rebuilt on the image of a covenant, should encapsulate and nourish. All are non-hierarchical and egalitarian partners to the covenant. Their political conduct is open, transparent, and does not transgress limits and capacity already agreed upon. The political community is poly-centric or multi-centric, which is one of the most important qualities for a state in plural societies that try to emerge out of ethinic conflicts over sovereignty. The practical, working implications of the covenantal proposal are not particularly complicated. Some of the procedural and institutional aspects required for its initial formation are already there. It suggests two basic steps.

First, there should be a peace treaty involving all communities. It should seek the termination of the conflict and inauguration of a new constitution redefining the foundations of the state. It should be conceived and written around the normative principles and political virtues that emanate from the concrete needs of peace, reconciliation, and democratization. For example, peace and reconciliation among all; distribution of democratic rights and entitlements on principles of ethnic justice and fairness, inclusion, and pluralism; sharing of state sovereignty; and fidelity to mutual political promises made by communities to others are some of the norms and virtues that can give collective ethical sanction to the terms of political re-association. In this approach, the constitution is both a peace treaty and a covenant. The actual peace treaty among conflicting parties is the normative preface to the constitution. The constitution in turn is the body of the covenant that embodies the virtues that binds together the political community of equals.

Second, both the peace treaty and the constitution form the overall covenant of the pluralistic political community. Therefore, they need to be legitimized through the plebiscitary consent of the people. The constitution should be drafted by a popularly elected constituent assembly and approved by the people at a referendum. This will make the people, not only the ethnic leaders who sign the peace treaty, stakeholders in the terms, institutions, and processes of peace-making and democratization. It is ultimately popular legitimacy that will turn a constitution into a covenant, according the covenant the character of a charter for political emancipation.

DEEP FEDERALIZATION AND NON-TERRITORIAL POWER-SHARING

In Sri Lanka's present debate on federalism and power-sharing, the principal focus continues to remain on political relations between the

Sinhalese majority community and the Tamil community, or the state and the Tamil community. This debate has a number of features that do not draw attention to the possibilities of multi-level, multi-community, power-sharing arrangements. First, there has been a peculiar, and of course incomplete, cartographic imagination of the special plurality of the island, which is often expressed in the idea that Sri Lanka's ethnic conflict is territorially constituted in terms of north-east and the south. Second, the two territorial entities of north and east, and the south are also often imagined as being ethnically undifferentiated social–geographical entities. Muslim communities in the eastern province have often challenged this particular political mapping of Sri Lanka, reminding us, sometimes in violent ways, that Muslims represent a third ethnic group in the equation in the political settlement to the ethnic conflict. Third, federalist options are understood primarily as constituting a bi-nation future for Sri Lanka in which Sinhalese and Tamil 'nations' would find a constitutional arrangement of regional autonomy through negotiations among Sinhalese and Tamil political elites. This constitutes the fourth characteristic of Sri Lanka's present debate on power-sharing: it is indeed a form of 'top–down federalism', or federalism from above.

Those limitations notwithstanding, the present federalist debate is indeed concerned with refashioning Sri Lanka's future political architecture. While recognizing the limits of the debate, it is important to generate a process of political thinking so that in the emerging new architecture of the Sri Lankan state, the regional/local ethnic minorities are not excluded from power-sharing entitlements. This calls for a form of inclusive and just federalism, or a structure of deep federalization. Before exploring the constitutional options capable of addressing the issue of multiple minorities leading to deep and inclusive federalist arrangements, let us first examine how the question of minority representation and participation in power-sharing has begun to figure in Sri Lanka's political debate as well as in constitutional theory.

In an insightful essay on the political-economy, cultural, and social consequences of Sri Lanka's protracted ethnic war, Rajasingham-Senanayake has drawn attention to the need in any devolution plan to 'eschew the dominant political wisdom' which had long believed the Sinhalese to be 'an absolute majority and Tamils, Muslims and all others as absolute minorities in Sri Lanka'. Rajasingham-Senanayake asserts that for devolution 'to work the magic of peace in Sri Lanka', it must 'focus on localized minorities'.[41] The concern he expressed is that Sri Lanka's devolution proposals that were drafted in the late 1990s did not take into account the rights of local minorities. In this critique, the devolution discourse, as evolved in Sri Lanka, has been founded along the logic of the 'ethnic nationalists' of Sinhalese, Tamil, and Muslim communities, with the consequence that it turned the concept of ethnic self-determination into territorialized ethnic enclaves or ethnic homelands. The outcome of that process would make official the ethnic enclave mentality as well as fears, suspicions, and cultural differences that have been built in the course of the protracted war and violence. In this argument, devolution for multiculturalism and pluralism should have arrangements to safeguard the rights of local minorities while ensuring their safety and security from the hegemonic desires of the local majorities.

Indeed, the question of the possibility of minorities persecuting or oppressing their own minorities under arrangements of federalism, or regional autonomy, has in recent years been a concern among political theorists. Defining the rights of the minorities in opposition to the majority, even against the legitimate claims of the majority, is only one side of the complex story of minority rights. The other side of it is that federalist power-sharing arrangements are intended, consciously and by design, to make a national minority a regional majority. Meanwhile, an ethnic minority can very well be a pluralist community in its ethno-social composition. As Green[42] points out, the minority groups whose claims are defined against the majority are rarely homogeneous. They often contain other minorities. Green calls them 'internal minorities'. We may also call them 'marginal minorities', in the sense that they are marginalized in the mainstream discourse of minority rights as well as in most of the constitutional arrangements of minority-oriented power sharing.

By posing the issue of 'internal' minorities, Green also seeks to address a theoretical concern about modern liberal constitutionalism: doesn't the contemporary liberalism's concern with the protection of minority collectivities or groups itself result in illiberal consequences? For instance, the social groups that it protects and promotes can themselves be enemies of liberal values. As feminists argue, liberal theory and practice secures the family from the interference of the state, but rarely protects women and children from the predations of the family. Liberalism also secures religious liberty but permits religions to suppress minority members. The discourse of minority rights assumes that minorities have rights *even when* they are minorities, as well as *because* they are members of certain minority groups. The protection of internal minorities from the predations of the larger minority is a complex challenge to modern liberalism, and Green concludes by saying that 'without respect for internal minorities, a liberal society risks becoming a mosaic of tyrannies ... The task of making respect for minority rights real is one that falls not just to the majority but also to the minority groups themselves.'[43]

There is, however, an inherent inadequacy of the conventional federalist model when it comes to the power-sharing possibilities for smaller, regional, and dispersed minorities. In a nutshell, the classical federalist principle is about spatial reorganization of state power. It is often required to mediate in conflicts between majority and minority ethnic communities within nation-states. In a way, the democratic ideal of minority protection is now being viewed as a particular task of federalism. When democratic and minority protection tasks of federalism are put together, and further, when both federalism and democracy are interpreted as constituting principles, an interesting problem arises: Can the equality of all citizens be understood in a way that permits also local—that is, group—liberty?.[44] If federal democracy's underlying basis is defence of liberty by preserving diversity, then it must be respectful to both individual and minority rights. However, territorial federalism has an inherent dilemma, because it operates with 'nested entities' without allowing overlapping constitutive units. As I noted earlier, although territorialized distribution and sharing of state power is viewed as a solution to conflict among major ethnic or national groups, it has a potential to leave out local, dispersed, or internal minorities. This question is clearer in the case of bi-national states. The mere fact that there are two national groups in a state does not necessarily mean that the state is a bi-national or multinational one.

The question of local minorities poses itself in another way, giving rise to their status of being what has been called 'double minorities'.[45] While the traditional idea of federalism is based on the notion of territory-based regional autonomy, in instances where the federal units are not ethnically homogenous, the territorial principle of federalism is likely to be inadequate to address ethnic heterogeneity. Indeed, it may even generate tension among communities living within the federal unit. A potential basis for such inter-ethnic tension within federal units would be the feeling among small ethnic communities of being a minority within their federal unit while being members of a national minority. They might remain unrepresented even within a system of power sharing and might feel their cultures to be under threat. More important, they might feel insecure and even unprotected. The other related question is that there is always the possibility of significant proportions of a minority living outside the federal unit that is controlled by their larger, federated community. In multi-ethnic societies with the freedom of movement and spatial mobility, and due to economic and historical reasons, as well as a result of how provincial or administrative units are territorially organized, there may exist 'dispersed minorities'.

Tamils and Muslims in Sri Lanka constitute such dispersed minorities in a number of provinces, particularly in the western, southern, Sabaragamuwa, Uva, and central provinces. One way of addressing the problem of such dispersed minorities is the redrawing of the initial internal boundaries of the federal system, as has been done in Nigeria, India, and Switzerland, so that the minority and constituent unit coincide better. This option can, however, be complex, depending upon the specificities of the context. Provincial boundaries in societies of deep ethnic cleavages can be contested by some groups while some others might view them as historically given, unalterable, and fixed. Altering internal borders in Sri Lanka's context is a difficult proposition to negotiate.

There is also the specific case of Sri Lanka's plantation Tamil community that has not been overtly discussed in the present debate on power-sharing. As we already noted, the focus of the dominant power-sharing debate has been on a bi-national, or bi-community, federalist arrangement. However, the peculiarity of the Sri Lankan case of power-sharing is that seven units of devolution have been established in the Sinhalese majority region of the island, on the territorial basis of provincial boundaries. In these seven provinces, representatives of the plantation community have found their way to the devolved provincial assemblies only in two provinces, in the central and Uva provinces. However, there are sizeable plantation Tamil minorities living in Sabaragamuwa (in Kegalle and Ratnapura districts), southern (in Matara and Galle districts), and western (Kalutara district) provinces. Political claims of the plantation Tamil community have not been an integral part of Sri Lanka's mainstream Tamil nationalist struggle either, although occasionally the citizenship issue relating to them has been raised. Even if the mainstream Tamil nationalism represented plantation Tamil interests and political aspirations, working out a system of power-sharing on the basis of the political homogeneity of the two Tamil communities would have been a complex issue, primarily due to the geographic separation of the regions they inhabit.

Even within federal units, linguistic and cultural minorities can be discriminated against. As Sri Lanka's own experience demonstrates, forming a bi-national state through federalist power-sharing is an exceedingly difficult issue, although at the heart of the conflict between the Sri Lankan state and Tamil nationalist is the question of two nations forming two separate states or a single federalist state. Even assuming that a bi-national federal state is formed with the consent of the two national groups, constitutional and political measures will have to be put in place to avoid the tyranny of the majority and the majority's control over the minority at sub-national levels. As political and constitutional theorists argue, this cannot be achieved through mere goodwill, but only by means of consensus that has institutional foundations. A combination of territorial and non-territorial forms of federalism is one creative option for institutionalizing consensus among multiple minorities in a system of power-sharing.

In Sri Lanka, there are three primary areas with which any future solution to the minority problems needs to be concerned. They are representational rights, security guarantees, and access to state power. The first calls for constitutional guarantees for all minorities to secure representation in the assemblies of governance in parliament, provincial councils, as well as local government bodies. To ensure the translation of such constitutional guarantees into institutional practices, it is necessary to reform the electoral system. There are mechanisms for special representation for smaller minorities, who would not stand a chance in the 'normal' electoral systems, which a new Sri Lankan system could creatively incorporate. The question of security guarantees for smaller minorities can be partially addressed by ensuring representational rights at the three levels of governance by assembly: national, provincial, and local. To ensure greater security for them, measures of affirmative action should be provided for, particularly through non-territorial mechanisms of federalism. Access to state power encompasses representation, legislative decision-making, and participation in executive process, all at national, provincial, as well as local levels. In concrete terms, this demands (i) territorial as well as non-territorial federalism and (ii) federalizing national, provincial, and local assemblies of governance. In framing these constitutional arrangements, the general principle that could be adopted is bi-national multi-community federalism. This principle can provide for power-sharing arrangements between the Sinhalese and Tamil communities on the basis of a two-nation approach while ensuring power-sharing rights to regional, local, and dispersed minorities as well. This requires a constitutional framework of bi-national and multi-ethnic federalism.

* * *

Sri Lanka's experience in recent decades points to a number of key paradoxes as well as possibilities in the politics of state reform in an ethnically divided society with a protracted ethno-political conflict. The country's modern political and constitutional debate has gone through a history of nearly a century within a framework of ethno-identity interests. Over 50 years of that debate has been on the question of unitarism versus federalism. However, even today the debate remains inconclusive, given the incommensurability of communication between the island nation's two principal ethno-nationalist projects. However, the country's constitution has incorporated the principle of power-sharing in its framework of devolution. This, as the chapter points out, has two key dimensions. First, even after nearly a century of constitutional and political debate, the opposition to power-sharing with minority communities continues to remain a major obstacle to the real federalization of the polity. Second, even though the constitution has created institutions of power-sharing in the form of provincial councils, the power-sharing arrangements remain weak, under-developed, and subject to central government control. The issue which this chapter raises in this context is that power-sharing in a deeply divided society in conflict is more than an exercise in altering or rewriting its constitution. It requires the reconstitution of political communities in equality and solidarity.

This chapter has also argued that federalist power-sharing in an ethnically divided society is a highly complex political exercise, because of the ethnic political fears generated by the presence in society of a protracted ethnic conflict. This paradox is further complicated by the fact that political communities think and act as ethnic communities first. Their political worth is believed to derive from their ethnicity. In other words, their worlds of political imagination and action are ethnicized. In such a political world of ethnicization, the discourse of federalism finds no legitimacy among ethnic majoritarian forces. Indeed, in Sri Lanka, the argument for federalization of the polity has emerged from the Tamil ethnic minority and the pressure for federalist reforms originates from outside entities, that is, the states and institutions of global civil society. Its consequence is felt in the way in which Sinhalese majoritarian political forces have successfully managed to delegitimize the very idea of federalism. Indeed, one conclusion one may arrive at through the Sri Lankan experience is that federalism is not an ethnically neutral concept of constitutionalism. It is an acutely ethnicized category. This chapter indeed argued for de-ethnicization of democratic solutions to ethnic questions while recognizing ethnicity as a mediatory dynamic for democratization.

However, a process of de-ethnicizing democratic solutions to ethnic grievances cannot even begin without framing the initial package of political-constitutional options partly in ethnic-identity terms. It means, as this chapter argued, working out, at the very outset of a settlement process, a system of federalist power-sharing among ethnic communities on the basis of their ethnicity. The paradox of ethnic politics is that while it has provided the framework for conflict and has failed to provide democratically emancipatory options, it is also the framework within which a solution to the conflict has to be initially conceptualized. This chapter argued for an acknowledgement of the limits of ethnic imagination in bringing about democratic alternatives to ethnic grievances. It also made a case for recognizing the validity of ethnicity as an organizing principle of post-conflict state power. The proposal for both territorial and non-territorial forms of federalism is based on this duplex nature of ethnicity's limitation as well as unavoidability. The idea of deep federalization, proposed in this chapter, is both the recognition of, and a way out of, this dilemma.

The challenge for Sri Lanka, as I assert in this chapter, is not just about reforming the existing constitutional structures of power-sharing, but merging the task of ethnic conflict resolution with the transition of the state to post-conflict conditions. This requires the state to be both the subject and object of change at the same time: to act as an agent of change while transforming itself. Sri Lanka's ruling parties as well as the international community have in the past viewed constitutional reform for power-sharing as a necessary precondition for ethnic conflict resolution. However, the constitutional reform project has been repeatedly stalled in Sri Lanka precisely because the ethnic conflict has produced dynamics against a constitutional settlement. The conclusion one may arrive at from this observation is that in Sri Lanka ethnic conflict resolution and constitutional reform are so closely interwoven that one cannot precede or follow the other. I have, however, argued that the link between ethnic conflict resolution and political reforms for ethnicity-based power-sharing is so fragile that its realization requires a qualitatively new political consensus, a sort of

new social contract, a fresh covenant for political association. Some
ideas concerning this symbolic social covenant have been outlined in
this chapter. I have argued that an imaginatively contractarian option
in the image of a new ethnic–social covenant would help radicalize the
inter-ethnic political consensus for conflict resolution as well as deeply
federalized power-sharing.

The discussion developed here also leads to a host of critical and
unconventional premises on the state, citizenship, ethnicity, ethnic
politics, constitutionalism, power-sharing, and the legal order. A few
may be restated as follows in order to recapture the flow of my analysis
and argument: Sri Lanka's experience of ethnic conflict as well as failed
attempts at constitutional reform suggest that the existing forms of
the nation-state as models of political association have already become
outdated in the historical context of a protracted ethnic conflict. This
has been a global historical tendency of state formation during recent
decades. New forms of political organization are likely to emerge out
of nation-states in crisis. Among the forms of the state likely to emerge
are mono-ethnic mini-states in post-conflict societies.[46] However, this
form of ethnic enclave state is unlikely to offer a democratic alternative.
A key challenge which any new form of the state will be compelled
to confront and negotiate concerns the democratic accommodation
of ethnic plurality and diversity while pushing to the background
exclusively ethnic imaginations of the political futures of communities.
In this chapter, I have developed an argument for 'just pluralism' to
address this dilemma.

I have pointed out that Sri Lanka's question of power-sharing
and federalism is integrally linked with ethnic conflict resolution and
a reconstitution of the post-colonial state. This state reconstitution
agenda is framed in the historical transition of Sri Lanka's post-colonial
state to a post-conflict state. In that transition, the resolution of Sri
Lanka's ethnic conflict requires democratic solutions to ethno-political
grievances and demands of a multiplicity of communities, not excluding
regional, dispersed, local, and marginal minorities. Thus, working
out democratic solutions to ethnic issues will also mean democratic
reconstitution of the modern state by reforming and federalizing it
from within, at its foundations, at its centre, and, importantly, also at
its periphery and the regions. There is therefore a compelling need to
re-imagine the project of the state in fresh and emancipatory terms.
As for my own contribution to this conversation, I have proposed a
mode of covenantal re-imagination of the state that would create a

political–constitutional framework of bi-national and multi-community federalism. This chapter argued for a federalizing polity, distinct from a static federal polity that should have a relentless capacity to re-invent itself in more, not less, democracy, autonomy, and justice.

Postscript

Since this chapter was written, its political context has changed. There have been some major shifts and developments in Sri Lanka's ethnic conflict. The key development is the military defeat of the LTTE in May 2009 at the hands of the armed forces of the Sri Lankan state. This was the culmination of the fourth phase of Sri Lanka's civil war, a phase that began in early 2006. The outright military defeat of the LTTE, and the annihilation of virtually its entire leadership in the war, is an outcome that surprised the world. The critical question that remains to be answered at present is: will the military defeat of the LTTE and the military victory of the Sri Lankan state constitute a new phase of Sri Lankan politics, enabling the Sinhalese and Tamil communities to resolve the ethnic conflict through political reforms? There is no easy answer to this question. In a way, it raises new, and no less difficult, questions about the extent to which the Sri Lankan state can be reformed in a post–civil war context.

The military defeat of the LTTE has obviously removed from Sri Lanka's political equation a key obstacle to a negotiated political settlement to the ethnic conflict. The LTTE's secessionist agenda has been a stumbling bloc to a political settlement within a framework of devolution, or even federalism. It is hardly necessary to emphasize that the end of the LTTE is not the end of the ethnic conflict. If it remains unresolved politically, the conflict can take new forms with a protracted life of its own. However, the question now is whether the absence of the LTTE and its military dimension would provide incentives for Sri Lanka's political elites to recognize the urgency of a political settlement with the remaining Tamil political entities. A somewhat uncomfortable observation one can make in this regard is that a unilateral military victory for the state in an ethnic civil war may not create new conditions for state reform. In the emerging post–civil war conditions, Sri Lanka seems to be facing a new dilemma of having no real incentives for state reform initiatives. The outcome of the war has not strengthened the state reform potential of the polity; rather, it has led to impulses towards re-strengthening the unitary and centralized ethnic state.

In the post-LTTE phase of the ethnic conflict, the debate for state reforms has been resurrected in the form of an argument for devolution and the full implementation of the 13th Amendment to the existing constitution which introduced devolution in 1987. Devolution provides a minimalist framework for power-sharing with the Tamil and Muslim minorities. However, the pressure for devolution does not seem to emerge from within the Sri Lankan polity, coming principally from external actors, notably India and USA, who have anticipated the defeat of the LTTE to provide new incentives for the Sri Lankan government to adopt a unilateral political reform agenda. The Sri Lankan government has been successfully resisting such external pressure for immediate political reforms. Meanwhile, there is no significant political force within the regime, or from among other domestic political actors, to bring devolution to the centre of the regime's agenda. Paradoxically, the argument now is in favour of further centralization of the state within the unitary framework with no reforms, ostensibly to consolidate national security and sovereignty that the war has secured for the people. In other words, the end of the war has not really widened but narrowed down the political space for state reforms in a direction of ethnic pluralization of the associational bases of the Sri Lankan state. Thus, Sri Lanka is likely to remain in a post–civil war trap for the foreseeable future with no prospects for reforming the state, notwithstanding the fact that state reforms in a federalist framework continue to be a good political path towards a durable resolution of the ethnic conflict.

Notes

1. Ketheshwaran Loganathan, *Sri Lanka: Lost Opportunities, Past Attempts at Resolving Ethnic Conflict* (Colombo: University of Colombo, 1996), p. 104.

2. Loganathan, *Sri Lanka*, pp. 144–62, especially 104.

3. Jayadeva Uyangoda and Morina Perera (eds), *Sri Lanka's Peace Process 2002: Critical Perspectives* (Colombo: Social Scientists' Association, 2003) p. 280.

4. Jayadeva Uyangoda, 'The State and the Process of Devolution in Sri Lanka', in Sunil Bastian (ed.), *Devolution and Development in Sri Lanka* (New Delhi: Konark Publishers, 1994).

5. V. Karalasingham, *The Way Out for the Tamil Speaking People* (Colombo: Young Socialist Publications, 1963).

6. John Burton, *Conflict: Resolution and Prevention* (New York: St. Martin's Press, 1990).

7. Johan Galtung, 'Violence, Peace, and Peace Research', *Journal of Peace Research*, 6 (3), (1969), pp. 167–91.

8. Kalevi Holsti, *The State, War and the State War* (Cambridge: Cambridge University Press, 1996), p. 21.

9. Kristian Stokke, 'Building the Tamil Eelam State: Emerging State Institutions and Forms of Governance in LTTE-Controlled Areas in Sri Lanka', *Third World Quarterly*, 27(6), pp. 1021–40.

10. Sankaran Krishna, *Postcolonial Insecurities: India, Sri Lanka, and the Question of Nationhood* (Minneapolis and London: University of Minnesota Press, 1999).

11. These observations are also based on my interactions with the LTTE leaders as well as sympathizers in January–April 1995 and in 2003.

12. Darini Rajasingham-Senanayake, 'The Dangers of Devolution: The Hidden Economies of Armed Conflict', in Robert I. Rotberg (ed.), *Creating Peace in Sri Lanka: Civil War and Reconciliation* (Washington DC: Brookings Institution Press, 1999).

13. John Darby, *The Effect of Violence on Peace Processes* (Washington DC: The US Institute of Peace, 2001), p. 8.

14. Barbara F. Walter, 'Designing Transition from Civil War: Demobilization, Democratization and Commitments to Peace', *International Security*, 24, pp. 127–55.

15. Ibid., p. 127.

16. I. William Zartman, 'Dynamics and Constraints in Negotiations in Internal Conflicts', in I. William Zartman (ed.), *Elusive Peace, Negotiating an End to Civil Wars* (Washington DC: Brookings Institution, 1995), pp. 3–27.

17. Ibid., p. 5.

18. Ibid., p. 3.

19. Ibid., pp. 21–2 [emphasis added].

20. P. Saravanamuttu, 'Sri Lanka: Civil Society, the Nation and the State-Building Challenge', in A. Van Rooy (ed.), *Civil Society and the Aid Industry* (London: Earthscan, 1999).

21. Krishna, *Postcolonial Insecurities*, p. 17.

22. Michael Walzer, 'Nation and Universe', in *The Tanner Lectures on Human Values, XI* (Salt Lake City: University of Utah Press, 1990), pp. 507–56.

23. Shane O'Neil, *Impartiality in Context: Grounding Justice in a Pluralist World* (Albany: State University of New York Press, 1997), p. 188.

24. Arendt Lijphart, 'Consociational Democracy', *World Politics*, 21, 1969, pp. 207–25; 'Consociational Democracy', in R.J. Jackson and M.B. Stein (eds), *Issues in Comparative Politics* (New York: St. Martin's Press, 1971); *Democracy in Plural Societies: A Comparative Exploration* (New Haven: Yale University Press, 1977).

25. Ibid.; Arendt Lijphart, *Democracy in Plural Societies: A Comparative Exploration* (New Haven: Yale University Press, 1977); Arendt Lijphart, *Power-Sharing in South Africa: Policy Papers in International Affairs, No. 24*, (Berkeley, California: Institute of International Studies, 1985).

26. Horowitz notes: 'In democratic conditions, grand coalitions are unlikely, because of the dynamics of intra-ethnic competition. The very act of forming a multiethnic coalition generates intra-ethnic competition—flanking—if it does not already exist; what is more, the Asian or African regime which declares that it has a grand coalition probably has, not a consociational democracy, but an ethnically exclusive dictatorship' (Donald Horowitz, *Ethnic Groups in Conflict* [Berkeley and London: University of California Press, 1985]).

27. Richard Bellamy, *Liberalism and Pluralism: Towards a Politics of Compromise* (London and New York: Routledge, 1999), pp. 126–7.

28. Siri Gloppen, *South Africa: The Battle over the Constitution* (Aldershot: Dartmouth, Ashgate, 1997), p. 58. Justice Albie Sachs was a member of the ANC's Constitutional Committee; after political transition he became a member of the Constitutional Court. He did not offer a fully-fledged 'model' as such, but his writings contain a framework for a justice-based constitutional model. This discussion on Sachs' model is largely indebted to Gloppen's work. Among Sachs' major writings are: 'Towards the Constitutional Reconstruction of South Africa', *Lesotho Law Journal*, 2, 1989; 'Post-Apartheid South Africa: A Constitutional Framework', *World Policy Journal*, 6(3), 1986; *Protecting Human Rights in a New South Africa* (Cape Town: Oxford University Press, 1990); *Advancing Human Rights in South Africa* (Oxford: Oxford University Press, 1992).

29. Gloppen, *South Africa*, p. 60.

30. Sachs, *Protecting Human Rights*, pp. 152–3.

31. Sachs' counter-federalist arguments ran parallel to some of the old socialist and contemporary Sinhalese nationalist arguments in Sri Lanka. To quote Sachs: '[The] concern about the importance of maintaining grass-roots democracy and avoiding the emergence of an over-centralized and unduly bureaucratic state has come strongly from community-based sections of the anti-apartheid movement, giving rise to the possibility that *strong forms of local democracy can be developed without dividing the country up into a myriad of political group areas*' (Sachs, *Protecting Human Rights*, p. 153, emphasis added).

32. Gloppen, *South Africa*, p. 71.

33. Sachs, *Protecting Human Rights*, p. 5.

34. Gloppen, *South Africa*, p. 215.

35. The contractarian argument I am presenting in this chapter has been developed over two previous endeavours: first a presentation in my SWRD Bandaranaike Memorial Lecture held in Colombo on 26 September 1992, and then a further development of that argument in a paper entitled 'Democracy and the State in Multi-Ethnic Societies in Conflict: Perspectives from Sri Lanka', presented at the international conference on 'Democracy and the Rule of Law in a Changing World Order', organized by the Library of Congress and the New York University School of Law on 6 March 2000 in Washington DC, and New York. For a critical response to my contractarian argument, see David

Scott *Refashioning Futures, Criticism after Postcolonialism* (Princeton: Princeton University Press), chapter 7.

36. Walzer, 'Nation and Universe'.

37. Jurgen Habermas, 'Jurgen Habermas: An Interview on Ethics, Politics and History', in David Ramussen (ed.), *Universalism vs Communitarianism* (Cambridge, Mass.: MIT Press, 1990), p. 210.

38. O'Neill, *Impartiality in Context*, p. 190.

39. For example, Sri Lanka's President Ranasinghe Premadasa invoked the Sri Lankan tradition of covenantal politics to authenticate his own interpretation of democratic governance as 'rule by consensus'. He argued that democracy was basically 'consensual politics'—*janasannathavadaya* in Sinhalese—which meant a form of authoritarianism derived from the society's total submission to the ruler.

40. Daniel J. Elazar, *Covenant and Constitutionalism: The Great Frontier and the Matrix of Federal Democracy* (New Brunswick and London: Transaction Publishers, 1998), pp. 2–3. This is the third volume of Elazar's four-volume series on *The Covenant Tradition in Politics*.

41. Rajasingham-Senanayake, 'Dangers of Devolution', 66–7.

42. Leslie Green, 'Internal Minorities and Their Rights', in Will Kymlicka (ed.), *The Rights of Minority Cultures* (New York: Oxford University Press, 1995).

43. Ibid., p. 270.

44. Thomas Fleiner and Lidija R. Basta Fleiner, 'Federalism, Federal States, and Decentralization', in Thomas Fleiner and Lidija R. Basta Fleiner (eds), *Federalism and Multiethnic States: The Case of Switzerland* (Fribourg: Institute of Federalism, 2000), p. 39.

45. John McGarry, 'Federal Political Systems and the Accommodation of National Minorities', in Ann L. Griffiths and Karl Nerenberg (eds), *Handbook of Federal Counties 2002* (Montreal and Kingston: McGill-Queen's University Press, 2002), p. 425.

46. Chaim Kaufman, 'Possible and Impossible Solutions to Ethnic Wars', *International Security*, 20 (1996), pp. 136–75.

6 Foreign Policy Reversal

The Politics of Sri Lanka's Economic Relations with India

Rajesh M. Basrur*

A relatively neglected puzzle in the discipline of international politics is the reversal of foreign policy by states against the expectations of the reigning theoretical paradigm. The realist approach, which has so far not only proved dominant but also remarkably resilient in the face of a constant stream of criticisms over the past two decades and more, does identify systemic or structural sources of change, but does not adequately explain significant policy change occurring as a consequence of other factors. This chapter attempts to comprehend the general problem of foreign policy reversal through an analysis of a specific issue: the change in Sri Lanka's policy orientation towards India from the mid-1990s onwards. Prior to that, Sri Lankan policy was driven by an essentially structural–realist outlook that viewed Indian power as inimical to Sri Lanka's economic and political security. This meant that India was to be kept at arm's length through the adoption of a strategy typical of small states vis-à-vis large neighbours—by balancing and distancing or 'moat-building'. Accordingly, economic relations with India were kept to a minimal level. During the 1990s, this policy underwent a radical transformation. The Sri Lankan leadership shed its fear of Indian dominance and sought and obtained a rapid expansion of economic ties, including a landmark Free Trade Agreement (FTA) in 1998. Why did this happen?

* The author is deeply grateful to Nanda Godage, Sridhar Khatri, and Jayadeva Uyangoda for facilitating his research in Sri Lanka, and to E. Sridharan and Teresita Schaffer for their comments on an earlier version of this chapter.

This chapter argues that Sri Lanka's policy reversal underwent a remarkable transformation only partly as a consequence of structural factors, and to a significant degree as a result of decisions taken at the level of the topmost policymakers. This essentially involved the revision of a long-standing negative image of India. The Sri Lankan national leadership was instrumental in rethinking the relationship. The change in its perceptions was propelled both by external factors—the changing power dynamics between the two countries—and a revised assessment of the situation on the part of Sri Lankan policymakers. This change can only be explained by a theoretically pluralist approach that combines analysis of power relations, which realists stress, with an understanding of state-level decision-making favoured by liberal theorists.

The analysis begins with a brief background of the history of Sri Lanka–India relations, followed by an outline of the change in Sri Lanka's economic and political relationship with India. In the following section, I outline two aspects of international relations (IR) theory that are relevant in this context. First, I discuss the dynamics of policy change through an elaboration of contemporary theoretical debates, principally the competing claims of realism and its liberal critics. The section goes on to examine models of foreign policy change. I then attempt to explain Sri Lanka's policy shift through a systematic examination of factors operating at the three levels of analysis that most scholars accept as standard: the systemic, the state, and the individual. This section of my analysis draws on a series of interviews with Sri Lankan policymakers, academics, and specialists in non-governmental organizations (NGOs). Unavoidably, several individuals in the government have preferred to remain anonymous. The chapter concludes that Sri Lanka's foreign policy reversal, which involved a fundamental reconstruction of its image of India, grew out of both external and domestic factors. A central aspect of the latter was a fundamental rethinking about India on the part of the country's policymakers. Theoretically, the chapter shows that structure does not determine policy outcomes, but that decision-makers can transcend it if they so choose. This has significant implications for India's relationship with other neighbours and, more broadly, for inter-state relationships in general.

Policy Trends and Change

Economic policy in relation to India cannot be separated from the politics of the relationship. From the beginning of the post-colonial era, the central dynamic was what one might call the problem of Indian hegemony. The sheer size and power of the Indian economy and the Indian state was a source of unease for all of India's neighbours.[1] At the time of India's independence, Sri Lanka (then called Ceylon) watched with some trepidation the Indian union's 'police action' in Hyderabad state, which aroused the small country's fears of being swallowed up by a large neighbour. Sri Lankan policy towards India charted a realist course of distancing and balancing. India was kept at arm's length by minimizing economic relations, even though it offered an obviously convenient and large market and was a major potential source of manufactured imports and services.

In the early years, Sri Lanka developed close ties with China, and during the India–China war (1962), criticized India for violating its non-aligned policy by rushing to USA for military aid. During the Bangladesh Crisis (1971), Sri Lanka voted in favour of a UN resolution antithetical to Indian interests notwithstanding the fact that, earlier the same year, New Delhi had provided Colombo with the military wherewithal to subdue a radical insurgency. By the late 1970s, Sri Lanka had chosen to build a close economic association with USA rather than with India in pursuit of a liberal economic strategy. An extension of the balancing strategy was the preference for multilateralism. During the 1970s and 1980s, Sri Lanka sought to associate itself with the Association of Southeast Asian Nations (ASEAN) rather than the India-dominated South Asian Association for Regional Cooperation (SAARC). It also supported the proposal to declare the Indian Ocean as a 'Zone of Peace' in the hope of establishing 'a sort of cordon sanitaire wrapped around the coastline'.[2]

All these are indicators of a consistent policy of maintaining a 'safe' distance from India by a balancing strategy and by avoiding interdependence with it, as interdependence in an unequal relationship tends in reality to be dependence of the weaker upon the stronger power. In practice, this was not very effective. As Marshall Singer put it in 1990, 'India is a major power and the paramount power in the region. Anything India does or does not do, in any situation, is going to have some impact on that situation.'[3] As it happened, Indian pressure compelled Sri Lanka to acquiesce reluctantly in India's direct involvement in the Sinhala–Tamil ethnic conflict on Sri Lankan territory. In May 1987, India resorted to a show of force when its Mirage 2000 fighters accompanied transport aircraft on a 'relief mission' over northern Sri Lanka without the latter's permission. At the same time, USA refused to intervene, preferring to let India play the role of regional policeman so long as American interests were not at stake. Thus, with India bent on intervention, Sri Lankan President J.R. Jayewardene had little choice but to sign the Indo-Sri Lanka Accord of July 1987. Under this agreement, an Indian Peace-Keeping Force (IPKF) was despatched to try and bring about a managed end to the Sinhala–Tamil conflict which had deeply divided Sri Lankan society and politics. This was the high point of across-the-board antipathy towards India.

The election of a new president, Chandrika Kumaratunga, in 1994 marked the beginning of a major change in Sri Lanka–India relations. Kumaratunga sought to expand economic relations with India and simultaneously encourage it to play a role in resolving the ethnic problem. Acknowledging that for geographical and economic reasons and 'everything else' India is 'the one country that would be justifiably interested in Sri Lanka', Kumaratunga asserted that 'India should play a role proactively' in her country's peace process.[4] India, having burnt its fingers in attempting fruitlessly to subdue with military force the secessionist Liberation Tigers of Tamil Eelam (LTTE), confined itself to low-profile security assistance to the Kumaratunga government. Nonetheless, economic relations expanded rapidly from the late 1990s. The FTA, signed in 1998, took effect in March 2000. Though the accord established only partial free trade, the quantum of trade shot up. Within a year, Sri Lankan exports to India rose by 138 per cent, and Indian exports to Sri Lanka by 39 per cent. Between 2001 and 2002, Sri Lanka's overall import/export ratio improved from 8.6:1 to 4.9: 1, and its overall import coverage ratio, which measures the extent to which export proceeds cover disbursements on imports, rose significantly from 11.6 per cent in 2001 to 20.23 per cent.[5]

A series of agreements were signed in 1998 to enhance inter-country air and sea transport services, and cooperation in information technology, space, telecommunications, and agriculture. Cooperation on political issues proceeded simultaneously. The vexed issue of Tamils of Indian origin was effectively met with the Sri Lankan government's decision in July 2003 to grant citizenship to 168,141 Tamils. In August 2003, Sri Lankan Prime Minister Ranil Wickremasinghe proposed a bridge between the two countries as a 'win-win development that could change the economic map of the region'.[6] In October 2003, the two nations agreed to begin talks on a Comprehensive Economic Partnership Agreement (CEPA). G.L. Peiris, spokesperson for the Sri Lankan cabinet, declared that the CEPA would 'diminish the borders between the two countries and put in place a borderless economy'.[7] The two nations also agreed in principle on a defence cooperation agreement. In 2005, India agreed to train Sri Lankan police officers at its own cost. During the last stages of the civil war in Sri Lanka (2007–8), defence cooperation was on a low profile owing to domestic political opposition in India, especially Tamil Nadu. Nevertheless, it was of considerable magnitude in terms of hardware, training and intelligence, and naval cooperation.[8] From time to time, Indian and Sri Lankan naval forces conducted joint exercises and by the summer of 2010, a defence pact was under discussion and a CEPA was on the anvil.

Theory and Policy Change

There are numerous ways of classifying the paradigms that seek to understand world politics.[9] Today, the literature as a whole centres around three: realism, liberalism, and constructivism. Constructivism, which stresses the central importance of identities and norms in determining what happens in international relations, has now become a standard 'paradigm' in textbooks on IR theory, but there is good reason to pass it over for present purposes.[10] In the current context, it need not be accorded a separate status because it is not distinguishable from liberalism in its identification of the dynamics of transformation.[11] The realist–liberal divide, on the other hand, is central to the issue.

Realism has a rich history, its many practitioners since the beginning of history paralleled by the writings of Kautilya, Thucydides, and Machiavelli.[12] These and later thinkers viewed the selfishness of human nature as the source of perpetual conflict among states.[13] Contemporary structural realism (or 'neo-realism') holds that international politics is a system of self-centred states compelled by the lack of a sovereign above them to privilege self-interest over collective interest, which makes cooperation difficult, and to seek power for the sake of security, which periodically results in tensions and war. The anarchic structure of the system creates typical patterns of power balancing, arms racing, alliance formation, and competition for influence. What states do is determined largely by their external structural relationships, not so much by internal factors such as leadership, party politics, interest groups, and ideological preferences. Much of the current literature dwells at length on the merit or otherwise of this structural explanation of international politics, which is widely attributed to the neorealist writing of Kenneth Waltz.[14] In this framework, the sources of policy change are structural, and, barring the end of anarchy, we may anticipate a shift in policy when the distribution of power changes. Thus, the emergence of an overriding threat from a third party tends to bring two hostile states together; or the insecurity that results from the growing power of a strong neighbour encourages a relatively weak state to try and reduce its dependence on that neighbour by balancing (enhancing its power capabilities, drawing closer to another state) or distancing (reducing interactions with the neighbour in question). Conversely, the absence of structural change means substantive change in policies is very unlikely.

Liberal theory, on the other hand, stresses cooperation and a growing sense of community on a global scale.[15] The notion of an essential harmony among states goes back to the eighteenth-century *philosophe*s, and to James Mill and Jeremy Bentham.[16] The four principal strands of liberal thought are commercial liberalism, which stresses the positive effects of free trade; democratic liberalism, which holds that democracies are essentially peaceable by nature; regulatory liberalism, which highlights the importance of rules and institutions in engendering cooperation; and sociological liberalism, which believes that expanding transnational contacts are changing national attitudes and interests.[17] From this perspective, change in policy may be dictated by a variety of factors, such as the growth of interdependence between states, changes in domestic political equations, and changes in perceptions and political attitudes among major domestic political actors. Here, change is attributed to both external and internal factors, though on the whole, even liberals who focus on the former do acknowledge the significance of domestic decision-making.

Neither approach fully explains the dynamics of inter-state politics. While realists see conflict as intrinsic to an anarchic world, liberals focus more on cooperation. The conflict between the two paradigms is less sharp than we might at first think. As Robert Jervis has observed, realists focus on state power and conflict because they are more interested in military–strategic issues, whereas liberals tend to look more at non-military issues, and hence stress interdependence.[18] Nevertheless, the difference between them is important, for it turns on whether decision-makers are prisoners of the structure of international politics or possess the capacity to transcend that structure. Neoclassical realists provide a bridge between the two. Unlike structural realists, who see structures as determining outcomes, neoclassical realists hold that structures in themselves do not shape state actions. Within the constraints established by a specific structural context, policymakers may choose from diverse options. For instance, states perceiving a nuclear threat may opt to go nuclear or may refrain from doing so.[19] As is well known, following the Chinese nuclear test of 1964, India did perceive a potential threat from China, but sought to enhance its capability to a limited extent rather than pushing hard for nuclear weapons. This remained true even after it had acquired the technical capability to go nuclear in 1974. In short, the extent of policy change depends on policy choices arrived at by decision-makers.

In an illuminating paper, Jakob Gustavsson critically examines as many as six different models of foreign policy change which explain varying degrees of transformation in policy, ranging from the incremental to the fundamental.[20] All the models posit three steps: (i) background factors conducive to policy change; (ii) cognitive factors and institutional-processual factors relating to the decision-making process; and (iii) the connection between these two and a foreign policy outcome in the form of a typology of foreign policy change. Gustavsson integrates and refines the models by identifying the basic sources of change (background factors) as international and domestic factors, which are inputs influencing a decision-maker, who channels his/her own cognitive learning into the decision process. The decision process produces an output which circles back to the background factors by way of feedback, thus producing a continuing and dynamic model of change. Gustavsson adds a crucial element: the availability of a 'policy window', or a moment of opportunity, which determines the timing of change. He sees this policy window as the space created by crisis situations, which alter the calculus of policy change, making the latter more feasible than in normal times.

Regarding the policy window, it may be added that, apart from crises, change may also occur in another way. When the disharmony between an existing policy paradigm and a changing international setting reaches a point of serious disequilibrium, a policy window may be said to have opened up. This is akin to Thomas Kuhn's conception of paradigm change in the sciences, when existing ways of doing things are found to be increasingly inadequate as evidence of anomalies mounts.[21] Thus, for example, Mikhail Gorbachev's monumental decision to transform Soviet policy towards USA was not propelled by a crisis, but rather by the growing inability of Soviet policy to come to terms with a changing world. A change in Sri Lanka's policy approach towards India may be attributed, accordingly, either to the occurrence of a crisis or to Sri Lankan policymakers' response to the accumulated weight of dysfunctional policy. It must be stressed that the appearance of a policy window does not automatically ensure a response that results in major policy change. Some decision-makers may choose to transform policy radically, others may opt for partial change, and yet others may do little or nothing at all.

EXPLAINING THE SHIFT

Levels of Analysis

What brought about the change in Sri Lankan policy towards India? A systematic investigation requires an assessment of factors at different levels of analysis. There is no unanimity among IR scholars as to who or what constitute the principal actors in international politics.[22] The widest consensus, employed in this study, is that there are three major levels: the international system, the state (including society and organizations within it), and the individual (extendable to small decision-making groups).[23] The structural realist approach confines itself to the first, while classical and neoclassical realists hold that the other two levels often have a determining effect on international outcomes. The analysis in this chapter, which highlights the relevance of both the systemic and individual levels of analysis, utilizes a framework that finds useful the explanatory power of the latter.

A recent comparative study of small state behaviour (not including Sri Lanka) shows how all three levels of analysis can and do influence policy.[24] Given the reality that power plays a significant role in inter-state relations, small state policy is heavily constrained by systemic factors. Yet, though there are definite limits to what a state can do, regimes and individual leaders can 'stand out as dynamic and effective'.[25] Regime type plays a significant role, in that developed states are more influential than developing ones. In several of the case studies, which encompass all the continents, the individual policymaker does make a difference, though 'leaders place their personal imprint on a set of predetermined choices'.[26] It is argued here that leadership choices are not necessarily restricted to what is predetermined. In the case of Sri Lanka, it was by no means foreordained that policy towards India would have to change drastically. A glance at Bangladesh's continuing reluctance to revamp its India policy illustrates this. Sri Lankan leaders chose both the content and timing of their policy shift just as their counterparts in Bangladesh, for whatever reason, have chosen to refrain from attempting such a shift.

System-Level Factors

At the level of the international system, there was no basic change in the distribution of power between Sri Lanka and India during the 1980s and 1990s. In every way—size, population, economic power, military attributes—Sri Lanka remained dwarfed by India's hegemonic presence.[27] India's much greater power was the principal factor that enabled it to intervene militarily in the civil conflict in Sri Lanka in 1987.[28] However, Indian policy did undergo change. Since the 1970s, India had intervened in Sri Lanka's ethnic conflict, first by covert support for Tamil secessionists (from the late 1970s to the mid-1980s), later by a policy of mediation and reconciliation, and finally by the exertion of military force.[29] This was motivated by domestic exigencies—strong pro-Tamil sentiment in the state of Tamil Nadu, and the fear of a domino effect in India—and by structural considerations, principally concerns that USA and Pakistan would obtain a foothold in Sri Lanka.[30] After its military failure against the LTTE, however, Indian policy retreated to cautious support for the Sri Lankan government. As it happened, the Tamil cause in India faded rapidly after the assassination of Rajiv Gandhi by the LTTE in 1991.[31] Prime Minister P.V. Narasimha Rao (1991–6) followed a policy of non-intervention and close cooperation on a range of economic and political issues.[32] The so-called 'Gujral Doctrine', attributed to I.K. Gujral, minister for external affairs in 1996–7 and prime minister in 1997–8, brought a markedly warmer Sri Lanka–India relationship. The rapid improvement of the relationship was reflected in Sri Lanka's relaxed response to India's nuclear tests in 1998.[33] The Indian High Commission in Colombo, formerly viewed with a mixture of apprehension and distaste, came to be regarded favourably in policy-making circles.[34]

The political aspect of structure thus played a major role in the rethinking that occurred in Sri Lanka. Once the political problem receded, economic relations were relatively easy to reshape. Here, one structural factor was basically favourable. Since Sri Lanka had chosen to liberalize its economy much earlier—in 1977—there was no sense of anxiety about opening up to India. The Sri Lankan economy was already open to much more powerful global economic forces, and concerns about external economic dominance no longer counted for much. Consequently, there was very little political opposition to the prospect of the regional hegemon increasing its economic presence in Sri Lanka.[35]

State-Level Factors

My inquiries reveal that major foreign policy decisions in Sri Lanka flow from the very top of the political hierarchy. The push for the FTA came essentially from the president and a handful of advisors, of whom some were from the bureaucracy, particularly the finance and foreign ministries. The bureaucracy, on its own admission, plays a largely advisory and implementation role rather than acting as a pressure group. On economic policy, it also acts as a channel of communication between business interests and policymakers. Business groups do not play a major role in the determination of economic policy either, though some individuals are close to the leadership and a consultative process for gauging the mood of private enterprise does exist. According to a senior official, the FTA was rushed through with very little business input. Initial protests from a surprised business community had no impact on policy.[36]

Political parties have not played a significant role other than providing broad support for the initiatives taken by the government. Both the principal parties, the United National Party (UNP) and the Sri Lanka Freedom Party (SLFP), together with their allies, have actively worked for enhanced economic cooperation with India. Initially, the left-wing Janatha Vimukthi Peramuna (JVP) opposed the FTA and the entry of Indian Oil into the Sri Lankan economy, but the party was not strong enough to influence policy. In any event, it eventually adopted a generally pro-Indian stance after it was cultivated by the Indian High Commission.[37] The Buddhist Sangha (Order), which represents the country's majority religious community, is broadly influential, and had played a significant part in mobilizing public opinion against Indian intervention in 1987.[38] In 2000, however, when the LTTE virtually controlled of the Jaffna Peninsula, the Sangha sent representatives to New Delhi to appeal for Indian assistance.[39] Thereafter, the Sangha has not been an obstacle to the forging of closer relations with India.

Public opinion, which sets the broad parameters within which policymakers take decisions, was also favourably inclined towards strengthening relations with India during the mid-1990s. This had not always been so. India was widely viewed with suspicion up to the early 1990s, and its military presence strongly opposed. The assassination of Rajiv Gandhi, however, was a watershed event which revealed that Indian interests were distinctly antithetical to those of the LTTE.[40] A recent national public opinion survey is indicative of the favourable public attitude towards India. In January 2003, when questioned about the need for India's involvement in the domestic peace process, 58.5 per cent of the respondents gave a positive response, while 21.4 per cent viewed the prospect in a negative light.[41] Even among the majority Sinhala community, which has been inclined to view India less favourably, the majority (54.3 per cent) was supportive of India, and a minority (23 per cent) opposed.[42]

The overall picture is that factors at the level of state and society were generally supportive of policy initiatives taken by the leadership to reverse policy towards India. Perhaps the one state-level factor that did play a critical role was the harsh reality of Sri Lanka's internal weakness. In interviews, more than one official acknowledged that, given the weakness of the state in the face of the Tamil insurgency, there was no option other than to draw closer to India. Building economic bridges with India was a way to strengthen the Sri Lankan state and society in the struggle to cope with a debilitating schism that simply would not go away.

The Individual-Level Factor

As observed earlier, political leadership played (and continues to play) a key role in policy-making. The change in Sri Lanka's orientation towards India began with the election of Chandrika Kumaratunga as president in 1994. Kumaratunga's reasoning was that India could be a part of the solution to the country's difficulties rather than a part of its problems. Economics was seen as the key. The president worked closely with Prime Minister Ranil Wickremasinghe (1994–5, 2001–2), Minister for Economic Reforms Milinda Moragoda (2001–4), Foreign Minister Lakshman Kadirgamar (1994–2001; 2004–5), and others to initiate and develop close economic links with India. Wickremasinghe forged direct links with the Indian leadership (partly to bypass anticipated resistance from the Indian bureaucracy) and was rewarded with reciprocal interest on the part of Indian leaders, notably Prime Minister I.K. Gujral, and later Prime Minister A.B. Vajpayee and his senior associates, especially National Security Advisor Brajesh Mishra.

An opinion piece by Foreign Minister Lakshman Kadirgamar in December 2003 is indicative of the rethinking that took place.[43] Kadirgamar lays down the basis of his country's policy: (i) recognition that security is not military alone, but has a vital economic component; (ii) acknowledgement of interdependence, particularly regional interdependence, in a globalizing world; and (iii) acceptance of India's pre-eminent role and 'responsibility' in fostering of regional peace. All these, it must be noted, relate to leadership perception of systemic factors. The overall effect of the change in perception is that rather than playing the old balancing-cum-distancing game, Sri Lanka has shifted to a bandwagoning approach that seeks to draw advantage from a closer relationship with a strong neighbour.[44] Such is the case with Canada and Mexico vis-à-vis USA. Indeed, the same may be said to be the case with respect to India and USA.

In the view of the leadership, Sri Lanka stood to gain from a closer economic relationship with India in several respects. India was seen as a huge market for Sri Lankan goods; tourism, a major industry, would be given a fillip. Though hard data is not available, Indian visitors were perceived to be the biggest spenders among tourists, outspending travellers from developed countries.[45] An expanding Indian economy would, it was felt, provide across-the-board investment in industry, infrastructure, energy, power, telecommunications, and financial services.[46] The long-range objective was to try and make Sri Lanka a gateway to India for cargo, financial services, software, and electronics, as Hong Kong is to China.[47] The focus was particularly strong on the four most physically proximate states of southern India: Tamil Nadu, Kerala, Karnataka, and Andhra Pradesh.[48] It was anticipated that in addition to the economic advantages accruing from increasing cross-strait interaction, the gains for the Tamil-dominated north would help weaken support for secessionist sentiment.[49]

* * *

The reversal of Sri Lanka's policy towards India from an arm's-length orientation to a close embrace is a remarkable and unusual phenomenon in inter-state relations. The brief review undertaken in this chapter shows that such a policy reversal was, in part, shaped by systemic factors. While there was no notable change in power distribution, the options open to Sri Lanka were limited by the sheer size, power, and proximity of India, and by the weakness of the Sri Lankan state as a consequence of an apparently ceaseless civil conflict. There was a more favourable systemic context for enhancing economic relations with a liberalizing India because of India's more cooperative approach towards Sri Lanka and because the Indian economy was opening up to the world. Here, it is important to distinguish between structure, or the distribution of power, and systemic interaction, which focuses on the ways in which power is exercised. The shift in Indian policy provided the systemic context in which Sri Lanka could exercise the option to build a closer relationship with India. This in turn was the consequence, as is well known, of India's adjustment to the requirements of the global economy, which Sri Lanka had already undergone much earlier. However, the systemic factor did not in itself determine the extent of policy change, which could just as well have been limited. State-level factors were conducive to the change, but the very fact that bureaucratic and business interests were weak, and that public opinion was broadly supportive of state policy means that they could have equally chosen *not* to reverse policy. Alternatively, they could have embarked on a much more cautious and incremental course. Clearly, the dramatic nature of the policy reversal can only be attributed to the choices made by the political leadership.

What are the theoretical implications of this case study? First, it strengthens the argument of both neoclassical realists and liberals that structures do not necessarily determine policy, but can be transcended to transform policy and hence inter-state relations. The implication of this is that the structural obstacles facing other relationships may also be overridden. I do not imply that it is simply a matter of 'where there's a will there's a way'. The extent of policy change is certainly likely to be shaped by the strength of inhibiting factors at work in a specific situation. In difficult cases, only partial change may be feasible so as to stabilize and incrementally improve rather than fully transform a relationship, as is the case with the India–China relationship.[50] The crucial point, however, is that structure *can* be transcended; a reality for which Sri Lanka's policy reversal towards India is a clear illustration. This has important implications for India's relationships with its neighbours. It points to the considerable scope for improving these relations if India's policy is less power-driven and interventionist, and if its smaller neighbours choose to bandwagon with rather than balance against it. Beyond lies the hope of greater coherence and meaningful cooperation in the SAARC.

Second, it is clear that a 'paradigm change' does not require a crisis to create a policy window. In the case of Sri Lanka, there was certainly an ongoing crisis in the form of the enduring civil conflict between the state and the LTTE, but that had not drawn India and Sri Lanka closer earlier. Besides, the negotiations for the FTA began well before the LTTE reached the peak of its success in 2000. The critical factor was the Sri Lankan leadership's perception that a policy of balancing and distancing was unproductive, that an opportunity was at hand, and that appropriate policy change could help make the most of it. Third, with regard to an understanding of small state behaviour, this chapter shows that small states are not necessarily tightly bound by systemic constraints. Sri Lanka's leaders responded to a particular situation by taking policy initiatives. Were they simply making the most of 'predetermined choices'? The evidence shows otherwise. Bandwagoning rather than balancing was a conscious choice that they need not have made.

Fourth, the role of politics in shaping economic relationships is undeniable. We know that the origins of both the European Union and ASEAN lie in the political imperatives of the Cold War. These were, of course, structural factors, that is, the threat perceived from the former Soviet Union and China. In the present case, while there was no comparable structural pressure on Sri Lanka and India to cooperate, the transformation in their economic relationship was possible largely because of a rethinking of political interests and preferences on the part of both countries. Apart from the expected gains derived from trade, both Sri Lanka and India have a common security interest in a negotiated end to the Sri Lankan civil war. Common, or at least compatible political interests, enhance the prospects for wider regional cooperation. It is not sufficient to argue, as some do, that South Asia's states need to work harder at economic cooperation. A security motive, or at minimum, the absence of security problems hindering cooperation, is necessary if one is to expect significant policy change.

Finally, a levels-of-analysis approach is of great utility in understanding key international political phenomena. In the present case, factors operating at all three levels were conducive to a specific outcome; in others this may not happen. For instance, if powerful national elites are unwilling to choose a particular policy course, it may matter little that such a policy would be in the interest of the nation as a whole. Alternatively, a leadership may lack the vision and confidence to grasp the nettle of policy change and may prefer to navigate a slow shift, or even do nothing.

Notes

1. For a more detailed review, see Rajesh M. Basrur, *India's External Relations: A Theoretical Analysis* (New Delhi: Commonwealth Publishers, 2000), chapter 3.

2. Nira Wickremasinghe, 'Sri Lanka: The Many Faces of Security', in Muthiah Alagappa (ed.), *Asian Security Practice: Material and Ideational Influences* (Stanford, CA: Stanford University Press, 1998), pp. 367–89, especially p. 370.

3. Marshall R. Singer, 'New Realities in Sri Lankan Politics', *Asian Survey*, 30(4), April 1990, pp. 409–25, especially p. 419.

4. Amit Baruah, 'India Should Play a Proactive Role', *The Hindu*, 12 April 2003.

5. Joint Study Group on India–Sri Lanka, *Comprehensive Economic Partnership Agreement*, October 2003, p. 13.

6. Jayaraj Sivan, 'A Bridge too Misunderstood', *Indian Express*, 1 September 2003. However, opposition from the Indian state of Tamil Nadu appears to have stalled the proposal.

7. V.S. Sambandan, 'Pacts with India not Pre-emptive: Peiris', *The Hindu*, 24 October 2003.

8. Nitin A. Gokhale, *Sri Lanka: from War to Peace* (New Delhi: Manohar, 2009).

9. Ken Booth and Steve Smith (eds), *International Relations Theory Today* (University Park, PA: Pennsylvania State University Press, 1995); Scott Burchill and Andrew Linklater, *Theories of International Relations* (Basingstoke: Macmillan, 1996); K.J. Holsti, *The Dividing Discipline: Hegemony and Diversity in International Theory* (London: Allen & Unwin, 1985); Charles W. Kegley, Jr (ed.), *Controversies in International Relations Theory* (New York: St. Martin's Press, 1995); A.P. Rana, 'Restructuring International Relations as a Field in India: A Programme for the Disciplinary Development of International Relations Studies', *Studying International Relations: The Baroda Perspective, Occasional Review*, I(1), March 1988: 17–26.

10. The pre-eminent constructivist treatise is Alexander Wendt, *Social Theory of International Politics* (Cambridge: Cambridge University Press, 1999). See also Stefano Guzzini, 'A Reconstruction of Constructivism in International Relations', *European Journal of International Relations*, 6(2), June 2000: 147–82.

11. Jennifer Sterling-Folker, 'Competing Paradigms or Birds of a Feather? Constructivism and Neoliberal Institutionalism Compared', *International Studies Quarterly*, 44(1), March 2000: 97–119. As Robert Jervis points out, constructivism, in stressing the role of identities in inducing cooperation, 'mistakes effect for cause: its description is correct, but the identities, images, and self-images are superstructure' and 'what is crucial is not people's thinking, but the factors that drive it' ('Theories of War in an Era of Peace', Presidential Address, American Political Science Association, 2001, *American Political Science Review*, 96(1), March 2002, pp. 1–14, especially p. 4).

12. B.B. Naik, *Ideals of Ancient Hindu Politics and the Arthashastra of Kautilya* (Dharwar: Self-published, 1932); Thucyides, *History of the Pelopponesian War*, trans. by Rex Warner (Harmondsworth: Penguin, 1954); N. Machiavelli, *The Prince*, trans. by W.K. Marriott (London: J.M. Dent & Son, 1908).

13. This view lay at the heart of the writings of Hans Morgenthau, indisputably the most influential post–Second World War thinker on international politics in the English language. See Hans J. Morgenthau, *Politics*

among Nations: The Struggle for Power and Peace, 3rd Edn (New York: Alfred A. Knopf, 1960).

14. Kenneth N. Waltz, *Theory of International Politics* (Reading, MA: Addison-Wesley, 1979). See also his 'Structural Realism After the Cold War', *International Security*, 25(1), 2000, pp. 5–41; and Barry Buzan, 'The Timeless Wisdom of Realism?' in Steve Smith, Ken Booth, and Marysia Zalewski (eds), *International Theory: Positivism and Beyond* (Cambridge: Cambridge University Press, 1996), pp. 47–65. For a sympathetic review, see Richard Little, 'The Timeless Wisdom of Realism?', in Steve Smith, Ken Booth, and Marysia Zalewski (eds), *International Theory: Positivism and Beyond* (Cambridge: Cambridge University Press, 1996).

15. See, for example, Hedley Bull, *The Anarchical Society: A Study of Order in World Politics* (London & Basingstoke: Macmillan, 1977); Robert O. Keohane, *After Hegemony: Cooperation and Discord in the World Political Economy* (Princeton, NJ: Princeton University Press, 1984); Robert O. Keohane and Joseph S. Nye, Jr, *Power and Interdependence: World Politics in Transition* (Boston: Little Brown, 1978); and Stephen D. Krasner (ed.), *International Regimes* (Ithaca, NY: Cornell University Press, 1983). For an overview, see Richard Little, 'The Growing Relevance of Pluralism?' in Smith, Booth, and Zalewski (eds), *International Theory*, pp. 66–86.

16. F.H. Hinsley, *Power and the Pursuit of Peace: Theory and Practice in the Relations between States* (Cambridge: Cambridge University Press, 1963), pp. 81–91; Holsti, *The Dividing Discipline*, pp. 27–30.

17. Joseph S. Nye, Jr, 'Neorealism and Neoliberalism', *World Politics*, XL(2), 1988, pp. 235–51, especially p. 83. For a more recent effort to build a 'scientific' liberal theory, see Andrew Moravcsik, 'Taking Preferences Seriously: A Liberal Theory of International Politics', *International Organization*, 51(4), 1997, pp. 513–53.

18. Robert Jervis, 'Realism, Neoliberalism and Cooperation: Understanding the Debate', *International Security*, 31(4), 1999, pp. 42–63.

19. The division between offensive and defensive realism also brings out this difference. Whereas offensive realists, notably John Mearsheimer, hold that the anarchic structure of the state system impels states to maximize power, defensive realists like Waltz argue that states primarily seek security rather than power, which may not require them to enhance power. John J. Mearsheimer, *The Tragedy of Great Power Politics* (New York and London: W.W. Norton, 2001); Waltz, *Theory of International Politics*. More broadly, defensive realists show that there is no fixed realist response to a specific situation. Policy depends on decisions taken as a result of factors operating at sub-systemic levels. See Stephen G. Brooks, 'Duelling Realisms', *International Organization*, 51(3), 1997, pp. 445–77; and Jeffrey W. Taliaferro, 'Security Seeking under Anarchy: Defensive Realism Revisited', *International Security*, 25(3), Winter 2000–1, pp. 128–61.

20. Jakob Gustavsson, 'How Should We Study Foreign Policy Change?', *Cooperation and Conflict*, 34(1), 1999, pp. 73–95.

21. Thomas S. Kuhn, *The Structure of Scientific Revolutions*, 2nd Edn (Chicago & London: University of Chicago Press, 1970).

22. For a seminal discussion of the issue, see J. David Singer, 'The Level-of-Analysis Problem in International Relations', in Klaus Knorr and Sydney Verba (eds), *The International System: Theoretical Essays* (Princeton, NJ: Princeton University Press, 1961), pp. 77–92.

23. For a detailed exposition, see Kenneth N. Waltz, *Man, the State and War: A Theoretical Analysis* (New York: Columbia University Press, 1959).

24. Jeanne A.K. Hey (ed.), *Small States in World Politics: Explaining Foreign Policy Behavior* (Boulder, CO & London: Lynne Rienner, 2003). The definition of small states is often disputed. Criteria include size, economic power, and vulnerability. See also Amalendu Mishra, 'An Introduction to the "Small" and "Micro" States of South Asia', *Contemporary South Asia*, 13(2), 2004, pp. 127–31. Perhaps the most appropriate criterion is their self-perception and 'role in the international hierarchy', Jeanne A.K. Hey, 'Introducing Small State Foreign Policy', in Jeanne A.K. Hey (ed.), *Small States in World Politics*, pp. 1–12, especially p. 3.

25. Jeanne A.K. Hey, 'Refining Our Understanding of Small State Foreign Policy', in Hey (ed.), *Small States in World Politics*, pp. 186–95, especially p. 187.

26. Hey, 'Refining Our Understanding of Small State Foreign Policy', p. 192.

27. Mohammad Humayun Kabir, *The 'India Factor' in Sri Lanka's Foreign and Security Policy* (Colombo: Bandaranaike Centre for International Studies, 1996), pp. 10–14.

28. Ibid., pp. 40–52; A. Sivarajah, 'Indo-Sri Lanka Relations and Sri Lanka's Ethnic Crisis: The Tamil Nadu Factor', in Shelton U. Kodikara (ed.), *South Asian Strategic Issues: Sri Lankan Perspectives* (New Delhi, Newbury Park, and London: Sage Publications, 1990), pp. 139–41.

29. Rajat Ganguly, *Kin State Interventions in Ethnic Conflicts: Lessons for South Asia* (New Delhi, Thousand Oaks, and London: Sage Publications, 1996), pp. 193–232.

30. J.N. Dixit, 'Sri Lanka,' in J.N. Dixit (ed.), *External Affairs: Cross-Border Relations* (New Delhi: Roli Books, 2003), pp. 47–96, especially p. 55.

31. Kabir, *The 'India Factor'*, pp. 216–18.

32. Shelton U. Kodikara, 'International Change and Regional Compulsions: Sri Lanka's Foreign Policy', *South Asian Survey*, 1(2), March 1995, pp. 77–100.

33. Vandana Chopra, 'Sri Lanka/Nuclear', Voice of America, 19 May 1998, http://www.fas.org/news/india/1998/05/980519-india.htm, accessed 20 July 2010.

34. Interview with Nanda Godage, former Sri Lankan diplomat, 10 September 2004.

35. Interview with Dushni Weerakoon, economist, Institute for Policy Studies, Colombo, 9 September 2004.

36. Confidential interview with a senior official, Colombo, 14 September 2004.

37. Interview with Jayadeva Uyangoda, Colombo University, a founding member of the JVP, 11 September 2004.

38. Wickremasinghe, 'Sri Lanka', pp. 386–8.

39. Interview with R.A. Ariyaratne, Senior Fellow, Regional Centre for Strategic Studies, Colombo, 6 September 2004.

40. Though I could not obtain hard data, this was a perception widely expressed by knowledgeable individuals both within the government and outside it.

41. 'India's Involvement: National Trend', Peace Confidence Index, *Social Indicator*, Centre for Policy Alternatives, Colombo, March 2003, p. 25. The positive view combines the response 'is essential' and 'will add a positive impact', while the negative view combines 'will add a negative impact' and 'is not essential'. The remaining categories were 'will have no impact' and 'don't know/not sure'. In May 2002, the positive total was higher and the negative total lower.

42. 'India's Involvement: Ethnic Breakdown', Peace Confidence Index, *Social Indicator*, Centre for Policy Alternatives, Colombo, March 2003, p. 25.

43. Lakshman Kadirgamar, 'Securing South Asia', *Hindustan Times*, 15 December 2003.

44. On bandwagoning, see Randall L. Schweller, 'Bandwagoning for Profit: Bringing the Revisionist State Back In', *International Security*, 19(1), 1994, pp. 72–107.

45. Interview with Milinda Moragoda, former minister for economic reform, Colombo, 15 September 2004.

46. Interview with a senior Sri Lankan official who was a key negotiator for the FTA, Colombo, 14 September, 2004.

47. Interview with Moragoda, 15 September 2004.

48. Ibid.

49. Interview with Uyangoda, 11 September 2004.

50. Rajesh M. Basrur, 'Nuclear India at the Crossroads', *Arms Control Today*, 33(7), 2003, pp. 7–11.

7 Domestic Bases of Foreign Policy

Bangladesh's Policy towards India

Nalini Kant Jha

Foreign policy, being a dependent variable, is conditioned by several factors,[1] of which domestic factors are particularly significant. The domestic sources of foreign policy are so many that the task of tracing the process that enables them to shape policy constitutes an important theoretical and empirical challenge. A comprehensive multidisciplinary approach is required to unearth how the domestic geographic, socio-cultural, and politico-economic environment of a country moulds its foreign policy.

This is especially true for a state like Bangladesh, whose most pressing problems are often domestic. The foreign policy of Bangladesh is a projection of its geographic, economic, socio-cultural, historical, and political compulsions in international politics. These compulsions are most vividly reflected in its policy vis-à-vis India. The ruling regimes in Bangladesh, brittle and strife-torn, have often sought external support to preserve their privileged position, with major repercussions for the state's foreign policy and regional relations. From the time of its creation, this factor has directly or indirectly constituted a vital element in the conduct of Bangladesh's external policy.[2]

However, a systematic effort to study the implications of Bangladesh's domestic environment for its policy towards India has not been undertaken so far. Most available studies are descriptive, chronological, and devoid of theoretical content. For example, a recent study on the subject[3] has documented India–Bangladesh relations but has not attempted to study the domestic inputs of Bangladesh's policy towards India. This chapter aims at filling this lacuna. It begins with an attempt to evolve a theoretical framework for studying linkages between

Bangladesh's domestic environment and her policy towards India and then presents an empirical overview of these linkages.[4]

Towards An Analytical Framework

It is important to clearly demarcate the boundaries between domestic and foreign policies. This is necessary to counter the belief expressed both by political leaders and scholars that the lines between domestic and international policy have blurred. Senator J.W. Fulbright wrote in 1959, 'If ever the line between domestic and foreign affairs could be drawn, it is now wholly erased.'[5] Hans J. Morgenthau similarly wrote in 1960: 'The traditional distinction between foreign and domestic policies tends to break down. One might be tempted to say that there are no longer any purely domestic affairs.'[6] There is, of course, increasing interdependence between internal and external affairs and, therefore, between domestic and foreign policies. The latter can nonetheless be analytically distinguished from the former.

Domestic policy, according to Roscoe Pound, is social control through law.[7] Domestic policies are embodied in legislation and administrative regulations that citizens are obliged to obey. Foreign policy, on the other hand, is usually executed through persuasion, negotiation, and compromise, or in some cases through coercion; foreign states or international organizations have no obligation to collaborate except in accordance with their own interests. Foreign policy may, however, be addressed principally to domestic interest groups.

Although the linkages between domestic politics and foreign policy had been discussed earlier, it was only in the 1960s that these began receiving serious scrutiny.[8] Since then, it has almost become a routine for foreign policy analysts to proceed on the basis of these linkages.[9] Alexander Dallin remarks, 'The domestic sources of foreign policy behaviour have indeed come to attract the attention of various analysts, observers and actors in international affairs.'[10]

A Critique of Dependency Theory

The growing interdependence between nations in the globalized environment, facilitated by technological advances, has made it increasingly difficult for them to remain isolated. There is hardly any country that can claim to be completely free in the conduct of its external relations. This is particularly true for a small, impoverished, and resource-strapped state like Bangladesh. This chapter therefore acknowledges the validity of the central argument of the dependency theory.[11] However, the dependency thesis is less satisfactory in explaining specific situations and developments. Perhaps because of its vagueness and its emphatic assertion that the problems of developing countries originate outside their boundaries, the 'dependency' explanations have become influential among scholars and statesmen from the developing world. Moreover, the propensity to pass the buck enables the Third World elite to preserve the status quo. Also, the dependency thesis neglects the role of domestic factors by attempting to explain the poverty and weakness of Third World countries solely in terms of the impact of the international system upon them.[12]

The focus of this chapter is the manipulation of foreign policy by the ruling elite as an instrument of domestic political competition, and the subsequent quest for the monopolization of power. It is, therefore, relevant to briefly review the debate on the significance of national versus regime interests in the making of foreign policy.

THE PRIMACY OF REGIME INTERESTS VIS-À-VIS NATIONAL INTERESTS

Several influential scholars, such as Morgenthau, Gibson, Modelski, Northedge, Haas, Whiting, and Appadorai, have emphasized the significance of national interest as the goal of foreign policy.[13] Implicit in this assumption is the belief that foreign policy is above and beyond the partisan politics of a country. James N. Rosenau's view, for example, that foreign policy is an adaptive behaviour, typically represents this belief.[14] However, in order to understand foreign policy, analysts have to move beyond generalizations and break the concept into specific components. The literature on foreign policy analysis appears to emphasize three points, a sort of 'holy trinity': physical survival, economic well-being, and the freedom of action or manoeuvrability at the international level.[15] However, this is where the problem begins.

First, the concept of national interest is extremely vague because its components are not well operationalized. For instance, does economic well-being mean economic self-sufficiency or does it follow the classical trade theory of comparative advantage? Second, the components can be incompatible, as some current debates reveal. The intense debate within

USA and India about the fallout of the India–US nuclear agreement statements of 18 July 2005 and 2 March 2006 vividly illustrates the subjectivity of the concept of national interest. Third, how does one integrate into the national interest trinity, a foreign policy objective such as prestige? Fourth, there is considerable ambiguity about immediate gains and long-term gains of a foreign policy move. While dealing with South Asian neighbours, including Bangladesh, Indian governments led by Indira Gandhi and Rajiv Gandhi, for example, insisted on reciprocity on their part, while the non-Congress regimes of I.K. Gujral and Atal Bihari Vajpayee attempted to improve ties with them without insisting on strict reciprocity in order to serve India's long-term interests.

At a fundamental level, the classical view about national interest ignores the following question: whose national interest are we talking about within the state? It is possible that given how vague the concept is, each government or elite group may so interpret a country's national interest as to serve its own interest. For example, the effects of a defence programme may trickle down to some among the rural unemployed or the marginalized urban populace. However, its primary benefit would go to the military of the country or to a foreign firm, in addition to middlemen.

Unlike the proclaimed goal of foreign policy—that is, national interest—the reality is that leaders are often more concerned with their own survival or the interests of their regime.[16] Under certain circumstances, such as in a stable democratic political system, the need to use, as well as the space to utilize, foreign policy for the sustenance and survival of a regime in power is far greater than in an authoritarian political system.[17] Indira Gandhi, for instance, utilized India's foreign policy as a tool to seek legitimacy during the Emergency.[18] Often, the regime's interest need not necessarily clash with national interest. For instance, Indira Gandhi's interest in political survival, as well as national interest, dictated a friendly policy towards the erstwhile USSR after the Congress split in 1969.[19]

The unclear conceptualization of the nature of regimes as a factor influencing foreign policy strikes at the very foundation of the classical approach, which ignores the fact that in the name of national interest, a state's foreign policy is actually formulated by individuals in power. This approach also underestimates human characteristics, such as fickleness and the errors of decision-makers. It excludes the complexity of state–society relations and the different aspects of the decision-making process.

If every decision-maker were to act with rationality, hardly any decision would fail. This, however, is rarely the case.

It is, therefore, necessary to go beyond the classical view and ask several questions. How many individuals are capable of viewing the world in a totally objective, unbiased manner? How many individuals undertake the effort to spell out goals and to come to grips with the often agonizing choices between equally desired but mutually incompatible benefits? How many have the time to carefully consider all conceivable options, or possess complete information to arrive at the best possible solution? These questions are particularly important in Third World countries such as Bangladesh that have weak institutions, where policy processes are usually personalized, and where governments change without any change in the overall framework of the political system. Although not the sole factors conditioning foreign policy, the influence of the leader and the nature of the regime should not be overlooked in any worthwhile analysis of foreign policy.[20]

This chapter, therefore, focuses on how Bangladesh's foreign policy has become a device to serve interests of a particular section, group, or political party in domestic politics. Often, there is a good fit between the interests of the domestic ruling elites and their external patrons, even though such policies might be at variance with national interests; and, not surprisingly, successive regimes have willingly accepted a dependency relationship to remain in power or, conversely, to deny power to their political opponents.

Inadequacies of the 'Linkage Politics' Model

The preceding discussion on the significance of regime interest in shaping the foreign policy of Bangladesh raises a theoretical question: when and why does regime interest acquire greater significance as a goal of foreign policy in comparison to national interests? To put it broadly, how can we identify conditions under which domestic political variables tend to be the predominant sources of foreign policy? Does the famous 'linkage' concept of Rosenau help us in answering this question? He coined the term 'linkage politics' in 1969 to provide a systematic framework to test connections between national and international political behaviour of states. To facilitate the convergence of the two fields, he proposed that linkages should serve as the basic unit of analysis, and defines it as 'any recurrent sequence of behaviour that originates in one system and is reacted to in another'.[21]

However, this model neither helps us answer the aforementioned questions nor does it answer another important question: what level of analysis should be adopted to probe the domestic bases of foreign policy? This is because Rosenau does not throw light on the distinction between linkage politics as a foreign policy model—that is, a model to investigate linkages between foreign policy and domestic politics of a country—and linkage politics as a system model—that is, a model for the investigation of relationships between the domestic system and the international system in general.[22]

In order to answer the first question regarding the relative significance of domestic politics and regime interests, we may proceed on the assumption that the relative significance of domestic vis-à-vis international catalysts of foreign policy can change according to the type of decision and in different domestic or international contexts. A hypothesis may be proposed to tentatively identify the conditions under which domestic political variables tend to predominate in the making of foreign policy: In circumstances where the ruling elites' retention of power depends upon its response to foreign policy demands of the competing elites, or various interest groups, or of those political entities on whose support its retention of power depends, the influence of internal constraints may become predominant in the shaping of foreign policy. These circumstances tend to exist in situations where the balance of political (and sometimes military) strength tends to favour political rivals, or where public support for the regime is relatively limited. Another, though related, hypothesis may also be proposed: the significance of regime interests as a goal of foreign policy tends to be greater than the national interests when the regime is closed, that is, when freedom of the press, opposition parties, and institutions are absent or weak.

As regards the second question—the appropriate level of analysis to investigate domestic compulsions in foreign policy—a study of the domestic bases of the foreign policy of Bangladesh must concern itself with an analysis of foreign policy at the state level; when doing so, it must use the perspective of the nation-state.[23] In addition, it must be recognized that while Rosenau's linkage politics focuses principally upon political factors, a country's strategic, socio-cultural, and economic attributes too condition its foreign policy. The analytical framework must therefore be wider than the linkage politics model at the state level.

PITFALLS IN DEVELOPING A GRAND AND GENERAL THEORY OF DOMESTIC BASES OF FOREIGN POLICY

The task of identifying domestic sources of foreign policy and measuring their relative significance is extremely difficult because the connections between internal situations and external policy are extremely complex, and also because the number of relevant domestic factors is very large. It is very difficult to suggest a common framework on the basis of which internal constraints on foreign policy issues of all the countries may be studied for all times.[24] Although facts can be stretched to fit a preconceived set of categories, generalizations based on such facts do not advance our understanding of the formulation of foreign policy. Such an approach that begins with general 'pre-theories' and 'theories' and seeks to force all research into a highly structured mould, stimulates endless arguments about whose definitions and categories are the best, and runs a serious risk of culminating in sterile categorization. One may, for example, raise a number of questions concerning Rosenau's attempt to build a general theory of foreign policy in his 'Pre-theories and Theories of Foreign Policy'.[25]

Thus, while I do not deny the value of models or theoretical frameworks in the study of foreign policy, I stress that the theoretical prospects will be greatly enlarged if each researcher devises an individual framework suited to his/her specific data and particular theoretical concerns. The opportunity for comparative analysis, I argue, depends less on the adoption of a common framework than on the willingness of case study writers to express their conclusions in the form of general hypotheses, using well-known, loosely defined variables that can be seamlessly translated from one study to the next.

I do not propose to evolve a general and comprehensive framework for studying internal compulsions in foreign policy, but only to find relevant explanatory propositions enabling an understanding of the domestic bases of Bangladesh's foreign policy. These explanatory variables are geography, economy, historical experiences and philosophical outlook, society, and politics. These factors are not mutually exclusive, with some inevitable overlaps. Cultural norms, for instance, may also be regarded as characteristics of the social structure. Similarly, natural resources may be categorized as geographical or economic factors. My classification of domestic sources of foreign policy is, therefore, designed only for analytical purposes.

Finally, the significance of a particular determinant of foreign policy tends to change under varying circumstances and in different countries. Though I have proposed a *tentative hypothesis* to identify under what situations domestic compulsions are likely to prevail, it is difficult to identify a permanent dominant input in a country's foreign policy. In a great many cases, it is simply impossible to discover which variable is the most important: often, even a decision-maker does not know. Even the author of one of the most comprehensive case studies of the foreign policy process found it 'premature' to rank variables on the basis of a single study alone.[26] If, however, it is impossible to rank variables in one case, how can they be ranked in relation to many?

The attempts made by most of the analysts of comparative foreign policy to rank the various domestic variables are likely to yield only inclusive results and are bound to open the floodgates of arguments and counter-arguments. Indeed, the preoccupation with ranking that has dominated research in comparative foreign policy obstructs any significant advancement in our understanding of foreign policy-making. Very little attention has been devoted to a more promising line of enquiry, that is, how factors such as geography, economy, historical–cultural setting, socio-political factors, and external pressures affect one another in relation to foreign policy. Rather than asking which determinant of foreign policy is more 'basic', we could ask, for instance, how economic compulsions lead to more or less permanent dependencies on aid donors in the case of many countries, but, in the case of others, that very compulsion leads to a vigorous pursuit of self-reliance; or how politics creates incentives to respond to some of the problems created by geography and history, but not to all of them. I do not, therefore, propose to examine here whether a particular domestic factor has been crucial in shaping Bangladesh's foreign policy but instead to analyse how various domestic factors interact with each other and thereby cumulatively shape Bangladesh's foreign policy in general and its policy towards India in particular.

THE GEOSTRATEGIC LOCATION

The geostrategic location of a country is one of the most discussed determinants of foreign policy. Although technological advancements have reduced the significance of geographical factors, various aspects of geography continue to influence the foreign policy of a country. In the case of Bangladesh, three aspects of its geography—location, size, and natural resources—are particularly relevant. As regards location, Bangladesh shares over 90 per cent of its international border with India alone. The Indian state of West Bengal borders Bangladesh to the west, Assam and Meghalaya to the north, and Tripura and Mizoram to the east. Although it has a common border with Myanmar in the south-east, this is very limited and insignificant. Out of total 4,246 km of land boundary, only 193 km with is shared with Myanmar and 4,053 km with India. In terms of size, the total area of Bangladesh is 144,000 sq. km, extremely small in comparison with India which has total land area of 3,287,263 sq. km.

Bangladesh has virtually no natural resources apart from some natural gas, its vast underutilized manpower, and alluvial farmlands, the potential of which is almost invariably ravaged each year by recurrent natural disasters (including devastating floods). Its natural gas, which is found in several small fields in the north-eastern part of the country, is not properly utilized due to lack of industrialization. India and Bangladesh are thus sharply contrasting in terms of their size, manpower, resource endowments, and international standing.

These constraints make for a fragile economy and a weak military, generating anxieties among the Bangladeshi elite about India, even though Bangladesh is vital for India too for the security of its north-eastern states. Its 'India-locked' position makes Bangladesh feel that its political stability is greatly dependent on India. In other words, Bangladesh fears that it is easy for India to alter its political situation through the states bordering Bangladesh. The extent to which India can penetrate Bangladesh was amply demonstrated during India's involvement in the crisis in Pakistan in 1971. Paradoxical as it may appear, the apprehension of Indian domination is perhaps germane in the very role that India played in the emergence of Bangladesh, and therefore Bangladeshis often suspect Indian intentions.[27]

These anxieties have contributed to Bangladesh's reluctance to grant India trans-shipment rights to facilitate the export of the latter's goods from the north-east via the Chittagong port. Allowing such trans-shipment will act as a source of revenue and may help to correct to a considerable degree Bangladesh's parlous balance of payments situation.[28] This phenomenon also explains Bangladesh's attempts to raise bilateral disputes with India at international forums in order to muster world sympathy for a small nation. Raising issues such as the Ganga waters dispute and maritime boundary discord at various international forums clearly demonstrates its determination to register its note of dissent against India. Besides, the unnatural boundaries created between the two nations during the partition of India in 1947 have contributed to several disputes between them.

ECONOMY

The economic situation of a country—as reflected in agricultural production, industrial and technological capacity, total revenue and expenditure of the government, balance of payments position, and the pattern and content of economic growth,—affects its foreign policy in numerous ways. The economic situation, for example, determines its power potential which in turn conditions a country's decision to opt for war or peace. More directly, a country's economic situation determines the degree of dependence on foreign aid and the boundary conditions within which such aid is to be sought and secured.[29]

As a small and impoverished state, an understandable consideration behind Bangladesh's foreign policy has been the pursuit of economic assistance, trade, and access to markets. The country was born in 1971 under tumultous circumstances. Nine months of war had all but destroyed its economy and infrastructure. It had no foreign exchange reserves, and inherited external debt from Pakistan. Moreover, the international economic environment was particularly difficult during that period: the first oil crisis hit the world in 1973; there was a sharp deterioration in the terms of trade, and a decline in the volume of international development assistance. Even before the new country had time to come to grips with these problems, the world economy slid into a recession; interest rates shot up, coupled with sharp exchange rate movements; the prices of commodities fell and, crucially for Bangladesh, the availability of soft loans shrank.

Bangladesh has not yet been able to overcome these difficulties. As one of the least developed countries, it still faces nearly all conceivable problems of development. According to the *Human Development Report 2008–9* of the United Nations Development Programme (UNDP), the Human Development Index of Bangladesh in 2007 was 0.543, which gave the country a rank of 146 out of 182 countries surveyed. According to this survey, the per capita income of a Bangladeshi citizen was $523, the adult literacy rate (ages 15 years and over) was 46.5 per cent, and life expectancy at birth was 62.84 years in 2007.[30] According a US Central Intelligence Agency (CIA) report of December 18, 2008, though the Bangladesh economy has grown 5–6 per cent over the past few years, the country remains a poor, overpopulated, and inefficiently-governed nation. Although more than half of GDP is generated through the service sector, nearly two-thirds of Bangladeshis are employed in the agriculture sector, with rice as the single-most-important product.[31]

Bangladesh is a predominantly agricultural country, highly dependent on monsoons. This makes people vulnerable to the hazards of poor harvests and famine in the event of a failure of the monsoons. Therefore, Bangladesh continues to generate very low levels of internal resources to finance development or manage non-developmental expenditures. Of late, macroeconomic indicators show some positive trends, such as a 6 per cent growth in gross domestic product (GDP) during 2007.[32] Even so, the overall economic scenario is grim, as spiralling prices of essential commodities have made the situation intolerable for the ordinary people. In fact, Bangladesh experienced a famine-like situation in the winter of 2005.[33]

At that same time (in the year 2005), the country suffered from balance of payment difficulties, with export earnings financing roughly about 35 per cent of import costs.[34] Bangladesh's exposure to the global economy is very low in terms of other aspects of external economic interaction such as trade and investment. Exports account for an abysmally low share of the country's GDP, a little over 6 per cent.

Under the circumstances, Bangladesh has had to depend heavily on foreign aid. By 1990, 96 per cent of Bangladesh's development budget was dependent on foreign aid (in comparison with 17 per cent in India's case), and approximately half of its total imports were financed by foreign aid. At the same time, the international aid climate deteriorated after 1987, reducing the rate of (inflation adjusted) 'real dollar' aid flows into Bangladesh. Consequently, much more of Bangladesh's aid is now received in the form of loans rather than grants, adding to the cost of debt servicing. Bangladesh's total outstanding debt has increased drastically over the past three decades, growing from $501 million in 1974 to $21.52 billion in December 2008.[35]

This reliance on foreign aid has greatly reduced the prospect of self-reliance,[36] providing leverage to the donor countries to influence domestic and foreign policies. As the World Bank's first resident representative in independent Bangladesh noted, 'The opportunity for the aid-givers to impose their views on Bangladesh was made all too clear when it became the accepted view that Bangladesh simply could not manage her economy without large amounts of aid.'[37] In a well-documented study, evidence pointed to the 'overriding concerns of the donors on the direction of both domestic and foreign policies in Bangladesh, their normative biases and their perceptions of their own particular interests in Bangladesh'. [38]

Bangladesh's policy towards India could not remain unaffected by its dependence on foreign aid. As long as India extended massive aid to Bangladesh during the period immediately after her independence, Dhaka maintained good relations with New Delhi. However, when New Delhi could not by itself bear the burden of reconstruction of the war-ravaged country, Dhaka had to diversify its sources of aid.[39] In the post-Mujib era Bangladesh slowly moved away from India towards other countries such as USA and China who were not sympathetic to India.[40] Not surprisingly, therefore, Bangladesh's extreme poverty, economic instability, and aid dependency directly or indirectly fuel Indian concerns about external interference in the region. The post-Mujib era rulers deepened these Indian apprehensions by emphasizing and exaggerating Bangladesh's strengthening links with USA, China, and the Arab states (long-standing allies of Pakistan, India's principal adversary).[41] An Indian writer, therefore, commented:

India has reasons to be wary about Bangladesh's potentially disruptive role in the north-east in the context of continuing uncertainty in that strategic region. India has also reasons to be uneasy about any major destabilization in Bangladesh, which would lead to the involvement of an extra-regional power in the area and have major repercussions in India. A hostile Bangladesh, in league with China and Pakistan, or both, will be able to exploit the turbulence in the north-east to India's patent disadvantage.[42]

Marcus Franda and Ataur Rahman advance a subtle, yet similar view on this issue:

The inability of Bangladesh to become economically self-sufficient together with its terribly restricted power position vis-à-vis India, significantly affect the security environment of Bangladesh. Possibilities for big power penetration are, therefore, considerable. Given the volatility of Bangladesh politics, the intensity and depth of Indo-Bangladesh differences, and Bangladesh's economic vulnerability, it is difficult to envisage an extensive period in the future when the big powers would not be tempted to at least probe Bangladesh's internal affairs.[43]

As the post-Mujib rulers in Bangladesh fostered, rather than allayed, Indian concerns regarding the adverse implications of Bangladesh's dependence on foreign aid, economic factors appear to have been manipulated by, rather than being instrumental in, the shaping of Bangladesh's policy towards India. India is likely to continue to view

Bangladesh's economic difficulties in terms of a blend of political and ideological concerns, despite Dhaka's economic dependence on countries which are no longer a threat to India, or organizations such as the World Bank to which India too is indebted.

Whatever may be the implications of Bangladesh's dependence on foreign aid for its India policy, its impoverished situation has given impetus to large-scale migration of Bangladeshi nationals to India since 1974 in the quest of better economic opportunities. Although the migrants have largely settled in Assam and West Bengal, causing severe demographic pressures, Delhi, Mumbai, and several cities of north India have also had to cope with the presence of a large number of Bangladeshi nationals. Bangladesh has flatly denied any exodus of its nationals to India. Although till 1982, it took back Bangladeshi nationals handed over by the Indian authorities, it has since categorically refused to accept back the 'aliens' sent by India. As a result, New Delhi approved an Indo-Bangladesh border road and fence project in 1986 to prevent illegal immigration from Bangladesh, though the progress of this project was very slow and irregular till 1998. Dhaka saw this as a humiliating and unnecessary provocative act by India, leading to exchanges of fire between the border forces, further vitiating the atmosphere. Although no efforts were subsequently made by India to press the issue of fencing to its logical culmination, it brought to the fore the enormity of the problem created by poverty in Bangladesh, which was further aggravated by a section of India's ruling elite seeking the votes of Bangladeshi migrants.[44]

HISTORY

The behaviour of any human system, be it an individual or a state comprising a complex society, results in part from the cumulative weight of past experiences. The residue of the past must be seen as one of the factors affecting the external behaviour patterns of a country. Contrary to the general impression prevailing in India, that Bangladesh's history began with East Bengal's struggle for liberation from West Pakistan, most Bangladeshi scholars trace the history of Bangladesh's independence in 1971 to the beginning of Bengali Muslim nationalism in the mid-1930s, which was aimed at establishing an identity separate from not only the non-Muslim Bengalis, but also from the fellow followers of Islam in other parts of India.[45] The cultural and religious differences between Hindus and Muslims, and the dominance of Hindu businessmen and landlords in East Bengal in undivided India, led the East Bengali

Muslims to enthusiastically support the cause of Pakistan. A section of Bengali Muslims even regard the cancellation of Bengal's partition (1905) in 1911 as a victory of Hindu domination over Bengali Muslims. However, even at the height of Muslim nationalism, Bengali Muslims were apprehensive, as A.K. Fuzlul Haq called for more than one state for Indian Muslims, thereby seeking to protect the rights and interests of Bengali Muslims in East Bengal.[46] After Partition, when Mohammad Ali Jinnah let down these expectations of the Bengali Muslims by declaring Urdu as a state language in 1948, the language movement received a fillip, culminating in the emergence of a secular Bangladesh in 1971 with friendly ties with India.

Anti-India feelings assiduously cultivated by the erstwhile Pakistani rulers, however, began to surface during the Mujib regime itself.[47] When the so-called 'honeymoon' period between the two countries ended with the murder of Sheikh Mujibur Rahman in 1975, the legacies of the past, especially Hindu–Muslim rivalry in undivided India, received a fillip in Bangladesh. During the liberation war and immediately thereafter, these tendencies existed but were dormant because of India's assistance in the war and its continued economic assistance. When India was no longer in a position to continue aid given its own economic constraints, anti-Indian sentiment came to the fore. A sense of indebtedness to India soon became a psychological burden, triggering resentment.

Factionalism among various groups that fought the liberation war, and the charge that India was selectively aiding groups close to the Awami League (AL), had already created grounds for an anti-India feeling.[48] An atmosphere resulted in which India's actions were seen by the rival and smaller political groups as serving the AL's political interests. Moreover, groups that operated outside the AL's leadership, but worked in tandem to achieve their common goal of independence, viewed with suspicion the close ties that the Bangladesh government in exile (BGE), based in Calcutta (now Kolkata), had with India. A point of irritation for some freedom fighters was the requirement that Bengali armed forces officers, formerly with the Pakistan army but later fighting the liberation war, send in reports to the Indian army to enable coordinated action. Some liberation forces were troubled by the induction of mostly Mujib loyalists into the armed Mukti Bahini when it was formed. It was indeed a difficult task for the Indians to bring groups with differing ideologies under a unified command.

India channelled its support to various groups through the BGE. Given the lack of support from India, the left parties in Bangladesh played a secondary role in the liberation struggle.[49] Another influential group, the Kader Bahini, fought the war on its own. Its leader, Kader Siddiqi, played a prominent role in the liberation war. He resented the presence of the Indian army during the ceremony held for the surrender of the Pakistan army, when none of the senior officers of the Bangladesh forces were present. This incident ruffled the ego of Bangladeshis. These groups played an important role in the post-liberation political development of Bangladesh. India became the favourite whipping boy and the source of all the woes that befell the young state.

SOCIETY

The formulation of foreign policy represents, on its domestic side, a continuing series of compromises and adjustments between the different elements of government and social forces.[50] The societal sources of foreign policy are therefore very significant. The social structure of Bangladesh too influences its foreign policy in several ways.

First, although the population of Bangladesh is predominantly Muslim, and considered to be a more homogenous society than other South Asian countries, there are significant religious and ethnic minorities such as Hindus in the plains and a substantial number of tribes in the Chittagong Hill Tracts (CHT). The most important among the tribes inhabiting the CHT are Chakmas, the Marmas, the Tipras, and the Mhos. Although constituting only 1 per cent of Bangladesh's population, yet given their distinct language, ethnicity, religion, and social organization, they present the most serious challenge to the national integration of Bangladesh.[51] The formation of Pakistan, with its emphasis on Urdu, Islam, and a unitary structure, eroded the autonomy thus far enjoyed by these groups. The Pakistan government not only permitted outsiders to settle in this heretofore prohibited area, it actually encouraged these settlements with monetary and other incentives. This policy continued after the formation of Bangladesh, leading to the transformation of the region's demography to the disadvantage of the tribal population. The development projects of the central government destabilized these tribes and adversely affected their economic, social, and cultural existence with new economic activities replacing traditional ones. The cumulative effect of these developmental and resettlement policies was the crystallization of a defiant stance among the tribal population, which was expressed, in the absence of a participatory democracy, in the growth of insurgency. Unfortunately, however, the successive governments, rather than addressing the grievances of these marginalized sections of their society, responded to their agitation by resort to repressive measures.[52]

These measures led to a large-scale migration of these tribes into India, particularly into the state of Tripura. Earlier, the Commissioning of the Karnafuli Hydro Electricity project in 1962 had displaced thousands of then East Pakistan's tribal people, who subsequently migrated to India and were eventually resettled in Arunachal Pradesh. This issue later generated tensions in India–Bangladesh relations, as the latter accused India of providing assistance and encouragement to the insurgency mounted by the Shanti Bahini, a tribal force. India, on its part, remains gravely concerned about the spillover effect of the insurgent activities on its own border states in the sensitive north-east. For instance, Tripura had to bear the brunt of not only the large-scale influx of Chakma refugees, but also of the disquieting implications of extremist groups such as the Tripura National Volunteers (TNV) seeking refuge across the border. Frequent clashes have been reported between Chakmas and the local population in Arunachal Pradesh too. Although several efforts have been made during the past years for the repatriation of Chakmas to Bangladesh, estimated to be between 50,000 and 60,000, the issue remains unresolved and a major irritant in India–Bangladesh relations.

The growing influence of Islamic fundamentalist forces in Bangladesh also affects India–Bangladesh relations. The Hindu–Muslim divide never ebbed even during the heyday of secular Bengali nationalism. Indeed, the AL's opposition to Punjabi domination was not rooted in any secular commitment as such; Mujib's emphasis on secularism was in all probability a reflection of his sense of gratitude to India for its assistance in the liberation of Bangladesh. That the replacement of his secularism was inevitable after his departure was foreseen as follows:

Historically, the duality of the Indian Muslim's culture had resulted in a conflict between his Indianness and his Muslimness and it may well be possible that once again Bengali Muslims will decide to claim their Muslim legacy.... After all, Bangladesh now is the next largest Muslim nation to Indonesia, and the very fact that it exists as a political entity separate from the culturally similar West Bengal is evidence enough of the survival of one form of Muslim nationalism.[53]

It is against the broad spectrum of Bangladesh's socio-cultural milieu that the resurgence of radical Islamic ideology in the post-Mujib era has to be viewed. Most of the post-Mujib rulers, including former prime minister Begum Khaleda Zia, attempted to consolidate their positions by taking recourse to fundamentalist Islamic ideology. Indeed, the 2001 elections and the return to power of Begum Zia's Bangladesh Nationalist Party (BNP) with the help of the Jamaat-e-Islami, considered by many to be the fountainhead of terrorism in Bangladesh, with a pathological hatred for India, revived Indian concerns about Bangladesh. Post-election violence directed against the minority Hindu community came in for severe criticism by India.

The Islamic terrorists demonstrated their strength and reach on 17 August 2005 by simultaneously setting off 475 bomb blasts in a span 45 minutes in 63 of the 64 districts of the country. A banned Islamic terrorist organization, Jama'atul Mujahideen Bangladesh (Organization of the Holy Warriors, JMB),[54] claimed responsibility for these well-coordinated attacks. Leaflets found near the blast sites demanded that Islamic rule be promptly established. Although there was not much loss of life, Islamist groups behind the attacks succeeded in attracting the attention of the government and the people at large.[55] That terrorists continued to operate without fear was evident when they attacked three local courts in October 2005 and again on 29 November 2005 in which at least nine persons were killed.

Rather than cracking down on these groups, the leaders of the then ruling coalition in Dhaka pointed their fingers towards the opposition party and external forces, especially India.[56] The initial drive to catch the masterminds of the 17 August bomb blasts and dismantle their networks slowed down within months, as reports revealed links between members of the then ruling coalition and the militants. For example, Mufti Abdul Hannan, leader of the Harkat-ul-Jihad[57] (a militant Islamist organization with connections to the Pakistani militant group with a similar name), who was sentenced in absentia in 2003 to life imprisonment and arrested on 1 October 2005, claimed that he had been given assurances by the former home minister that he could safely stay within the country.[58] It was ironical, therefore, that during her New Delhi visit in March 2006, Begum Zia agreed with Prime Minster Manmohan Singh that both being 'victims' of terrorism, Bangladesh and India should join hands to fight the menace. The former ruling coalition's dependence on fundamentalist forces led to doubt about the sincerity of this commitment.[59]

It is, however, heartening to note that ever since the new government led by Sheikh Hasina came to power in Dhaka after the December 2008 elections, it has been determinedly rounding up terrorists and cleansing its state institutions of extremist sympathizers who had flourished under the previous BNP–Jamat-e-Islami regime. In a welcome development in the year 2009, authorities in Bangladesh have arrested six members of the terrorist organization Harkat-ul-Jihad Islami as part of Sheikh Hasina's drive against Islamic militancy in that country. The benefits to India from Bangladesh's tough stance on extremism are obvious. Separatists and jihadi groups alike have used the porous Indo-Bangladesh border to successfully evade the law and carry out their nefarious activities. That now there is a regime in Dhaka that believes that both India and Bangladesh are fighting a common enemy is a source of great relief for New Delhi. In line with this thinking, both countries have decided to take significant steps to enhance bilateral ties and implement joint security measures, such as coordinated patrolling of the border.[60]

Third, Islamic predominance in Bangladeshi society makes it react to Hindu–Muslim relations within India. To cite an example, the Bangladeshi reaction to the demolition of the Babri Masjid in 1992 shows how social structure moulds Dhaka's India policy. Khaleda Zia, the then prime minister of Bangladesh, proclaimed: 'The situation arising out of the demolition of the Babri mosque is fraught with a possibility of an adverse impact on Indo-Bangladeshi relations.'[61] M.R. Nizami, the secretary of Jammat-e-Islami, called upon the Muslims of the world to boycott India economically unless the Babri Masjid was rebuilt.[62] He also observed that the Babri incident showed that India could not accept the existence of an independent Bangladesh, wanting to see Bangladesh subservient to it.[63] Some of the leading Bangladeshi newspapers too joined the chorus. *Bangladesh Observer* (Dhaka), in its editorial of 11 December 1992, for instance, commented:

As far as Bangladesh and other SAARC members are concerned, it is time they got together, put all their grievances down on paper and let the world know how the Indians have behaved, to crush each of them culturally, economically and politically. India, the bully of the subcontinent, has at last exposed itself to be nothing but a crude Hindu state.

However, while attacking India, these critics forgot that a vast number of Hindus in India and elsewhere rose against the Ayodhya incident and four state governments led by Hindu nationalist Bharatiya Janata Party were dismissed, even though three of them were not responsible for protecting the Babri Masjid.

Fourth, while the liberation of Bangladesh demolished the validity of the two-nation theory based on religion, it raised afresh the problem of identity of the people of Bangladesh.[64] What is difference between a Bangladeshi and an Indian from West Bengal? Is Islam the only difference? Then what happens to Bengali or Bangladeshi nationalism in assertion of which the liberation war was fought? The answer that people of the same ethnic origin and culture can belong to two different nation-states due to differences in religious affinity appears to be too simplistic.

Bangladesh is still grappling with the question of defining its identity. While religious affinity brings Bangladesh closer to Islamic brotherhood, its language and cultural heritage bring it closer to India's West Bengal. Not surprisingly, the basis of Bangladesh's identity has been oscillating between ethnicity and religion. A Bangladeshi scholar expresses this dilemma of Bangladesh's identity in these words:

Bangladesh emerged as a sovereign state on the basis of Bengali nationalism, and in the 1972 constitution, the citizens were defined as 'Bengalis'. However, in 1977, Ziaur Rahman substituted 'Bangladeshis' for 'Bengalis'. This has raised a great controversy in the country. Some hold that the emergence of Bangladesh was nothing but the consequential product of the Lahore Resolution of 1940, which had envisaged two Muslim 'Independent States' in India. Others challenge this view, and believe that the emergence of Bangladesh was the logical conclusion of the historic urge of the Bengalis to be independent of external control. Bengali nationalism is emphasized more by the secularists and the leftists, whereas Bangladeshi nationalism is espoused by those who emphasize fundamental differences between the Bangladeshis and the Bengali-speaking people in the neighbouring states of India (West Bengal, Bihar, Meghalaya, Tripura and Assam), or to whom Bangladesh roughly corresponds to a Muslim Bengal. The confusion remains: Bengali nationalism is discarded in favour of Bangladeshi nationalism, then the basis of the liberation war—the Bengali language and culture is questioned; if Bengali nationalism rather than Bangladeshi nationalism is accepted, it, on the one hand, fails to integrate the non-Bengali speaking tribal peoples (more than a dozen in number) within the framework of the nation in Bangladesh, and the other an 'over-arching' Bengali nationalism, banishing cultural distinction between Bangladesh and West Bengal, tends to erode the force of geographical nationalism of Bangladesh.[65]

While Mujibur Rahman emphasized secularism and the Bengali identity of the people of Bangladesh, Ziaur Rahman called for a distinct Bangladeshi nationalism to ostensibly denote a distinction from both the Bengali and Islamic identities. In reality, however, he laid greater emphasis on reviving Islamic values in national life. The slogan 'Joy Bangla', which was an expression of secular Bengali nationalism, was discarded as 'un-Islamic' and in its stead the slogan 'Bangladesh Zindabad' was popularized, largely by Ziaur Rahman and his followers.

At the social level, a new trend was encouraged to assert the Muslim characteristics of the Bengali language, as against the Hindu ones, by increasing the use of Arabic and Persian words to replace Sanskrit words associated with Hindu culture, a trend reminiscent of the programme in Tamil Nadu to purge from the Tamil language terms of non-Dravidian origin.[66]

Bangladesh's foreign policy in general and its India policy in particular could not have remained unaffected by this shift from Bengali to Islamic identity. Post-Mujib Bangladesh introduced a new thrust in its foreign policy by amending the Constitution to proclaim, 'The state shall endeavour to consolidate; preserve and strengthen fraternal relations among Muslim countries based on Islamic solidarity.'[67] Simultaneously, a growing Islamist tendency revived insecurity among the Hindu minorities in Bangladesh. The process of encouraging Islamic resurgence in Bangladesh which began during the Ziaur Rahman period, continued more or less during the subsequent non-Awami League regimes. There were reports of discrimination against them, as they were subjected to partisan application of vested property laws. Their sense of insecurity was manifested in their refusal to 'acquire property or many material goods because they feel they should remain mobile in case they are forced to move to India'.[68] They made the Indian position delicate by complaining to the Indian High Commission in Dhaka.[69] The resurgence of Islamic identity in Bangladesh thus became the core of resistance to Indian predominance. An Islamic scholar commented that in Bangladesh 'anti-Indianism and communalism are connected with each other deeply'.[70] This internal tension over Bengali versus Islamic identity has become a significant variable in Indo-Bangladesh relations.[71] Accordingly, the return to power of Bengali nationalists in Dhaka, for whom national, cultural, and linguistic identity supersedes loyalty to an Arab-dominated Wahhabi Islam augurs well for India–Bangladesh relations.

POLITICS

The political system and processes of a state have a significant bearing on its foreign policy. It is generally assumed that the foreign policy decision-making process in an authoritarian political system differs from that in a democratic system. As the decision-making power in the former rests with an individual (aided by a clique), decisions can be made quickly in accordance with the will of the person and clique in power.[72] Democratic political systems, on the other hand, have a far more complicated decision-making process, where the views of several constituencies are usually taken into account before arriving at any decision.

A reading of the literature on the politics of foreign policy in non-American settings, however, suggests that the aforesaid assumptions regarding democratic versus authoritarian systems overlook the fact that the actual character of the regime is more important than the formal structure of a political system.[73] This is especially true in countries like Pakistan and Bangladesh where the military plays a vital role in the sustenance and survival of any regime. It is, therefore, necessary to examine the actual nature of the regime rather than simply looking at the openness of a political system for its implications for foreign policy.[74]

Bangladesh, like other smaller South Asian states, has often been plagued by political instability and military takeovers. This has created a crisis of legitimacy for political regimes. When a regime faces threats to its survival, it may cite external threats to divert people's attention from growing difficulties at home.[75] Indian leaders, too, have used this strategy to strengthen their regimes while dealing with countries like the USA. However, this tendency to use foreign policy for the sustenance and survival of regimes is much more pronounced in India's neighbouring countries like Bangladesh because of the narrower political base of the ruling elite, chronic political instability, and crisis of governance aggravated by the undeveloped nature of political institutions. This applies not only to military-led governments but also to elected ones. As pointed out by noted Bangladeshi scholar Iftekharuzzaman:

Very few of the numerous political parties active in the country are strictly organized, well-knit and spread into grass-roots levels having definite policies and programmes of action. Intense factionalism and polarization among social groups and classes which are formulated along the prevailing inequitable distribution of wealth and power coupled with a widespread network of patron–client relationships pervading the whole society have resulted in a system devoid of institutional virtues. Parties are born of factions and party politics is almost universally characterized by factional and parochial interests, while policies and decision reflect strong subjective bias, which leaves the interest of the masses at bay. Whether in the government or in the opposition parties and their organizational set-ups lack democratic values and the leadership caters to the maximization of the interest of the influential élites and power bases at the cost of the interest of the common people.[76]

Indeed, factionalism is pervasive not only within Bangladesh's political parties, civil service, and armed forces, but also between each of these groups. The problem of factionalism was particularly destabilizing during the first decade of Bangladesh's existence. However, throughout the country's history, factionalism has fostered state insecurity and led the various ruling regimes to foment an anti-India attitude as a component of its foreign policy. Anti-Indianism appears to be a ready tool for the government to divert the attention of the people from pressing issues such as abysmal poverty, unemployment, and political instability. This also serves as a cover to shield martial law regimes. This form of foreign policy behaviour can be seen in each phase of Bangladesh's relationship with India, when bilateral disputes have intensified during periods of internal stress in the former's political set up.

For example, once Ziaur Rahman emerged as a military strongman and consolidated his hold over the unruly cantonments, he sought to create a broad coalition against the AL. However, lacking in legitimacy and unable to address the economic and political problems confronting the nation, Zia resorted to the one convenient card that he held: stepping up anti-Indian sentiments to not only distract popular attention from real issues, but to also discredit the AL and rally the support of the Islamist forces. In order to achieve this, Zia drew upon an assortment of stereotypical imagery running high on emotions:

We will not tolerate any interference from any quarter that can create obstacles in the way of fulfilment of this aim ... Certain circles forgetting their past misdeeds, are engaged in trying to join hands with the forces opposed to [the] country's sovereignty. These elements have clearly indicated that they are active with the help of external forces ... Foreign agents engaged in conspiracy against our independence are warned that the heroic people of Bangladesh would frustrate all their evil designs. There is no place for Mir Jafars[77] on our soil. Find out the Mir Jafars and foreign agents and cooperate in inflicting adequate punishment on them. Allah is with us.[78]

The forcefulness of this rhetoric illustrated Zia's determination to consolidate his regime by raising the bogey of the threat posed by India and tarnishing the image of the pro-Mujib freedom fighters by portraying them as Indian agents. At the same time, Zia used the Islamic card to seek legitimacy for his illegal regime. His public stand vividly illustrates this:

Dear brother and sisters, our people seek justice which emanates from Allah, and they must get their justice otherwise the people will fight for it ... We want to practice our respective religion and to live under the umbrella of religion. This government of yours is determined to satisfy this requirement of the people ... A handful of miscreants in our country are carrying on loot and plunder in the villages ... So I want to tell you that the entire nation has to be determined to root out and destroy these miscreants [who] ... claim to bring independence with foreign help ... we want that no other country will interfere in the internal affairs of Bangladesh ... We have religious, historical and cultural relations with all the Muslim countries of the world and we want to further our relations with them ... If there is aggression on us the seven and a half-crore people of this country will rise to one man and resist it and defend the independence.[79]

The strategy of making a scapegoat of India by combining accusations of territorial aggression with the cry of 'Islam in danger' not only deflected domestic criticism, but it also reinforced the notion of Bangladeshi nationalism that he was attempting to foster.[80] While doing so, he was unconcerned about the long-term consequences such as communal conflict and Indian retaliation by way of withdrawal of economic cooperation. Similarly, while blaming India for abetting the Chakma Shanti Bahini, he overlooked the fact that India was forced to extend shelter to the Chakmas as for two decades they were being subjected to what the Amnesty International in London in its report in September 1986 described as 'unlawful killing and torture'.[81] For him, finding an Indian scapegoat was the easier option than trying to address the demand for autonomy of these marginalized tribes.

Zia's attempt to involve the United Nations in the Farakka barrage dispute with India too reflected his domestic compulsion to consolidate his regime by demonstrating his 'commitment to Bangladesh' as against Mujib's 'loyalty to India'. Though technical in nature, this dispute was, in the sense, that both the countries were sorely in need of the Ganga waters and this could be amicably sorted out only through dispassionate discussion and in a spirit of give-and-take, Zia's bid to legitimize the usurpation of power through presidential elections in 1979, and his apprehension of strong opposition to any mutually beneficial accord on sharing of Ganga waters obliged him to once again stir up anti-India hysteria. He, therefore, cautioned his foreign minister to go slow on finding a negotiated solution of the Farakka barrage issue until the presidential elections were over.[82]

After Ziaur Rahman's assassination in 1981, the second military regime under General H.M. Ershad came to power. As with Zia, Ershad's successful bid for power influenced the course of Bangladesh's policy towards India, though to a relatively limited degree. This was so because although, like Zia, Ershad too did not have a popular mandate to rule the country, and political life remained volatile and precarious, certain conditions offered opportunities for an ambitious and shrewd

individual like him. While Zia usurped power under dangerous circumstances and in the face of Indian disapproval and indignation, Ershad
had ample time to choose an opportune moment to take over the reins
of government from a civilian acting president, Abdus Sattar. By opting
to delay the bid for direct rule, Ershad was able to concentrate on the
task of consolidating his position as leader of the armed forces and,
at the same time, minimizing civilian apprehension. His attempt to
deal with these problems was encapsulated in his open commitment
to ensure that the military be given a decision-making, stabilizing role
in Bangladesh's political life,[83] governed by constitutional means and
theoretically subject to popular approval.

Unlike Zia, therefore, Ershad had sufficient time to implement
his political designs cautiously, deliberatively, and methodically,
synchronizing his coup with the most politically advantageous domestic
and regional conditions. Ershad's comparatively assured bid for leadership
did not compel him to drastically alter the direction of foreign policy,
as Zia had been obliged to do given his more turbulent debut. Ershad
was in a position to draw upon his predecessor's accomplishments and
consolidate the more effective changes, which had already been put in
place by Zia, rather than having to run the risk of treading an untested
path.

The difference in the political circumstances between Zia's and
Ershad's assumption of power had fallouts for India–Bangladesh relations.
Though Ershad's initial decision to support the civilian government in
Dhaka aroused some suspicion in India about his intention to 'cover up
something',[84] his astute move to postpone his coup not only provided
him greater scope for political gain at home, but also created a favourable
environment for improvement of Bangladesh's ties with India.[85] There
was a temporary upswing in India–Bangladesh relations during 1981–
2.[86] Although Ershad's assumption of power per se might not have been
a primary cause of improvement in India–Bangladesh relations, it did
not have the effect of impairing the relationship. Indeed, the reaction
of the Indian press to the non-violent coup was quite favourable and
optimistic.[87] The move towards restoration of normalcy in India–
Bangladesh relations was reflected during the Indian Foreign Minister
Narasimha Rao's visit to Dhaka in May and Ershad's visit to New Delhi
in October 1982. Two memorandums of understanding on Ganga water
sharing were also signed in 1982 and 1985.[88]

This auspicious beginning notwithstanding, relations between the
neighbours could not be significantly strengthened during the Ershad

regime for several reasons, including domestic politics in India and Bangladesh. In India's case, the agitation in Assam resulting from the influx of refugees, and its decision to erect barbed wire fencing on the India–Bangladesh border invited Dhaka's wrath.[89] In the case of Bangladesh, the growing opposition to Ershad's rule and gradual coming together of Shiekh Mujib's daughter, Sheikh Hasina Wajed, and widow of Zia, Begum Khaleda Zia, on a single platform (notwithstanding their deep differences) to 'deal a death blow to martial men in power',[90] compelled Ershad to engage in anti-India rhetoric to divert people's attention from issues of governance and his political illegitimacy. Ershad's quest for political legitimacy and survival also led him to rely on Islam, culminating in his decision to declare Islam as the state religion of Bangladesh through 8th Amendment of the Constitution formalized on 7 June 1988.[91] Domestic politics thus necessitated the direction of Bangladeshi nationalism, which was essentially based on Islam and anti-India attitudes and policies. This was reflected in non-ratification of the 1974 Treaty signed by Indira Gandhi and Sheikh Mujibur Rahman for comprehensive settlement of outstanding border issues between the two countires and delay in handing over the Tinbigha corridor to India. The issue of leasing the Tinbigha corridor became a political albatross for India. Factionalism within the government and the political imperatives of the ruling elite, especially during the Ershad's regime, hampered an early resolution of the Farakka barrage dispute with India,[92] even though the Farakka stalemate benefited India at the cost of Bangladesh's national interest.[93]

Military rulers apart, politics has guided the foreign policy approach of civilian leaders too. After the end of the Ershad regime, India became an issue in Bangladesh's domestic politics during the 1991 elections. The AL manifesto spoke of secularism and a return to the 1972 Constitution. Begum Zia's BNP attacked this stance as a sell-out to India. It based its electoral discourse on the theme of being 'a saviour' who had saved the country from Ershad's autocratic regime and loss of sovereignty to its powerful neighbour India. This caused apprehension in India about the nature of bilateral relations under the BNP regime. Though relations began on a positive note, as Begum Zia spoke of joint endeavours to strengthen Indo-Bangladesh relations, no common ground could be found on various issues such as border fencing and Bangladeshi immigration into India. She publicly supported the separatist movements in India's north-east by referring these as 'freedom movements.'[94] Her visit to India in March 2006 again generated hopes of improvement in Bangladesh's ties with India. In reality, however, both her tenures as prime minister (1991–6 and 2001–6) proved to be difficult in terms of Dhaka's equation with New Delhi.

Sheikh Hasina's first tenure as prime minister (1996–2001) did not fulfil India's reasonable expectations from Dhaka on several issues: controlling support by anti-India forces within Bangladesh to rebel groups in India's north-east; acting effectively against Pakistan's Inter-Services Intelligence Directorate and terrorist organizations like the Harkat-ul Jihad-e-Islami Bangladesh using Bangladesh's territory for terrorist strikes against India; granting Indian goods transit facilities from the rest of the country to the north-eastern states through its territory; and the sale of Bangladesh's natural gas to India. Dhaka did, of course, sign an agreement with New Delhi in December 1996 on sharing of Ganga water which, unlike the past agreements on this subject, has proved to be durable. The major credit for this agreement should, however, go to the then West Bengal chief minister, Jyoti Basu, who actively participated in the negotiations and it was due to his approval that West Bengal, which earlier opposed any major concession to Dhaka on this issue, permitted New Delhi to be more generous on this occasion.[95]

On the other hand, domestic political constraints prevented Sheikh Hasina from acting tough against anti-India forces within Bangladesh. This was because the previous rulers had swamped the bureaucracy, the armed and paramilitary forces, and the intelligence agencies with pro-Pakistan and anti-India elements, while systematically trying to Islamize Bangladesh. Any government committed to secularism and friendly ties with India could have been hobbled by Bangladesh's power structure. Overhauling the latter would have required a majority, which the AL that won 146 out of 300 seats in the Jatiya Sansad in the 1996 elections, lacked. On the other hand, the BNP of Begum Zia acted as an effective opposition with 110 seats in the national parliament. This forced Sheikh Hasina to try to co-opt the Jama'at during the opposition boycott of parliament, which in turn considerably enhanced the legitimacy of the Islamists in Bangladesh politics to the detriment of Dhaka's ties with New Delhi.[96]

However, growing attacks by the Islamic terrorists on NGOs (non-governmental organizations), liberal intellectuals, and politicians, especially the AL leaders—including the grenade attack on Awami League rally in Dhaka on 21 August 2004,[97] in which Sheikh Hasina escaped miraculously—bred in her a steady determination to wipe out terrorism. The massive majority achieved by her in the December 2008 elections facilitated her resolve to wage war against terrorism. This is on full display with the arrest of Lashkar-e-Taiba terrorists and Dawood Ibrahim's men. The rebels of north-eastern India are also under pressure. The mystery of the massive arms haul in Chittagong on 2 April 2004 is being unravelled. The Jamat and its leaders are facing prosecution as war criminals with the government responding positively to the widespread demand for the trial of those who committed unspeakable atrocities while collaborating with Pakistanis during the 1971 liberation war. Her handling of the mutiny by Bangladesh Rifles personnel in Dhaka in February 2009 shows a remarkable blend of courage, political wisdom, and leadership.[98] India has everything to gain from further deepening its ties with Bangladesh under her leadership.

* * *

The events and issues discussed earlier illustrate the way in which Bangladesh's policy towards India has evolved. While some of these stimuli have helped to improve ties, others have had an adverse impact on cooperative relations. Domestic factors, such as Dhaka's sense of insecurity, arising from its small size and 'India-locked' location, its underdevelopment and dependence on foreign aid, problems emanating from its colonial past and the state's subsequent political underdevelopment, the dilemma of national identity, half-hearted accommodation of the religious and linguistic minorities, the political insecurity of ruling elites, and acute factionalism within the ruling establishment, have interacted with each other and together shaped the country's foreign policy in general and its India policy in particular.

The preceding discussion therefore proves the hypothesis that in a situation where the ruling elites' support base is narrow, they lack political legitimacy, and their survival is uncertain, domestic politics is accorded greater salience in the making of foreign policy in comparison to the external environment. At the same time, regime interests override national interests. However, when a regime is relatively stable with open politics, a free press, and strong institutions, the need and scope you resorting to foreign policy for sustenance and survival tend to be much less. It needs to be clarified that regime interest may not necessarily clash with national interest; there could be convergence between the two. For instance, Zia's effort towards South Asian cooperation was beneficial for Bangladesh (indeed for South Asia) as also for establishing the legitimacy of his regime by demonstrating his acceptability to the international community.

In the case of Bangladesh, however, regime interests often clashed with national interests. This is true not only in the context of making India a scapegoat in the regime's search for sustenance and thereby contributing towards jeopardizing a mutually beneficial partnership with India, but also in the context of seeking foreign aid. Even though foreign aid failed in its basic objective of facilitating development, it became a vital instrument in internal power play. The availability of aid augmented the meagre resources of the state and enabled the military to consolidate its hold through massive patronage. This explains how and why military rulers could retain power for over 15 years by establishing an elaborate clientelistic regime and co-opting some of the opposition groups into the power structure, notwithstanding the failure of successive military rulers to gain legitimacy. In the process, however, democratic institutions and civil society were greatly emaciated and the autonomy of the state was greatly circumscribed.

This is not to absolve the elected governments of their responsibilities in acting against the national interests of Bangladesh. Political parties in Bangladesh have not learnt to live and work with political opponents. Though they came together to a degree due to massive popular, especially students' pressure, during the last phase of the anti-autocratic movement, they were unable to carry forward this flexibility after the 1991 elections. Thus, Bangladesh today faces two basic and interrelated challenges: first, sustaining the process of democratic transition and its institutionalization; second, ensuring a process of sustainable participatory development that places the interest of the people at the core of all policy and decision-making.

Viewed in this perspective, the thrust of Bangladesh's foreign policy should be to count on what it can bargain you and earn abroad by projecting what it is capable of, rather than what it may deserve and obtain because of its impediments. It is after all the strengths and weaknesses of the geography, economy, society, polity, and leadership of a country that ultimately define its position in the international community. This is not to suggest that Bangladesh should compromise its dignity or to deny India's role in contributing to tensions in their bilateral relations.[99] Here one is only stressing the point that to be able to strengthen Bangladesh's position in the world in general and in South Asia in particular, the first priority should be to build national resilience to ensure uninterrupted development. For this, a reasonable degree of economic growth with equitable distribution of resources, and spontaneous and active popular participation are indispensable.

Notes

1. See, for example, Patric J. McGowan and Howard B. Shapiro, *The Comparative Study of Foreign Policy: A Survey of Scientific Findings* (Beverly Hills, California: Sage Publications, 1973); Michael Brecher, *The Foreign Policy System of Israel: Setting Images, Process* (London: Oxford University Press, 1972), pp. 1–4; as also, Michael Brecher, Blema Steinberg, and Janice Stein, 'A Framework for Research on Foreign Policy Behaviour', *Journal of Conflict Resolution*, Michigan, 1 March 1969, pp. 75–101; David O. Wilkinson, *Comparative Foreign Relations: Framework and Methods* (Belmont, California: Dickenson Pub. Co, 1969); J.N. Rosenau, 'Pre-theories and Theories of Foreign Policy', in R. Barry Farrell (ed.), *Approaches to Comparative and International Politics* (Evanston: North-western University Press, 1966), pp. 27–92; and Jonathan Wilkenfeld, Gerald W. Hopple, Paul J. Rossa, and Stephen J. Andriole, *Foreign Policy Behaviour: The Interstate Behaviour Analysis Model* (Beverly Hills, California: Sage Publications, 1980).

2. Kathryn Jacques, *Bangladesh, India and Pakistan* (New York: St. Martin Press, 2000), p. 3.

3. See Smruti S. Pattanaik, 'Internal Political Dynamics and Bangladesh's Foreign Policy towards India', *Strategic Analysis*, New Delhi, 29(3), July–September 2005, pp. 395–426.

4. For details regarding theoretical framework for studying domestic sources of India's foreign policy, see Nalini Kant Jha, *Domestic Imperatives in India's Foreign Policy* (New Delhi: South Asian Publishers, 2002), chapter I.

5. *The Reporter*, 20(10), 14 May 1959, p. 19.

6. Hans J. Morgenthau, *Politics among Nations* (New York: Alfred A. Knopf, 1960), p. 148. See also, views expressed by Norman Hill, *International Politics* (New York: Harper & Row, 1963), p. 198; E.L. Morse, 'The Transformation of Foreign Policies: Modernization, Inter-dependence and Externalization', *World Politics* (Princeton), 22(3), April 1970, pp. 371, 374; and C.J. Friedrich, 'International Politics and Foreign Policy in Developed (Western) System', in R. Barry Farrell (ed.), *Approaches to Comparative and International Politics* (Evanston: North-western University Press, 1966), n. 1, pp. 97–119.

7. Roscoe Pound, as quoted in F.S. Northedge, *The Foreign Policies of Powers*, 2nd Edn (London: The Free Press, 1974), p. 11.

8. See Jha, *Domestic Imperatives in India's Foreign Policy*, n. 4, pp. 4–5.

9. For instance, see views expressed by Henry, A. Kissinger, 'Domestic Structure and Foreign Policy', in Stanley Hoffman (ed.), *Conditions of World Order* (Boston: Houghton Mifflin, 1968), p. 164; L. Jensen, 'Post-war Democratic Politics: National–International Linkages in the Defence of the Defeated States', in J.N. Rosenau (ed.), *Linkage Politics: Essays on the*

Convergence of National–International System (New York: Free Press, 1969), pp. 304–23; J.N. Rosenau (ed.), *Domestic Sources of Foreign Policy* (New York: Free Press, 1967); Stanley Hoffmann, *Contemporary Theory in International Relations* (New Delhi: Prentice Hall of India, 1964), p. 4; and R.H. Dawson, *The Decision to Aid Russia, 1941 Foreign Policy and Domestic Politics* (Chapel Hill, North Carolina: University of North Carolina Press, 1959), p. xi.

10. A. Dallin, 'The Domestic Sources of Foreign Policy', in Seweryn Bailer (ed.), *The Domestic Context of Soviet Foreign Policy* (Boulder, CO, 1981), p. 340. See also, J.N. Rosenau, *The Adaptation of National Societies: A Theory of Political System Transformation* (New York: McCaleb-Seiler, 1970), p. 1.

11. As against modernization theory, which views politico-economic debilities in Third World countries as an outcome of internal characteristics such as political culture, domestic conflicts, political organizations, and the like, dependency theory attempts to explain 'distortions' and 'deformities' of these countries in terms of various 'constraints' arising from their 'dependent' relations with developed countries. In this sense, dependency theory may be regarded as an attempt to establish an alternative paradigm to Western modernization theory. For a general review of these theories, see Philip O' Brien, 'A Critique of Latin American Theories of Dependency', in Ivar Oxaal, Tonny Barnot, and David Booth (eds), *Beyond the Sociology of Development: Economy and Society in Latin America and Africa* (London: Routledge, 1975), pp. 7–27; and Gabriel Palma, *Dependency and Development: A Critical Reassessment* (London: Frances Pinter, 1981), pp. 20–78.

Western thinking that views the problems in Third World countries as a consequence of their domestic structure and process can be found in Western literature on political modernization and development. See, for example, Lucian W. Pye, *Aspects of Political Development* (Boston: Little, Brown and Co, 1966); L.W. Pye and Sidney Verba (eds) *Political Culture and Political Development* (Princeton, NJ: Princeton University Press, 1965); and S.P. Huntington, *Political Order in Changing Societies* (New Haven: Yale University Press, 1968).

12. Gowher Rizvi, 'Bangladesh Foreign Policy: Domestic Compulsions', in Baladas Ghoshal (ed.), *Diplomacy and Domestic Politics in South Asia* (New Delhi: Konark, 1996), p. 161.

13. See Morgenthau, *Politics Among Nations*, n. 6; Hugh Gibson, *The Road to Foreign Policy* (Garden City, NY: Doubleday, Doran, and Company Inc., 1944), p. 9; George Modelski, *A Theory of Foreign Policy* (London: Praeger, 1962), pp. 6–7; Northedge, *The Foreign Policies of Powers*, n. 7; E.B. Hass and A.S. Whiting, *Dynamics of International Relations* (New York: McGraw-Hill, 1956), pp. 59–70; and A. Appadorai and M.S. Rajan, *India's Foreign Policy and Relations* (New Delhi: South Asian Publishers, 1985), pp. 2–7.

14. See J.N. Rosenau, 'Comparing Foreign Policies: Why, What, How?' in J.N. Rosenau, (ed.), *Comparing Foreign Policy: Theories, Findings and Methods* (New York: Sage Publications, 1974), p. 4. See also J.N. Rosenau, 'Adaptive Strategies for Research and Practice in Foreign Policy', in F.W. Riggs (ed.),

Design for International Studies: Scope, Objectives and Methods (Philadelphia: Nichols Pub. Co., 1971), pp. 218–85.

15. F. Pearson and J. Rochester, *International Relations* (Mass: Addison-Wesley, 1984), pp. 145–241.

16. For one of the best illustrations of this thesis, see Donald Hindley, 'Indonesia's Confrontation with Malaysia: A Search for Motives', *Asian Survey*, Berkeley, California, 4 June 1964, pp. 904–13. See also Daniel Lerner's discussion of the Egyptian President Gamal Abdul Nasser in *The Passing of Traditional Society: Modernizing the Middle East* (New York: Free Press, 1958), pp. 247–8; and William Zartman's contention that leaders of newly liberated countries cast their foreign policies in an anti-Western mould to generate the temporary solidarity experienced prior to Independence, in William Zartman, 'National Interest and Ideology', in Vernon Mckay, (ed.), *African Diplomacy: Studies in the Determinants of Foreign Policy* (New York: Praeger, 1966).

Also, Graham T. Allison, *Essence of Decision: Explaining the Cuban Missile Crisis* (Boston: Longman, 1971); M.H. Halperin, 'Why Bureaucrats Play Games', *Foreign Policy*, New York, 50, 1971, pp. 70–90; and G.T. Allison and M.H. Halperin, 'Bureaucratic Politics: A Paradigm and Some Policy Implications', *World Politics*, 24, Spring 1972, Supplement: *Theory and Policy in International Relations* (New York: Cambridge University Press), pp. 40–79; Edward Shills, 'The Intellectuals in the Political Development of the New States', in John H. Kautsky (ed.), *Political Change in Underdeveloped Countries: Nationalism and Communism* (New York: Wiley, 1962), p. 211; Peter Calvert, *The Foreign Policy of New States* (Brighton: Wheatsheaf Books, 1986), pp. 154–71; W.H. Wriggins, *Rulers' Imperative: Strategies for Political Survival in Asia and Africa* (New York: Columbia University Press, 1969); and Shashi Tharoor, *Reasons of State: Political Development and India's Foreign Policy under Indira Gandhi, 1966–77* (New Delhi: Vikas, 1982).

17. Nalini Kant Jha, 'Coalition Governments and India's Foreign Policy', in M.P. Singh and Anil Mishra (eds.), *Coalition Politics in India: Problems and Prospects* (New Delhi: Manohar, 2004), pp. 295–325.

18. Nalini Kant Jha, *Internal Crisis and Indira Gandhi's Foreign Policy* (New Delhi and Patna: Janaki Prakashan, 1985).

19. Jha, *Domestic Imperatives in India's Foreign Policy*, n. 4, p. 136–7.

20. Bhagat Korany, 'When and How Do Personality Factors Influence Foreign Policy?', *Journal of South and Middle Eastern Studies*, 9(3), 1986, pp. 35–60.

21. Rosenau, *Linkage Politics*, n. 9, p. 45.

22. Yaacov Bar-Simon-Tov, *Linkage Politics in the Middle East: Syria between Domestic and External Conflicts, 1961–1970* (Boulder, CO: Westview Press, 1983), pp. 10, 38.

23. M.M. and S.K. Sharma, 'Domestic Determinants and Foreign Policy Analysis: Need for a Framework', *Journal of Political Studies*, Jalandhar, 25(1), February 1987, pp. 1–12.

24. Surprisingly, however, scholars like Michael Brecher, Blema Steinberg, and Janice Stein make an unrealistic claim that 'all data regarding foreign policy can be classified in one of the categories', and that 'all foreign policy issues may be allocated to four issue areas'. See their, 'A Framework for Research on Foreign Policy Behaviour', n. 1, pp. 80 and 87. As against this claim, Ralph Pettman rightly remarks, 'A general theory of foreign policy in the study of world affairs is probably not feasible'. See Ralph Pettman, *Human Behaviour and World Politics* (London: Macmillan, 1975), p. 61.

25. Rosenau, 'Pre-theories and Theories of Foreign Policy', n. 1, pp. 27–92. For these questions and criticisms of Rosenau, see Jha, *Domestic Imperatives in India's Foreign Policy*, n. 4, pp. 12–13.

26. Bernard C. Cohen, *The Political Process and Foreign Policy: The Making of the Japanese Peace Settlement* (Princeton: Princeton University Press, 1957), p. 281.

27. My interview with Abdur Rob Khan, research director, Bangladesh Institute of International and Strategic Studies, Dhaka, on 20 July 2005.

28. According to Mustafizur Rahman, Bangladesh can earn about 800 crore taka by way of freight and other charges levied on Indian goods if Dhaka provides transit corridor facilities to India. See his Mustafizur Rahman, 'Bangladesh–India Economic Relations: Current Status', *Peace Initiative*, 17(1–3), January–June 2001, p. 173.

29. The term 'foreign aid', as economists point out, is an ambiguous concept. However, following the new accepted practice, 'foreign aid' may be defined as 'the normal value of the direct and indirect flow of financial and other resources from governments of rich countries to those of poor countries'. See I.M. Little and J.M. Clifford, *International Aid* (London: Transaction Publishers, 1965), p. 13.

30. http://hdrstats.undp.org/en/countries/country.../cty_fs_BGD.html, accessed on 7 August 2010.

31. Central Intelligence Agency, *The World Fact Book, Bangladesh: Economy*, *http://www.umsl.edu/services/govdocs/wofact2008/geos/bg.html#top*, accessed on 7 August 2010.

32. https://www.cia.gov/library/publications/the-world factbook/print/bg.html, accessed on 24 July 2010.

33. Ibid. See also Ali Riaz, 'Bangladesh in 2005: Standing at the Crossroads', *Asian Survey*, California, Berkeley, 46(1), January–February 2006, p. 111.

34. CIA Fact Book, n. 32. Also, World Bank, *World Development Report, 1991* (New York: Oxford, 1991).

35. http://www.indexmundi.com/bangladesh/debt_external.html, accessed on 7 August 2010. Also see, Anisul Islam, 'Foreign Aid and Economic Development', in H. Zafarullah, M.A. Taslim, and A. Chowdhury (eds.), *Policy Issues in Bangladesh* (New Delhi: South Asian Publishers, 1984), pp. 98–101.

36. Sobhan Rehman (ed.), *The Decades of Stagnations: The State of Bangladesh Economy* (Dhaka: UPL, 1991).

37. Cited in Sobhan Rehman and Debapriya Bhattacharya, 'Donor Perspectives and Influence on Domestic Economic Policy', in Rahman Sobhan (ed.), *From Aid Dependence to Self-Reliance: Development Options for Bangladesh* (Dhaka: UPL, 1990), p. 177.

38. Ibid., p. 178.

39. In contrast to initial period between 1971 and 1975, when India had considerable political stakes in Bangladesh's survival and supplied Bangladesh with the extraordinary sum of US$304.3 million in aid when India itself was a major aid-recipient, its subsequent aid to Bangladesh was negligible. See Rahman Sobhan, *The Crisis of External Dependence: The Political Economy of Foreign Aid to Bangladesh* (London: Zed Press, 1982), pp. 142, 240.

40. Nalini Kant Jha, 'India–Bangladesh Relations: A Perspective', *India Quarterly*, 56(3–4), July–December 2000, pp. 15–34.

41. Jacques, *Bangladesh, India and Pakistan*, n. 2, pp. 22–3. The Bangladeshi press too contributed towards this Indian concern. For instance, the Chinese links with Bangladesh were continually published with great fanfare in *Bangladesh Observer* (Dhaka), 4 November 1983, 16 June 1987, and 11 December 1988.

42. Nancy Jetly, 'India and the Domestic Turmoil in South Asia', in Urmila Phadnis (ed.), *Domestic Conflicts in South Asia: Political Dimensions*, Vol. I (New Delhi: South Asian Publishers, 1986), p. 73.

43. M. Franda and A. Rahman, 'India, Bangladesh and the Superpowers', in Paul Wallace (ed.), *Region and Nation in India* (New Delhi: Oxford & IBH Pub. Co, 1985), p. 263.

44. My interview with Iftekharuzzaman, head of Transparency International of Bangladesh in Dhaka on 20 July 2005.

45. Hasan Zaheer, *The Separation of East Pakistan: The Rise and Realization of Bengali Muslim Nationalism* (Karachi: Oxford University Press, 1994), pp. 17–18.

46. Dilara Chowdhury, *Bangladesh and South Asian International System* (Dhaka: Kazi Publications, 1992), pp. 6–7.

47. Jha, 'India–Bangladesh Relations: A Perspective', n. 40. For a detailed discussion of Hindu–Muslim rivalry in the Bengal province of undivided India, see P.S. Ghosh, *Cooperation and Conflict in South Asia* (New Delhi: Manohar, 1995), pp. 57–60. See also, Sanjay Bhardwaj, 'Bangladesh's Foreign Policy vis-à-vis India', *Strategic Analysis*, 27(2), April–June 2003, pp. 265–6.

48. Anisuzzaman, *Identity, Religion and Recent History* (Calcutta: Naya Udyog for Maulana Abul Kalam Azad Institute of Asian Studies, 1995), p. 54.

49. Talukdar Maniruzzaman, *Radical Left and the Emergence of Bangladesh* (Dhaka: Bangladesh Books, 2003), p. 101.

50. F.S. Northedge, 'The Nature of Foreign Policy', in F.S. Northedge, *The Foreign Policies of Powers*, 2nd Edn (London: The Free Press, 1974), n. 7, p. 27.

51. It may be recalled that, after the emergence of Bangladesh, when Sheikh Mujibur Rahman advised them 'to do away with ethnic identities' and

emphasized 'Bengali nationalism and culture', the then Chakma MP from the CHT, Manabendra Narayan Larma, protested vehemently. Challenging the idea of Bengali nationalism, he argued that the CHT had ethnicity, culture, traditions, and language different from those of the Bengalis. See M.Q. Zaman, 'Crisis in Chittagong Hill Tracts: Ethnicity and Integration', *Economic and Political Weekly*, Bombay, 17(3), 16 January 1982, p. 78.

52. Much literature has been produced on the causes of the Chakma problem, its consequences for the integration of Bangladesh and the governmental response. See, for instance, Zaman, 'Crisis in Chittagong Hill Tracts: Ethnicity and Integration', pp. 75–80; R.H.S. Hutchinson, *Chittagong Hill Tracts* (Delhi: Vivek Publication Co., 1978); Syed Nazmul Islam, 'The Chittagong Hill Tracts in Bangladesh: Integrational Crisis between Center and Periphery', *Asian Survey*, Berkeley, California, 21(12), December 1981, pp. 1211–22; Kazi Montu, 'Tribal Insurgency in Chittagong Hill Tracts', *Economic and Political Weekly*, Bombay, 15(36), 6 September 1980, pp. 1510–12; and Ghosh, *Cooperation and Conflict in South Asia*, n. 47, pp. 73–81.

53. Saleem M.M. Qureshi, 'Pakistan Nationalism Reconsidered', *Pacific Affairs*, Vancouver, 45(4), Winter 1972–3, p. 570.

54. http://news.bbc.co.uk/2/hi/south_asia/4158478.stm, accessed on 22 September 2010.

55. Riaz, 'Bangladesh in 2005', n. 34, p. 108.

56. 'RAW Behind Blasts: Claims Nizami', *New Age*, 21 August 2005, Dhaka, p. 1. The Research and Analysis Wing (RAW) is the external intelligence service of the Indian government. Also see, 'Indian and Local Criminals Jointly Staged August 17 Blasts: BDR Chief Alleges as Delhi Talk Conclude', *Daily Star*, 1 October 2005, Dhaka, p. 1.

57. The Bangladesh government banned Harkat-ul=Jihad in 2005. http://www.newsnetwork-bd.com/UI/Public/NewsDetail.php?LogID=10064, accessed on 22 September 2010.

58. 'Mufti Hannan Captured: Militant Kingpin Tells of Altaf's Assurance of "No Fear"', *Daily Star*, 2 October 2005. A court convicted mufti Hannan in 2003 for attempting to kill the then Prime Minister Sheikh Hasina, in 2000.

59. *The Pioneer*, 23 March 2006, New Delhi.

60. Editorial, 'Dhaka Cracks the Whip', *The Pioneer*, 6 August 2009, Lucknow.

61. 'Public Opinion Trends (POT), New Delhi', *Bangladesh Series*, 47(284), p. 3728.

62. *Daily Star*, 12 December 1992.

63. Suchita Ghosh, *China–Bangladesh Tangle Today* (New Delhi: Sterling Publishers, 1995), p. 54.

64. Some Bangladeshi scholars argue that Bangladesh's nationhood preceded its achievement of statehood. See, for instance, Mizanur Rahman Shelley, 'Nation-Building and Political Development in Bangladesh', in M. Abdul Hafiz and Abdur Rob Khan (eds), *Nation Building in Bangladesh: Retrospect and*

Prospects (Dhaka: Bangladesh Institute of International and Strategic Studies, 1986), p. 190. A closer look, however, reveals that the country continues to be far from having achieved the objectives of nation building. The critical factors appear to be the endemic weakness of the state, deep-rooted crisis of governance, suppression of minorities, and conflict of identity.

65. Azizul Haque, 'Politics in Bangladesh: Conflict and Confusion', *Regional Studies* (Karachi), 3(2), Spring 1985, p. 59. While Professor Imtiaz Ahmed of Dhaka University explained the shift from Bengali to Bangladeshi nationalism in terms of Ziaur Rahman's attempt to integrate the tribal minorities into the Bangladeshi nation, a noted scholar of the Bangladesh Institute of International and Strategic Studies agreed that it was party directed towards demonstrating Bangladesh's distinctiveness from Indian West Bengal. My interview with the above scholars at Dhaka University on 12 July 2005 and at BIISS on 13 July 2005.

66. Jananbrata Bhattacharya, 'Aspects of Cultural Policy in Bangladesh', *Economic and Political Weekly*, 26 March 1983, pp. 501–2.

67. *Asian Recorder*, 14–20 May 1970, New Delhi. See also, Rounaq Jahan, *Bangladesh Politics: Problems and Issues* (Dhaka: University Press, 1980), pp. 215–17.

68. Marcus Franda, 'Ziaur Rahman and Bangladeshi Nationalism', *Economic and Political Weekly*, 16(10–12), Annual Number, March 1981, p. 377.

69. S.K Datta Ray, 'India and Bangladesh', *The Statesman*, 27 May 1980, Calcutta.

70. Badruddin Umar, 'Anti-Indianism and Communalism', *Saptahik Swadhikar*, 17 September 1972.

71. For a detailed analysis of this problem as a factor in India–Bangladesh relations, see Chandrika J. Gulati, *Bangladesh: Liberalism to Fundamentalism: A Study of Volatile Indo-Bangladesh Relations* (New Delhi: Commonwealth Publishers, 1988), chapter I.

72. Indeed, much of the current empirical knowledge about political influences on foreign policy centres around a single variable-accountability, and in particular the distinction between democratic and authoritarian or open and closed regimes. See S.A. Salmore and C.F. Hermann, 'The Effect of Size, Development, and Accountability on Foreign Policy', as cited in J.D. Hagan, 'Regimes, Political Oppositions and the Comparative Analysis of Foreign Policy', in Charles F. Hermann, Charles W. Kegley Jr, and James N. Rosenau (eds), *New Directions in the Study of Foreign Policy* (Boston: Allen & Unwin, 1987), p. 340; B.G. Salmore and S.A. Salmore, 'Political Regimes and Foreign Policy', in *M. East, S.A. Salmore, and C.F. Hermann (eds), Why Nations Act? Theoretical Perspectives for Foreign Policy Studies* (Beverly Hills, CA.: Sage Publications, 1978), pp. 103–22; Bruce M. Russett and R. Joseph Monsen, 'Bureaucracy and Oligarchy as Predictors of Performance: A Cross National Examination', *Comparative Political Studies*, 8(1), April 1975, pp. 5–131; and C. Friedrich

and Z. Brzezinski, *Totalitarian Dictatorship and Autocracy* (New York: Harvard University Press, 1956).

73. See Franklin B. Weinstein, *Indonesia's Foreign Policy and Dilemma of Dependence* (London: Equinox Publishing, 1976).

74. For an elaboration of this, see Hagan, 'Regimes, Political Oppositions and the Comparative Analysis of Foreign Policy', n. 70, pp. 339–65. See also, Salmore and Salmore, 'Political Regimes and Foreign Policy,' n. 70.

75. Nalini Kant Jha, *Internal Crisis and Indira Gandhi's Foreign Policy* (Patna: Janki Prakashan, 1985), chapter I; see also, Wriggins, *Rulers' Imperative*, n. 16; Robert C. Good, 'State-Building as a Determinant of Foreign Policy in the New States', in Lawrence W. Martin (ed.), *Neutralism and Non-Alignment: The New States in World Affairs* (New York: Greenwood Press, 1962); and Franklin B. Weinstein, 'The Uses of Foreign Policy in Indonesia: An Approach to the Analysis of Foreign Policy in Less Developed Countries', *World Politics*, 24, April 1972, pp. 356–81.

76. Iftekharuzzaman, 'Bangladesh in the Post-Cold War Era: Primacy of Domestic Imperatives', *Journal of International Relations*, Dhaka, 1(1), July–December 1993, p. 41.

77. Also spelt 'Meer Jafar', has remained a symbol for treachery in the Bengal region because of his opportunistic arrangement with the British under Clive during the Battle of Plassey in 1757.

78. *Bangladesh Observer*, Dhaka, 24 November 1975.

79. Ibid., 2 May 1976.

80. The Zia regime took numerous other steps to mobilize Islamic support for his government, such as the display of Quranic verses and the Prophet's edicts on public places, flying Eid Mubarak festoons bearing the national flag on Eid festivals, propagation of Islam and the Shariat over television and radio, creation of a new administrative division for religious affairs with a fully-fledged minister, and on the like. See, for details, Emajuddin Ahmed, 'Current Trends in Islam in Bangladesh', *Economic and Political Weekly*, 18 June 1983, pp. 114–18.

81. 'Bangladesh-Insurgency in the Chittagong Hills,' www.mongabay.com/.../bangladesh/bangladesh/*insurgency_in_the_chittagong_hills.html*, cached accessed on 2 August 2010.

82. Gowher Rizvi, n. 12, pp. 165–6.

83. Zia's policies, tending towards civilian rule, had intensified the sense of insecurity amongst the powerful Bangladeshi military establishment. See Z.R. Khan, 'Bangladesh in 1981: Change, Stability, and Leadership', *Asian Survey*, 22(2), 1982, p. 165.

84. See editorial, *The Times of India*, 25 March 1982, New Delhi.

85. Jacques, *Bangladesh, India and Pakistan*, n. 2, p. 124.

86. Ibid., chapter 3. Also see Nalini Kant Jha, 'India and Bangladesh: The Track Back to Normalcy', in Nalini Kant Jha (ed.), *India's Foreign Policy in*

a Changing World (New Delhi: South Asian Publishers, 2000), pp. 174–92; and Shyamali Ghosh, 'India–Bangladesh Relations', in Nalini Kant Jha and V.T. Patil (eds), *India in a Turbulent World: Perspectives in Foreign and Security Policies* (New Delhi: South Asian Publishers, 2003), pp. 112–20.

87. See *The Times of India*, 25 March 1982.

88. Ishtiaq Hossain, 'Bangladesh-India Relations: The Ganges Water-Sharing Treaty and Beyond', *Asian Affairs: An American Review*, Philadelphia, PA, 25(3), Fall 1998, p. 139.

89. For details of implications of Indian domestic factors in impairing India–Bangladesh ties during the Ershad regime, see Jacques, *Bangladesh, India, and Pakistan*, n. 2, ch. 3. Also, Jha, n.18, chapter 6.

90. For details regarding domestic opposition to the Ershad regime, see Ghosh, 'India–Bangladesh Relations', n. 47, pp. 92–4.

91. Soon after assuming power, Ershad proposed setting up a 'Zakat' fund (Islamic welfare fund) under the supervision of the government. He introduced Arabic and Islamiat from Class I in the school. In a mammoth meeting of the Bangladesh Jamiatul Mudderessin (BJM) in January 1983, he emphasized that the cultural life of Bangladeshis should be firmly based on Islamic principles. Shortly thereafter an Islamic bank with 10 branches was opened in Bangladesh with 13 Arab sponsors subscribing 70 per cent of the equity. That very year, he questioned some of the practices associated with the Martyr's Day at Dhaka Shahid Minar in memory of those students killed while protesting against Pakistan's imposition of Urdu. He ordered that Qur'an should be read at that function in order to establish an Islamic state. See Ghosh, 'India–Bangladesh Relations', p. 71.

92. Ben Crow, Alan Lindquist, and David Wilson, *Sharing the Ganges: The Politics and Technology of River Development* (New Delhi: Sage Publications, 1995).

93. Jacques, *Bangladesh, India and Pakistan*, n. 2, chapters 2–3.

94. Begum Khaleda Zia, while in opposition had described the insurgents in India's North East are 'freedom fighters' and that Bangladesh should help them, instead of curbing their activities. See, Pattanaik, 'Internal Political Dynamics and Bangladesh's Foreign Policy towards India', n. 3, p. 406. See also, Deepender Kumar, 'Growing Network of Terror in Bangladesh: How Real is the Threat?', *Journal of Peace Studies*, New Delhi, 9(6), November–December 2006, pp. 36–41.

95. See, for details, Nalini Kant Jha, 'Foreign Policy Making in Federal States: Indian and Canadian Experiences', *India Quarterly*, New Delhi, 55(3–4), July–December 1999, pp. 1–16.

96. Sreeradha Datta, 'Bangladesh's Political Evolution: Growing Uncertainties', *Strategic Analysis*, 27(2), April–June 2003, p. 236.

97. http://www.idsa.in/strategicanalysis/AttackonSheikhHasina_sdutta_0704, accessed on 22 September 2010.

98. These arrests took place in September 2009. See, Hiranmay Karlekar, 'Reach out to Bangladesh', *The Pioneer*, 4 September 2009, Lucknow. Also, Amitava Mukherjee, 'Sheikh Hasina's Resolve to Foil the Conspiracy of Destabilisation in Bangladesh', *Mainstream*, New Delhi, 47(48), 14 November 2009. Anand Kumar, 'Bangladesh Cracks Down on Terror', *Asia Sentimental Consulting*, http://www.asiasentinel.com/index.php?option=com_content&task=view&id=2339&Itemid=369, accessed on 7 August 2010.

99. Karlekar, 'Reach out to Bangladesh', n. 95; Indeed, through its highhandedness, India too has contributed much to Bangladesh's sense of insecurity. As a much larger neighbour, India must respect Bangladesh's sensibilities and try to earn its goodwill through positive gestures, such as the grant of tariff concessions to Dhaka to enable it to reduce its trade gap with New Delhi. This aspect has however not been discussed in this chapter because it does not fall under its scope.

Part III

POLITICAL ECONOMY AND REGIONAL COOPERATION

8 The Political Economy of Preferential Trade in South Asia
The Indo-Sri Lanka Free Trade Agreement

*Rahul Mukherji**

This chapter argues that the Indo-Sri Lanka Free Trade Agreement (ISLFTA), which was signed in December 1998 and came into force in 2000, was an excellent opportunity to examine the conditions under which a large country with a diversified economy could enter into a fruitful bilateral trade relationship with a small country with a less diversified economy in South Asia. Intra-South Asian trade constituted a small proportion of the region's trade with the world. India did not have robust trade relations with two other important neighbours, Pakistan and Bangladesh, illegal rather than legal trade dominating exchanges of goods with these two neighbours. Second, this perception of vulnerability was evident when Sri Lanka's trade with India declined after its independence in 1948 and when it decided to engage Western countries more proactively in the aftermath of its balance of payments crisis in 1977. I will also show in this chapter that there was hostility to the ISLFTA within Sri Lanka in 1998, which was not easy to overcome.

* The author would like to thank Sitaram Kumbhar, Siddhartha Mukerji, and Taberez Ahmed Neyazi for excellent research assistance, and Anjali Mukherji for editorial comments. E. Sridharan, I.N. Mukherji, Saman Kelegama, Bibek Debroy, and Lal Jayawardana helped with discussions, comments, and contacts. I am grateful to Vinod Aggarwal for involving me in a project that aided thinking on this essay. This research benefited from conversations with J.B. Kelegama, Patrick Amarasinghe, Jayadeva Uyangoda, S. Jayanetti, Douglas Jayasekhara, Ken Balendra, Sridhar Khatri, and Stanley Jayawardena in April 2003. The shortcomings, as usual, rest with the author.

Why then did Sri Lanka proceed with a free trade agreement (FTA) with India in 1998?

Indo-Sri Lanka trade has grown remarkably despite the problems posed by the negative list[1] of items of Indian and Sri Lankan goods and the high transaction costs. According to Sri Lankan customs figures quoted by Saman Kelegama,[2] ISLFTA had made a clear impact on Sri Lanka's improvement of trade with India. The ratio of Sri Lanka's imports from India to its exports to India, which was 16:1 in 1998, fell to 5:1 in 2002. Sri Lanka's exports to India as a percentage of its total exports, which were 1 per cent in 1998, were 3.6 per cent in 2002. According to Saman Kelegama's analysis of the 2002 data, preferential exports amounted to 68 per cent of the total exports to India. India's Ministry of Commerce's website revealed that India's exports to Sri Lanka increased by 48.13 per cent in 2002–3 and by 36.01 per cent in 2003–4.

The implication of this is that the smaller country, which was more dependent on a larger and more diversified economy, was benefiting relatively more greater extent from the trade relationship institutionalized under the FTA than the larger country in the relationship. For its part, India, which had a larger and more diversified economy, was nonetheless benefiting. These are some of the classic characteristics of a positive sum relationship between large and small countries in international relations.

I argue in this chapter that the ISLFTA poses a puzzle for standard realist approaches to an understanding of international economic relations and, in a conditional way, strengthens the claims of the neoliberal institutional view. The chapter will first pose the theoretical puzzle and then use an alternative theoretical framework as a plausible explanation. The subsequent section will attempt to marry the political data with a modified neo-realist institutional approach to explain the political dynamics of the ISLFTA.

The Puzzle

Realist and neo-realist approaches to international political economy suggest that rules reflect the global distribution of power. Powerful states in the international system would attempt to maintain their relative power in relation to other states in the international system. International rules reflect the interests of the powerful rather than any legitimate collective purpose.

They argue that states in the international system operate in the absence of a legitimate supranational authority, which produces an environment that Hobbes described as anarchy. States rely on themselves for survival and build up their economic and military power to defend their interests in a hostile world. They pursue the objective of relative gains in relation to other similarly placed states in the international system, and often utilize their economic power for military purposes and vice versa.

The Hobbesian metaphor is a powerful rationale you the proposition that international rules reflect the distribution of power. If states worried about relative gains in the absence of a supranational authority, the chances were that the relative economic gains of their competitors within the system could be used to exploit the weak both militarily and economically. The pursuit of relative power, wealth, and relative gains was intimately related to the question of survival in the global political economy.[3]

To give one example: no international regime could protect the sovereign rights of states in relation to the cross-border transmission of radio signals. The reason why there was no agreement over the right to transmit radio signals across state boundaries was because the industrialized countries wished it and the developing countries could not stop it. As industrialized countries got their way without any cooperation, there was no imperative for cooperation with developing countries.[4] The rules reflect power.

The logic of conflict and cooperation within realism suggested that smaller and weaker countries within the international system should prefer multilateral to bilateral settings. In a bilateral relationship between a large and a small economy, chances were that the large country could exploit the smaller one's vulnerability. For example, if a country A's exports to a country B were 60 per cent of its exports, whereas the country B's exports to country A were only 5 per cent of its exports, then the threat of trade withdrawal would hurt country A to a greater extent than country B. Albert Hirschman had first pointed out that trade was not only about specialization and growth but also about vulnerability.[5] This could be one reason why China accepted the adjustment demanded by the industrialized countries before it was allowed to join the World Trade Organization (WTO). India opposed the Trade Related Intellectual Property Rights regime within the WTO but eventually acquiesced to a deal that would benefit pharmaceutical companies in the rich countries. China and India probably realized that multilateralism gave greater voice to the smaller economies in the world economy than asymmetrical bilateral deals.

The standard version of realism seemed to explain rather well the trade relations between India and Bangladesh, on the one hand, and India and Pakistan, on the other. The India–Bangladesh export–import ratio, which is defined as India's exports to Bangladesh as a proportion of India's imports from Bangladesh, was about 15.5 in 1997–8. The same figure had risen to over 27 in 2004–5.[6] An Indo-Bangla Free Trade Agreement was nowhere near the horizon, even though there had been a warming of relations in 2007. The figures for Indo-Pakistan trade relations were even more dismal, with Pakistan refusing to offer India even the regular multilateral most favoured nation (MFN) treatment.[7]

The realist logic based on vulnerability seemed to work for Indo-Sri Lanka relations till recent times. Sri Lanka had suffered from the vulnerability syndrome for many years. In colonial times, Indo-Sri Lanka trade flourished. In 1938, Sri Lanka spent 42.5 per cent of its import bill on India, its export basket dominated by coconut oil and copra. By the late 1940s, immediately after independence and the severance of the connection of a common colonial master, this figure dropped to 15 per cent and Sri Lanka's exports to India were about 2 per cent of its total exports. The Sri Lanka–China trade agreement of 1952 diverted trade away from the India–Sri Lanka trade relationship, as Sri Lanka attempted to diversify its dependence away from one large neighbour. The Chinese agreed to buy rubber at higher than international prices in return for an assured supply of rice, also agreeing to supply coal at lower than international prices and restrict the entry of Indian garment exports. India's contribution to Sri Lanka's exports dropped to 10 per cent in 1960. Following the pessimism regarding a large neighbour, Sri Lanka tried to diversify its trade basket in order to avoid becoming overly dependent on a single country.[8]

Trade between India and Sri Lanka stagnated between 1948 and 1967 notwithstanding the Indo-Sri Lanka Treaty in October 1961. An Indo-Lanka Joint Committee on Economic Cooperation was set up in 1968 with the objective of increasing cooperation in trade, industry, agriculture, and tourism. This was later upgraded to an Indo-Sri Lanka Joint Commission for Economic, Trade, and Technical Cooperation, which met regularly in the early 1970s. Issues were taken up by senior officials at the sub-committee levels and by the respective ministers of foreign affairs at the level of the Commission. Despite these efforts, the system of controls in both countries did not allow trade to grow.

After 1977, when the Sri Lankan economy was opened up, the Indo-Sri Lanka Joint Commission lay largely dormant. The ethnic politics and mistrust of the 1980s helped reinforce an anarchic environment of pessimism over Indo-Sri Lanka trade relations. Attempts to revive the Commission after the Indo-Sri Lanka Political Accord of July 1987 did not succeed. The Commission was unable to play a significant role in promoting the Indo-Sri Lanka trade potential until mid-1991.[9]

There was considerable opposition to the ISLFTA among technocrats and the business houses of Sri Lanka, small and medium firms feeling threatened by the ISLFTA of 1998. Patrick Amarasinghe, heading the Federation of Chambers of Commerce and Industries, opposed the move on the grounds that the ISLFTA would result in de-industrialization and unemployment. Agricultural producers were also concerned about the competitiveness of Indian agriculture. Ken Balendra, heading the Ceylon National Chambers of Commerce, representing large industry, was the only prominent industry leader who was in favour of the ISLFTA.[10]

A prominent technocrat, commerce secretary, and economist, J.B. Kelegama was opposed to the agreement on the basis of largely mercantilist objections to trade between a large diversified economy and a small less diversified one. The objections were on the following grounds. First, Kelegama argued that Sri Lanka needed to strengthen the South Asian Association for Regional Cooperation (SAARC) and South Asian Preferential Trading Agreement (SAPTA) frameworks rather than adopt a bilateral framework, which could increase its vulnerability. Second, Kelegama was concerned that in the post-liberalization phase between 1993 and 1997, India's exports doubled at the existing tariffs, even without any preferential trade. He did not see much scope for a reciprocity-based FTA to bring about a substantial increase in Sri Lanka's exports. He was pessimistic about Sri Lanka's ability to compete with the Indian economy, with rules of origin, which specified that Sri Lanka's exports needed to have had at least 35 per cent value addition in Sri Lanka. Kelegama worried that the FTA would divert Sri Lanka's trade away from its major trading partners such as USA and the UK, with which Sri Lanka enjoyed surpluses. This would inhibit good trade relations with these countries. In a similar vein, Kelegama argued that Sri Lanka needed to improve trade relations with Pakistan, to which there was a possibility of increasing its exports of tea.[11]

The puzzle therefore was: why did the relations improve after 1992 when the Joint Commission was revived? It was true that Indian goods were becoming increasingly competitive after the liberalization of its economy in 1991, creating a trade surplus in India's favour. Why did Sri Lanka respond by holding out the hand of friendship rather than keeping the level of economic integration in relation to India at a low level? Pakistan and Bangladesh could also have secured economic gains by freeing their trade to many Indian items that were available from geographically proximate sources. The fear of economic vulnerability led these countries to keep their domestic costs high by importing expensive goods from more distant regions.

AN ALTERNATIVE ARGUMENT

A second important proposition in international cooperation concerned how states might realize their interests by evolving certain norms for rational self-interested reasons. Norms such as reciprocity could evolve in international relations in a manner that would promote everyone's gain. Unlike the realist's world described earlier, this was an environment of a positive sum game, where institutions could help realize such gains. The absence of international institutions would lead to sub-optimal outcomes.

Rationality-based arguments about international cooperation draw an analogy from the Prisoner's Dilemma (PD) game. This game presents an interesting scenario. In it, cooperation was inhibited by the fact that the two prisoners had no communication with each other. Two prisoners were caught for a minor crime, but the police suspected a major crime. If the prisoners squealed or sneaked about the major crime, they would receive a sentence of three years' imprisonment (punishment for the major crime). If both cooperated and did not confess to the police, they would be imprisoned for two years (punishment for a minor crime). If one confessed and the other did not, then the one who confessed would receive only a one-year sentence as a reward. The second prisoner, who did not confess, would remain in prison for four years. Lack of communication led to a situation where both prisoners were imprisoned for three years because they confessed, when they could both have benefited from a two-year sentence had they cooperated. The dilemma in this game was that the prisoners would have an incentive to reduce their prison sentence by cooperating but the logic of the situation would drive them to cheat each other.

Robert Axelrod found that communication among prisoners could evolve if the prototypical prisoners were allowed to play the PD game over an infinite number of plays.[12] In computer tournaments organized at the University of Michigan, Axelrod found that the strategy of reciprocity won two successive computer tournaments modelled after the PD game. The strategy used was beginning the game by cooperating, and thereafter rewarding a cooperative move with cooperation and punishing defection (confession) with defection. In this manner, the persistent use of reciprocity led to cooperation. The prisoners ceased to squeal and learned to live with each other by developing a reciprocity norm.

Axelrod found that trench warfare during the First World War was played as a cooperation game, because soldiers on both sides learnt to live with each other over a period of time.[13] The German and the French armies learnt to fire their shots in the air pretending that they were fighting, lest their commanders realized that they were really not doing so. In this case, if the soldiers fired in air and the superiors did not realize this, then the soldiers on each side could live. If, on the other hand, they kept killing each other, then many more soldiers would lose their lives.

What lessons did cooperation in the PD game, based on rational self-interest, have for students of international cooperation? Institutions could perform two critical functions. They could repeatedly bring interested parties to the bargaining table to enable reciprocity to evolve as a strategy. In the words of game theory, they could turn a one shot PD game into one that involved an infinite number of plays. Second, they could provide information to the concerned parties about which state was cooperating and which one was defecting. Often international relations were characterized by situations where cooperation could not easily be differentiated from defection. International institutions could monitor the behaviour of states and make their responses public for other members of the club. If states were aware that they would repeatedly have to meet at the bargaining table and could discern the moves of other states, cooperation could evolve. The unrealized positive sum in the relationship could evolve through the strategy of reciprocity.[14]

Could the institutionalization of trade between India and Sri Lanka have come about due to the evolution of reciprocity between 1992 and 1998? For reciprocity to arise as a viable strategy, we needed three conditions. The first condition was the availability of common interests. Second, another condition for the success of this strategy was that the parties needed to come repeatedly to the bargaining table. Third, there needed to be one party that would begin the game by cooperating and reward every move of cooperation with cooperation.

One of the problems of the PD game analogy was that the prototypical prisoners were equally vulnerable. In our case, if the players were not equally vulnerable, one could infer that the less vulnerable would need to make more concessions because they would be more threatening to the smaller and more vulnerable partner. The third condition was the quintessential one. The availability of common interests arising out of increased trade orientation of the two countries did not materialize till 1992. This is because Sri Lanka's concerns regarding vulnerability with respect to India took precedence over its common interests till 1992. Joint commissions were futile exercises in cooperation till 1991. What had changed from 1992 that persuaded India to grant greater than equal concessions to Sri Lanka, and pledge itself at the very least to a strategy of reciprocity through the ISLFTA?

Two factors could increase a country's interest in promoting a strategy of economic interdependence rather than autarky. First, there is evidence to suggest that the concern for relative gains and vulnerability was affected by the nature of the security relationship between the countries involved in trade. It mattered whether a country is perceived as being a friend or a foe. Trade among allies, it has been argued, added to collective relative economic power, while the same among adversaries increases asymmetric interdependencies. By the early 1950s, trade between USA and the Eastern Bloc had become negligible. Mansfield and Bronson found that trade between allies who participated in preferential trading arrangements was 120 to 140 per cent greater than that between non-allies.[15] When China's relations warmed with USA and in opposition to the former Soviet Union, so did its trade with USA grow. This could explain why relatively small countries like Nepal and Bhutan could trade with India during the Cold War. I argue that an improvement in India's security relations with Sri Lanka was essential in promoting reciprocity-based strategies leading to economic cooperation between the two countries.

Second, global economic interdependence becomes important when a country begins viewing trade as an important element of its development strategy. Almost all developing countries, including those of South Asia, followed an inward-oriented model of development based on a logic that was very different from that mentioned earlier. Post-colonial states with comparative advantages in primary production worried that export earnings would not grow with increased production given changes in global income and the price inelasticity of demand for primary commodities. Therefore, these states began concentrating their resources on manufacturing, but the infant manufacturing industries of the developing world were unable to compete with the mature ones of the industrialized countries. Manufacturing in the developing world had to be promoted by a protected home economy, and protectionism was lifted when an industry was sufficiently mature to exploit economies of scale.[16]

The difference between India and many of the successful Asian economies was that India persisted with import substitution for a longer duration than many other Asian countries. If India was pessimistic about the prospects of trade until the late 1980s, why would it need preferential trade arrangements that would help promote its exports? The end of the Cold War coincided with the end of import substitution in India. I demonstrate later how India's political economy transformed itself from one based on inward orientation towards one that began depending upon the promotion of external economic relations.

I argue that exogenous shocks, such as the end of Cold War, the assassination of Rajiv Gandhi on 21 May 1991, the Asian financial crisis of 1997, and the Indian nuclear tests of May 1998 increased the imperative for India to negotiate an agreement with a neighbouring country which would be sympathetic to the concerns of the small neighbour. External shocks such as these have the propensity to affect the nature of the security relationship, which in turn could affect the trade relationship. An improvement in the security relationship may lead to the success of reciprocal cooperation in trade as relative gains considerations become less salient. External shocks may also make trade a more important need when the domestic economy becomes incapable of dealing with exogenous shocks in the absence of a viable trade strategy.[17]

The end of the Cold War coincided not only with the demise of the *historical* Union of Socialist Soviet Republics (USSR) but also a liberalization drive, which drove India to search for markets. Rajiv Gandhi's assassination by the Liberation Tigers of Tamil Eelam (LTTE) in May 1991 and the blacklisting of the LTTE by the Indian government rapidly helped to improve the security relations between India and Sri Lanka. The Asian financial crisis of 1997 and India's nuclear tests and the consequent sanctions of May 1998 restricted India's markets both in Asia and in the rest of the world. India's need for economic cooperation at this juncture inspired a model of cooperation between the two countries.[18] At this juncture in the late 1990s, when India's exports to Sri Lanka were growing much faster than Sri Lanka's exports to the latter, it was prudent for a small trade-dependent country like Sri Lanka to lock India into a deal where the Indian side would be sympathetic to Sri Lanka's major concerns.

The Evolution of Common Interests

Common Interests due to Interdependence Concerns

Given India's size, which is larger than that of all the other South Asian countries put together, her trade strategy during the Cold War could have had a liberalizing effect.[19] India adopted an import-substitution industrialization (ISI) model of development, which persisted until the balance of payments crisis of 1991.[20] India's model of ISI was based on import, production, and foreign exchange controls, and selective finance that aided the domestic industry in the public and private sectors to sell within the large and protected home market.[21]

These policies systematically biased production towards the home market and raised the costs of exports. The lack of competition reduced India's competitiveness and cushioned the Indian industrial sector which was faced with low levels of productivity. According to an influential study on comparative productivity, Indian productivity grew much slower than productivity in South Korea and Taiwan between 1963 and 1993.[22]

The import-substitution model, which began being challenged from the mid-1980s, had a powerful political economy supporting it, which could not be overcome during the Cold War years. Organized business wanted freedom to play within the protected Indian market but were averse to risking foreign markets and higher profits. Organized labour, which constituted less than 10 per cent of India's workforce, was happy with job security and labour laws that protected it while the majority of the workers in the unorganized sector endured hardships.[23] India's low levels of productivity were sustained by an underperforming industrial sector and job security for a minority of the labour force that was protected by labour laws. Inviting competition from other countries within or outside the region needed the support of a political economy that could adjust to competition.

The government's reports from the late 1970s had acknowledged the problem of low levels of productivity, the dearth of development finance, and the need for export promotion. Indira Gandhi's second tenure (1980–4) had taken note of these problems.[24] Rajiv Gandhi had tried to initiate economic liberalization from 1985, but substantial promotion of competitiveness and exports could not be achieved in the 1980s. Even Rajiv Gandhi's comfortable majority in Parliament could not overcome the political impediments in the way of India's tryst with globalization, India remaining one of the most autarkic economies in the world at a time when China was embracing global economic integration and the Soviet model was crumbling.[25]

India's integration with the global economy began in a surefooted way after 1991 in the aftermath of a balance of a payments crisis sparked by the Gulf War-driven oil price shock. This, in conjunction with India's fiscal profligacy, discouraged short-term lenders who had become essential for financing India's development. Trade and investment liberalization ensued when a convinced pro-trade technocracy used the crisis and the consequent need to strike a deal with the International Monetary Fund (IMF) to push for far-reaching pro-competition policies. I have argued elsewhere that changed executive orientation driven by the policy puzzles of the 1980s were at least as important as the external shock and the consequent dependence on the IMF.[26]

The pro-autarky policymakers did not exploit the balance of payments crisis of 1966 to change policy in a trade and investment-friendly direction. At that time, donor advice owing to the balance of payments crisis was consumed as a bitter pill that was swallowed momentarily. However, India reverted to its severest version of autarky between 1969 and 1974. In 1981, at the time of the second oil shock, India had utilized resources from the IMF to build its public sector assets. In 1991, on the other hand, the policymakers surprised even the IMF by their willingness to reform. India's reforms were gradual and steady, and like its relations with USA, were able to survive both the United Front coalition government (1996–8) and the National Democratic Alliance coalition governments of 1998–9 and 1999–2004.[27]

What were the dimensions of the export-oriented globalization programme? The rupee was devalued and a market-driven exchange-rate regime was introduced. The weighted average duty was reduced from 72.5 per cent in the 1980s to 29 per cent in 2002–3. Quotas were abolished ahead of the World Trade Organization's (WTO) stipulated date. Industrial licensing was abolished. The stock market was reformed and portfolio investment was welcomed. The foreign direct investment regime was liberalized. Infrastructure areas such as telecommunications became efficient.[28] As a consequence, India's dependence on trade, which was 15.1 per cent of the gross domestic product (GDP) in the 1980s, rose to 24.8 per cent in 2000. Indian products won acclaim in areas such as information technology, outsourcing of services, and gems and jewellery. The post-reforms growth rates, which have consistently averaged over 6 per cent per annum, have accelerated to over 8 per cent in recent years.[29] Given India's promise as a rapidly growing economy, the IMF–World Bank Annual Meetings held in Singapore in 2006 were dedicated to the rise of China and India. The IMF had predicted in 2004 that the Indian economy could grow at about 10 per cent in the coming years.[30]

The harbinger of common interests was the strategy of trade-oriented growth adopted by India since 1991. The devaluation of the rupee, the abolition of industrial licensing, and capital market reforms, all rapidly increased India's competitiveness in relation to its South Asian neighbour. In 1986, India supplied 3.8 per cent of Sri Lanka's import needs and Japan's share was 14.2 per cent. In 1996, India became the pre-eminent exporter to Sri Lanka, surpassing Japan, after almost six decades. That year India supplied 10.4 per cent of Sri Lanka's import requirements in comparison to Japan's 9.2 per cent.[31]

The most important export items from India that accounted for imports worth Sri Lankan Rs 1 billion or more included cotton, iron and steel, vehicles and transport equipment, paper, drugs and pharmaceuticals, and Bombay onions. India's low cost of production and low freight rates proved to be the sources of its competitive advantage. High quality products being produced by Japanese and other multinationals firms and Indian firms in India reduced the need for products from Japan or other countries that were farther away. To give some very interesting examples based on prices prevalent in the late 1990s, the Hero Honda motorcycle was available in Sri Lanka for Rs 78,000 in comparison to the original Honda motorcycle priced at Rs 149, 000. A 31-seat Ashok Leyland bus cost Rs 1,750,00 as against the cost of Rs 3,000,000 for a similar Mitsubishi Rosa bus.[32]

Exogenous shocks increased India's propensity to look for new trading partners. The end of the Cold War reduced the importance of the USSR as a market for India's exports. About 20 per cent of India's exports went to the USSR in 1985 but the same figure was just over 3.5 per cent in 1995.[33] The 1997 Asian financial crisis reduced the potential for Indian exports in Asian markets, and the currency depreciation in the crisis-hit countries made their exports even more competitive in Indian markets. India's exports to ASEAN (Association of Southeast Asian Nations) as a proportion of its total exports declined from 7.6 per cent in 1995 to 5.4 per cent in 1998.[34] Even friendly ASEAN leaders like

Singapore's Prime Minister Goh Chok Tong seemed unhappy about the progress of India's Look East policy in the aftermath of the Asian crisis. Integration with Asia as a route to trade-led growth seemed to be less relevant between 1998 and 2000. Last, but not the least, USA trade sanctions on India after the nuclear tests of 1998 increased India's resolve to look for alternative markets.[35]

On the other hand, Sri Lanka's exports to India were not doing well. In 1997, out of a total trade of $560 million, Sri Lanka's exports contributed only $42.7 million. Sri Lanka's exports to India as a share of its overall exports declined from 1.1 per cent in 1990 to 1.0 per cent in 1996.[36] The reasons for this were twofold. First, Sri Lanka's exports were geared to service the high-end requirements of industrialized countries. Second, and more significantly, non-tariff barriers in India guarded many exportable items of interest to Sri Lanka. Sri Lanka had an incentive to negotiate an agreement that would remove some of the barriers to its possible exports to India and also wanted to promote itself as a base from where Indian multinationals could export to India and the rest of the world.[37]

This common interest was discerned through scholarly economic research. The World Institute of Development Economics Research (WIDER) commissioned a study in 1991 to examine the possibility of stimulating Indo-Sri Lanka trade. The WIDER study was conducted in New Delhi under the auspices of the Research and Information System for Non-Aligned and Other Developing Countries. One of Sri Lanka's foremost policy economists and civil servants, Lal Jayawardena, and other prominent intellectuals worked on this idea and suggested that the two countries needed to move away from a commodity-by-commodity approach towards one that would necessitate reciprocal trading concessions across the board, with the provision of a small negative list of items.[38]

Common Interests due to Strategic Concerns

Interdependence concerns alone are not sufficient to explain the evolution of reciprocity in trade. I have argued earlier that security relations are closely tied with the issue of trade. As security relations improve, countries begin to think more about interdependence gains and worry less about the costs of vulnerability due to trade. Indo-Lanka security relations were hostage to the Cold War-driven divergence of interest since the early 1980s. The Cold War became a major issue in Indo-Sri Lankan relations. When India worried about USA and Western influence in the region, it tried to destabilize Sri Lanka's internal situation by aiding the cause of the LTTE. Security relations improved dramatically after the withdrawal of the Indian Peace-Keeping Force (IPKF) by 31 March 1990 and the assassination of Indian Prime Minister Rajiv Gandhi in May 1991 by the LTTE. The end of the Cold War was a background condition that facilitated cordial security relations between India and Sri Lanka. As India's relations with USA improved after the loss of the special Soviet security and trade partnership, so did its relations with Sri Lanka.

The United National Party (UNP) government in Sri Lanka since 1977, which went to the IMF at the time of an economic crisis, improved its relations with the West, a fact that was not appreciated by the Congress government in India since the 1980s. Promoting US presence in the region was considered antithetical to India's interests at that time. Sri Lanka's tryst with non-alignment and ISI ended with the end of dominance of the Sri Lanka Freedom Party (SLFP), which lasted from 1956 to 1977. This had been a period when Sri Lanka took its non-alignment and ISI seriously.

The government of J.R. Jayawardene, which became dependent on the IMF since 1977, promoted US interests. There were attempts to lease a Trincomalee oil farm to a US concern. To push the economic reform programme away from autarky and towards greater export orientation, Jayawardene worked more closely with his finance minister and undermined his commerce minister, encouraging the foreign ministry towards greater international commercial orientation. Commerce Ministers in autarkic dispensations are often influenced by industrialists who are comfortable with the privileges of a closed market. Singapore's export orientation was the model, rather than the self-sufficient economy model, that Sri Lanka had pursued under the SLFP governments. The Sri Lankan government was dependent on the West for military assistance to fight the Tamil rebels. It allowed Mossad and the US Central Intelligence Agency (CIA) to help out with its internal problems, and was supportive of the US naval presence in the Indian Ocean. It attempted to join the pro-US camp of ASEAN nations and agreed to host a Voice of America station.[39]

Indira Gandhi did not appreciate Jayawardene's outlook towards USA. With a greater US and Western presence in the region, which India considered her sphere of influence, she pushed India's security agency, the Research and Analysis Wing, to intensify its monitoring of Sri Lanka. India became actively involved in training the Tamil rebels with a view to destabilizing an unfriendly regime in the neighbourhood. The big brother approach continued during Rajiv Gandhi's regime.[40]

Rajiv Gandhi and Jayawardene did not enjoy cordial relations. Communication between the Indian and Sri Lankan governments was dismal when the Indo-Sri Lanka Accord was being negotiated during July 1987, largely with the LTTE in the picture as being supported by India. This is evident from the Sri Lankan government's concerns about the Accord. It was unhappy with India's discouragement of the proposed Voice of America station. Second, foreign military personnel and experts were discouraged from engaging with the Sri Lankan army. It is reported that when the IPKF left for Sri Lanka, the government of Tamil Nadu gave a cheque of Rs 40 million to the LTTE (whom India at that time still supported). On the other hand, President Premadasa, who was elected in December 1988, secretly supplied weapons to the LTTE to fight the IPKF during 1989–90[41] (fighting broke out between the IPKF and the LTTE from early October 1987, just over two months after the introduction of the IPKF, for reasons that included mutual suspicions of intentions that are still not quite clear).

The return of the IPKF, the assassination of Rajiv Gandhi by the LTTE in 1991, and the simultaneous end of the Cold War, all aided the warming of Indo-Sri Lanka relations. This was the first time that the government of India lost all sympathy for the LTTE. The governments of the two countries worked together to help the Indian Special Investigation Team to bring to book Rajiv Gandhi's assassins. Such was the level of Indo-Sri Lanka cooperation that even the LTTE understood that it had erred in orchestrating the assassination of Rajiv Gandhi. The Sri Lankan government under President Chandrika Kumaratunge (1994–2005) also became more serious about accommodating the LTTE's and the Sri Lankan Tamil community's aspirations for regional autonomy and power-sharing.[42] This fitted in with India's understanding of the Tamil problem in Sri Lanka, that the root of the problem was the denial of due rights and share of power to the Tamils, an understanding that has been reiterated by every Indian government since 1983. The end of the Cold War provided a benign structural context for friendly Indo-Sri Lanka relations. In the past, US involvement in the region was viewed with scepticism by India. Most recently, Indo-US cooperation during the 2004 tsunami demonstrated how trust between the two governments has evolved over a period.

The increasing convergence of the security interests of India and Sri Lanka pushed the trade agenda between the two countries. Security problems could have increased the vulnerability perceptions in Sri Lanka in relation to its large neighbour. With the LTTE irritant in Indo-Lanka relations gone, as both viewed it as a terrorist organization; with peace-oriented Sri Lankan governments since 1994, willing in principle to accommodate Tamil aspirations and therefore fitting in with India's policy perspective on the problem; and with greater cooperation between India and USA, the path was now cleared to pursue common interests by bringing trade issues to the bargaining table.

The Bargaining Table

Common interests cannot be realized when there is a lack of communication. The Joint Commission had provided the venue for negotiations since 1968. Till the mid-1970s, India's economy was not sufficiently competitive to demand Sri Lanka's attention. From the mid-1980s, as the economy began gaining momentum, the political problems with Sri Lanka also began to rise. The assassination of Rajiv Gandhi was perhaps the turning point in Indo-Sri Lanka trade relations too. The arrival of the IPKF and the tenure of J.N. Dixit as high commissioner in Sri Lanka were not appreciated in that country. People from all walks of life felt a malevolent hegemonic Indian presence in Sri Lanka during this period. Indian high commissioners after the assassination of Rajiv Gandhi, such as Shiv Shankar Menon and Gopal Gandhi, created a friendlier image of India.

Saman Kelegama pointed to the advent of P.V. Narasimha Rao as India's prime minister as the turning point in political relations. The Prime Minister's Office (PMO) in India could now deal directly with the Sri Lankan government. The new Joint Commission came into being with two sub-committees: one dealing with trade, finance, and investment; the second dealing with culture, education, and social activities. A third committee on science and technology was added in 1993. The progress of the sixth and seventh meetings of the economic sub-committee had been mired by debates on market access by Sri Lanka. India needed to make greater than reciprocal concessions to convince a relatively small neighbour that the agreement would not only promote Sri Lanka's trade but also reduce its vulnerability.[43]

More than Simple Reciprocity

Common interests were not being realized because India was bogged down with market access issues. What changed the negotiation dynamics was a changed strategy of cooperating with neighbours that I.K Gujral brought about, first as foreign minister in 1996 and then prime minister in 1997. During his short tenure (1997–8) as prime minister, Gujral tried to practise a policy of reciprocal or greater than reciprocal gestures to be made by India in dealing with Bangladesh's Farakka barrage problem and other issues in South Asian relations. What this meant was that any negotiation dynamic would be governed by generous first moves by India to which the smaller neighbours would have to respond. PM Vajpayee was known to have worked towards better relationships with all South Asian neighbours, including Pakistan. The Asian financial crisis of 1997 and the US trade sanctions on India after the nuclear tests of May 1998 increased India's imperative and incentives to promote preferential trade with its neighbours.

Lal Jayawardena, one of the architects of the Indo-Sri Lanka FTA, explained to me how this changed strategy of negotiating with neighbours had an excellent impact on the Indo-Sri Lanka FTA. Once the strategy of engagement was changed to reciprocity after providing unequal concessions, sympathetic officials and committees aided it. Shiv Shankar Menon, the Indian high commissioner, played a key role in winning the confidence of the Sri Lankan elite. According to one account, some pro-liberal Sri Lankans even used the office of the Indian High Commission to pursue their agenda with a less liberal Sri Lankan ministry of commerce. This was a far cry from the days of J.N. Dixit. Foreign Minister Jaswant Singh and Finance Secretary Montek Singh Ahluwalia also played an active facilitators' role on the Indian side.[44]

The ISLFTA signed in December 1998 was an example of asymmetrical concessions made by India. It was rare in South Asian history that India's trade policy had shown such a liberal orientation. This inspired the confidence of the smaller neighbour that India's intention was to promote trade with Sri Lanka without making it more vulnerable. Statistics given earlier in this chapter have shown that India's intentions and Sri Lanka's negotiations built on the positive sum that the relationship had to offer.

What were the asymmetrical concessions made by India? India provided zero duty concession on 1,000 items when Sri Lanka provided the same concession on approximately 300 items. India would bring down tariffs to zero within three years. The adjustment period given to Sri Lanka was eight years. There was some discipline on the negative list, which could not exceed 20 per cent of the tariff lines. Positive lists in non-competing sectors were easy to prepare. In competing sectors like potatoes, chillies, and onions, the negative list protected Sri Lankan jobs. Similarly, Indian rubber and tea producers were not willing to compete with the Sri Lankans. Sri Lankan tea was subject to a 50 per cent duty and a quota of 15 million kg. India offered 8 million pieces of garments at 50 per cent duty.

India placed 24 per cent of the total goods—428 out of 1,788—in the negative list. Sri Lanka placed 13 per cent of the products on its free trade list and 49 per cent (1,183 out of 2,391) on the negative list. This meant catering to medium, small-scale agricultural and industrial producers. Even imported items such as wheat and flour were protected. Wheat was imported from USA under the PL-480 programme by the state-owned Co-operative Wholesale Establishment (CWE), and its processing into wheat flour was controlled by the Singapore multinational Prima Ceylon. CWE was a loss-making enterprise. The shortage of fish in Sri Lanka could have been alleviated by imports from India. Freeing mass consumption items like toothbrushes, ballpoint pens, pencils, combs, and hair slides could have worked to the benefit of the common consumer. Sri Lanka was, therefore, able to protect a variety of interests before getting into an FTA with India.

The preceding discussion shows that India made more concessions than Sri Lanka. Therefore, it is not surprising that Sri Lanka's exports have done well in relation to India after the FTA. Preferential exports grew by 620 per cent in 2002. The biggest winner was copper-related products such as refined copper, copper alloys, unwrought copper, copper wires, copper bars, copper rods, copper profiles, copper waste, and scrap. These grew at 2,854 per cent; the other preferential products at 192 per cent. New products, such as multi-wall paper sacks, marble slabs, ceramic ware, jewellery, ice cream machines, and furniture, expanded during this phase. Between 1999 and 2005, Sri Lanka's exports to India rose from 1 per cent of its total exports to 9 per cent, and its imports from India increased from 8.5 per cent of its total imports to 20.7 per cent. The FTA, by expanding traditional exports and bringing new exports into Sri Lanka's trade basket, was able to reduce India's import–export ratio from 16:1 to 5:1 between 1998–9 and 2002–3. The same figure was further reduced to 3.7:1 in 2004–5. This experience has increased Sri Lanka's confidence in a positive sum trade relationship with its large neighbour and at the same time has promoted India's trade. India and Sri Lanka are negotiating a comprehensive economic partnership agreement covering areas such as services and infrastructure.[45]

THE DOG THAT DID NOT BARK: ABSENCE OF PREFERENTIAL TRADE BETWEEN INDIA AND BANGLADESH

Why did Indo-Bangladesh trade not improve despite the end of the Cold War and gains to be reaped from trade and investment cooperation? The two neighbouring countries conduct robust informal trade worth about $900 million in 2002 (according to Gary Pursell and Zaidi Sattar[46]). This informal trade flourished in the face of substantial tariff and non-tariff barriers to formal trade. According to one study,[47] the rules of the game in informal trade were quite well institutionalized. This was characterized by the non-anonymity of transactions. The majority of the firms involved in it were stable entities that had been trading for a period in excess of five years. Traders on both sides did not perceive substantial risk posed by the enforcement agencies. The transactions costs were typically between 10 per cent and 20 per cent of the turnover, which enriched border officials. There was a regular payment mechanism on both sides.[48] One senior former minister in Sheikh Hasina's cabinet informally shared the information that the lack of informal trade would hurt Bangladesh as this would raise the price of essential commodities such as meat, milk, and eggs, which contributed to the nutritional enrichment of Bangladeshi citizens.

The perception of vulnerability was a major factor that debilitated formal trade between India and Bangladesh. Bangladesh worried that if trade with India became freer, it would be flooded with Indian goods. As India's competitiveness increased, so did its ability to export to neighbouring countries like Sri Lanka and Bangladesh. The ratio of India's exports to Bangladesh to its imports from Bangladesh increased from 13.9 in 1995–6 to 27.1 in 2004–5. In 2004–5, while India's official imports from Bangladesh were to the extent of $59 million, its exports were worth $1.6 billion.[49] Indian exports to Bangladesh had thus risen to a much greater degree than Bangladesh's exports to India. As things stood, it was much easier for Bangladesh to politically admit an imbalance in informal trade than an imbalance in formal trade.

The reason for this lack of enthusiasm for preferential trade between India and Bangladesh was due largely to the problems in their security relations. Bangladesh was unhappy about the way in which India shared river waters with it (India is the upper riparian for all the rivers that enter the Bay of Bengal through Bangladesh); there were unresolved border disputes; and India worried about illegal migrants from Bangladesh.

Most important, India worried that Bangladesh had become a sanctuary for nurturing terrorism in the post-9/11 world.[50]

Common interests could not be realized under conditions of adversarial security relations, and therefore a preferential trade and investment pact, as in the case of the ISLFTA, was not feasible. A gas pipeline from Myanmar to India via Bangladesh and the possibility of selling Bangladeshi gas to India have not taken shape, notwithstanding the potential of positive sum economic gains on both sides. Bangladesh could have gained from the transit fees by just permitting the movement of Myanmarese gas to India. A $3 billion investment proposal by India's Tata group, which could be the one major foreign investment in Bangladesh with a potential for increasing its exports to India, has been awaiting approval for a long time.[51] Last but not the least, trade is related to the free movement of people and capital. Bangladesh is not willing to offer transit facilities to India that could increase the rest of India's connectivity with its north-eastern states.

Were there any reasons for hope regarding the evolution of cooperation based on greater-than-simple reciprocity? It may be too early to say. There is reason to suspect that India was happy about the anti-terrorism actions taken by the interim government of President Iajuddin Ahmed, which showed boldness by executing six of the seven Jamaat-ul Mujaheedin Bangladesh militants on 30 March 2007. These militants had orchestrated a string of 63 simultaneous bomb blasts across Bangladeshi cities, including Dhaka and Chittagong, on 17 August 2005. There is a possibility that these actions inspired India to respond with unilateral zero duty concessions for the least developed countries of the SAARC in August 2008.[52] This concession would primarily benefit Bangladesh, as Nepal and Bhutan have enjoyed such privileges under bilateral treaties. India could be pursuing via multilateral fora such as SAARC, the logic of greater-than-simple reciprocity, which pushed the ISLFTA. This Indian move has been appreciated by Bangladesh, especially because it symbolizes more than a gesture of simple reciprocity from the Indian side.

* * *

Tables 8.1 and 8.2 suggest that Bangladesh's trade with India grew significantly in 2007–8. Sri Lanka remains the more significant trading partner. This is despite the fact that the size of the Sri Lankan economy is less than half the size of Bangladesh's economy. Besides, Sri Lanka has enjoyed easier market access into India than Bangladesh. The war with

TABLE 8.1 Department of Commerce Export Import Data Bank (Bangladesh)

Dated: 17 August 2009; Values in US$ million; Country: The People's Republic of Bangladesh

Year	2003–4	2004–5	2005–6	2006–7	2007–8
EXPORT	1,740.74	1,631.12	1,664.36	1,626.58	2,918.22
% Growth		-6.30	2.04	-2.27	79.41
India's Total Export	63,842.55	83,535.95	103,090.54	126,262.67	162,983.90
% Growth		30.85	23.41	22.48	29.08
% Share	2.73	1.95	1.61	1.29	1.79
IMPORT	77.63	59.37	127.03	228.31	257.12
% Growth		-23.52	113.96	79.73	12.62
India's Total Import	78,149.11	111,517.44	149,165.73	185,604.10	251,562.26
% Growth		42.70	33.76	24.43	35.54
% Share	0.10	0.05	0.09	0.12	0.10
TOTAL TRADE	1,818.37	1,690.49	1,791.39	1,854.90	3,175.34
% Growth		-7.03	5.97	3.54	71.19
India's Total Trade	141,991.66	195,053.38	252,256.27	311,866.78	414,546.15
% Growth		37.37	29.33	23.63	32.92
% Share	1.28	0.87	0.71	0.59	0.77
TRADE BALANCE	1,663.11	1,571.75	1,537.34	1,398.27	2,661.10
India's Trade Balance	-14,306.56	-27,981.49	-46,075.20	-59,341.43	-88,578.36
Exchange rate: (1 US$ = Rs)	45.9516	44.9315	44.2735	45.2849	40.2410

Source: The Department of Commerce, Government of India.

Notes: The country's total imports since 2000–1 do not include import of Petroleum Products (27100093) and Crude Oil (27090000).

TABLE 8.2 Department of Commerce Export Import Data Bank (Sri Lanka)

Dated: 17 August 2009; Values in US$ million; Country: The Democratic Socialist Republic of Sri Lanka

Year	2003–4	2004–5	2005–6	2006–7	2007–8
EXPORT	1,319.20	1,413.18	2,024.67	2,253.82	2,826.54
% Growth		7.12	43.27	11.32	25.41
India's Total Export	63,842.55	83,535.95	103,090.54	126,262.67	162,983.90
% Growth		30.85	23.41	22.48	29.08
% Share	2.07	1.69	1.96	1.79	1.73
IMPORT	194.74	378.40	577.70	470.26	631.42
% Growth		94.31	52.67	-18.60	34.27
India's Total Import	78,149.11	111,517.44	149,165.73	185,604.10	251,562.26
% Growth		42.70	33.76	24.43	35.54
% Share	0.25	0.34	0.39	0.25	0.25
TOTAL TRADE	1,513.93	1,791.58	2,602.37	2,724.07	3,457.97
% Growth		18.34	45.26	4.68	26.94
India's Total Trade	141,991.66	195,053.38	252,256.27	311,866.78	414,546.15
% Growth		37.37	29.33	23.63	32.92
% Share	1.07	0.92	1.03	0.87	0.83
TRADE BALANCE	1,124.46	1,034.79	1,446.97	1,783.56	2,195.12
India's Trade Balance	-14,306.56	-27,981.49	-46,075.20	-59,341.43	-88,578.36
Exchange rate: (1 US$ = Rs)	45.9516	44.9315	44.2735	45.2849	40.2410

Source: The Department of Commerce, Government of India.

Notes: The country's total imports since 2000–1 do not include import of Petroleum Products (27100093) and Crude Oil (27090000).

the LTTE, Sri Lanka's balance of payments problems, and opposition from domestic industry in Sri Lanka has ensured that India and Sri Lanka have made progress but not signed a Comprehensive Economic Partnership Agreement, which would include services in addition to trade in goods. Indo-Sri Lanka relations have been able to stand the strain of the Sri Lankan army's assault on the LTTE in 2009.

What lessons can be learnt from the story of the Indo-Sri Lanka FTA? First, the existence of common interests in trade was essential. If India had continued its import-substitution path, it might have been difficult to convince Sri Lanka to enter into an FTA with it. It was India's rise as a trading nation that made the opportunity costs for Sri Lanka's staying out of its trade with India very high. Increased trade volume but low export potential motivated Sri Lanka to improve its export basket through an FTA. Herein lay the opportunity for Sri Lanka, and India needed markets at a time when it had moved away from import-substitution towards export promotion as a key element in its development strategy. The 1997 Asian financial crisis and the US trade sanctions on India in the aftermath of the 1998 nuclear tests further strengthened India's resolve to implement an FTA in the neighbourhood. Common interests required a cordial strategic setting. The end of the Cold War, the assassination of Rajiv Gandhi by the LTTE, and the Sri Lankan government's turn to a peace process with the Tamil rebels since 1994, provided the strategic background that facilitated the realization of common interests arising from India's globalization.[53]

Second, regular meetings helped the participants to realize that the positive sum in a trade relationship was necessary but not sufficient to conclude an FTA. What was essential was a change in India's mindset to allow for greater than reciprocal concessions to a small neighbour. As India began to be perceived as a friendly country with an ability to make asymmetrical concessions, the prospect of an FTA became evident. Strategies of trade cooperation in South Asia, such as strategies of engendering cooperation within the PD game, will have to be based on reciprocity. In this case, the first move by India may require greater than reciprocal concessions because its smaller neighbours feel vulnerable vis-à-vis a large neighbour. India's relations with its neighbours is not a game among equals. There is reason to believe that this logic may be beginning to work in the case of Indo-Bangladesh relations, even though it may be too early to tell. Much will depend on whether Bangladesh will be able to signal reciprocity with some friendly moves towards India's unilateral tariff concessions.

Reciprocity is likely to remain a dominant theme in bilateral South Asian trade. We have noted that no country will allow another country to become rich at its expense. Free trade works when all countries open their markets to one another. Like the PD game, which does not work if one player cooperates but the other does not, the trade game will not work if mutual advantages are not reaped. A certain degree of trust based on rational self-interest can reduce transaction costs and institutionalize the norm of reciprocity to move towards freer trade. The strategy of reciprocity was moving India and Sri Lanka towards deeper integration through an economic partnership agreement.

If the evolution of reciprocity and trade cooperation were plausible, why did South Asia not witness similar arrangements between India and Pakistan, or even a robust South Asian Free Trade Agreement (SAFTA) which has formally existed since 2006? Was it because India could not pursue a similar rational course of the reciprocity plus[54] strategy that worked with Sri Lanka? Alternatively, was it because reciprocity could evolve as a strategy of cooperation under conditions of interdependence, when states desired absolute rather than relative gains, in an environment where the conflictual effects of the Hobbesian world were somewhat mitigated? Adversarial security relations heightened relative gains considerations. The context of improved security relations between India and its neighbours was an important precondition for efflorescence of strategies of reciprocity that could have increased the gains from regional economic cooperation.

Notes

1. A negative list connotes those items excluded from a free trade arrangement.

2. Saman Kelegama, 'Sri Lankan Exports to India', *Economic and Political Weekly*, 38(30), 26 July 2003, pp. 3153–4.

3. Kenneth Waltz, *Theory of International Politics* (Reading, MA: Addison-Wesley, 1979), chapter 7; Joseph Grieco, 'Understanding the Problem of Cooperation', in David A. Baldwin (ed.), *Neoliberalism and Neorealism* (New York: Columbia University Press, 1993), pp. 301–38.

4. Stephen D. Krasner, 'Global Communications and National Power: Life on the Pareto Frontier', in Baldwin (ed.), *Neoliberalism and Neorealism*, pp. 234–49.

5. Albert O. Hirschman, *National Power and the Structure of Foreign Trade* (Berkeley: University of California Press, 1980).

6. I.N. Mukherji, 'India's Economic Diplomacy Towards its Neighbours', in I.P. Khosla (ed.), *Economic Diplomacy* (New Delhi: Konark Publishers, 2006), p. 106.

7. There was nothing discriminatory about the most favoured nation (MFN) clause within the WTO. It implied that once a country defined its trade concessions within the multilateral system, the same should be available to all the other parties in the system. Pakistan has also not been a keen participant in ensuring progress within either the SAPTA or the SAFTA.

8. Saman Kelegama, 'Indo-Sri Lanka Economic Relations: Trends and Outlook', *Business Today*, New Delhi, November 1998, pp. 68–71.

9. Sisira Jayasuriya and Dushini Weerakoon, 'India–Sri Lanka Trade and Investment Links', in Partha Shome (ed.), *India and Economic Cooperation in South Asia* (New Delhi: ICRIER, 2001), pp. 111–37; Saman Kelegama 'Indo-Sri Lanka Trade and the Bilateral Free Trade Agreement: A Sri Lankan Perspective', *Asia Pacific Journal*, 6(2), December 1999, pp. 87–106.

10. Interviews with Patrick Amarasinghe and Ken Balendra in Sri Lanka, April 2003.

11. Interview with J.B. Kelegama, April 2003, Colombo. See also J.B. Kelegama, 'Indo-Sri Lanka Free Trade Agreement', *South Asian Survey*, 6(2), 1999, pp. 283–96.

12. Robert Axelrod, *The Evolution of Cooperation* (New York: Basic Books, 1984).

13. Ibid.

14. Ibid.; Robert Axelrod and Robert Keohane, 'Achieving Cooperation under Anarchy', in Baldwin (ed.), *Neorealism and Neoliberalism*, pp. 85–115.

15. On the relationship between alliance and trade, see Edward D. Mansfield and Rachel Bronson, 'Alliances, Preferential Trading Arrangements, and International Trade', *American Political Science Review*, 91(1), 1997, pp. 94–107. See also Edward D. Mansfield and Rachel Bronson, 'The Political Economy of Major-Power Trade Flows', in Edward D. Mansfield and Helen V. Milner (eds), *The Political Economy of Regionalism* (New York: Columbia University Press, 1997), pp. 188–208; Baldev Raj Nayar, *The Geopolitics of Globalization* (New Delhi: Oxford University Press, 2005).

16. For the relationship between import substitution and late development, see Alexander Gerschenkron, *Economic Backwardness in Historical Perspective* (Cambridge, Mass: Harvard University Press, 1962). This literature is reviewed in Anne O. Krueger, 'Trade Policy and Economic Development', Cambridge, MA, NBER Working Paper 5896, 1997.

17. Vinod K. Aggarwal and Rahul Mukherji, 'India's Shifting Trade Policy: South Asia and Beyond', in Vinod K. Aggarwal and Min Gyo Koo (eds), *Asia's New Institutional Architecture: Evolving Structures for Managing Trade and Security Relations* (New York: Springer, 2008), pp. 215–58.

18. Ibid.

19. In 2001, India accounted for 80 per cent of the region's exports and 6 per cent of its imports.

20. This crisis was precipitated by the Gulf War when short-term lenders decided to quit India during a phase when the state practised fiscal profligacy at the time of rising oil prices.

21. On India's import substitution model, see Jagdish N. Bhagwati and Padma Desai, *India's Planning for Industrialization* (Bombay: Oxford University Press, 1970) and Sukhamoy Chakravarty, *Development Planning* (Oxford: Clarendon Press, 1987), especially chapter 2.

22. On Indian productivity, see Isher J. Ahluwalia, *Productivity and Growth in Indian Manufacturing* (New Delhi: Oxford University Press, 1991); and Marcel P. Timmer and Adam Szirmai, 'Productivity Growth in Asian Manufacturing: The Structural Bonus Hypothesis Examined', *Structural Change and Economic Dynamics*, 11, 2000, pp. 371–92.

23. On India's inflexible labour laws, see Roberto Zagha, 'Labor in India's Economic Reforms', in Jeffrey D. Sachs, Ashutosh Varshney, and Nirupam Bajpai (eds), *India in the Era of Economic Reforms* (New Delhi: Oxford University Press, 1999), pp. 160–85.

24. On Indira Gandhi's second tenure and a critical look at past policy, see P.N. Dhar, 'The Indian Economy', in Robert E.B. Lucas and Gustave F. Papanek (eds), *The Indian Economy* (New Delhi: Oxford University Press, 1988), pp. 3–22; and Arjun K. Sengupta, *Reforms, Equity and the IMF* (New Delhi: Har Anand, 2001).

25. On the political economy of import substitution opposing trade orientation in the 1980s, see Atul Kohli, *Democracy and Discontent* (New York: Cambridge University Press, 1990), chapter 11.

26. Rahul Mukherji, 'Economic Transition in a Plural Polity: India', in Rahul Mukherji (ed.), *India's Economic Transition: The Politics of Reforms* (New Delhi: Oxford University Press, 2007), chapter 5, pp. 117–45; Arvind Panagariya, *India: The Emerging Giant* (New York and New Delhi: Oxford University Press, 2008), chapters 3–5.

27. On the 1966 crisis, see Rahul Mukherji, 'India's Aborted Liberalization—1966', *Pacific Affairs*, 73(3), 2000, pp. 375–92. On 1981, see John G. Ruggie, 'Political Structure and Change in the International Economic Order: The North-South Dimension', in John G. Ruggie (ed.), *Antinomies of Interdependence* (New York: Columbia University Press, 1983), pp. 423–504. On 1991, see Mukherji, 'Economic Transition in a Plural Polity'.

28. See Rahul Mukherji, 'Managing Competition: Politics and the Building of Independent Regulatory Institutions', *India Review*, 3(4), 2004, pp. 278–305.

29. See Mukherji, 'Economic Transition in a Plural Polity', p. 133. This is not to suggest that economic reforms were devoid of political problems, such as the growing fiscal deficit, inflexible labour laws, and poor human and physical infrastructure in many areas. See Suresh D. Tendulkar and T.A. Bhavani,

Understanding Reforms: Post 1991 India (New Delhi: Oxford University Press, 2007), chapters 7–8.

30. 'WB, IMF at Odds on India's Growth Potential', *The Economic Times*, New Delhi, 11 November 2004, at http://economictimes.indiatimes.com/articleshow/919484.cms (URL no longer available).

31. Kelegama 'Indo-Sri Lanka Economic Relations', pp. 92–4.

32. Ibid.

33. Aggarwal and Mukherji, 'India's Shifting Trade Policy', p. 225.

34. Ibid.

35. Ibid.

36. Kelegama 'Indo-Sri Lanka Free Trade Agreement', p. 88; Kelegama 'Indo-Sri Lanka Economic Relations', pp. 68–71.

37. Initially, there was opposition to Indian investment. Saman Kelegama, in a conversation in Colombo in April 2003, explained how this problem was resolved. Initially, when Harrisons Malayalam came as investors in tea gardens, there was much opposition to foreign investment. Workers subsequently realized that foreign investment actually improved their conditions. There was no major worker protest on the eve of the ISLFTA. See also Kelegama, 'Indo-Sri Lanka Economic Relations'; and Kelegama, 'Indo-Sri Lanka Trade and the Bilateral Free Trade Agreement'.

38. L. Jayawardena, *Indo-Sri Lanka Economic Cooperation: Facilitating Trade Expansion through a Reciprocal Preference Scheme* (Helsinki: The United Nations University–WIDER, 1993).

39. Neil DeVotta, 'Sri Lanka's Structural Adjustment Program and Its Impact on Indo-Lanka Relations', *Asian Survey*, 38(5), 1998, pp. 457–73.

40. Ibid., pp. 460–3.

41. N.N. Jha, 'India and Sri Lanka: From Uncertainty to Close Proximity', in Atish Sinha and Madhup Mohta (eds), *Indian Foreign Policy: Challenges and Opportunities* (New Delhi: Academic Foundation and Foreign Services Institute, 2007), pp. 641–57.

42. Ibid., pp. 650–3.

43. Various discussions with Saman Kelegama, April 2003. See also, Kelegama, 'Indo-Sri Lanka Trade and the Bilateral Free Trade Agreement', pp. 1991–2.

44. This view is based on discussions with Saman Kelegama and Lal Jayawardane in Colombo in April 2003, and with Milinda Moragoda in Dhaka in March 2000. Milinda Moragoda was a member in the cabinets of Prime Minister Ranil Wickramsinghe and President Rajapakse.

45. Saman Kelegama and I.N. Mukherji, 'India–Sri Lanka Bilateral Free Trade Agreement: Six Years Performance and Beyond', *RIS Discussion Papers # 119* (New Delhi, RIS, 2007); Kelegama, 'Sri Lankan Exports to India'; Kelegama, 'Indo-Sri Lanka Trade and the Bilateral Free Trade Agreement', pp. 95–103.

46. Gary Pursell and Zaidi Sattar, 'India Bangladesh Bilateral Trade and Potential Free Trade Agreement', *Bangladesh Development Series Paper No. 13* (Washington: World Bank, 2002), pp. XXIV–V.

47. Sanjib Pohit and Nisha Taneja, 'India's Informal Trade with Bangladesh: A Qualitative Assessment', *The World Economy* 26(8), 2003, pp. 1187–1214.

48. Ibid.

49. I.N. Mukherji, 'Indo-Bangladesh Trade: Analyzing Impact of Trade Preference on Growth and Structure of Bilateral Trade', *Artha Vijnana*, 46(3–4), 2004, pp. 197–22; Rahul Mukherji, 'Managing Competition: Politics and the Building of Independent Regulatory Institutions', in Rahul Mukherji (ed.), *India's Economic Transition: The Politics of Reforms* (New Delhi: Oxford University Press, 2007), pp. 278–305.

50. Mukherji, 'Economic Transition in a Plural Polity', pp. 557–68. This view is also based on a series of interviews in Dhaka in May 2003 with eminent Bangladeshis such as Rehman Sobhan, Reza ul Karim, Saber Hussain Choudhury, and Mustafizur Rehman.

51. BBC News, 'Tata halts Bangladesh investment', 10 July 2006, London, see: http://newsvote.bbc.co.uk/mpapps/pagetools/print/news.bbc.co.uk/2/hi/south_asia/5164926.stm, accessed on 28 September 2010.

52. India is also planning to reduce its list of sensitive goods by the end of the year. See, Dushni Weerakoon, 'The Political Economy of Trade Integration in South Asia', *The World Economy*, 33(7), 2010, p. 924.

53. For a more general explication of this argument, see Aggarwal and Mukherji, 'India's Shifting Trade Policy'.

54. By reciprocity plus strategy, I imply a strategy that needed to be based on greater than reciprocal concessions.

9   Obstacles to Bangladesh–India Cooperation

An International Relations Theory Perspective

Mohammad Humayun Kabir

Bangladesh and India are contiguous neighbours, sharing over 4,000 km of common border. Having been parts of a single, huge entity in South Asia until 1947, these two independent, sovereign countries share a common history, ethnic origins, language, religions, and culture. India played a crucial role in Bangladesh's war of liberation against Pakistan and, therefore, in the emergence of its eastern neighbour as a sovereign country in 1971. India also provided massive and critical assistance to war-ravaged Bangladesh in the initial years of rehabilitation and development, when Dhaka was unable to enlist the support of many rich and powerful friends elsewhere in the world.

This bond and mutuality of interests was sealed with the signature of the Treaty of Friendship, Cooperation, and Peace between Bangladesh and India in 1972, having heralded enormous promise of a period of close and cordial neighbourly ties. The two friendly countries also concluded several other agreements during the first half of the 1970s, including agreements on border demarcation, trade, and the Joint Rivers Commission. However, the full potential of this relationship never came to fruition. Indeed, the initial warmth in their relationship began to peter out and show signs of friction within a few years of the new nation's independent existence. The bilateral relationship became strained following the brutal overthrow and assassination of Bangladesh's father of the nation, President Bangabandhu Sheikh Mujibur Rahman, on 15 August 1975 and the eventual military rule in that country. Although two landmark agreements on sharing the

Ganges waters—the 1977 Agreement and the 1996 Treaty—have been concluded between the two close neighbours, there remain visible stresses in their bilateral relations, inhibiting consolidation of friendly ties and development of extensive cooperation. The questions that arise are: Why does cooperation not significantly fructify between Bangladesh and India, and what are the factors thwarting cooperation? What affects Bangladesh's perceptions and policies about India? Can economic cooperation between Bangladesh and India be separated from the political and security issues between them?

This chapter aims at providing answers to these part-theoretical, part-empirical queries. In these attempts, I explore the use of some concepts, such as relative gains, cumulative relative gains, lock-in effects, trust and reassurance, geopolitics, and geo-strategy, from international relations theory. This is not an exercise in theory per se but a study of Bangladesh–India relations. The chapter is divided into six sections, including the introductory and the concluding sections. The second section deals with some relevant theorizing, while the third deals with some select areas of potential cooperation between Bangladesh and India. The fourth section examines the problems of cooperation on the utilization of the waters of the common rivers. The fifth section brings in a comparative perspective by drawing upon the water cooperation experiences of USA, Canada, and Mexico. The final section makes some concluding remarks relating to the outlook for the relationship.

INTERNATIONAL RELATIONS THEORY ON INTER-STATE COOPERATION

When and why do states cooperate and when and why do they not? Let us first begin with the concepts of relative gains and cumulation effects. The crux here is the impact of relative gains on a state's preferences for cooperation. It is, therefore, important to comprehend why relative gains concerns vary. John Matthews defines 'gain' as a benefit derived from cooperation. In economic cooperation, this will generally take the form of monetary benefits. In security cooperation, the primary benefit is a decrease in the capability of a potential adversary to inflict damage to one's own state or its physical assets. An absolute gain is the total award received by a state for a transaction; the comparative measure of absolute gains is the same state relative to itself at different times. A 'relative gain' is a disproportionate benefit that changes the balance between two states. Relative gains create 'advantages' when they allow the state that benefits more to secure additional gains not directly linked to the terms of the original agreement or outcome. Advantages accrue when relative gains can be used to influence other outcomes.[1]

Matthews introduces the concept of 'cumulation effects'. He argues that

concerns over relative gains both in security and political economy vary according to the cumulation effects inherent in the issue under consideration for cooperation. If a relative gain in a current round of interaction creates advantages that allow additional gains in future rounds, relative gains will be more important. If, however, a relative gain in a current round produces only absolute gains in that round and does not have implications for future interactions, relative gains concerns will be more muted.[2]

Grieco uses the term 'cumulative' to describe increasing returns to early relative gains. However, his brief usage essentially refers to the potential for relative losses to restrict independent action of states at a later date in their political decisions.[3] This concept seems to clarify why states are sometimes concerned about relative gains for their impact on the future and also explains state behaviour, depending upon the variation in the sensitivity to relative gains.

The predominant explanations for variation in concern over relative gains are that the sphere of security is more prone to concern than the sphere of the economic, and that a state's relative gains' concerns will vary with the degree to which another state's relative gains can be turned into military capabilities that threaten the first state.[4] However, Matthews convincingly shows that such arguments cannot account for behaviour based on relative gains where security is not an apparently pressing concern, and also cannot account for efforts at pure security cooperation, such as arms control agreements, in which relative gains were relatively moderate and manageable.[5] Matthews' argument reconnects what have come to be seen as two analytically distinct spheres in international relations literature, and his hypothesis of relative gains cumulation applies to both frameworks as it offers a way to link them. He states that the emphasis placed on discord in security and on cooperation in international political economy (IPE) are overdrawn; security cooperation may not always be impeded by relative gains' concerns, and IPE interactions will often be characterized by high levels of relative gains concerns that thwart cooperation, even when the security implications are low and absolute gains are the ultimate objective.[6]

Matthews argues that cumulation is of broader applicability, and that the key to the problem of relative gains is the future interactions states face. Relative gains' concerns vary both within and across issue areas. In other words, relative gains in one issue area can also cumulate into advantages in related areas. Besides, cumulation is measured by examining whether the issue gives evidence of characteristics that allow a state to demand or acquire additional benefits later. When an issue evidences many such characteristics, the cumulation is high; when it evidences few, cumulation is low.[7]

Peter Liberman highlights the point that theoretical analyses of relative gains in the literature have argued that relative-gains' sensitivity is affected by (i) the political-military relationship between the nations involved, (ii) the offence–defence balance, and (iii) system structure. According to these analyses, relative-gains' sensitivity should be attenuated by a low likelihood of war, by defence dominance, and by multipolarity, and that it should be heightened by the converse of these factors.[8] However, in one of his studies, Liberman argues that relative economic gains are unlikely to interfere with cooperation in multipolar international systems; that the threat posed by a particular nation depends largely upon its power, geographic proximity, offensive capabilities, and hostile intentions; that sensitivity to relative gains is affected by the specifics of the partners' political relationship; and that resistance to unequal gain depends on the magnitude of the asymmetry as well as the sensitivity factor.[9]

Two other cooperation-related concepts that may be discussed here are the 'strategy of reassurance' and 'costly signalling theory of reassurance'. Obviously, the concepts are related to mistrust, which, coupled with fear, plays a crucial role in explaining international conflict. Indeed,

at the heart of the security dilemma is mistrust, a fear that the other side is malevolently inclined and bound to exploit one's cooperation rather than reciprocate it...[and therefore] the possibility that conflict may result from exaggerated perceptions of hostility makes the issue of reassurance important... If the force driving two states into conflict is a set of false beliefs, it would be very beneficial for both sides to dispel these beliefs through strategies of reassurance...reassurance is the flip side of the security dilemma coin.[10]

How does one side dispel the disbeliefs of the 'other' side? Andrew Kydd develops what can be called the 'costly signalling' theory of reassurance, because it focuses on sending and interpretation of costly signals. Costly signals, in this context, are signals designed to persuade the other side that one is trustworthy by virtue of the fact that they are so costly that one would hesitate to send them if one were untrustworthy.[11] This theory has two main implications: first, to reassure, a signal must be adequately costly, that is, gestures with substantive risks attached; second, in order to be willing to send a signal that is so costly that the untrustworthy type finds it too risky to mimic, the trustworthy type must be willing to take greater risks for peace than the untrustworthy type. Thus, reassurance through costly signals can reduce mistrust and lead to full cooperation.[12] There are, of course, differing views in the literature on conflict and cooperation that reassurance is, by and large, a risky strategy that will seldom succeed because of the implicit danger that concessions will be taken advantage of by the other side if they are uninterested in cooperation.[13] However, it is more convincing that trust can be established and fostered by small, unilateral cooperative gestures that initiate chains of mutually rewarding behaviour.[14] Equally importantly, the commitment of one side to the other must be credible, that is, ready to be implemented fully, not in a revised and partial way, and without resort to procrastination.

Concepts of interdependence and lock-in effects are also relevant in understanding conflict and cooperation. Copeland poses a fundamental question: Does economic interdependence increase or decrease the probability of war among states? He attempts to resolve this by presenting his theory of trade expectations, fusing the liberal insight that the benefits of trade give states an incentive to avoid war with the realist view that the potential costs of being cut off can push states to war to secure vital goods.[15] Without delving into the details of this theory here, this chapter highlights the possible implications of the situations when states get locked-in by signing agreements. What are the possible lock-in effects? While cooperation generates benefits, interdependence exacts costs. There is sensitivity interdependence and there is vulnerability interdependence. The former entails costs that go hand-in-hand with high trade, while the latter entails costs that are experienced if trade is cut off. Interdependence may result in loss of autonomy for the contracting parties. It may put constraints on exit options once deals are contracted, which in turn may affect the relative gains calculus. As interdependence is actually mutual dependence on the partner country's economy and decisions, it makes parties vulnerable. Indeed, highly interdependent nations might be tempted to regain lost markets and resources by force and thus ensure continued access to necessary materials and goods. As such, high interdependence can be war-inducing as well as peace-inducing, depending upon the expectations of future trade and the relative gains' sensitivity.[16]

Apart from the theoretical exposition set out earlier, there are some practical aspects in the context of Bangladesh and India that tend to enter into their relative gains calculus. The Indo-centricity of South Asia, with the neighbours on the periphery having borders only with India, is of strategic significance. The asymmetry in size and power between India and her regional neighbours is often awe-inspiring. Bangladesh, a small state by comparison, is constrained to develop a self-image of such a state in juxtaposition to India. Bangladesh's fear of India is engendered by this asymmetry in size, resources, and power. It is also generated by the fact that Bangladesh is bounded by India on three sides, while its southern oceanic frontier may easily be choked off by the giant neighbour's navy. Yet another fear-inducing factor is India's regional security doctrine. This doctrine is based on India's assumptions that South Asia is one single strategic as well as civilizational unit and that her neighbours are just integral to it. New Delhi's policy objective is to establish India as the custodian of the region's security, even if this means interfering in the internal affairs of other South Asian countries.[17] This naturally generates a sense of insecurity amongst its smaller neighbours. In this context, what are the implications of the Indo-centric structure of the South Asian subsystem for Bangladesh? How does the 'India factor' impinge on Bangladesh's relative gains' concerns vis-à-vis the regional Goliath?

Let us now focus on some issue areas concerning Bangladesh and India with a view to examining the extent of application of the theories and concepts discussed earlier.

ISSUE AREAS OF COOPERATION BETWEEN BANGLADESH AND INDIA

The list of issue areas is fairly extensive. However, only three of these— the issues of transit, gas export, and sharing of the waters of the common rivers—are discussed here.

The Transit Issue

India had transit facilities through the territory of Bangladesh across waterways to its seven north-eastern states until these were disrupted following the India–Pakistan war in 1965. Actually, India has been more interested in road and railway transit facilities in order to gain easy access to its distant north-east, particularly since the birth of

Bangladesh. India's desire for cooperation from Bangladesh on such transit facilities became keener since the 1990s. Granted transit rights, India would be able to send goods to its north-eastern states at a much lower cost, and this would help in integrating the economies of these states with the mainstream Indian economy. India's north-east would also have access to Bangladesh's Chittagong seaport. In other words, India's objective is to mainstream, politically and economically, its insurgency-wracked, isolated north-eastern federating units through a comprehensive development package. India considers that transit through Bangladesh would cost it a great deal less in implementing its development strategy.

India tends to present to Bangladesh a tantalizingly rosy picture of the transit/transhipment issue in terms of financial benefits from revenue and transportation, employment generation within Bangladesh, and increase in bilateral trade. However, the transit issue is extremely controversial in Bangladesh. Those who favour granting transit facilities to India argue in terms of global economic trends and geo-economic perspectives. They view inter-state road networks as infrastructure that is crucial for development.

However, those who oppose granting transit facilities to India sound the alarm bell. The foremost argument is that it would impinge upon Bangladesh's sovereignty, as it would facilitate India's interference in the internal affairs of the smaller neighbour. They also argue that if Indian vehicles use Bangladesh's territory, it would curtail the country's freedom. India, with its geographical and locational advantages, might be tempted to draw all kinds of mileage from the transit facility. The point they make is that India cannot be trusted, as evidenced by Dhaka's bitter experiences with New Delhi regarding the issue of the lease of the Tin Bigha Corridor and, in general, the implementation of the 1974 Mujib–Indira Border Agreement.[18] The consequent perennial movements of Indian vehicles are likely to flood Bangladesh's market with Indian goods. Any probable transit agreement is suspected of being another Indian attempt to lock-in Bangladesh, like the now-lapsed 25 Year Friendship Treaty. It is feared that the transit facility would make India's influence and trade interests in Bangladesh so predominant that it might lead to a virtual deconstruction of the Partition of 1947. India might abuse/misuse the transit facility for military purposes. It is suspected that India would send troops to its north-eastern states in order to suppress the insurgency movements there. Taking advantage of this opportunity, Indian troops might penetrate into Bangladesh. Finally, a related fear is that, in the event of an India–China war, India might very well occupy Bangladesh in order to wage the armed conflict.[19]

It is clear from the aforementioned that, in relation to the transit issue, Bangladesh shows relative gains sensitivity: that it is fearful of Indian dominance and loss of sovereignty, that it mistrusts India, and that it feels vulnerable to Indian motives and military action under certain eventualities. An uneasy deep-seated and lingering feeling in Bangladesh is that India is deliberately not doing anything to reassure Bangladesh. Such studied inertia on India's part might be explained by her self-confidence borne out of a sense of impunity in a big power–small power framework. The result is that there is no tangible progress in matters of cooperation on the transit issue between Bangladesh and India.

However, there has apparently been a perception and policy-level change on both sides since the military-backed caretaker government took over in Bangladesh on 11 January 2007. One prominent Bangladesh analyst has captured the changed bilateral ambience in a few apt words: 'We have had four high-profile visits from India in the last six months, more than what we had in the five years of the Bangladesh National Party (BNP) alliance government.'[20] Pranab Mukherjee, then India's external affairs minister, paid a visit to Bangladesh in late February 2007, within about one-and-a-half months of the assumption of office by the caretaker government in Dhaka. Talking to newsmen prior to his return to New Delhi, Mukherjee said that both sides had agreed to take steps to place bilateral relations on an 'irreversible higher trajectory', and that both sides had discussed all outstanding issues of mutual interest.[21] Echoing his minister's views, India's high-profile high commissioner to Bangladesh, Pinak Ranjan Chakravarty, subsequently described the bilateral relations between Bangladesh and India as 'very good' and stressed the need to enhance cooperation between the two countries in all sectors.[22]

Expectations of a vastly improved relationship with India have also been expressed from Bangladesh side. Fakhruddin Ahmed, chief adviser (CA) of the caretaker government of Bangladesh (head of the caretaker government), said that his country would like to see cooperation from India on a larger scale on key issues. He conveyed this desire on Bangladesh's part to the visiting Indian foreign secretary, Shiv Shankar Menon.[23] Barrister Mainul Hosein, an influential adviser of the caretaker government, said that the two countries were anxious to improve the overall relationship to move forward together for a better future, and that his government appreciated the genuine need for good and constructive relations with India.[24] Some analysts in Bangladesh hold the view that Dhaka too should play its role in putting its relations with New Delhi on an 'irreversible higher trajectory' by, for example, being sensitive to India's security concerns and by coming out of 'the box'.[25] In 2008, speakers at a roundtable discussion in Dhaka on 'Bangladesh–India Economic Cooperation' said that all kinds of relationships, including political, social, cultural, economic, and diplomatic ones, and cooperation between Bangladesh and India would have to be forged even for Bangladesh's own interests and benefit.[26] Therefore, the general thrust in the Bangladesh–India relationship of the time was: 'Trust can be built up through actions, not merely words... We can no longer afford to remain a captive to misperception and a hackneyed mind-set.'[27]

The Bangladesh Awami League (AL)-led grand alliance that swept the polls on 29 December 2008, capturing about four-fifths of the 300-strong parliament, formed a democratic government on 6 January 2009, ending the two-year-long unelected caretaker government. The positive feelings generated during the caretaker government in the Bangladesh–India relationship seem to have received a boost under the AL government in Dhaka and the Congress government in New Delhi. Indeed, there have been expectations of a growing and deepening bilateral relationship between the two neighbouring countries on both sides. Even before the December 2008 election in Bangladesh, the then Indian minister Mani Shankar Aiyar had expressed the hope that the year 2009 would be a year of India and Bangladesh. He indicated a shift of India's policy towards Bangladesh after the parliamentary elections in that country.[28] This view was echoed in the first reaction to the media by S.M. Krishna, who was appointed India's minister of external affairs following the electoral victory of the Congress-led alliance in May 2009. He said that India wanted to have friendly and peaceful relations with its neighbours as it was essential for its main goal of achieving the economic growth rate of 9–10 per cent.[29]

With new governments in Dhaka and New Delhi, Bangladesh's Prime Minister Sheikh Hasina also wants ties with India to thrive. The foreign minister of Bangladesh, Dipu Moni, has also stated that Delhi is important for Dhaka's foreign policy priorities, while her former deputy, Hasan Mahmud, has said, 'Bilateral relations between Dhaka and New Delhi will deepen with the new governments in Bangladesh and India.'[30] Expectations in Dhaka for a close, cordial, and mutually beneficial relationship are quite high. An English daily in Dhaka ran an editorial as follows:

We hope the two sides will approach the host of outstanding disputes with a view to a resolution rather than manipulation for political mileage as has too often been the case...We hope, therefore, that the new regime in Delhi will use its historic opportunity to work with Dhaka to resolve outstanding disputes and set the tone for future negotiations, as powerful neighbour and not as regional hegemon.[31]

In a similar vein, the former adviser for foreign affairs in the immediate past caretaker government of Bangladesh (2007–8) has written: 'India must be the elder, not the big, brother, with a special responsibility. It must not only be the largest country in the heart of South Asia, but also the country with the largest heart. It is as simple, or as difficult, as that.'[32] Another similar view of India may also be pertinent here: 'Given her historical ties with us, it is only natural to expect India to be way more responsive to our problems than we saw she has been.'[33]

It is in this favourable scenario of regime compatibility between the AL-led government in Bangladesh and the Congress-led government in India that the relationship is likely to grow and deepen across the board, including the issue of transit. Indeed, in a major breakthrough in the bilateral relationship during the Bangladesh foreign minister's visit to India from 8 September to 10 September 2009, India agreed to transit facilities for Bangladesh to Nepal and Bhutan, provide at least 100MW power on a priority basis, increase trade and communication facilities, and resolve other outstanding issues. Recognizing the importance of bilateral and regional connectivity, Bangladesh discussed the possibility of allowing India to use Chittagong Port and designating Ashuganj as a new port of call under the Inland Water Transit and Trade Agreement.[34] It is a movement forward on the transit issue, but the devil lies in the detail and, of course, in implementation. Whether the favourable signals from New Delhi, in terms of meeting Bangladesh's demand for overland access to Nepal and Bhutan, will assuage the political and civil society opposition to granting transit facilities to India remains to be seen. The issue of an Asian highway, recently approved by the Sheikh Hasina government, is also very controversial in Bangladesh as the opposition forces there tend to equate it with granting transit facilities to India, only in a different way. Although Prime Minister Hasina has made a categorical statement in parliament dispelling the perceived security threat over the Asian Highway,[35] the issue nonetheless remains highly sensitive in Bangladesh. The fears and apprehensions in Bangladesh need to be outweighed by Bangladesh's tangible gains from any deal as well as by a definitive shift in India's perception of and policy towards Bangladesh.

Export of Bangladesh's Natural Gas to India

Bangladesh is reported to have plentiful reserves of natural gas. Several international oil companies (IOCs) were engaged in exploration and exploitation activities here, and there was international pressure for export of gas from Bangladesh to India. Most Bangladeshis do not have access to gas and they seldom enjoy the benefits of development derived from various forms of gas use. As such, the issue of gas export became a hotly debated national issue in Bangladesh. There were three concerns here: whether Bangladesh has sufficient gas for export in the first place; if yes, whether it should be put to domestic use first, including household use and industrialization; and whether a strategic resource like natural gas should be exported to a big, powerful neighbour like India, with which the relationship has not always been congenial.

While government sources in Dhaka say that the country does not have an exportable surplus of natural gas, an impression has been created by a section of the international media and by those who are interested in having this resource exported to India that Bangladesh is literally floating on gas. One might recall the reports to this effect on the British Broadcasting Corporation (BBC) and in USA, in both the print and electronic media. Donors are even ready to increase aid if Bangladesh exports gas to India.[36] M.L. Tripathi, former high commissioner of India to Bangladesh, said that gas export and transit facilities would help the India–Bangladesh trade balance.[37] However, whatever may be the economic rationale for gas export, political sensitivity in Bangladesh stands in the way of striking a deal. A former senior Bangladesh cabinet minister has said that it is politics and not business that is a barrier to gas export to India.[38] Whichever government of Bangladesh decides to export gas to India is likely to be dubbed as being subservient to New Delhi, a label considered suicidal in the country in terms of electoral politics. The people of Bangladesh do not appreciate India's strong, persistent preference for reciprocity from her smaller neighbours. They expect affordable generosity from a country that is immensely powerful and has plenty of resources. The least they expect from New Delhi is access to the vast Indian market for their commodities,[39] transit facilities through the Indian territory to Nepal and Bhutan, a fair and equitable share of the waters of the common rivers, the conduct of inter-state relationship on the basis of sovereign equality, no interference in Bangladesh's internal affairs, no bias for any particular regime in

Bangladesh, and accommodation of Bangladesh's security concerns and foreign policy preferences.

Be that as it may, the truth of the matter is that Bangladesh does not have sufficient natural gas for its own consumption, let alone for the purpose of export. There are frequent gas supply shortages to the fertilizer factories, power plants, and for household use. At the present rate of consumption, Bangladesh's proven natural gas reserve, without any addition to the total, would last only till 2011. Even though the probable reserve could be converted into proven reserve, it would only meet the demand up to 2015. To face the crisis, the government of Bangladesh opened in 2008 a bid for offshore oil and gas exploration. Two companies were selected: ConocoPhillips and Tullow Energy. However, as the disputes over the respective maritime boundaries between Bangladesh, India, and Myanmar remain unresolved, the commissioning of the project and finally supply of gas to the national pipeline do not seem probable in the near future.[40] Under the circumstances, the question of Bangladesh exporting gas to India is obviously no longer on any agenda. The government of Bangladesh is currently seized of the imperative of enhancing the energy security of the country and its people.

Bangladesh had, however, agreed to join a tri-nation gas pipeline transit scheme. Bangladesh, India, and Myanmar agreed to cooperate in gas exploration and an overland pipeline project to pump offshore natural gas from western Myanmar to energy-hungry India through Bangladesh. An international consortium, to be formed on the basis of a tripartite agreement, would export the Myanmar offshore gas to India through a pipeline across Bangladesh. The route of the pipeline would be mutually finalized ensuring each party's access, maximum security, and optimum economic utilization. Bangladesh and India will reserve the right to access the pipeline as and when required, including the injection of and siphoning off their own natural gas.[41] The 290-km pipeline is planned run through Arakan province of Myanmar and the Indian states of Mizoram and Tripura before passing through Bangladesh to Kolkata (India).[42] Under the plan, Tripura will pump gas in the pipeline that will be transmitted to West Bengal through Bangladesh. The three nations agreed, eight years after the project was conceived, in a meeting at Yangon on 27–8 February 2005, to sign a Memorandum of Understanding (MoU) in March or April 2006 in Dhaka. In the negotiations, Bangladesh's concern was to ensure a balance among the three countries. That is why Bangladesh insisted on involving an international consortium to set up the gas pipeline. It would be easier for Bangladesh to ask for the due wheeling charge from a company rather than from a nation like India.[43]

Bangladesh added some conditions for allowing gas pipeline to pass through its territory.[44] It wanted a trade corridor and power transit from Delhi: Bangladesh's access to the low-cost hydroelectricity of Nepal and Bhutan, using India's power grid, and a trade corridor to the Himalayan kingdom through Indian territory. The arrangement would also provide for measures to reduce the trade imbalance between India and Bangladesh.[45]

It is significant here that Bangladesh agreed to cooperate with India on a project on a gas pipeline in a *multilateral framework*. In this way, Bangladesh felt more comfortable and expected to reduce its relative gains concerns. Also, Bangladesh attempted to reduce her sensitivity by seeking to address an important bilateral problem with India, while opening up new vistas of possible cooperation with two other regional countries. Bangladesh thus attempted to establish trans-issue linkages as a price for cooperation with a vastly asymmetric neighbour. Clearly, no Bangladesh–India issues are purely economic; they are viewed through the prism of national security and strategic lenses. However, it may be noted here that the India–Bangladesh–Myanmar MoU has been in limbo ever since the Yangon meeting held in 2005. In fact, Bangladesh is itself trying to obtain gas from Myanmar, while India is trying to cut bilateral deals with that ASEAN country.

Let us now turn to the utilization of common water resources, an issue of crucial importance to Bangladesh in its relationship with India. Therefore, the issue demands detailed discussion in a separate section.

BANGLADESH–INDIA INTERNATIONAL WATERCOURSES: PROBLEMS OF COOPERATION

Water is a strategic resource which, unlike many other resources, flows across political boundaries, often leading to conflict over international watercourses between and among riparian states. As the stakes are high, inter-state cooperation for the management of common water resources is most desirable. One of the most intractable cases of conflict in hydropolitics is that of Bangladesh and India, plaguing their relationship for nearly four decades. The two countries share as many as 54 rivers (border and across boundaries), including some of the mightiest in the world such as the Ganges, the Brahmaputra, and the Meghna. The principal water problem, from Dhaka's point of view, is that India unilaterally extracts waters from these rivers upstream without any concern for the needs and rights of Bangladesh, and often to the detriment of the lower riparian state. India, on the other hand, contends that unless the Ganges water is augmented from other sources, the water needs of Bangladesh can scarcely be met in the long run. The common water resources have been so politicized that 'hydro-cooperation' between the two neighbours has so far been minimal. Conflict and cooperation have mostly been limited to water sharing, neglecting other issues such as flood control, navigation, hydro-power generation, water quality, and other environment-related issues. The water-sharing arrangement too has been limited to the case of the Ganges river. Repeated attempts on the part of Bangladesh to engage India in water talks concerning the other common rivers, particularly the Teesta, have not yet led to any significant breakthrough, to the frustration of the former. Recent reports about India's plan to divert water from its eastern Himalayan rivers to the country's water-stressed western and southern regions through inter-basin link canals have raised deep concerns in Bangladesh over the impact of this massive Indian project on the lower riparian state.

This section seeks answers to such questions as: What makes cooperation possible between a weaker lower riparian state and a more powerful upper riparian neighbour? What makes such cooperation mutually beneficial and sustainable? Before undertaking that, however, a few words may be relevant regarding the imperatives and potentials of water harnessing.

There are obvious imperatives for Bangladesh and India, as also for Nepal and Bhutan, to harness their water resources for sustainable socio-economic development. The countries are poor and their need for all-round development is extremely compelling. The sub-region of eastern South Asia is the most backward area in the region and one of the poorest in the world. There, the economy is predominantly agrarian, savings rate and investment flows are low, population growth rates are high, infrastructure is dismally inadequate, natural disasters are frequent, institutional capabilities to promote sustained socio-economic development are limited, and human resource development is very poor.[46] Even so, the sub-region is not altogether without resources. Among other things, it has a vast reservoir of water resources in the form of a multitude of rivers, including the Ganges, the Brahmaputra, the Meghna (GBM), and their tributaries, criss-crossing these countries from the Himalaya in the north to the Bay of Bengal in the south. It is estimated that the GBM area carries about 214 million hectometres of water annually to the sea, and, if properly harnessed, could generate about 162,600 MW of energy.[47] Most experts believe that the prosperity in the sub-region is dependent upon harnessing the great Himalayan rivers for irrigation, flood control, and energy.

There have been attempts over the past several years to harness the waters of the common rivers between India and Nepal, and Bangladesh and India. Water being a key resource, the Bangladesh–India relationship has been a classic case of hydropolitics in South Asia. A brief account of the history of the Bangladesh–India water dispute and cooperation is given in the following.

A Brief History of Bangladesh–India Water Conflict and Cooperation

The origin of the water dispute between Bangladesh (then East Pakistan) and India may be traced back to the Indian decision in 1953 to construct a barrage at Farakka, about 15 miles upstream from the Bangladesh–India border in Rajshahi, ostensibly to flush out silt from the Calcutta (now Kolkata) port. It was strongly felt in (East) Pakistan that the upstream diversion of the Ganges through a feeder canal into the Bhagirathi river would reduce the flow into Bangladesh through the Padma river.

Despite protests from Pakistan, the construction work on the Farakka barrage began in 1960–1 and was completed in 1975. The Bangladesh government agreed in April 1975 to the test run of the feeder canal for 41 days, but India continued to unilaterally withdraw water at Farakka, to the utter dismay of the lower riparian state, and to its detriment in terms of the negative impact on irrigation, flood control, navigation, employment, fisheries, salinity intrusion, and the ecology in the south-west of the country.[48] The dispute came to be known as the Farakka Barrage issue.

Bangladesh, having been unsuccessful in convincing India about the severity of the problem, raised the issue in 1976 in several international forums, including the United Nations. However, the two countries signed a five-year bilateral agreement in 1977 on sharing the Ganges waters to the satisfaction of both the parties. For Bangladesh, a guarantee clause of 80 per cent of the minimum flow in the lean season (January–May) to the lower riparian was important.[49] India would not renew the agreement in 1982; instead the two co-riparians signed that very year a three-year MoU, followed by a similar MoU in 1985.

Augmentation of the Ganges flow in the dry season, as well as the formula to share this became the bone of contention and the principal focus of negotiation between the two countries. India's link-canal proposal to divert water from the Brahmaputra river in the east to a point above Farakka through Bangladesh territory and Bangladesh's proposal for water reservoirs in upstream India and Nepal did not lead to any settlement of the dispute. As there was no bilateral understanding between the two countries on sharing of the Ganges waters, India continued its unilateral withdrawal of the river flow from 1988 until a 30-year treaty was signed with Bangladesh in 1996.

The 1996 Ganges Water Treaty

The Treaty on Sharing of the Ganges Waters at Farakka was signed by an Indian government that was considered relatively more liberal towards South Asia and by a government of Bangladesh that was viewed in New Delhi as more friendly towards the regional giant.[50]

The sharing of the Ganges waters at Farakka through 10-day periods from 1 January to the 31 May every year will be with reference to an agreed upon formula given in Annex I of the treaty, and an indicative schedule citing the implications of the sharing arrangement under Annex I is in Annex II. Annex I assures both sides of half the flow when the availability is 70,000 cusecs or less; 35,000 cusecs to Bangladesh and the balance to India when availability is between 70,000 and 75,000 cusecs; and 40,000 cusecs to India and the balance to Bangladesh when the availability is 75,000 cusecs or more. This formulation is subject to the condition that both parties are guaranteed 35,000 cusecs in alternate 10-day periods between 1 March and 10 May. The indicative schedule is based on the calculation of 40 years (1949–88) 10-day period average availability of water at Farakka. In the event that the flow at Farakka falls below 50,000 cusecs in any 10-day period, the two governments will enter into immediate consultations to make adjustments on an emergency basis, in accordance with the principles of equity, fair play, and no harm to either party.[51]

The Treaty has set up a Joint Committee consisting of representatives nominated by the two governments in equal numbers. The Joint Committee set up teams at Farakka and Hardinge Bridge to observe and record at Farakka the daily flows below Farakka Barrage, in the

Feeder Canal, and at the Navigation Lock, as well as at the Hardinge Bridge. The Joint Committee submits to the two governments the data collected and also submits an annual report. Any difference or dispute, if not resolved by the Joint Committee, is to be referred to the Indo-Bangladesh Joint Rivers Commission set up in 1972. If the difference or dispute still remains unresolved, it shall be referred to the two governments, which shall meet urgently at the appropriate level to resolve it by mutual discussion.[52]

The treaty has several positive aspects. One, the unhindered assured minimum Ganges flow will now serve the water needs of south-western parts of Bangladesh. Two, as it is a long-term treaty assuring a reasonable quantum of water for the lower riparian state, development partners of Bangladesh are now more agreeable to finance various water-related projects within the country, including the multipurpose mega project, the Ganges Barrage in south-west Bangladesh. Three, following the signing of the treaty, Bangladesh–India relations witnessed tangible improvement. Fourth, the contracting parties declare adherence to the principles of equity, fairness, and no harm to either party with regard to harnessing common rivers.[53]

However, there are certain shortcomings in the treaty. One, the treaty is essentially only about sharing the waters, although there are vague references in the preamble to the need for a solution to the long-term problem of augmenting the Ganges flows and to the optimum utilization of the water resources of the other international rivers in the areas of flood management, irrigation, river basin development, and generation of hydro-power for the mutual benefit of the peoples of both the countries. Two, significantly, the quantum of waters agreed to be released by India to Bangladesh will be at Farakka. On Bangladesh's part, this is a huge investment in trusting India, as 'every effort would be made by the upper riparian to protect flows of water at Farakka as in the 40-years average availability as mentioned above'.[54] However, in the very first year of the treaty, tensions ran high between the two governments following New Delhi's failure to maintain the quantum of water at Farakka. This has happened in some later years too. Third, in the event of low flows, the interim releases of waters by India, pending an agreement through emergency consultation, remain unstated.[55] This might periodically render the treaty dysfunctional. The Ganges Treaty has also not been followed up in terms of addressing the disputes concerning several other common rivers between Bangladesh and India.

Indeed, Bangladesh and India had no interaction on water issues after 2005, as the overall relationship had actually stagnated over the last half a decade. However, with the Congress-led government in New Delhi and the AL-led government in Dhaka, the two countries are likely to take their relations to a new height. In a Joint Statement in New Delhi by the foreign ministers of Bangladesh and India on 10 September 2009, both sides recognized the need to expedite negotiations with a view to finalizing an agreement for sharing of the waters of the Teesta river. Towards this end, they agreed to mandate their respective foreign offices to meet and discuss the technical and other parameters of this issue. They agreed to immediately commence joint hydrological observations on the river by a team comprising experts from Bangladesh and India in order to prepare a draft on water availability and other related issues. In March 2010, Delhi and Dhaka exchanged draft agreements on sharing of the Teesta waters during the Bangladesh Prime Minister's visit to India, and an agreement is expected to be signed in a year.[56]

However, the Tipaimukh dam, a new but critical and controversial issue in Bangladesh–India relations, has been bedevilling the already sour ties between the two countries since 2008. The controversy surrounds India's proposed Tipaimukh dam project over the Barak River in Manipur in the north-east. The Barak flows westwards into Bangladesh and bifurcates into the Surma and Kushiyara rivers that merge with the Meghna river system in the downstream country. The Tipaimukh dam is a $1.7 billion project that aims to generate 1,500 MW of hydroelectric power. However, experts in Bangladesh and India tend to disagree on the purpose and impact on both the countries. A perception prevails in Bangladesh that India is carrying out the project without any prior consultation with the lower riparian country that is likely to bear the brunt of the adverse impact of the dam.

Bangladesh sent a parliamentary delegation to India in late July 2009 in order to convey Dhaka's concerns and obtain necessary information from discussions with concerned political quarters in New Delhi as also from a visit to the dam site in Manipur. The delegation, boycotted by members of the principal opposition party, Bangladesh National Party (BNP), returned to Dhaka 'satisfied' with the assurances given by the Indian authorities. A delegation member said, 'During meetings, Indian ministers told us that India would not do anything harming the interests of Bangladesh. We have more than what we wanted in respect of information from the Indian side.'[57] Jairam Ramesh, Indian minister of state for environment and forests, said that India should address Bangladesh's concerns over the proposed Tipaimukh dam on the Barak river.[58]

Foreign Minister Dipu Moni of Bangladesh, during her visit to India from 8 September to 10 September 2009, also received similar assurances from her hosts. She even welcomed India's assurance of not taking steps that would adversely impact Bangladesh.[59] There is, however, a widespread perception in Bangladesh that India, in the first place, has violated the provisions of the 1996 Ganges Water Sharing Treaty in that it has not consulted or informed Dhaka of the Tipaimukh dam project before embarking on it, that India is still not providing sufficient information on the project, and that India's current assurances are not substantive, lacking costly signalling meant to reassure Bangladesh.[60]

It is now relevant to highlight the problems hindering cooperation between the two immediate neighbours.

Impediments to Cooperation between Bangladesh and India

There are a number of challenges militating against cooperation between Bangladesh and India with regard to their common rivers. Let us first look at the geographical setting of the common rivers.

Geographical Setting of the Common Rivers

Originating in the Himalaya, either in India or in China, there are as may as 54 rivers that primarily flow southwards through Bangladesh before emptying themselves into the Bay of Bengal. As such, India, with its 'tyranny of geography', is the upper riparian state vis-à-vis Bangladesh in the west, north, and east. Withdrawal of water by India in the upper reaches and the construction of various water-related projects make Bangladesh helplessly dependent on the giant upper riparian. Bangladesh is the largest active delta, some describing it as 'the best attended swamp', in the world. It is the lowermost riparian in the GBM systems, with all the attendant disadvantages. There is an interesting seasonal variation in Bangladesh in terms of water availability. In the low-lying alluvial flood plain that Bangladesh is, water is in plenty during the monsoon while it is scarce in the dry season.

Another important factor relates to the extent of the drainage basins that each of the co-riparian nations share. The GBM ecological region stretches across Bangladesh, Bhutan, Tibet region of China, India, and Nepal. The total drainage is about 1.75 million sq. km, of which 62.90 per cent lies in India, 19.11 per cent in Tibet, 8.02 per cent in Nepal, 7.39 per cent in Bangladesh, and 2.58 per cent in Bhutan.[61] Such a physical configuration at times leads to the espousal of certain kinds of water use doctrine, water rights/claims, basin-wide development, or integrated basin management. I elaborate on this in the following.

The Location and Role Perception Factor

South Asia is Indo-centric in terms of location and power potential. India is not only the most powerful but also by far the largest and centrally located in the heart of the region and sharing land or maritime borders with all the regional neighbours. The six other regional countries are located on its periphery, none sharing borders with one another except India. This often leads to certain kind of world-view and role perception. Driven by such locational advantage, buttressed by size and power, India has propounded its regional security doctrine, called the 'Indira Doctrine',[62] claiming power status and leadership in South Asian affairs. India is also known for its preference for bilateralism in its dealings with regional neighbours, and is usually averse to the involvement of extra-regional powers and/or donor agencies. Such attitudes and policies also have a bearing on issues of water harnessing with neighbouring countries.

Water Policy

The international river water policy of a nation is based on its approach towards water rights, water needs and water use, power status, riparian position, status of relationship with co-riparian states, national legal system, sensitivity to the international comity of nations and to the co-riparians' needs, etc.

Initial claims to water in negotiations are often justified in terms of one of several legal doctrines. These doctrines seek to formulate a general approach to division of the scarce resource of river water. There are five such theories or legal doctrines: (i) the theory of absolute territorial sovereignty; (ii) the territorial integrity theory or natural water flow theory; (iii) the theory of prior appropriation; (iv) the theory of community interest; (v) the theory of equitable utilization of inter-state river waters, or the equitable apportionment theory.[63]

The *territorial sovereignty theory* is also known as the Harmon doctrine as it was propounded by US Attorney General Judson Harmon in 1896 in connection with the controversy between USA and Mexico over the use of the waters of River Rio Grande. This theory holds that riparian states have exclusive or sovereign right over the waters flowing through their territory. According to this doctrine, a riparian state can do what it pleases with its waters without regard to its effect on co-riparian states and no riparian state has a right to demand the continuing flow of water from other states. The *natural water flow theory* holds that every lower riparian is entitled to the natural flow of the river without any interference from the upper riparian. According to the *theory of prior appropriation*, the first user who puts the water to beneficial use establishes a prior right, and subsequent users can only appropriate what is left by the first user. This doctrine allocates property rights to water on the basis of historical use. Under the *community of interest theory*, the entire basin is regarded as a single economic unit. It cuts across all state boundaries and the water can be utilized to the maximum benefit of all in an integrated manner. The *theory of equitable utilization of inter-state river water* stresses that there should be equitable utilization of common rivers by mutual agreement among the parties concerned. The equitable utilization and community of interest theories are closely interrelated.[64]

India, in theory at least, seems to uphold the theories of absolute territorial sovereignty and prior appropriation, resulting in the establishment of her water rights and benefits on the basis of numerous water projects and denying these to downstream Bangladesh. India views the GBM systems as one single unit and prefers harnessing the resources and dispute settlement management in an integrated manner. India once even held the view that the Ganges was not an international river in the first place, as most of its drainage basin falls within its territory. Bangladesh has often accused India of procrastination in negotiation, negotiating from a position of strength and resorting to pressure tactics, attempting to link water with non-water issues and making the water issue a political instrument. And also of offering no financial or technical/technological help, and not sharing her vast experience in the water sector, even withholding information in the field of flood forecasting and several other meteorological aspects, and preference for bilateralism as opposed to multilateralism, even in respect of international rivers flowing through more than two countries. However, the long-term Ganges Water Treaty of 1996 with Bangladesh amply demonstrates that

India is politically able to alter its doctrinal orthodoxy and recognize the water rights and needs of the lower riparian state.

Bangladesh, for obvious reasons, used to adhere to the theory of natural water flow or the territorial integrity theory. Having signed the Convention on the Non-Navigational Uses of International Water Courses of 1997, Bangladesh now officially upholds the theory of equitable utilization of international river water. Bangladesh does not view the GBM systems as one single unit, but rather approaches these as three separate units of river systems. Bangladesh prefers multilateralism in water talks in order to offset the adverse effects of bilateralism.

Lack of Follow-Up in Water Negotiations

The 1996 treaty includes only one river: the Ganges. The hope in Bangladesh was that this was only the beginning of a process of continuing cooperation on the water issue, leading to agreements on several other common rivers like the Teesta, Dharla, and Muhuri. The treaty actually bears indications in this direction and also established the principle of equity, fair play, and no harm to either party. Bangladesh is now somewhat disappointed by India's protracted manner of negotiations over these rivers. Moreover, it is horrified by India's renewed river-linking project because of the disaster it is thought to be causing to the lower riparian. Some details on India's proposed mega plan will be most relevant here.

India's River-Linking Project

India's river-networking venture has been designed to connect 38 rivers through 30 links, 9,000 km of canals, 74 reservoirs, and several embankments by 2016 to store water during monsoons to create irrigation potential for an additional 150 million hectares of land. The project will in fact divert water from the Brahmaputra towards the Ganges, thereafter driving it into the Mahanadi and the Godavari. The Godavari will be linked to the Krishna, and then to the Pennar and Cauvery. The Narmada will flow into the Tapi and the Yamuna into the Sabarmati. The interlinking proposals essentially comprise three links:[65]

1. Southern Water Grid: interlinking the Mahanadi, Godavari, Pennar, Cauvery, and Vaigai in peninsular India;

2. interlinking the Brahmaputra with the Ganges, Subernarekha, and Mahanadi; and

3. interlinking the Gandak, Ghaghara, Sarda, and Yamuna through Rajasthan to Sabarmati.

Besides these three major links, a number of minor links will be made under the peninsular and Himalayan components. It is proposed that, at the final stage, the Himalayan links from the Brahmaputra to the Ganges would be integrated with the peninsular link from the Mahanadi to the Vaigai. A number of large dams and canal systems are proposed to be constructed to store and transfer the flood water of the surplus rivers. In order to transfer the surplus waters of the Mahanadi and Godavari, dams are proposed to be constructed at Manibhadra on Mahanadi, and Inchampali and Polavaram on Godavari. Similarly, dams on the Manas and Sankosh rivers in Brahmaputra basin (Bhutan) and Kosi, Gandak, Ghaghara, and Sarda in the Ganges basin (Nepal) are proposed to store and transfer water to water-deficit areas.[66]

This massive inter-basin transfer is to be completed by 2016. The Indian Supreme Court, in an extraordinary observation in 2002, had suggested that the government should complete the project in a time-bound manner (against the original estimates of 45 years to complete it) within 10 years, starting from 2007. The Brahmaputra diversion plan is a mega-project worth about US$ 40–125 billion and it will take 14 years to implement. The World Bank is likely to collaborate on the project. Up to one-third of the flow of the Brahmaputra and other rivers could be diverted to southern Indian rivers to provide 173 billion cubic metres of water a year, providing millions of people in the states of Uttar Pradesh and Karnataka with more reliable drinking and irrigation water.[67]

The proposed river-linking project in the upstream has significant impacts on the socio-economic, ecological, environmental, biological, and eventually morphological characteristics of the river systems in Bangladesh. The negative impacts of the river-linking project on Bangladesh depend upon three principal issues: the areas from where the water is transferred, the amount of water that will be transferred, and the time of year when the water will be transferred. Some of the adverse impacts are:[68]

1. The river-linking project would have a disastrous impact on the economy of Bangladesh. In the long run, it will also lead to the internal displacement of millions of its citizens.

2. The implementation of such a project would most certainly lead to more severe flooding during the monsoons and worse droughts in the lean season.

3. It would increase salinity across the country and cause a sharp fall in sweet water levels. Eventually, the largest mangrove forest in the world, the Sundarbans, might be destroyed.

4. The natural flow of the Ganges to Bangladesh was barred by the Farakka Barrage, and if the Brahmaputra waters are diverted with the river-linking project, the Yamuna river in Bangladesh will lose flows.

5. Desertification of a substantial part of Bangladesh will intensify, many rivers have lost their navigability, and salt water is intruding into farming areas.

6. The dependence of over 80 per cent of Bangladesh's 20 million rice growers on water flowing from the two international rivers has already made it difficult for farmers to subsist and survive. The river-linking project would worsen their condition by affecting the water flow.

7. India's project would endanger the agro-based life of about 100 million people in Bangladesh by impacting their livelihood negatively and drastically.

8. The water quality is progressively deteriorating due to increased withdrawals for various uses, leaving insufficient flows for dilution of pollutants during lean periods.

9. The saline content in the surface and groundwater would increase due to distress use since freshwater will be less available. Groundwater levels would be adversely affected, resulting in a lack of freshwater due to diversion of waters upstream, which will increase excessive use of groundwater for irrigation. This may aggravate arsenic contamination in Bangladesh.

10. Depletion of freshwater fish and disruption of waterways are the other adverse consequences feared.

11. The long-term effects of the proposed project will be drastic changes in the ecology and the hydraulic characteristics of rivers in Bangladesh.

12. If the project is implemented, the Brahmaputra's flow will be reduced to 40,000 cusecs from its normal flow of 1,40,000 cusecs, while the combined flow of the Padma and Brahmaputra at the Maowa point will also be reduced to 30,000–40,000 cusecs from the normal flow of 2,00,000 cusecs.

13. Finally, there will be drastic reductions in the flows of rivers Dharla, Dudkumar, Teesta, and Mahananda even during normal monsoon. Flows in Madhumati, Nabaganga, Ichhamati, Mathabhanga, Kapotakhya, and Betna will also fall substantially.

The Mistrust Factor

What follows from the aforementioned is a bilateral relationship between Bangladesh and India that may be characterized by lack of mutual confidence and will to cooperate with each other. The upper riparian tends to become insensitive and, occasionally, even overbearing towards the lower riparian, while the latter develops a sense of helplessness and frustration. Consequently, the need to view the water issue as a shared problem is either overlooked or neglected.

Lack of Funds

Water development requires huge financial resources that countries like Bangladesh and India, particularly the former, often find difficult to muster. Given the differences in the will and policy between the two co-riparians, which prevent a joint approach between them for funding, the donors are often found to be reluctant to make any financial commitments.

Let us now turn to examine the situation in North America with regard to shared water resources management between USA and Mexico, and USA and Canada.

TRANSBOUNDARY WATER MANAGEMENT IN NORTH AMERICA: EXPERIENCES OF USA, CANADA, AND MEXICO

The US–Mexico Transboundary Water Management: Colorado–Rio Grande Rivers

The US–Mexico transboundary waters include the Colorado, Rio Grande, and Tijuana rivers. Beginning in the state of Colorado in USA, the Rio Grande flows through New Mexico, marks the international border between Texas and Mexico, and empties into the Gulf of Mexico. It is the fifth longest river in North America, with two interconnected basins: the Colorado–Tijuana basin in the west and the Rio Grande–Rio Bravo basin in the east. It serves as the Texas–Mexico border region's principal source of water.[69]

The US–Mexico water dispute began in 1896 over international water rights concerning the Rio Grande. USA wanted to use the water from the river for irrigation, and this encountered opposition from its southern neighbour. The American attorney general at that time, Judson Harmon, declared his country's position on the use of international waters, which came to be known as the 'Harmon Doctrine'. He rejected 'a servitude which makes the lower country dominant and subjects the upper country to the burden of arresting its development and denying to its inhabitants the use of a provision which nature has supplied entirely within its own territory'. According to this doctrine, 'the fundamental principle of international law is the absolute sovereignty of every nation, as against all others, within its own territory'.[70]

However, the US Supreme Court struck down the Harmon Doctrine in a ruling on *Wyoming vs Colorado* in 1922. Eventually, the two countries signed a water treaty in 1944, under which USA conceded water rights to Mexico.

The US–Mexico Water Treaty of 1944

The Water Treaty of 1944 began as a treaty of freshwater allocation, eventually evolving into a system concerned with issues of water quality, water shortages, and sanitation.

The treaty governs and divides the flow of water in the Rio Grande Basin from the Rio Grande and certain tributaries in USA and Mexico. It provides the framework for sharing between the two countries the water resources of the Rio Grande–Rio Bravo, from Fort Quitman to the Gulf of Mexico, and the waters of the Colorado river. According to the treaty provisions, Mexico obtained rights to 1.5 million acre-feet of Colorado river water per year. During periods of extraordinary drought, the treaty provides for reductions in that allocation proportional to reductions in the US consumptive use. In exchange for 1.5 million acre-feet of the Colorado river water, USA is entitled to an annual average minimum of 350,000 acre-feet from treaty tributaries before Mexico's entitlement to any water. Under the treaty, USA is credited one-third of water, which reaches the main channel of the Rio Grande from the Conchos, San Diego, San Rodrigo, Escondido, and Salado rivers, and from the Las Vacas Arroyo. Mexico receives two-thirds of that water.[71] As the treaty provides for emergency deliveries of water, USA has on several occasions made five-year 'emergency' deliveries of the Colorado river waters to Tijuana, Mexico.

Institutional Framework: Cooperation and Dispute Settlement

Article 2 of the 1944 Water Treaty between USA and Mexico establishes the International Boundary and Water Commission (IBWC), creating an institutional mechanism for implementation of the treaty. Indeed, the treaty authorized the IBWC for the application of its terms, the regulation and exercise of the rights and obligations assumed by the two governments, and dispute settlement mechanism. The IBWC is made up of one 'engineer commissioner' representing each government, who also leads the country Section. The Sections may include two additional principal engineers, a legal adviser, and a secretary designated by each government. The US Section reports to the Department of State of the US government. The commissioners and the core staff are accorded diplomatic status and immunity.[72]

Article 25 of the treaty provides for a 'minute' process through which the terms and conditions can be altered. Decisions of the IBWC, expressed in minutes and signed by the commissioners from both countries and not disputed by either of the governments within 30 days, have the force of treaty. It is through this process that the two governments have negotiated dispute resolutions and addressed issues on water management that were not anticipated when the treaty was signed. Article 24 contains the general powers of the IBWC relating to compliance system mechanisms.

The IBWC has the power to invoke the national courts to support the enforcement of the treaty provisions, and to settle disputes subject to the approval of the two governments. The IBWC is required to furnish information to the parties but not the public. The flexibility of this procedure has allowed the IBWC to respond to changing conditions without the need to re-negotiate the treaty. This evolving practice is one of the strengths of the US–Mexico water treaty of 1944.[73]

US–Canada Common Water Resources Management

The Boundary Waters Treaty of 1909

USA and Canada share one of the longest boundaries in the world: about 4,000 miles along the 49th Parallel and about 1,500 miles between Alaska and the Canadian Northwest Territories. About 150 lakes and rivers are transcended by this boundary. These include the Great Lakes, which have been vital to the economy of North America since their discovery in 1618 by Etiene Brule. The Great Lakes—

Superior, Michigan, Huron, Erie, and Ontario—are the largest group of freshwater lakes in the world, with a total surface area of 245,000 sq. km and containing about 20 per cent of the world's surface fresh water. Eight US states and one Canadian province (Ontario) border these vast water bodies.[74]

Prior to 1905, only ad hoc commissions had been established to deal with issues relating to the shared water resources. Both USA and Canada felt it necessary to establish a more permanent body for the joint management of their shared water resources. Negotiations commenced from 1905 between them, culminating in the signing of the Boundary Waters Treaty in 1909. Understandably, the negotiations were not easy as the oft-divergent views and interests of the stronger lower riparian and the weaker upper riparian had to be accommodated.[75]

Treaty Provisions   Some relevant treaty provisions are:[76]

1. There should be no obstructions or diversions of boundary waters affecting the natural level or flow without the approval of the International Joint Commission (IJC), or special agreements between the contracting parties.

2. Parties may undertake governmental works that do not materially affect water levels and flows.

3. There should be no works on transboundary waters that raise levels upstream on other side of the boundary without the approval of the IJC or special agreements between the governments.

4. The IJC is obligated to protect the interests on each side of the boundary from actions on the other side.

5. The boundary and transboundary waters are not to be polluted on either side to the injury of health or property on the other side.

The 1909 Water Treaty between USA and Canada is considered to be a model of the success of cooperation between riparian states on water resources management. This is largely the result of the institutional mechanism the two parties have so prudently put in place. Let us briefly examine it.

IJC   The treaty has established IJC with extensive power and an elaborate structure, with a view to implementing its provisions, preventing disputes over boundary waters, and providing a mechanism for dispute settlement.[77]

1. The IJC has six commissioners, three appointed by the government of each side.

2. They declare faithfulness to the treaty and impartiality in their actions.

3. The IJC provides an opportunity for all parties to be heard.

4. It operates without instructions from governments.

5. The IJC has a balanced membership: three commissioners from each country, and equality on its boards and working groups, the commissioners serving in a personal and professional capacity.

6. There is a system of joint fact-finding; the IJC independently regulates the operation of structures in boundary/transboundary waters.

7. It addresses disputes at the request of the governments concerned.

8. It provides periodic alerts to the two governments on transboundary air and water issues.

9. It acts as 'quasi-judicial' authority: any project likely to affect the 'natural' flow of the boundary waters has to be approved by both governments.

10. It has the mandate to arbitrate agreements.

11. It also has investigative authority: it may have development projects submitted for approval, or be asked to investigate an issue by one or another of the governments.

12. The commissioners act independently and not as representatives of their respective governments.

As stated, experts view the US–Canada IJC as a model of international cooperation. The IJC has indeed evolved more effectively than the IBWC (US–Mexico) over time and truly functions as a water council.

The 1961 Columbia River Treaty: Cooperative Synergism

The Columbia river is the fourth largest river in North America, originating in Canada's British Columbia and flowing 1,214 miles to the Pacific Ocean near Astoria, Oregon of USA. Its basin spans 260,000 sq miles, about the size of France, of which only 15 per cent lies in Canada. The Columbia is the most dammed river in North America, with nearly 250 reservoirs and 150 hydroelectric projects in the basin.[78]

USA and Canada signed the Columbia River Treaty in 1961. The International Joint Commission played a key role in it by conducting the necessary engineering and technical investigations and by formulating a set of principles for determining the likely benefits and their apportionment between the contracting parties. Notable here is the application of the principle of equal apportionment in terms of cost and benefit sharing. The Columbia Treaty provides for the establishment of a Permanent Engineering Board consisting of two members from each side. Differences between parties are to be settled by the International Joint Commission, and if they persist, by resort to arbitration or by reference to the International Court of Justice. The treaty stipulates that, barring specified diversions, neither side may divert the Columbia's waters for a period of 60 years without the consent of the other. The principle of downstream benefit evolved by the US–Canada International Joint Commission in 1959 and incorporated in the Columbia River Treaty in 1961 is a valuable addition to evolving water law.[79]

Under the Columbia River Treaty, in return for building power-generating and flood-controlling dams along the Columbia river, the Province of British Columbia of Canada is to receive 'downstream benefits': a portion of the power generated by American power plants below the international border. British Columbia[80] sold this power to a US utilities group over a 30-year period for revenues exceeding $250 million. As the terms expired in the 1990s, the Province maintains sales revenues for the remaining 30 years of the treaty.[81]

This is how the co-riparian states in North America are sharing and managing their common water resources. No relations between sovereign entities are without occasional problems, but given the good neighbourly attitude and policy, appropriate channels of communication, and dispute settlement mechanisms, these countries have been able to forge extensive, mutually beneficial networks of cooperation in relation to their common international watercourses.

Prospects for Cooperation between Bangladesh and India

The reasons for limited cooperation between Bangladesh and India are clear from the preceding exposition. The factors bearing on Bangladesh's perceptions and policies about India have been thoroughly examined. It has been argued how Bangladesh's relative gains and cumulation sensitivities and lock-in fears, and lack of trust given India's lack of reciprocity and reassurance have impeded cooperation between the two immediate neighbours, particularly in the areas of transit, gas export, and water resources.

A widespread perception in Bangladesh is that India, being the upper riparian, drives a hard bargain and obtains disproportionately greater benefits from water agreements with lower riparian Bangladesh. Bangladesh's cumulation sensitivity manifests itself in the view that India manages to cut such water deals with Bangladesh in order to be in a position to impact upon the future and influence other outcomes. There is a lurking fear that India is out to get Bangladesh's limited but vital natural resources for a meagre economic package. This explains Bangladesh's attempts to convert the issue of the gas pipeline into a multilateral issue by seeking trade and power corridors with Bhutan and Nepal.

Bangladesh is bounded by India in three sides, with the result that it is virtually India-locked. The insurgency-affected Indian territory lying east of Bangladesh is larger than Bangladesh itself. As such, Bangladesh shows a tremendous fear of a lock-in effect from any proposal of transit or corridor facilities through its territory to connect the Indian mainland with its distant, isolated areas. Bangladesh's concerns relate to its perceived loss of autonomy and constraints on its exit options in terms of the manoeuvrability of its foreign and security policy. Here, Bangladesh also entertains a sense of physical vulnerability in the event of a war between India and China. Similar lock-in sensitivities relate to the export of gas from and through Bangladesh to India.

From Bangladesh's point of view, the question of trust is absolutely crucial in its relationship with India. As viewed from Dhaka, the history of the relationship between the two countries does not seem to inspire confidence in New Delhi's reliability. In April 1975, Bangladesh had agreed to allow India to test-run the feeder canal at Farakka for only 41 days. To its utter dismay, New Delhi continued with the withdrawal of waters right up to the time when an agreement was reached in November 1977. The agreement on the Tin Bigha corridor was only partially implemented by India after a lapse of 18 long years, while Bangladesh honoured its international obligations soon after the signature of the border agreement in 1974. Even after the historic Ganges Water Sharing Treaty was signed in 1996, India has on several occasions failed to release the stipulated quantum of water downstream to Bangladesh. The elements of non-reciprocity in terms of commitment to international obligations on India's part are glaring. The mistrust factor is compounded by India's persistent tactics of procrastination in negotiating the various bilateral issues with Bangladesh. All this stands in the way of forging closer, cordial, and extensive cooperation between the two countries.

In Bangladesh there is a glaring perception that India is doing very little to reassure it. India appears totally unconcerned about taking any steps to dispel Bangladesh's concerns, suspicion, and perceptions about it and the latter sees no signs of any costly signalling coming from India in the form of unilateral, credible concessions, cooperative gestures, and commitments on any vital bilateral issue with a view to establishing trust with it.

Besides the policy-induced factors, Bangladesh–India relations are also affected by the structural givens in terms of the tyranny of geography and the asymmetry in extant and potential power. Therefore, even socio-economic interactions between the two neighbours can at times be scarcely separated from their politico-security issues. However, while the structural constants cannot be wished away, attitudes and policies may be modulated and adjusted in spatial and temporal terms.

It was implied in the argument in the foregoing discussion that there are compelling developmental imperatives, as also vast potential, for Bangladesh and India to enhance and intensify cooperation and graduate their relationship to a much higher level in terms of the extent and nature of ties in bilateral and multilateral contexts. Such cooperation may take place in the field of sharing and harnessing their common international watercourses. Indeed, win-win sharing/harnessing arrangements are essential and possible between Bangladesh and India. The challenge lies, however, in effecting a shift from a conflict mindset to a cooperative attitude.

In the light of the best practices, as seen in North America, one could highlight some of the preconditions for successful cooperation between Bangladesh and India in relation to their common rivers. These are:

1. Strengthening the position of the weaker party/riparian (knowledge of basin characteristics, astute diplomacy, and negotiations) and the will of the upper and stronger riparian states to cooperate and not create scenarios of prior appropriation.

2. Sensitivity to each other's needs, rights, and urgency. Avoiding unilateralist proclivity in favour of international cooperation.

3. Reciprocity in benefits from cooperation.

4. Technical/technological and financial assistance by the upper/richer riparian.

5. Measures to de-politicize issues and play down the disparity in power between parties.

6. Institutionalization of cooperation efforts; enduring agreements.

7. Setting up river commission(s) with an extensive mandate and elaborate structures/mechanisms for cooperation.

8. Efficient dispute settlement mechanisms, including recourse to arbitration and the International Court of Justice.

9. Independence of the commissioners (not government representatives, rather in a personal and professional capacity, impartial, and de-politicized).

10. Adherence to the principles of equity, fairness, and no harm to either party.

The obstacles in the way of an ever-expanding and deepening relationship between Bangladesh and India are indeed many but these are not insurmountable over time. At the risk of sounding normative, it may be said that a habit of cooperation between the two neighbouring countries needs to be patiently and carefully cultivated, leading to a culture of cooperation. The alternative to cooperation should be yet greater cooperation.

Notes

1. John C. Matthews III, 'Current Gains and Future Outcomes: When Cumulative Relative Gains Matter', *International Security*, 21(1), Summer 1996, pp. 112–46, especially p. 114.

2. Ibid.

3. Joseph Grieco, 'The Relative Gains Problem for International Cooperation', *American Political Science Review*, 87(3), September 1993, pp. 729–35, especially p. 734.

4. Matthews, 'Current Gains and Future Outcomes', p. 113.

5. Ibid.

6. Ibid., p. 115.

7. Ibid., p. 122.

8. Peter Liberman, 'Trading with the Enemy: Security and Relative Economic Gains', *International Security*, 21(1), Summer 1996, pp. 147–75, especially p. 148.

9. Ibid., pp. 149, 151, 153.

10. Andrew Kydd, 'Trust, Reassurance, and Cooperation', *International Organization*, 54(2), Spring 2000, pp. 325–57, especially p. 325.

11. Andrew Kydd has given examples of how to reassure your opponent or adversary. He writes: 'Soviet "new thinkers", most importantly Mikhail Gorbachev himself, used a strategy of reassuring concessions such as the 1987 Intermediate-range Nuclear Forces (INF) Treaty, the 1988 withdrawal from

Afghanistan, and the 1989 non-interference in the Eastern European revolutions to radically change Western perceptions of Soviet motivations and build trust', Ibid., p. 327.

12. Ibid, p. 326. Actually, Glaser introduced the costly signalling concept in the context of reassurance without developing it much. See Charles L. Glaser, 'Realists as Optimists: Cooperation as Self-Help', *International Security*, 19(3), 1994: 50–90.

13. See, for details, George W. Downs and David M. Rocke, *Tacit Bargaining, Arms Races, and Arms Control* (Ann Arbor: University of Michigan Press, 1990); Joel Watson, 'Starting Small and Renegotiation', *Journal of Economic Theory*, 85(1), 1999, pp. 52–90.

14. Kydd, 'Trust, Reassurance, and Cooperation', p. 333.

15. Dale C. Copeland, 'Economic Interdependence and War: A Theory of Trade Expectations', *International Security*, 20(4), Spring 1996, pp. 5–41, especially p. 6.

16. See, for details, ibid., pp. 5–51; Liberman, 'Trading with the Enemy'; and E. Sridharan, 'Economic Cooperation and Security Spill-Overs: The Case of India and Pakistan', in Michael Krepon and Chris Gagne (eds), *Economic Confidence-Building and Regional Security*, Report No. 36 (Washington DC: The Henry L. Stimson Center, 2000), pp. 321–40, especially p. 92.

17. For details of the doctrine, see Bhabani Sengupta, 'The Indira Doctrine', *India Today*, 31 August 1983; Bhabani Sengupta, 'Maldives Confirms India's Lead Role in South Asia', *Dhaka Courier*, 18–23 November 1988; Sunanda K. Dutta-Ray, 'The Rajiv Doctrine: India as Mini Superpower?', *Statesman*, 13 November 1988. For the Bangladesh perspective, see Iftekharuzzaman, 'The Indira Doctrine: Relevance for Bangladesh', in M.G. Kabir and Shaukat Hassan (eds), *Issues and Challenges Facing Bangladesh Foreign Policy* (Dhaka: Bangladesh Society of International Studies, 1989), pp. 18–43. Also see, Mohammad Humayun Kabir, 'Development, Regional Co-operation and Security in South Asia', in Mukesh Kumar Kayathwal (ed.), *Security and Foreign Policy in South Asia* (Jaipur: Pointer Publishers, 1999), pp. 1–9; Iftekharuzzaman and Mohammad Humayun Kabir, 'The Indo-Sri Lanka Peace Accord: An Assessment', *BIISS Journal*, 8(4), October 1987; Iftekharuzzaman, 'Maldives: Small, Beautiful and Vulnerable', *Dhaka Courier*, 11–17 November 1988.

18. There are as many as 192 enclaves along Bangladesh's north-western border with India. Of the total, Bangladesh has 119 enclaves inside India and India has 73 in Bangladesh. There were also unresolved boundary issues, such as boundary demarcation. On 14 May 1974, an agreement concerning the demarcation of the land boundary and related matters was signed in New Delhi by Prime Minister Bangabandhu Sheikh Mujibur Rahman of Bangladesh and Prime Minister Indira Gandhi of India. This came to be known as the Mujib–Indira Border Agreement of 1974. Under the Agreement, while the Berubari union would remain in India, Bangladesh would retain the Dahagram and Angarpota enclaves. To connect Dahagram with Panbari Mouza of Patgram

in mainland Bangladesh, India would lease *in perpetuity* a land corridor measuring 178 metres by 85 metres (about three *bigha*s or nearly an acre; and the passage came to be known as 'Tin Bigha' Corridor) to Bangladesh. The Bangladesh parliament ratified the agreement soon after it was signed and the government of Bangladesh handed over the relevant part of South Berubari to India in 1974. However, the handing over of the Tin Bigha corridor was delayed as a consequence of long constitutional and legal wrangles in India. India's inability/unwillingness to honour the obligations of an international undertaking generated enormous distrust and frustration in Bangladesh. The situation continued for about two decades until Bangladesh had to sign another protocol with India on 26 March 1992 relating to security, control, and use of the corridor for movement of people and vehicular traffic between the enclave and mainland of Bangladesh. Two provisions in the new protocol fundamentally altered the exchange status of the passage. India now would not hand over the corridor in perpetuity and the control of the passage would now rest fully with Indian authorities. Moreover, 6.5 km of land boundary between the two countries still remains non-demarcated, reportedly due to India's procrastination. For details, see S.S. Bindra, *India and Her Neighbours: A Study of Political, Economic and Cultural Relations and Interactions* (New Delhi: Deep & Deep Publications, 1984), pp. 153; Avtar Singh Bhasin (ed.), *India–Bangladesh Relations, Documents 1971–1994*, Vol. 1 (Delhi: Siba Exim Pvt. Ltd, 1996), Introduction, pp. cI–cIiv; http://banglapedia.search.com.bd/HT/E_0054.htm, accessed on 27 November 2007.

19. For details on the transit issue, see Sabbir Ahmed, 'Transit Issue: Nature and Direction of the Debate', *Bangladesh Foreign Policy Survey*, 2(3), July–September 1996, pp. 6–8; ABM Ziaur Rahman, 'Bangladesh–India Relations in 1999: An Overview', *Bangladesh Foreign Policy Survey*, 5(4), October–December 1999, pp. 9–11; M.M. Akash and Khandokar Mohammad Istiak, 'Transit Facilities for India: Past Experience and Future Prospects', and Md Nuruzzaman, 'Transit, Jatiya Sarbobhoumatya o Atmanirbhorsheel Unnayaner Prashna [in Bangla]', both unpublished research papers.

20. Shahedul Anam Khan, 'Captive to Misperception and Mind-set', *Daily Star*, 26 July 2007, Dhaka.

21. Syed Muazzem Ali, 'Pranab Mukherjee's Visit: New Impetus to Bangladesh–India Ties—Challenges Ahead', *Daily Star*, 27 February 2007, Dhaka.

22. 'Need to Increase Dhaka–Delhi Cooperation Stressed', *Daily Star*, 8 November 2007, Dhaka.

23. 'Dhaka Expects Enhanced Cooperation from India: CA; Great Potential for Improving Ties: Menon', *Bangladesh Today*, 27 June 2007, Dhaka.

24. Indo-Bangladesh Dialogue: Strengthening Cultural, Media Cooperation to Dispel Mistrust, Suspicion', *Daily Star*, 7 March 2007, Dhaka.

25. Kazi Anwarul Masud, 'Mending Indo-Bangladesh Relations', *Daily Star*, 25 February 2007, Dhaka; Syed Muazzem Ali, 'Pranab Mukherjee's Visit: New

Impetus to Bangladesh–India Ties: Challenges Ahead', *Daily Star*, 27 February 2007, Dhaka.

26. The Roundtable was organized by Bangladesh–India Citizens' Council (BICC). See *Daily Star*, 3 August 2008, Dhaka.

27. Shahedul Anam Khan, 'Captive to Misperception and Mindset', *Daily Star*, 26 July 2007, Dhaka.

28. 'Indian Minister Indicated Shift of Policy towards Bangladesh', *Daily Star*, 10 November 2008, Dhaka.

29. 'India to Push for Friendly Ties with Neighbours', *Daily Star*, 24 May 2009, Dhaka.

30. See, for their statements, *Daily Star*, 18 May 2009, 22 June 2009, and 22 July 2009, Dhaka.

31. 'Congress Govt Needs to Reinvent Regional Foreign Policy', Editorial, *New Age*, 24 May 2009, Dhaka.

32. Iftekhar Ahmed Chowdhury, 'How Neighbours View the Elephant', *Daily Star*, 3 June 2009, Dhaka.

33. Md Ali Akbar, 'Re-Inventing Friendship with India', *Daily Star*, 22 May 2009, Dhaka.

34. See for details, *Daily Star*, 11 September 2009, Dhaka.

35. For details of Prime Minister Sheikh Hasina's statement in the Bangladesh parliament, see *Daily Star*, 10 September 2009, Dhaka.

36. 'Donors to up aid if gas is exported to India', *Daily Star*, 4 June 2003, Dhaka.

37. *Bangladesh Observer*, 9 February 2003.

38. For comments made by M. Saifur Rahman, former finance and commerce minister of Bangladesh, see *Daily Star*, 21 May 2003, Dhaka.

39. In July 2006, India reduced tariff on 380 lines of imports from South Asian LDCs (least developed countries), including Bangladesh. The items that saw a cut in customs duties include motorcars, motorcycles, golf carts, pharmaceutical products, fertilizers, paints, routers, modems, iron and steel, a host of textile items, certain edible vegetables, cut flowers, cocoa and cocoa preparations, and lactose, maltose, and sugar syrups. What is significant here is that the South Asian LDCs are, in any case, not in a position to export many of these items to India. However, Bangladesh has signed a bilateral agreement with India to export duty-free garments worth $40 million annually.

40. For details on the shortage of natural gas in Bangladesh, see, A.B.M. Ziaur Rahman, 'Renewable Energy Resources in Bangladesh: Opportunities and Challenges', Md Maqbul-E Elahi, 'Energy Issues in Bangladesh', Md Shawkat Akbar, 'Nuclear Energy in Bangladesh: Opportunities and Challenges', papers presented at a national seminar on energy, 'Issues, Challenges and Options for Bangladesh', organized by BIISS in Dhaka on 25 June 2009. Also see, papers of a seminar on 'Energy Security of Bangladesh: Challenges & Options', held in Dhaka on 21 January 2009, available from http://www.biiss.org/epls_pro.pdf, accessed on 22 September 2010.

41. 'Dhaka Agrees to Gas Pipeline Transit', *Daily Star*, 14 January 2005, Dhaka.

42. 'Dhaka, Yangon, Delhi to Sign Deal in March', *Daily Star*, 28 February 2005, Dhaka.

43. 'Delhi Agrees to Dhaka's Strings to Gas Pipeline', *Daily Star*, 1 March 2005, Dhaka.

44. 'Dhaka to Tag Strings to Allowing Gas Pipeline', *Daily Star*, 5 December 2004, Dhaka.

45. 'Gas Pipeline Deal to be Inked by April', *Daily Star*, 16 January 2005, Dhaka.

46. Concept Paper on Sub-Regional Cooperation in South Asia, presented by Bangladesh at the Kathmandu meeting of the foreign secretaries of Bangladesh, Bhutan, India, and Nepal on 2 April 1997, p. 2. Also see other citations in Mohammad Humayun Kabir, 'Sub-Regional Cooperation in South Asia', *BIISS Journal*, 19(3), July 1998, Dhaka.

47. R.B. Shah, 'Ganges–Brahmaputra: The Outlook for the Twenty-first Century', in Asit K. Biswas and Juha I. Uotto (eds), *Sustainable Development of the Ganges–Brahmaputra–Meghna Basins* (New Delhi: Oxford University Press, 2001), pp. 17–45. See also B.G. Verghese, Ramaswamy R. Iyer, Q.K. Ahmad, S.K. Malla, and B.B. Pradhan (eds), *Converting Water into Wealth: Regional Cooperation in Harnessing the Eastern Himalayan Rivers* (Dhaka: Academic Publishers, 1994); B.G. Verghese and Ramaswamy R. Iyer (eds), *Harnessing the Eastern Himalayan Rivers: Regional Cooperation in South Asia* (New Delhi: Konark Publishers Pvt. Ltd., 1993).

48. For details see, B.M. Abbas, *Ganges Water Dispute* (Dhaka: University Press Limited, 1982). Also see, Md Shah Alam, 'Farakka Barrage: Laws and Politics', *BIISS Journal*, 4(4), October 1983, pp. 140–3, Dhaka; M. Rafiqul Islam, 'The Effects of Farakka Barrage on Bangladesh and International Law', *BIISS Journal*, 5(3), July 1984, pp. 249–73; Nahid Islam, 'The Ganges Water Dispute: Environmental and Related Impacts on Bangladesh', *BIISS Journal*, Dhaka, 12(3), July 1991.

49. M. Rafiqul Islam, *Ganges Water Dispute: Its International Legal Aspects* (Dhaka: University Press Limited, 1987); and 'The Ganges Water Agreements: A Comparative Study', *BIISS Journal*, 7(3), July 1986, pp. 287–306, Dhaka.

50. For general discussion on the treaty, see Surya P. Subedi, 'Hydro-Diplomacy in South Asia: The Conclusion of the Mahakali and Ganges River Treaties', *American Journal of International Law*, 93, October 1999, pp. 631–40; Surya P. Subedi, 'The Legal Regime Concerning the Utilization of the Water Resources of the River Ganges Basin', in *German Yearbook of International Law*, 46, 2003, pp. 452–93.

51. See the Treaty between the Government of the People's Republic of Bangladesh and the Government of the Republic of India on Sharing of the Ganga/Ganges Waters at Farakka, signed in New Delhi on 12 December 1996,

available at http://www.jrcb.gov.bd/attachment/Gganges_Water_Sharing_treaty,1996.pdf, accessed on 3 August 2010.

52. The 1996 Ganges Water Treaty between Bangladesh and India, available at http://www.jrcb.gov.bd/attachment/Gganges_Water_Sharing_treaty,1996.pdf, accessed on 3 August 2010.

53. See, for details, Ahmed Tariq Karim, 'The Bangladesh–India Treaty on Sharing of the Ganges Waters: Genesis and Significance', *BIISS Journal*, 19(2), April 1998, pp. 216–35, Dhaka.

54. Ibid.

55. See, for details, Nazrul Islam, 'Indo-Bangladesh Water Treaty', in Farooq Sobhan (ed.), *Strengthening Cooperation and Security in South Asia Post 9/11* (Dhaka: University Press Limited, 2004), pp. 125–48.

56. For details on the Bangladesh foreign minister's visit to India during 8–10 September, see Pallab Bhattacharya, 'India Assures of Tipai Talks', *Daily Star*, 11–12 September 2009, Dhaka.

57. *Daily Star*, 4 August 2009, Dhaka.

58. He said, 'Bangladesh's concerns over the proposed Tipaimukh Dam are quite obvious and they must be addressed.' See *Daily Star*, 29 August 2009, Dhaka.

59. *Daily Star*, 12 September 2009, Dhaka.

60. The Tipaimukh Dam project is likened in Bangladesh to the Farakka Barrage, evoking Bangladesh's unhappy memories and experiences with India. See, for example, Abdullah A. Dewan, 'Tipaimukh Dam: Trust, But Verify', *Daily Star*, 20 August 2009, Dhaka.

61. Verghese *et al.* (eds), *Converting Water into Wealth*, p. 1; Q.K. Ahmad, Nilufar Ahmad, and K.B. Sajjadur Rasheed (eds), *Resources, Environment and Development in Bangladesh, With Particular Reference to the Ganges, Brahmaputra and Meghna Basins* (Dhaka: Academic Publishers, 1994), p. 1.

62. Bhabani Sen Gupta, a leading Indian scholar, has specified the parameters of this doctrine following India's military intervention in May–July 1983. He asserts: 'India will not tolerate external intervention in a conflict situation in any South Asian country if the intervention has any implicit or explicit anti-Indian implication. No South Asian government must, therefore, ask for military assistance with an anti-Indian bias from any country...If a South Asian country genuinely needs external help to deal with a serious internal conflict or an intolerable threat to a government legitimately established, it should ask help from a number of neighbouring countries including India. The exclusion of India from such a contingency will be considered to be an anti-Indian move on the part of the government concerned.' See, for details, Bhabani Sen Gupta, 'Regional Security: The Indira Doctrine', *India Today*, 31 August 1983, p. 20, New Delhi.

63. Alan Richards and Nirvikar Singh, 'Water and Federalism: India's Institutions Governing Inter-State River Waters', paper written under a Cooperative Agreement with the US Agency for International Development

(USAID), Department of Economics, University of California, Santa Cruz, June 1996, pp. 4–6. Some scholars maintain that there are four theories, excluding the theory of prior apportionment. See, for example, http://www.unu.edu/unupress/unupbooks/80a03e/80A03E0j.htm, accessed on 17 October 2003, pp. 3–6.

64. http://www.unu.edu/unupress/unupbooks/80a03e/80A03E0j.htm, accessed on 17 October 2003, pp. 3–6.

65. For details, see http://nrlp.iwmi.org/main/Default.asp, accessed on 5 and 12 January 2007; http://nrlp.org/main/reports.asp, accessed on 16 September 2006; www.sdnpbd.org/river_basin/bangladesh/national_workshop-river_linking_project_india.htm, accessed on 10 September 2006.

66. Ibid.

67. Indian River Linking in Supreme Court, available at: http://nwda.gov.in/indexmain.asp?linkid=978langid=1, accessed on 15 February 2007.

68. For details, see M. Feroze Ahmed, Qazi Kholoquzzaman Ahmad, and Md Khakequzzaman (eds), *Regional Cooperation on Transboundary Rivers: Impact of the Indian River-Linking Project*, published by a number of organizations—Bangladesh Poribesh Andolon (BAPA), Bangladesh Environment Network (BEN), Bangladesh Economic Association (BEA), Institution of Engineers, Bangladesh (IEB), Bangladesh University of Engineering and Technology (BUET), and University of Dhaka (DU)—which organized an international conference on the subject in Dhaka in December 2004; Mohammad Nurunnabi Chowdhury, 'River-Linking Scheme: Looming Doom for Bangladesh', *IRD Review*, 1(3), January–March 2004, pp. 8–10, Dhaka; Shamim Ahsan, 'India's Giant River-Link Project: Will Bangladesh Dry Up?', *Star Weekend Magazine*, 10 October 2003, pp. 4–8, Dhaka; Jasim Uddin, 'Upstream Water Diversion: A Disaster for Bangladesh', *New Nation*, 11 September 2006, Dhaka; Shawkat Alam, 'The Proposed Indian River-Linking Project: Infringement of Rights', *Daily Star*, 22 September 2007, Dhaka.

69. Irasema Coronado, 'The Challenge of Equitable Allocation: Water Conflict in the Borderlands', *Borderlines 57*, 7(6), July 1999, available at http://www.americaspolicy.org/borderlines/1999/b157/b157oview_body.html, accessed on 23 October 2003.

70. B.G. Verghese, *Waters of Hope: From Vision to Reality in Himalaya–Ganga Development Cooperation*, 2nd updated Edn (New Delhi: Oxford & IBH Publishing Co. Pvt. Ltd., 1999), p. 309.

71. *An Update of Surface Water Availability in the Rio Grande Basin of Mexico*, A Report Based upon Satellite Remote Sensing Analyses and Information from the Mexican Section of the International Boundary and Water Commission, prepared for Susan Combs, Texas Commissioner of Agriculture, by the Center for Space Research, The University of Texas at Austin, September 26, 2003', Executive Summary, available at http://magic.csr.utexas.edu/Projects/MXWaterResources2003/doc/rgbasin_report_102703.pdf, accessed on 3 August 2010.

72. See, Treaty between the United States of America and Mexico signed at Washington on 3 February 1944 and Protocol signed at Washington on 14 November 1944, at http://www.ibwc.state.gov/html/body_1944_treaty. html, accessed on 3rd August 2010; http://www.ibwc.state.gov/ORGANIZA/ about_us.htm, accessed on 3rd August 2010

73. Ibid.; *U.S.–Mexico Transboundary Water Management: The Case of the Rio Grande/Rio Bravo: Recommendations for Policymakers for the Medium and Long Term*, report of the U.S.–Mexico Binational Council, Center for Strategic and International Studies (CSIS) & Instituto Tecnologico Autonomo de Mexico (ITAM), University of Texas at Austin, CSIS Mexico Report, January 2003, pp. 4–6, available at http://csis.org/files/media/csis/pubs/binational_council. pdf, accessed on 3rd August 2010.

74. The International Joint Commission: Canada and the United States of America, available at http://www.transboundarywaters.orst.edu/projects/ casestudies/ijc.html, accessed on 12 November 2003; Lars Joachim Jacobsen, Frank Ove Seth, and Katrien Van Eerdenbrugh, 'North America: The United States and Canada, Water Resource Problems', available at http://www.bygg. ntnu.no/ivb/stud/fag/vassdrpl/gruppe/N-america/n-america.html, accessed on 17 October 2003, p. 5; Rivers and Lakes of Canada, Canadian Council for Geographic Education, available at http:/www.ccge.org/ccge/english/ teachingResources/rivers/tr_rivers.htm, accessed on 1 December 2003, p. 1.

75. Verghese, *Waters of Hope*, p. 321; The International Joint Commission: Canada and the United States of America, available at http://www. transboundarywaters.orst.edu/projects/casestudies/ijc.html, accessed on 12 November 2003.

76. The International Joint Commission; also see the text of the 1909 Boundary Waters Treaty, Government of Canada, Department of Foreign Affairs and International Trade, available at http://pubx.dfait-maeci.gc.ca/A_ BRANCH/AES/Env_commitments2.nsf/Commitment?, accessed on 24 September 2003.

77. The 1909 Boundary Waters Treaty.

78. 'What Makes the Columbia River Basin Unique and How We Benefit, Foundation for Water & Energy Education, 2000', available at http://www. fwee.org/c-basin.html, accessed on 23 October 2003; 'The Columbia River, Great Canadian Rivers', available at http://great canadianrivers.com/rivers/ columbia/species-home.html, accessed on 1 December 2003.

79. Verghese, *Waters of Hope*, pp. 322–3.

80. Ibid.

81. See the text of the Treaty between USA and Canada Relating to Cooperative Development of the Water Resources of the Columbia River Basin, 1961, available at http://mgd.nacse.org/qml/watertreaty/textdocs/ international/99.html, accessed on 23 October 2003; 'The Columbia River, Great Canadian Rivers'.

Contributors

RAJESH M. BASRUR is Senior Fellow, S. Rajaratnam School of International Studies, Nanyang Technological University, Singapore.

APARAJITA BISWAS is Professor, Centre for African Studies, University of Mumbai, India.

NALINI KANT JHA is Professor and Director, Madanjeet Singh Institute of South Asia Regional Cooperation (MISARC), Pondicherry (Central) University, India.

MOHAMMAD HUMAYUN KABIR is Senior Research Director, Bangladesh Enterprise Institute (BEI), Dhaka, Bangladesh.

PRATAP BHANU MEHTA is President, Centre for Policy Research, New Delhi, India.

RAHUL MUKHERJI is Associate Professor, South Asian Studies Programme, Faculty of Arts and Social Sciences, National University of Singapore, Singapore.

VARUN SAHNI is Vice-Chancellor, University of Jammu, Jammu and Kashmir, India.

AYESHA SIDDIQA is Senior Visiting Fellow, School of Advanced International Studies, Johns Hopkins University, USA.

E. SRIDHARAN is Academic Director, University of Pennsylvania Institute for the Advanced Study of India, New Delhi, India.

JAYADEVA UYANGODA is Professor of Political Science, University of Colombo, Sri Lanka.